Blood Over Different Shades of Green
East Pakistan 1971: History Revisited

Blood Over Different Shades of Green

East Pakistan 1971: History Revisited

IKRAM SEHGAL

BETTINA ROBOTKA

OXFORD

UNIVERSITY PRESS

OXFORD
UNIVERSITY PRESS

Oxford University Press is a department of the University of Oxford.
It furthers the University's objective of excellence in research, scholarship,
and education by publishing worldwide. Oxford is a registered trade mark of
Oxford University Press in the UK and in certain other countries

Published in Pakistan by
Oxford University Press
No. 38, Sector 15, Korangi Industrial Area,
PO Box 8214, Karachi-74900, Pakistan

ISBN 978-0-19-070227-4

Typeset in Adobe Garamond Pro
Printed on 80gsm Offset Paper

Printed by Mas Printers, Karachi

Acknowledgements
Annexures 3 and 4 have been reproduced from the following book:
Major General (Retd.) Khadim Hussain Raja, *A Stranger in My Own Country*
(Karachi: Oxford University Press, 2012), Annexures B and C, pp. 114–26.

Owing everything to Allah Almighty

Dedicated
to
my beloved parents **Majeed** and **Bano Sehgal**
because of them I am today what I am
and my family is what they are

my wife **Shahnaz**
being a wonderful and patient life partner through years
of vicissitudes and successes

my son **Zarrar**
his tremendous achievements beyond our wildest dreams

Kashmala
a daughter more than a daughter-in-law
a wonderful stupendous life partner for my son

my daughters **Haya** and **Nefer**
outstanding in whatever they do

my granddaughters
Amaani and Elena
excelling in their accomplishments

and
last but not the least
Suleiman Sehgal
showing early signs of **living** up to
his **chosen** name from history

Contents

Annexures

Preface

My interest in South Asian history probably has its roots in the fact that my mother was a history teacher, as a result of which, discussions on historical topics were common during breakfast and lunch. Later, when thinking about subjects to study, I decided to go for history. I was offered study at the State University in St. Petersburg (at that time Leningrad)—a far-away place given the travel restrictions at that time in East Germany. In order to study there a good command of the Russian language was a prerequisite because all the teaching was in that language. Fortunately, I had been a good student of languages in school, particularly of Russian, which was the first foreign language in East German schools.

From 1973 to 1978, I studied South Asian history and languages (Hindi, Sanskrit, and Urdu) at Leningrad A.A. Zhdanov State University. Back in Germany, I did my PhD on Indian colonial history from the Berlin Humboldt University in 1983. I was offered a teaching position in the Department of South Asian Studies at the same university where I continued to work until retirement. I started specialising in Pakistan history and politics. After the fall of the Berlin Wall and re-unification of Germany in 1997, I was invited to monitor the general election in Pakistan as part of the EU team of election observers. It was my first visit to the country and ushered in a turn of events in my professional life. I was so intrigued by Pakistani people, politics, and society that I returned every year for a couple of weeks between semesters. I would start from Islamabad and visit Peshawar, Lahore and finally, Karachi.

Karachi, with its harbour and vivid urbanity became my love. Living in one of the apartments near the sea, I joined a group of people who went for walks along the beach, early in the morning. The discussions at dawn on people and politics gave me a lively insight into Pakistani society and brought me into contact with other walkers. Ikram Sehgal was one of them, though he was not a member of our group. I remember my first visit to his office on Zamzama, around 2001, when I interviewed him on the possibility of there being a reorganisation in the provincial structure of Pakistan and the demands of a newly formed organisation called the Pakistan Oppressed Nations' Movement (PONAM). The discussion proved fruitful and from then on, Ikram's publications and commentaries in the media became a signpost in my work.

During my visits, I was uneasy with the VIP treatment I was accorded—I longed to experience the 'real' Pakistan. In 2004, I applied for a professorship to the Higher Education Commission's Foreign Faculty Hiring Programme and was invited by the Dean and Director of the Institute of Business Administration (IBA), Professor Danishmand, to teach history and the social sciences at the institution. Taking leave from Humboldt University, I arrived at IBA in March 2005, and taught there until 2009. I was then transferred to the Institute of Business Management (IoBM), where I spent two more years, from 2009 to 2010 and 2012 to 2013. Eventually, I had to return to Humboldt University if I wanted to hold on to my job there and did so with a heavy heart.

My years teaching in academic institutions in Pakistan taught me invaluable lessons about academia in Pakistan. I became aware of the fact that in Pakistan, history is mostly used as a political tool to justify political decision-making. My history students did not accept historical writing as an academic endeavour, but rather, a political one that did not have much power of persuasion. Consequently, it was of little interest to them. I was convinced that one way to strengthen the national identity of young Pakistanis was to offer them a realistic view of the historical events that influenced the development of their country, based on primary sources.

My collaboration with Ikram reached new heights when he asked that I join him in writing a book on the break-up of Pakistan and the 1971 war. I was excited—here was a person who personally and intimately knew all the main characters of that drama and had been at the centre of all the action! I had read his book, *Escape from Oblivion: The Story of a Pakistani Prisoner of War in India*, and through our many discussions, was aware of his interest in history. Such a project would give me the chance to evaluate critically the way this event had been portrayed in history textbooks in Pakistan. It would also enable me to incorporate the experiences and recollections of the participants of that war, including previously unpublished material. I agreed to work on the project and started my research on the events during and leading up to 1971.

In 2017, I took early retirement from Humboldt University in order to commit more of my time to the project and began writing. The result of our work is now in front of you; it is the fruit of a cooperation between East and West.

BETTINA ROBOTKA

Introduction

Born of a Punjabi father and a Bengali mother, my sister Shahnaz and I grew up in three worlds. First was the wonderful, all-embracing world of our home, which our parents made for us. Second was West Pakistan, a world where we were dubbed Bengali. Third was East Pakistan where miraculously we transformed into Punjabis. Even the most experienced and intellectually astute of my closest friends, from both wings (East and West), found it difficult to explain this incongruity.

As an escapee from a prisoner of war (POW) camp at Panagarh, West Bengal, India, I was interrogated at the 434 Field Interrogation Centre (FIC) in Dhaka, from mid-August until early November 1971. However, the information I revealed then—regarding developments in East Pakistan—ran contrary to the official narrative. One thing I am unable to understand is why the facts revealed by me during my interrogation in Dhaka, that India had established a regular POW camp since 25 April, was never revealed publicly during 1971 and afterwards. While India had a valid reason to keep it secret, why was this for Pakistan? It should have been used in the media and in the United Nations Security Council to prove India's longstanding involvement in the East Pakistan crisis. This fact was not mentioned even to the Hamoodur Rehman Commission. Understandably, confidentiality had to be maintained in diplomatic circles, regarding the 'unofficial' help I received from the Americans in Calcutta (now Kolkata). But why was this fact being kept a state secret that dozens and dozens of Pakistani officers and men were detained as early as April 1971 in a regular POW camp run by India's Eastern Command with troops drawn from 430 Field Company of 203 Army Engineer Regiment? One reason could be that some in the army could not stomach how I had managed to escape from the camp in Panagarh when others had been unable to do so. This propaganda weapon could have been used to convince a sceptical world about India's deep involvement in the East Pakistan crisis. It could not have been simply an oversight. Perhaps it would not do to portray the first person to escape from an Indian POW camp as a 'national hero' because he was half-Bengali from his mother's side. In hindsight, personally, this was good for me as I was able to get on with my life. Nevertheless, Pakistan missed the boat in publicly revealing the amount of information that I had brought back.

According to my father, he was drafted in by the Adjutant General Lt. Gen. Khudadad Khan and Maj. Gen. Ghulam Omar, the National Security Advisor (NSA)—with the blessings of Gen. Yahya Khan—to visit East Pakistan and 434 FIC 'to correct my stance'. When he flew into East Pakistan, he was naturally emotional having given me up for lost! He scolded me as to why I was being obstinate when I was in line to receive a decoration for having escaped from a POW camp. I responded by reminding him why he had shifted from East Pakistan to West Pakistan in 1966 despite having a good civilian job after his retirement from East Pakistan Industrial Development Corporation, as a General Manager at Thakurgaon Sugar Mills. He had told me then that things were going from bad to worse, and that since he was no longer in the army, he could only protect my mother in West Pakistan, whereas she would not be able to protect him in East Pakistan, her home turf. That was why he had moved, in 1966, to Lahore. Moreover, he had no answer when I asked him why he did not accept Gen. Yahya Khan's repeated offers, prior to the 1970 elections, to make him Governor of East Pakistan (Lt. Gen. Khudadad Khan and Maj. Gen. Ghulam Omar had recommended him for the post). My father had accompanied Gen. Yahya to East Pakistan, but finally declined the offer. I told him how much I loved him, but that we were very different as individuals. He said, 'Look in the mirror, can anybody refute our resemblance?' I replied, 'Father, there is a difference; your mother was a Punjabi, my mother is a

Bengali.' Stunned into silence and with tears in his eyes, he embraced me and left. I could see he had given up the hope of seeing me alive again. This was in East Pakistan, in September 1971.

In a very tragic way, my 'mixed blood' makes me uniquely qualified to make an objective rendition of the facts, and with the help of Bettina Robotka, to make the correct analysis thereof. To write this introduction, extracts were taken from *Leave the Army Alone*, a collection of articles I wrote up until 2010, namely 'Dedication to 2 East Bengal', 'Army Aviation', and '44 Punjab' (now 4 Sindh). Extracts were also taken from *Converting Garbage into Dreams* and *Till Debt Do Us Apart*, which I dedicated to my parents, Lt. Col. Abdul Majeed Sehgal and Bano Sehgal, and *Power Play*, which I dedicated to my sister, Shahnaz. (*See* Annex 1.)

From the time I first became aware the army was 'The Army', I knew only the 2 East Bengal Regiment (2 EB). In 1949, when I was less than three years old, the GHQ in Rawalpindi decided that my mother's Bengali lineage was enough reason to post my father, Major Abdul Majeed Sehgal, to East Pakistan. He did not go quietly; being a die-hard 7/16 Punjab (later 19 Punjab), he went kicking and screaming, in protest, to lead a company-sized contingent from 'Sat Sola', and to raise the second battalion of the East Bengal Regiment (2 EB).

He went on to command the Junior Tigers in Comilla from early 1956 to 1958. Two of his adjutants, Captain K.M. Shafiullah and Captain Hossain Mohammad Ershad, rose to the rank of COAS in the Bangladesh Army post-1971. Two of his officers, Ziaur Rahman and Ershad, became presidents of Bangladesh. At least six others became major generals in Bangladesh while in Pakistan, Maj. Gen. (retd.) Nasrullah (his second-in-command in 2 EB), and Lt. Gen. (retd.) Sardar F.S. Lodi, a former governor Balochistan, who came to him in 2 EB as a subaltern, were present on 22 May 2000 on the '*dua*' for my mother. Lt. Gen. Iqbal Khan, a former chairperson, Joint Chiefs of Staff Committee (1980–4), was attached as a captain with two companies (2 FF with 2 EB) for over six months' time, and in late 1957, functioned as his adjutant during the military's anti-smuggling mission titled, Operation Close Door, in East Pakistan.

My mother, Bano, was from Bogra, in the heartland of Bengal. She was married in September 1944 in pre-partition Bengal to a Punjabi army officer from Sialkot—the heartland of Pakistan. A story too long to be told in a few paragraphs, suffice it to say that, Huseyn Shaheed Suhrawardy and J.A. Rahim (my mother's uncles), had something to do with my parent's marriage and their vision of the Pakistan-to-be. The year 1944 is important—coming after the 1940 Resolution, and before the 1946 Resolution—as it showed the resolve and bent of most Muslims. Maj. Gen. Q.G. Dastgir, originally part of the first battalion of the East Bengal Regiment (1 EB) and later Bangladesh's ambassador to Pakistan, was my mother's cousin. Meanwhile, the family of Ziaur Rahman (President of Bangladesh 1977–81), settled on my grandfather's estate near Bogra, after re-locating from Cooch Behar, later moved to Karachi.

My most enduring and vivid recollection of my mother is in *shalwar kameez*, riding a bicycle, with my infant sister, Shahnaz, in a basket on the front handle, my father and myself pedalling furiously on either side on separate bicycles. This was during the time when my father's postings was in different cantonments, from 1949 to 1953, successively in Sialkot, Kurmitola, Jessore, Quetta, and Comilla.

My mother was always an 'original', whether teaching classical dance or music, playing cards or just socialising, proud of being Bengali and proud of being Pakistani, never afraid to say what she felt and without a care to whom she said it or in the manner she said it. My father was far more reticent and always discreet.

Until my mother's death in 2000, I did not discover the Asalong Papers—documents on the six-week-long battle with the Indians in 1962. My father's command included 1 East Pakistan Rifles (EPR) battalion (since called the Asalong Mouza Battalion), with two companies of the regular army's 6 FF from the 53 Brigade in Comilla, in close support.

The operation, which was the biggest one, prior to the Rann of Kutch (1965), was conducted in rugged, forested, and mountainous terrain and considered an outright victory for Pakistan, because it evicted the Indians across the Feni River. Being among the few, if not the only successful combat officer at that time, my father was envied. This, along with the fact that he had married a Bengali, ultimately derailed what appeared to be a promising career in the army. He was about to be approved for an 'accelerated promotion' in 1964, but a heart attack sealed his fate. At that time, a candidate with a low medical category could not hope to be promoted. He never once complained about how this ended his professional career.

My sister Shahnaz (my wife's namesake), who was born in Sialkot on 24 January 1949 and died in Dhaka, on 26 October 1977, left behind two children. She was two-and-a-half years younger than me. In our early years, while growing up, I could never have guessed that the quiet, almost glum child would blossom into a beautiful, vivacious woman who became the life of the party wherever she went. She hated getting up for school in the morning and on her very first day at Our Lady of Fatima Convent, Comilla, in January 1953, she proceeded to tear apart Sister Mary Leo's white robe. Shahnaz must have been the only four-year-old child in history to be detained after school on her very first day there. Sister Mary Joan of Arc, who succeeded Sister Leo as principal in 1963, rescued her. Eleven years later, Shahnaz passed her Senior Cambridge.

Shahnaz came and stayed with me when I was undergoing Army Aviation training in Rawalpindi, making more friends in four months than I did in my three years there. As all good-looking women are apt to do, my sister had many proposals, but in the end married a man of her own choice and not necessarily the right one. His name was Omar Hayat Khan, nicknamed Lama, the son of Abdus Salam Khan, a distant maternal uncle of Sheikh Mujibur Rahman, an eminent lawyer and chairperson of the Pakistan Democratic Party. Sheikh Mujibur Rahman had a soft corner for Shahnaz.

My love for 2 EB explains my unstinting love for 44 Punjab (now 4 Sindh). It is not that I loved one more than the other. For me, 2 EB was a set-piece love that I grew into; 4 Sindh, on the other hand, gave me a home that no one was prepared to grant in 1971. It was, simply, amazing—a tremendous salvation for the burning torture of my heart and soul. My country comprised both East and West Pakistan; how many Pakistanis have lost their country the way I did, in 1971? I had been sent to 4 Sindh a condemned man; it was meant to be a transit camp to see me out of uniform. Fate and the men of 4 Sindh, however, had other ideas. God's hand works in mysterious ways. Of all the battalions in the Pakistan Army, destiny brought me to 4 Sindh. It remains my home to this day. I will always love the Junior Tigers and they will always be a part of me, but my love for 4 Sindh is a different matter altogether. The 4 Sindh was a body of men who accepted me without prejudice and without any reservations, despite my 'reputation'. I must state, however, that I can never forgive those who forever sullied the name of 2 EB, by ordering and carrying out the brutal murder of Subedar Ayub's wife and daughters, who, owing to their close friendship with Shahnaz, I viewed as my own sisters. I still remember them cheering me on vociferously from the side-lines of the parade ground and the sports field. Had I made it to the site 24 hours earlier, the massacre could perhaps have been prevented.

One of those who survived was Captain (later Major) Afsar Hussain Naqvi. In fact, Afsar joined 44 Punjab (now 4 Sindh) after his return from the POW camp. After retirement, he joined me in my business, where he remained until his death. Whatever I am today, I owe to this magnificent unit of the Pakistan Army. The officers of 4 Sindh are a different breed altogether. Brigadier (later Lt. Gen.) Javed Ramdey attended the Royal College of Defence Studies in the UK and was, for a time, the favourite for the slot of chief of army staff. Lt. Col. (later Brigadier) Shahid Jawad topped his class at the Malaysian Staff College, while Fayyaz, after topping his class at the Canadian Staff College, rose to become an instructor at Staff College, Quetta. He took over the unit after Jawad was transferred out. Whereas Fayyaz is presently a major general, Jawad was less fortunate and not promoted. Colonel Mohabbat, who preceded Jawad, but did not qualify for the Staff College, was one of the most outstanding professional soldiers that I have had the privilege to meet. As a second lieutenant in Siachen, he carried a wounded man in his patrol, through the snow, under fire, to safety, refusing to leave him behind. After retirement, he briefly joined me before doing a stint for the Defence Housing Authority and is expected to return after his tenure there ends. The rank and file of today's commanding officers of 4 Sindh are even more outstanding.

4 Sindh has signboards denoting 'Delta Company' as 'Sehgal Coy'. For my detractors, this is very difficult to stomach. Some of them were on my dole for over twelve years, until I gave up selling ammunition and equipment to the armed forces. On my visit to Command 5 Corps, the Corps Commander, Lt. Gen. Naveed Mukhtar (who later became the DG ISI), was gracious enough to allow me to meet my Company, which was detailed to guard the Corps Headquarters. They assembled with an ad hoc 'Sehgal Coy' sign—one of my most treasured photographs.

When my daughter and I visited 2 EB in Dhaka in 2008, the CO, who was born in 1971, gave me a photograph of my father that bore the signatures of all the officers of 2 EB. My own photographs, from the pre-1971 era, were on display in the NCO's Mess. I may have been of mixed ethnicity, but my father was a pure Punjabi. Why was it that they loved and respected him so much that they held on to his photograph for two generations and then handed it to his son, fifty years after he had left the unit's command? Ask Lt. Gen. Lehrasab Khan, one of the bravest and most professional soldiers in the Pakistan Army, who served in the 1965 and 1971 wars with distinction, how 1 EB reacted when he visited it with the president of Bangladesh in the early 1990s. Although 90 per cent of the soldiers had never served with him, his name and reputation were still very much alive.

Whoever is appointed the CO of 4 Sindh, keeps me informed about the unit to whatever extent possible in his professional capacity. As usual, 4 Sindh has been in the thick of battle, performing admirably in the region formerly referred to as FATA. Soldiers in any part of the world are remarkable souls for their willingness to sacrifice their lives for their country.

IKRAM SEHGAL

1

The Cultural Identity of East Bengalis

Like the complex weave of the *jamdani*, or the silken softness of muslin, the culture of Bengal—East Bengal in particular—has an intricacy of its own. Its unique fabric has been woven over the ages, with the threads of race, religion, belief, nature, humanity, the soil, and its people. Like the innumerable rivers that crisscross the delta perched on the Bay of Bengal, the culture of the land runs through the veins of Bengalis and their heart beats to a tune of its own.

Over the centuries, the riches of South Asia have been the subject of both envy and ambition. The subcontinent had witnessed invasions long before Alexander the Great crossed the mountains and entered the plains of India. While Alexander's army fell prey to fatigue and homesickness, and were filled with apprehension by lurid tales of black magic as they ventured deeper into South Asia, many conquerors came to plunder and loot. Some stayed to rule and continued to plunder over an extended period of time.

Perhaps history's most important lesson is that no one ever learns from history. This may be more true in the case of South Asians, than anyone else in the world. Despite the machinations of the colonial mind, the inherent culture of a people continues to endure in their lifeblood, rivers, forests, and in the sheaves of their paddy. The recognition and appreciation of a culture is a far more enduring mechanism of entrenchment than attempts to obliterate it. The British were hardly seeking rapprochement; they were simply looking to impose imperial rule. As a nation of shopkeepers, they went about it in a steadily measured manner. It took them almost a century, from

1

1757 to 1857, to establish their dominion across India and subjugate it. The East India Company then gave way to the rule of the Raj.

While the British were still loath to the idea of giving the subcontinent independence, it was clear, even before the Second World War that the mode of British governance had to change in India. The war had vastly reduced British colonial power overseas and British India underwent a vital transition, resulting in the creation of two separate independent states—India and Pakistan.

Much has been said about the case of East and West Pakistan. Historians and social scientists tend to see cultural differences as the wedge that was driven between what were once two wings of the same country. These differences may not be the major reasons why East Pakistan broke away to become independent Bangladesh, but they certainly catalysed the process and were used adroitly by the actors involved in re-mapping the region.

The Pakistan that came into existence in 1947 consisted of two parts distanced from each other by over a thousand miles and a territory that tried to unite people who may have been mostly Muslims, but differed vastly from each other as far as ethnicity and culture were concerned. Unfortunately, the rulers of the newly founded state perceived this diversity as a liability instead of an asset; they mistook the undisputable need for unity as a need for uniformity, which was to be achieved through a specific model of Islamic culture and a single language. This attempt to bring about national unity through cultural and religious uniformity is one of the central problems that lies at the very heart of the concept of Pakistan.

Situated in the eastern end of the subcontinent, Bengal has a rich history. It had been a province in the Delhi Sultanate of the fourteenth century and later, in the Mughal Empire, which helped it develop a strong regional identity. The eastern portion of Bengal that had been cast in with Pakistan comprised the largest ethnic community and one that was both ethnically and culturally consistent.

What exactly do we mean when we say 'culture'? One simple definition is that it is a way of doing things; the way we dress, speak, what we eat, sing, love, or hate. Throughout history, Bengal had enjoyed a great deal of autonomy in the subcontinent. This had led to the creation of a distinct culture, which included art and poetry. While Islam became the glue that bound the Muslims of Pakistan, the manner in which they practice the religion differed depending on their cultural background. Culture, therefore, shaped all aspects of life, including religious practices not only in Bengal, but also in other regions, such as Sindh and the North-West Frontier Province (now Khyber Pukhtunkhwa).

It is the very persistence of this unique and distinctive Bengali Muslim culture that prevented Bangladesh from being swallowed up by its more powerful neighbours, whether it was India, or Pakistan.

To this day, India is wary of a potential movement for a United Bengal that would include Assam and the many adjacent tribal states. The Association of Eastern States of South Asia (AESSA) is a concept that could very well have become a reality had history played out differently in 1947. Moreover, India's neglected north-eastern states, known as the Seven Sisters, are, today, a hotbed of insurgency, thus adding to India's wariness.

The partition of Bengal, in 1947, resulted in a considerable exchange of population, upsetting Bengali society and its economy. In East Bengal, the majority of Muslims lived in the rural areas. They were agricultural labourers belonging to the lower and lower-middle classes. Bengali Hindus, meanwhile, mostly educated and entrepreneurs were leaving East Bengal for Calcutta and other parts of West Bengal. Non-Bengali Muslims, from the surrounding eastern and northern territories, were moving into the newly founded state of East Pakistan. Among them were the so-called 'Biharis', a group that included Urdu-speaking non-Bengali Muslim refugees from Bihar and from other parts of northern India, such as Assam and Orissa. They numbered about a million in 1971, but decreased to approximately 600,000 by the late 1980s. Prior to Bangladesh's independence, they had dominated the upper echelons of society in East Bengal; being educated and of urban descent and because of their cultural preoccupations they got preference in the administration and dominated business enterprise. Many of them worked in the railway sector and in industry. As such, they stood to lose from Bangladesh's independence and sided with Pakistan during the 1971 war, having sided with West Pakistanis before. They shared an urban culture that is characterised by a stricter, Deobandi strain of Islam, and an allegiance to West Pakistan instead of Bengal.

East Pakistan was a land of Bengalis, a nation culturally different from all the ethnicities of not only West Pakistan, but also South Asia as a whole. It shared a large part of its culture with West Bengal, its separated 'other'. Bengal was the land of Rabindranath Tagore and Kazi Nazrul Islam, of dance and poetry, of song and music, of literary richness and folklore. At the same time, however, the culture was uniform throughout; West Bengal consisted predominantly of a Hindu population. The juxtaposition of East Pakistan's Muslim and Bengali identities gives it a unique disposition.

In any case, the nineteenth century 'Bengal Renaissance' that has been described in some detail in the chapter on the language movement, did a great deal to bring Bengalis to the forefront of a quest for identity and triggered the development of an all-inclusive Bengali nationalism—the predecessor of Indian nationalism. In fact, it was Bengalis like Surendranath Banerjee, who were among the founders of the Indian National Congress in 1885, together with the retired British administrator, Allan Octavian Hume. This history became part of the intellectual culture of Bengal and of East Bengal, after Partition.

West Pakistan, on the other hand, consisted of ethnically and culturally diverse regions. Here, the largest ethnic group was Punjabis, who occupied a prominent place in the army and possessed a strong self-esteem; they were industrious, crafty, and proud of their warrior-like image. The Punjabis, along with the Pashtuns, who are among the largest tribal societies in the world, and whose rugged habitat necessitated a semi-nomadic, warring lifestyle, were different from the Bengalis in every aspect and can be described as their complete opposite. The Bengalis were subjugated to British rule as early as the seventeenth century and were categorised by the administrators as being better educated, peaceful if not meek, yet sly. These characteristics—accurate or not—along with a lack of cross-cultural understanding and assimilation, became the crux of the clash between East and West Pakistan. The rulers of both sides not only failed to grasp the complexity of the situation and give it due recognition, but actively tried to impose a different culture on the population. In hindsight, this ignorance is mindboggling and can be attributed to an arrogance and superiority complex.

Cultural pride is a strong emotion that courses through the Bengali veins. They may not have the image of a martial race like the western region of the subcontinent imagine themselves to have, but they have fierce pride. I personally saw it first hand in my own mother. They rejected the condescending and patronising attitude of West Pakistanis and resented attempts at domination. This had its roots in the pre-Mughal and Mughal periods, when the area comprising Bangladesh was ruled by conquerors from the region now referred to as Afghanistan. My father understood this pride and was therefore able to manage effectively my mother's sensitivities, just as he was able to handle the officers of the East Bengal Regiment.

At the time of the 1981 census, just over one per cent of East Bengal's population was tribal and lived primarily in the Chittagong Hills and in the regions of Mymensingh, Sylhet, and Rajshahi. Most of these tribes folk are of Sino-Tibetan descent and have distinctive Mongoloid features. They differ in their social organisation, marriage customs, birth and death rites, cuisine and other customs, from the people of the rest of the country. They speak Tibeto-Burman languages and are mainly Hindus, Buddhists, or Christians. Their culture, although distinct from that of Bengalis, has nevertheless acquired many similarities with it, after centuries of cohabitation.

The culture of East Pakistan was therefore a mix of diverse influences, including pre-Islamic and contemporary Hindu ones, though given the Muslim majority of the country, it was dominated by the culture of the Bengali Muslim community as is seen in its architecture, dance, literature, music, painting and attire.

Religion is a strong binding factor, particularly in a region that had been rife with communal rioting and discrimination during colonial rule. Being a Muslim majority area, it was natural that Bengal got drawn into the controversy between the Indian National Congress and the Muslim League, in their fight for political power. Unfortunately, after the possibility of a united and independent Bengal had been discarded in 1947, the region was partitioned. One little-known yet significant fact is that the Muslim majority members of the pre-partition Bengal Assembly, voted overwhelmingly against partition, preferring instead to have a united Bengal, with a significant number of Hindus. On the other hand, the Hindu members of parliament voted for partition and preferred to remain with India.[1] That was why the Muslim majority had no option but to become part of East Pakistan. While their major concern regarding the Hindu domination of the economy was removed, their exposure to a streamlined and exclusive interpretation of Islam caused a great deal of unease.

Muslims in the eastern parts of Bengal are converts from Hinduism and Buddhism and for centuries have lived peacefully alongside followers of these two faiths. For this reason, most of the Muslims living there identify with the folk traditions of Bengal. This includes the belief in shamanism and the powers of *fakirs* (Muslim holy men who are exorcists and faith healers), *ojhaa* (shamans with magical healing powers), and *bauls* (religious mendicants and wandering musicians). Music, dance, and literature also reflect the classical devotions of Hindu and Muslim religious ideas. Tribal dances are popular with all Bengalis; women living in the rural areas traditionally dance to folk music.

This tradition is deemed somewhat controversial and un-Islamic, by the Deobandi, Ahle Hadith, and Jamaat-e-Islami schools of thought, which are mostly followed by literate residents of urban areas. With the degeneration of this Islamist strain of thought into potential militancy, these differences have become more pronounced and are challenging the harmony of Bangladeshi society. Instead of allowing different interpretations and practices of Islam to co-exist as they have done for centuries, the rulers of West Pakistan chose Deobandi Islam as a tool to streamline and unite the newly-founded Pakistani nation, while Urdu was chosen as the country's national language. This interpretation of Islam, which was by no means a representation of the wider faith, has only served to divide Pakistanis instead of uniting them. Islam as it was practiced in Bengal came under criticism for being too influenced by Hinduism and Hindu culture and this further estranged relations between East and West Pakistan. There was a joke doing the rounds during Bangladesh's struggle for independence in 1971. It was said that the West Pakistani soldiers were pulling down pictures of the long-haired, bohemian-looking Muslim poet, Kazi Nazrul Islam, thinking he was a Hindu, and showing a reverence for the portraits of the bearded Rabindranath Tagore, thinking he was a Muslim! This may have been a joke, but it effectively captured the lack of cultural comprehension.

Over 98 per cent of the inhabitants of Bangladesh are Bengalis, predominantly Bangla-speaking Muslims. They are primarily of Indo-Aryan, Mongol, and Dravidian origin, with Austro-Asiatic, Assamese, Sinhalese, Munda and Tibeto-Burmese influences as far ethnicity and linguistics are concerned. Speakers of Arabic, Persian, and Turkic languages have also contributed to the characteristics of the people. In the time of the Delhi Sultanate and the Mughal Empire, Muslims of Central Asian and Afghan descent—military adventurers, administrators, sheikhs, and artisans—migrated to Bengal and settled there, mixing in with the local population.

The oldest work of literature from East Bengal is over a thousand years old, dating back to the fourteenth century. It is not explicitly Islamic in nature, though traditional Islamic writing also exists in the region. The literature developed considerably during the medieval period, with the rise of popular poets such as Chandidas, Daulat Qazi, and Syed Alaol. East Bengal shares the heritage of Bengal Renaissance and the legacy of the Tagore family. It is worth noting that the national anthems of both India and Bangladesh were written in Bengali and by the same poet, Nobel Laureate Rabindranath Tagore, thus bearing witness to the cultural closeness of East Bengal to its Hindu heritage. Poet Kazi Nazrul Islam does well to encapsulate this in his work. He wrote of Radha and Krishna frolicking in the forests of Brindaban and was, at the same time, a prolific writer of Bengali *hamd* and *naat*. He summed up his own beliefs and the characteristics of the Bengali nation when he championed the cause of humanity over structured orthodoxy.

Theatre has been a tradition in Bangladesh for hundreds of years. More than a dozen theatres in Dhaka regularly stage locally-written plays, as does Dhaka University. Many theatres have also started adapting European plays. Dhaka's Bailey Road was known as 'Natak Para' and has now been extended to the Shilpakala Academy in Segun Bagicha, where plays are regularly staged.

Another important aspect of local culture is clothing. Bengali women usually wear *saris*, made of the world famous muslins, silks, and finely hand-embroidered fabric, produced by women in villages. *Saris* worn in villages would be simpler and made of cotton, while the *lungis* worn by the men resemble chequered wrap-around skirts, much like those worn by the Burmese. These are, however, different from the *dhotis* worn by Hindu men in the rural areas. In 'Pakistani culture', *saris* were given a Hindu epithet and *shalwar kameez* was declared the 'national dress' for both men and women, with the result that people who preferred *saris* were looked down upon as being less patriotic. Such sentiment became more pronounced in the post-1971 era.

The staple Bengali dish is, invariably, rice and fish and there is no shortage of the latter in the numerous, rivers, ponds, canals, and marshes across the country. Rice has traditionally been cultivated in the East Bengal delta and the adjoining areas of Burma and Thailand. This diet is a testimony to the closeness of Bengali culture to that of its eastern neighbours. And it is yet another factor that distances them from West Pakistanis, who generally prefer wheat. Though *roti* has never been declared the 'national' food of Pakistan and rice dishes are popular, the Bengalis' preference for rice and fish was sometimes commented upon with derision by West Pakistanis.

Owing to the historical diversity of the region, the intellectual culture of East Bengal is inclusive in nature and, as a result, clashed with exclusivity of the state-promoted Pakistani culture. The attitude on the Pakistani side may have had its roots in the martial mind-set of Pashtuns and Punjabis, who had a longstanding military background. It was one of the reasons why Bengalis were made second-class citizens, thus preventing the development of a united Pakistani national identity and sense of community.

One major contributor to the tensions between West and East Pakistan was the belief that Bengalis were racially and culturally inferior to West Pakistanis. Examples of this attitude can be found in Pakistan and India till this day. Bengalis are ridiculed for their eating habits and clothing style; they are characterised as cowardly, inefficient and dirty. When talking to people in India and Pakistan, until today this attitude is still visible and many people express low esteem for them.

Discrimination against Bengalis has a long history in the subcontinent. The division of India into 'martial' and 'non-martial' races was a British concept and a result of the Indian Mutiny of 1857 that had been started by a mutiny among Indian soldiers in the British Indian Army. One great travesty of perception becoming a fact was that, though some of the mutinying units were from the Bengal Native Infantry and the cavalry units, the British saw Bengalis on the whole as disloyal and unreliable. No one took account of the fact that the British themselves had restricted the recruitment of Bengalis into their army, because they had fought against them at Plassey (1757) and Buxar (1764) and did not trust them as a result. The administrators, who had strong anthropological leanings, labelled them as 'non-martial'. What double standards! On the one hand, they were not considered a threat to their rule, while on the other, they were not to be recruited into the British Indian Army because they were deemed untrustworthy. Warren Hastings decided to recruit most of the soldiers from the Rajput and the Brahmin classes of Awadh (also Oudh) and Bihar. Therefore, even the Bengal Army, which ceased to exist in 1857, had very few Bengalis, if any. After 1857, educated Hindu Bengalis were preferred for civilian administration postings and for the councils that were introduced in the second half of the nineteenth century.

Muslims, however, faced much more discrimination than Hindu Bengalis. This was because the British saw the Rebellion of 1857 as essentially a Muslim mutiny, since the symbol used by the rebels was that of a Mughal emperor. The Hindus among the Bengalis were trusted more and happened to be better educated. Given the fact that much of modern educational institutions and administrative jobs were situated in Bengal, around Calcutta, the oldest base of British rule in India, the Hindus were far more fortunate in receiving and accepting modern education provided by those institutions compared to the Muslims. Owing to their lively literary and reformist tendencies, the Bengalis were considered by the British to be less backward than the other 'races' of India. This created a stir among those who were called 'martial' by the British such as Rajputs, Pashtuns, and others, and were thus less trusted by them and mostly less educated—mainly Muslims who in themselves were considered by the British to be more violent, dangerous, and untrustworthy than Hindus because of their religious affiliation.

Perhaps the success of the Bengalis in service and education and their closeness to the British roused a degree of jealousy in other Indians. In any case, this feeling seems to have been quite common in the northern part of the subcontinent. Even a prominent public figure like Sir Syed Ahmed Khan was affected by it. Criticising the concept of competitive exams in the Indian Civil Service in a speech delivered in Lucknow, in 1887, he said:

> Think for a moment what would be the result if all appointments were given by competitive examination. Over all races, not only over

Mahomedans, but over Rajas of high position and the brave Rajputs who have not forgotten the swords of their ancestors, would be placed as ruler a Bengali who, at sight of a table knife, would crawl under his chair. (*Uproarious cheers and laughter.*) There would remain no part of the country in which we should see at the tables of justice and authority any face except those of Bengalis. I am delighted to see the Bengalis making progress, but the question is—what would be the result on the administration of the country? Do you think that the Rajput and the fiery Pathan, who are not afraid of being hanged or of encountering the swords of the police, or the bayonets of the army, could remain in peace under the Bengalis?[2]

Coming from a renowned scholar and intellectual, and someone held in high esteem by a majority of upper class Muslims, this is a significant statement. It found reverberations much later, in 1970–1, when West Pakistan could not swallow a Bengali victory in the general elections. The same attitude can be found in a book penned by G.W. Choudhury, an East Pakistani bureaucrat, who served as a member of the Pakistan's cabinet from 1967 to 1971. He argued, 'Bengalis are noted for a negative and destructive attitude rather than for hard work and constructive programmes; they also have a tremendous tendency to put the blame on others.'[3]

Evidence of a bias against Bengalis can also be found in the literature of the Mughal period. Pashtun tribes—the Lodhis, Suris, Rohillas and others—migrating from what is now Afghanistan and Central Asia, towards Bengal, from the eleventh to sixteenth centuries, would have encountered a settled, agrarian community very different to the tribal society of northern India, that relied on warfare and pillaging for a livelihood.

There was a widespread sentiment in West Pakistan and its army, that East Pakistanis were not true Muslims, that their version of Islam was closer to Hinduism and, therefore, they must be brought onto the correct path. This failure to recognise and accept cultural difference played a vital role in shaping Bengali disillusionment with West Pakistan.

The poetry of Rabindranath Tagore has, to a large extent, shaped the inclusive nature of religion practiced by Muslim Bengalis. Tagore dominated the Bengali literary scene since the late nineteenth century, while the revolutionary, brash poetry of Kazi Nazrul Islam represented the spirit of Muslims in Bengal from the 1920s onwards. Yet the Hindu elite did all it could to relegate him well below Tagore. Nazrul had no problem with this and nor did the Bengalis who revered both poets in their separate niches. But the West Pakistanis did not understand this. They went as far as to ban Tagore's songs on Radio Pakistan—a fatal blunder, considering Tagore was so deeply embedded in the Bengali psyche. India was quick to use this move to their own advantage, pointing out to the Bengalis of East Pakistan that their culture was being 'robbed' from them. According to Lt. Gen. (retd.) Kamal Matinuddin, 'Qazi Nazrul Islam (1893–1976) gave an Islamic tinge to Bengali literature, but he did not write much.'[4] Someone who had not read Nazrul Islam could only have made this false statement. The remark echoes the anti-Bengal bias common among military men and reveals an abysmal lack of understanding of Bengali literature and Nazrul on the part of General Matinuddin.

Nazrul wrote prolifically and from an early age. Unlike Tagore, he did not cater to the English readership, or have his works translated and, as a result, was not internationally acclaimed. He did not give an 'Islamic tinge' to Bengali literature. He wrote with the broad-minded psyche of a Bengali Muslim, encompassing the versatility of the culture that surrounded him.

Like little drops of water that make an ocean, little incidents here and there, seemingly innocuous, built up a tangible feeling of cultural repression. One such example was when a certain Brigadier Hafiz who served in the Pakistani Army as a captain, recalls going for Eid prayers at the Sialkot cantonment prayer grounds. A senior officer sneered at his scraggy beard, traditional kurta, and loose pajamas, 'What sort of beggarly clothes are you wearing?'[5] Hafiz was naturally insulted. This is just one of many small instances where West Pakistanis openly displayed their disdain for their Bengali counterparts in the army.

Viewed independently, each incident may seem like an insignificant one-off, but collectively they take the shape of an inverted cultural hegemony—not necessarily an imposition of alien culture, but a negation of an existing one. Bengalis were depicted as the weaker, dark-skinned, inferior race of Dravidian origin, as opposed to the fair-skinned and physically formidable West Pakistanis.

There was, also, a grudging jealousy about the superior academic qualifications of the Bengalis of East Pakistan; Dhaka University was reputed to be the 'Oxford of the East'. Unfortunately, West Pakistanis were unable to feel proud of Bengali achievements and attributes, as they failed to see them as one of their own. Bengalis, too, simmered in barely repressed anger at the manner in which they were treated; they insulted the Punjabis and Pathans as ignoramuses/halfwits.

Of course, there was an awareness among various West Pakistani politicians and leaders, of this latent cultural volcano and that it was on the verge of erupting. Zulfikar Ali Bhutto, the late chairperson of the Pakistan Peoples Party (PPP), was well-versed in Pakistan's cultural divide. He said that in Pakistan, 'It was not a case of culture and unity flowing from the fountainhead of a single nationality.'[6] He believed that cultural unity was being wrongly forced on the provinces of the country. He said, 'There is a fundamental difference between unity willingly forged by a people and that forcibly imposed…..'[7] Unfortunately, such a realisation was not translated into a pragmatic policy.

Bengali Muslim intellectuals could have been encouraged and given financial patronage. After all, they were perceived to be secular and their faith was as strong as that of their counterparts in West Pakistan, if not stronger. West Pakistanis perceived their social customs as un-Islamic, as they did not conform to their social norms. According to G.W. Choudhury:

A federal union can be strengthened by giving [it] cultural freedom and autonomy, but Pakistan's attempt to impose uniformity where diversity was desirable[,] had unfortunate consequences. Every attempt made by the Pakistan Government to foster a cultural uniformity based on Islamic culture in East Pakistan, produced a sharp reaction....[8]

Global connectivity in media and communications has resulted in a degree of amalgamation between different cultures. Traces of Pakistani culture still exist in Bangladesh, blending in with ease. Strolling down the streets of Old Dhaka, one will still hear the *qawwali* of the Sabri Brothers and the *ghazals* of Mehdi Hasan wafting from the windows. Urdu words still find their way into the Bengali language.

The political leaders of Pakistan and Bangladesh may continue to play the 1971 card, but the people are learning to look ahead and let go of the past. Culture, after all, is a reflection of life's natural progression and a manifestation of intellectual achievement. It is a wonderfully complex integration of art, life, the environment, and so much more. Culture contains all the potential ingredients of a force of reconciliation. However, the commonalities have not been capitalised upon. Vested quarters, unfortunately, have highlighted only the differences, not the versatility.

Notes

1. Haimanti Roy, 'A Partition of Contingency? Public Discourse in Bengal, 1946–1947'. *Modern Asian Studies*, 43, 2009, pp. 1355–1384, doi:10.1017/S0026749X08003788.
2. Speech of Sir Syed Ahmed Khan at Lucknow, 1887, http://www.columbia.edu/itc/mealac/pritchett/00islamlinks/txt_sir_sayyid_lucknow_1887.html.
3. G.W. Choudhury, *The Last Days of United Pakistan* (Karachi: Oxford University Press, 1993), p. 10.
4. Lt. Gen. (retd.) Matinuddin, *Tragedy of Errors: East Pakistan Crisis, 1968–1971* (Lahore: Wajidalis, 1994), p. 54.
5. Ibid., p. 55.
6. Zulfikar Ali Bhutto, *The Myth of Independence* (Oxford University Press, 1969), p. 30.
7. Ibid., p. 13.
8. G.W. Choudhury, *The Last Days of United Pakistan*, p. 11.

2

The Language Movement

Language occupies a central place in the matrix of nations and perhaps in no other country of the world has language played as important a role in its identity, even its *raison d'être*, as in East Bengal. While there were many factors that instigated the anger of East Pakistanis, yet today, Bangladesh stands as an independent nation. Undoubtedly, the movement to establish Bengali as its state language catalysed its quest for independence.

The question of what Pakistan's national language would be was an important one. The failure of the Pakistani leadership to grasp the intricacies of this question sowed the seeds of the Language Movement, aimed at establishing Bengali as one of the state languages of Pakistan. At no time in the history of the movement was there any attempt to displace Urdu as a national language; the movement only demanded that since Bengali was spoken by a majority of Pakistanis, it should be given equal status. A lack of understanding about the national language issue and the response to it became increasingly apparent by the beginning of 1948.

On 23 February 1948, the Constituent Assembly of Pakistan went into session at Karachi, which was then the capital of Pakistan. It was proposed that the members would have to speak either in Urdu, or in English, in the Assembly. This was a ludicrous proposition, as very few Bengali members spoke Urdu. Dhirendranath Datta, a member from the East Pakistan Congress Party, moved an amendment motion to include Bengali as one of the languages of the parliament. He noted that out of the 69 million-strong population of Pakistan, 44 million (64 per cent) were from East Pakistan, with Bengali as

their mother tongue.[1] In fact, even in Sindh, the NWFP (now Khyber
Pukhtunkhwa), and Balochistan, Urdu was not the first language,
while in Punjab it was the most common means of communication.
The leaders of the Pakistan government, including Prime Minister
Liaquat Ali Khan and Chief Minister of East Bengal, Khawaja
Nazimuddin, strongly opposed the motion. On receiving the news
that the motion had been rejected, the students, intellectuals and
politicians of East Pakistan broke out in protest and agitation.

LOOKING FURTHER BACK

Some scholars believe that the name '*bangalah*' is derived from the
word '*banga*', which originally described a few south-eastern districts
at the mouth of the Ganges River. According to another opinion, it is
believed to be derived from the Dravidian-speaking tribe, Bang, which
settled in the area that is now Bengal, around 1000 BC. Bangalah
(Bengal) became the name of the eastern-most provinces in the early
thirteenth century, during the reign of the Delhi Sultanate, which
comprised a larger territory that roughly encompasses the former
British province of Bengal and territories of neighbouring provinces.

The Bengali language, or Bangla, as it is now officially referred
to, has played an important role since the nineteenth century, in the
development of the Bengali identity comprising all Bengali speakers
regardless of their religious affiliation. Ethnically, modern Bengalis
have quite a diverse background that includes Aryan, Dravidian,
Tibeto-Burman, and Austro-Asiatic (mostly tribal) peoples. Many
features of the people and their culture, including their diet, are
strongly connected to their eastern and south-eastern neighbours.
It can safely be said that the modern Bengali ethnicity is a mix of
a variety of racial groups that migrated to the region in pre-historic
and proto-historic times. Bengalis have varying physical features,
ranging from Tibeto–Burman to light-skinned Aryan, to darker
Dravidian. There is even an Afghan connection: in 1538, Sher Shah
Suri invaded Bengal and made it part of his empire as a result quite

a few Persian and Urdu-speaking Afghans became an integrated part of the local population.

Being the eastern-most province of India, Bengal did not have a prominent Persian and Urdu-speaking elite like the western provinces and Uttar Pradesh, the centre of the Mughal rule. Alongside a small number of Persian and Urdu speakers (all of whom also had to be able to speak Bengali), there was a strong Bengali-speaking, educated elite, known as 'bhadralok' (literally translating into 'gentlemen'), who traditionally sought employment in the field of administration, education, and other intellectual professions. Language has been a matter of discord in British India since the nineteenth century, when the British abolished Persian as the official language in India and substituted it with English—and Bengali in Bengal, thus realising the importance of the latter in that province.

Bengali was acknowledged by the British due to the rapid development of the language during the nineteenth century and the 'intellectual awakening' of educated Bengalis, who opened up to European ideas of equality and rationalism. This process was referred to as the Bengal Renaissance. The new development was not really a rebirth; it was not in the first place rooted in their own ancient scriptures and subcontinental philosophy, but was essentially a positive response to imported European ideas.

From the early 1820s, various socio-religious reform movements were initiated in Bengal. The most famous among these was the Brahmo Samaj, founded by Raja Ram Mohan Roy, which opposed the caste system and local customs like sati (the Hindu tradition of burning widows alive on the pyre of their deceased husbands). Later, revivalist reform movements like the Ramakrishna Mission emerged in Bengal, rejecting the need to borrow from western values and insisting that reformist ideas could be found in ancient Indian scriptures such as the Vedas.

These new ideas needed to be communicated and this resulted in the development of the Bengali language with a host of new words, capable of expressing new social, philosophical, and scientific ideas.

This impetus led to the creation of a new type of literature and a host of newspapers and journals. The Bengali language saw a revival in the second half of the nineteenth century, in the literary works of Bankim Chandra Chatterjee and others. The Tagore family and other famous writers, contributed largely to this. The Bengal Renaissance gave rise to a Bengali nationalism that identified with the modernisation of the Bengali language long before the idea of an all-Indian nation arose.

In provinces like the Bombay Presidency, for instance, Persian was first substituted with Urdu and later Hindi, written in the Devanagari script. There was another clash of languages in the nineteenth century, namely the Hindi–Urdu controversy. Concerned about their employment and social status, the Muslim bureaucracy resented Hindi, as they did not know the Devanagari script. Thus, the Hindi–Urdu controversy had economic and social implications for the Urdu-speaking Muslim upper class that prevailed in northern and western India. As such, the whole question became politicised. The upper class had suffered a loss in prestige, jobs in the administration, and political influence, after the fall of the Mughal Empire.

In 1906, the Muslim aristocracy created the All India Muslim League (AIML) to demand a separate electorate for Muslims, which would secure their representation in a majority-based political system in the newly emerging political power structure created by the British. The preservation of Urdu as the official language and later, as the 'national language' of Muslims, became one of the central demands of the AIML. The AIML used Urdu to mobilise Muslims and founded Urdu committees across British India, including in Bengal.

The Anjuman Taraqqi-e-Urdu, founded in 1886 by Maulvi Abdul Haq, played an important role in the popularisation of Urdu in Bengal and Bihar. There was, however, a strong critique of the AIML's Urdu policy by Bengali Muslim intellectuals, who argued, as early as 1919, that Urdu could never be a 'national' language for Bengali Muslims and that only Arabic could occupy such a role, as the only semblance of a national community would be the *ummah*.

The Urdu-speaking elite had always been a minority in Bengal; those Bengalis who knew and spoke Urdu mostly preferred Bengali as their colloquial and literary language. The rejection of the Urdu policy of the AIML was strongest in East Bengal, probably because there were hardly any urban centres and modern educational institutions (places where an Urdu-speaking class could have found a living) located there. The Urdu–Bengali controversy continued until Partition. While supporters of Urdu understood that the language was a vehicle to emancipate Bengali Muslims culturally, away from Bengali Hindus, they started promoting a kind of Urdu-influenced version of Bengali, which was subsequently rejected by a large segment of Bengal's Muslim intellectuals, who criticised the efforts to amend Bengali with Urdu words and create the so-called 'Musulmani Bangla'. They insisted that a joint cultural and literary heritage in Bengal did not allow any division between its Hindu and Muslim parts.

Undeniably, Muslim Bengalis have a unique, distinguished identity that makes them stand apart from non-Muslim Bengalis, as well as Muslim non-Bengalis. It is this identity that has, over time, been open to a natural infusion of Urdu, Arabic, and Farsi words, into its mother tongue. This is not the politically enforced induction of Urdu into Bengali, but a natural progression, which comes from the Muslim study of Arabic—the language of the Holy Quran. Like Urdu, Farsi, too has an affinity to Arabic. A wide array of Islamic academia is conducted in these languages and it is, therefore, only natural that Bengali would have been influenced by them.

The Hindu Bengali elite was unhappy with this incursion of Urdu and Arabic. In fact, Tagore was displeased with what he felt was a contamination of the language. Nazrul, meanwhile, had no such compunction about the use of foreign languages and his Bengali poetry is replete with words from Farsi, Arabic and Urdu, making his verses all the more forceful. Tagore went as far as to publicly condemn the use of the word 'khoon' (Urdu for blood) in Nazrul's poems, rather than the Bengali word 'rakta'. Yet today, 'khoon' is an accepted word in Bengali. This is only natural, as one can see in the English language,

French, Italian, German, and even Urdu and Hindi influences. In the case of the Bengali–Urdu nexus, there was a clear awareness of religious connotations, particularly by the Hindu Bengali elite class.

The consciousness that united Bengali Hindus and Muslims, on the other hand, was mainly based on the rich literature and sophisticated nature of the Bengali spoken and written by Hindus and Muslims. It was only in the 1920s that Mohandas Gandhi, while insisting on the need of a 'national language', started an initiative to create new Hindi/Urdu terms, drawn from Sanskrit, to express scientific and political concepts.

It is worth mentioning that there has been a fair amount of Urdu-bashing long before the Urdu–Bengali controversy came to the fore. It was said that Urdu, as a language, lacked pedigree and was a *laskhari zaban* or 'camp-language'. While this theory was proven false a long time ago, it continues to linger and some Urdu teachers are among those who believe in its validity. According to the theory, Urdu came into existence in cantonments during the Mughal era, and was a fusion of Hindi, Arabic, Persian, and other languages and that it was a means of communication for soldiers hailing from different linguistic and ethnic backgrounds. But this is hardly plausible. If this were indeed the case then Urdu would have been based on the Turkic languages spoken by the soldiers in those camps and by their superior officers. While 75 per cent of Urdu words have their etymological roots in Sanskrit and Prakrit, the language also has a strong connection to Persian and Arabic—the official languages of northern India under the Delhi Sultanate and Mughal rule.

Thus, Urdu was a language formed through a natural process of linguistic evolution. But the point here is that language has and continues to be a bone of contention. Just look at the British derision of American English and the American's snide attitude towards the Queen's language! Even though it is the same language! It is evidence of the fact that language is more than just a means of communication; it can be a sensitive factor in a nation's identity.

THE PARTITION OF INDIA

The issue of language took a new turn when the Partition of British India was announced in June 1947 and it became clear that East Bengal would become part of Pakistan. Now, the question of Urdu becoming the national language of the newly formed state was viewed as an attempt at 'foreign domination' over East Bengal, by West Pakistan. In such a scenario, Urdu speakers would dominate the administration and other fields of employment and Bengalis would have to give more attention to mastering Urdu than to their mother tongue. For Pakistan, the need of the hour, in 1947, was to find common ground that would stabilise the new structure. Urdu, like Islam, was promoted as a symbol of unity. The rulers of the new nation believed that its survival depended on cultural and religious unity. This meant supressing centuries-old ethnic and cultural identities and Islamic variations. While Urdu was the language of all Muslims, a vast majority of Muslims in the subcontinent only spoke, and still speak, local languages.

East Pakistan inherited a Muslim League government consisting of upper-class Urdu speakers. Both East and West Pakistan witnessed an influx of Urdu-speaking refugees from India, most of them educated and possessed with the technical skills, or commercial experience. They referred to as 'Biharis', even though only a part of them came from Bihar. They became the main supporters of the Muslim League and its demand for Urdu as a national language. They not only spoke Urdu, but also came with a staunch belief in Pakistan and thus felt politically and culturally much closer to West Pakistani bureaucrats and army officers in East Pakistan, than to Bengalis.

Being of urban background, Biharis followed the more stricter, Deobandi School of Islamic ideology and this widened the gulf between the two communities. There was a misconception among the Bengalis that West Pakistani rulers wanted to install Biharis in privileged positions, which led to widespread resentment. The ultimate tragedy was that the real Biharis, who were the strongest proponents of Pakistan, were looked down upon by other Urdu-speaking Muslims who settled in East Bengal after Partition, and who, because they were better educated, were the ones actually favoured by West Pakistani rulers. In fact, the Nawab of Dhaka's family and their Urdu-speaking Bengali supporters detested the ethnic Biharis.

This insistence on an 'Urdu only' policy had its roots in the very concept of nationhood, which was essentially European in origin and had been transplanted in the subcontinent. Unlike European countries, the Indian subcontinent did not have a single universal language, or religion, nor did it go through a process of industrialisation, secularisation and individualisation. The nationalism of the Indian independence movement was of a local variety and had to take into account various ground realities. As a result, this secular concept took the form of Hindu and Muslim nationalisms and other regional nationalisms, including Bengali and Tamil. However, in order to create an all-Indian nationalism, the need was felt to overcome cultural diversity, which was seen as a threat to 'unity' and therefore suppressed.

Secondly, the idea of there being unity in diversity is yet to be understood and appreciated in Pakistan. The federation must be built on the pillars of cultural, linguistic and religious freedoms; the negligence of these can only have disastrous consequences, as was witnessed in the case of East Bengal in 1971 and in Balochistan today.

The Bengali–Urdu controversy, as we have seen, was not a creation of the Pakistani state per se, but a legacy of a short-sighted policy of the Muslim League on language. The party's leadership, which hailed mainly from Uttar Pradesh and West India, did not take heed of the rejection of Urdu by Bengali Muslims.

While Pakistan's leaders and the Urdu-speaking intellectuals declared that Urdu would be the state language of Pakistan, the students and intellectuals of East Pakistan demanded that Bengali be made a second state language. Despite this, however, serious preparations were underway in various forums of the central government of Pakistan, under the initiative of Fazlur Rahman, the then Federal Minister for Education, to make Urdu the only state language of the country.[2] On receipt of this information, students in East Pakistan grew agitated and held a meeting on the Dhaka University campus, on 6 December 1947, demanding that Bangla be made one of the state languages of Pakistan. The meeting was followed by student processions and more agitation. The first Rashtrabhasha Sangram Parishad (National Language Action Committee) was formed at the end of December, with Professor Nurul Huq Bhuiyan, of the Tamaddun Majlis, as the convener. Professor Abul Kasem was also a prominent leader of the Tamaddun Majlis. The final demand from East Pakistan was that Bengali must be made the official language and the medium of instruction in East Pakistan and for the central government it would be one of the state languages, alongside Urdu. Gradually, many other organisations joined the agitation, turning it into a mass movement.

Tamaddun Majlis published a booklet titled *Pakistan's State Language: Bengali or Urdu* (*Pakistaner Rashtra Bhasha: Bangla Na Urdu*), which included the writings of Kazi Motahar Hossain and Abul Mansur Ahmed. The writers strongly advocated that Bengali be accepted as a state language of Pakistan. They said that, if need be, a nationwide movement would be initiated to bring this demand home. The booklet contained a proposal put forth by Tamaddun Majlis, which stated:

1. The Bengali language would be:
   (a) The official language of East Pakistan
   (b) The medium of education in East Pakistan
   (c) The language used in the courts in East Pakistan
2. The central government of Pakistan would have two state languages—Bengali and Urdu.
3. Bengali would be the first language of East Pakistan's Education Department.
4. In the interests of governance and science education, for the time being, both English and Bengali would be used in the

governing of East Pakistan. The Bengali language would undergo reforms as necessary. The language in which the people could easily, and in the shortest time, write, read and speak, would be the state language.

This logic was the basis for the above proposal. Even though the Tamaddun Majlis later distanced itself from the nationalist movement, it played a significant role in the initial stages of the language movement.[3]

The first session of the Constituent Assembly in Karachi, began on 23 February 1948. As stated earlier, Dhirendranath Datta put forward the proposal at this session that, along with English and Urdu, Bengali also be adopted as an official language of the Assembly. A number of members delivered fiery speeches in support of this proposal. Prime Minister Liaquat Ali Khan, however, opposed the proposal. He said that he had initially seen the motive behind this proposal as innocent, but later deemed it to be a move to divide the people of Pakistan and to use a simple language issue to break up the unity of Muslims.

Liaquat Ali Khan's speech seemed to hint at a Hindu conspiracy and in fact, only served to divide the community. At this session, Khawaja Nazimuddin, Chief Minister of East Pakistan, alleged that the majority of East Pakistanis were willing to accept Urdu as the state national language. This was false, a complete negation of the facts on the ground; his speech evoked a sharp reaction in East Pakistan. In fact, the so-called 'leaders' of East Bengal led both Governor General Mohammad Ali Jinnah and Prime Minister Liaquat Ali Khan, astray. As events later show, the Nawab of Dhaka's family, for their own selfish purpose, contributed immensely to the demise of Pakistan by providing two of its principal leaders with bad advice.

The 27 February 1948, *Dainik Azad*, a Calcutta-based publication, carried an editorial in this regard, titled, 'The Bengali Language and Pakistan'. It read, 'This statement [of Khawaja Nazimuddin] is not at all true. We believe that if a referendum is held, not less than 99 per cent of the votes will go in favour of Bengali. By passing such an irresponsible remark, not only has he harmed the basic interests of East Pakistan, he has also tarnished his right to represent the people of this country.'[4]

A new committee was formed to fight for Bengali as the state language, with Shamsul Huq as convener. On 11 March 1948, a general strike was observed in the towns of East Pakistan, in protest against the omission of Bengali from the languages of the Constituent Assembly, the absence of Bengali letters on Pakistani coins and stamps, and the use of only Urdu in recruitment tests for the armed forces. The movement also reiterated the earlier demand that Bengali be declared one of the state languages of Pakistan and the official language of East Pakistan. Amidst the processions, picketing and slogans, arrests were made. Under such circumstances, the government had little choice but to give in and Khawaja Nazimuddin signed an agreement with the student leaders. And while he agreed to some of their terms and conditions, he did not comply with the demand that Bengali be made a state language.

Jinnah visited East Pakistan on 19 March 1948. In the two meetings he addressed in Dhaka, he reiterated that Urdu would be the only state language of Pakistan. On 21 March, he said, 'Now I ask you to get rid of this provincialism, because as long as you allow this poison to remain in the body politic of Pakistan, believe me, you will never be a strong nation...'.[5] Even after this, many Bengalis remained hopeful because of their faith in the Quaid and were confident that he would be fair and just.

In his speech at the Dhaka University Convocation days later, on 24 March 1948, he once again equated the demand for Bengali with provincialism that undermined the unity of Pakistan. He said,

> The recent language controversy, in which, I am sorry to make note, some of you allowed yourselves to get involved even after your Prime Minister had clarified the position, is only one of the many subtle ways whereby the poison of provincialism is being sedulously injected into this Province. Does it not strike you rather odd that certain sections

of the Indian Press, to whom the very name of Pakistan is anathema, should in the matter of language controversy, set themselves up as the champion of what they call your 'just rights'? Is it not significant that they very persons, who in the past have betrayed the Musalmans, or fought against Pakistan, which is, after all, merely the embodiment of your fundamental right of self-determination, should now suddenly pose as the saviours of your just rights and incite you to defy the Government on the question of language? I must warn you to beware of these fifth-columnists. Let me restate my views on the question of a State language for Pakistan. For official use in this Province, the people of the province can choose any language they wish. This question will be decided solely in accordance with the wishes of the people of this Province alone, as freely expressed through their accredited representatives at the appropriate time and after full and dispassionate consideration. There can, however, be only one *lingua franca*, that is, the language for inter-communication between the various provinces of the State, and that language should be Urdu and cannot be any other. The State language, therefore, must obviously be Urdu, a language that has been nurtured by a hundred million Muslims of this sub-continent, a language understood throughout the length and breadth of Pakistan and above all, a language which, more than any other provincial language, embodies the best that is in Islamic culture and Muslim tradition and is nearest to the language used in other Islamic countries.… These facts are fully known to the people who are trying to exploit the language controversy in order to stir up trouble. There was no justification for agitation but it did not suit their purpose to admit this. Their sole object in exploiting this controversy is to create a split among the Muslims of this State, as indeed they have made no secret of their efforts to incite hatred against non-Bengali Musalmans. Realizing, however, that the statement that your Prime Minister made on the language controversy, on return from Karachi, left no room for agitation, in so far as it conceded the right of the people of this Province to choose Bengali as their official language if they so wished, these persons changed their tactics. They started demanding that Bengali should be the State language of the Pakistan Centre and since they could not overlook the obvious claims of Urdu as the official language of a Muslim State, they proceeded to demand that both Bengali and Urdu should be the State languages of Pakistan. Make no mistake about it. There can be only one State language, if the component parts of this State are to march forward in unison, and that language, in my opinion, can only be Urdu.[6]

In an emotionally charged environment, these words did not reach the audience. From 1948 onwards, the Bengali Language Movement became a symbol for East Pakistan's struggle for political, economic, and cultural equality with West Pakistan. This exacerbated tensions, ultimately leading to secession from Pakistan.

The Language Movement spread throughout East Pakistan. The Dhaka University Language Action Committee was formed on 11 March 1950, with Abdul Matin as its convener. By the beginning of 1952, the movement took a serious turn. By this time, Jinnah had passed away, Liaquat Ali Khan had been assassinated and Khawaja Nazimuddin had succeeded the former as Prime Minister of Pakistan. With the political crisis becoming more intense, the economic condition in East Pakistan deteriorated sharply. People started losing faith in the Muslim League. A new party, the Awami Muslim League, later to be simply called the Awami League, was formed under the leadership of Maulana Abdul Hamid Khan Bhashani, in 1949. With the growing sense of deprivation and exploitation in East Pakistan, the movement got fresh impetus in 1952.

The *Pakistan Observer* was the mouthpiece for the language movement at that time. The government banned it on 13 February and its editor, Abdus Salam, was arrested. The weekly *Ittefaq* stepped up to fill that gap and promoted the movement. On 27 January 1952, Nazimuddin came to Dhaka from Karachi. Addressing a meeting at Paltan Maidan, he said that the people of the province could choose the provincial language, but that only Urdu would be the state language. There was, instantly, a negative reaction to this speech among the students, who responded with the slogan, '*Rashtra Bhasha Bangla Chai!*' (We want Bangla as the state language). A strike was observed at Dhaka University on 30 January and the following day, the representatives of various political and cultural organisations held a meeting chaired by Maulana Bhashani. An All-Party Central Language Action Committee was formed with Kazi Golam Mahboob as its convener. At this time, the government also proposed that Bangla be written in Arabic script—a suggestion that was vehemently opposed. The Language Action Committee decided to call a general strike and organise demonstrations and processions on 21 February throughout East Pakistan.

As preparations for the protests were underway, the government imposed Section 144 in the city of Dhaka, banning all assemblies and demonstrations. A meeting of the Central Language Action Committee was held on 20 February 1952. The students were determined to violate Section 144 and held a student meeting at 11 a.m. on 21 February, at the Dhaka University campus, then located close to the Medical College Hospital. When the meeting started, the vice-chancellor, along with a few university teachers, came to the spot and requested the students not to violate the ban on assembly. But the students were adamant. Thousands from different schools and colleges of Dhaka assembled on the university campus, while armed police waited outside the gate. When the students emerged in groups, shouting slogans, the police resorted to baton charge. The students then started throwing brickbats at the police, who retaliated with tear gas. Unable to control the agitation, the police fired upon the crowd, which was proceeding towards the Assembly Hall. Police action got out of control; and 19 students were killed at the Dhaka Medical College hostel campus.

There are first-hand accounts of that fateful day, a vital turning point in the region's history. A veteran leader of the Language Movement, A.N.M. Gaziul Haque, a student leader at the time, presided over the rally held at the Dhaka University campus on 21 February 1952. Many of the students who were present at the meeting, are alive today. They are known as the *Bhasha Sainik*, or Language Soldiers. At the time, Shamsul Huq and several other student leaders had been against violating Section 144. However, the pressure from the student body was too great to ignore.

Gaziul Haque wrote:

> It is true that, at the meeting, Shamsul Huq spoke against violating Section 144. However, when the decision was taken to violate Section 144, Shamsul Huq said to me, "I agree to this decision and I am with this struggle". So on that day, most of those who had not been in favour of violating Section 144 for one reason or the other, finally accepted our decision. Shamsul Huq was later arrested and spent a long time in jail.[7]

Student leader Muhammed Sultan was given the responsibility of listing the names of those who were going to violate Section 144 and emerge through the gates of the campus, out onto the streets. He was sitting at the gate, writing the names of the students. Habibur Rahman Shelley led the squad and was the first to pass through the gates. Habibur Rahman later went on to become the Chief Justice of Bangladesh, as well as the chief advisor in the caretaker government.

Police were arresting those who emerged to violate Section 144 and taking them, in their vehicles, to the police station. Among the girl students who violated Section 144 on that day, were Safia Khatun, Sufia Ibrahim, Rawshan Ara Bachchu, Shamsunnahar and others. They tore off the police barricade and assembled under the mango tree (Amtola) in the Dhaka University campus premises to join the movement. However, their contributions are not yet written in details nor properly documented.

There were a number of women including Dr Halima Khatun, Dr Sufia Khatun, Rawshan Ara Bachchu, Sufia Ibrahim, Fazilatunnessa, Rani Bhattachariya, Pratibha Mutsuddi, Sofia Khan, Zulekha, Nuri, Sara Taifur, Sufia Ahmed, Safia Khatun and others among them. Police charged batons brutally and around eight schoolgirls including Sufia Ibrahim and Rawshan Ara Bachchu got injured.[8] Shamsunnahar recounted, 'We emerged a little after Safia Apa. There was a police cordon in front of us. City Superintendent of Police, Masood Mahmood, was standing to one side. Sufia and I skirted around the cordon and went ahead. Many girls followed us.'

This same Masood Mahmood went on to become Director General of Bhutto's Federal Security Force (FSF) and ordered the elimination of some prominent politicians. Later, when a case pertaining to this was under investigation, Mahmood turned approver and provided hearsay evidence that led to the hanging of Bhutto. Some FSF officials who worked under him, confessed their guilt and were also hanged, while Mahmood himself left for the US without being held accountable for his many crimes.

Meanwhile, on 21 February 1952, the Legislative Assembly session was about to begin. Hearing the news of the shooting, some members of the Assembly, including Maulana Abdur Rashid Tarkabagish and members of the Opposition, went out and joined the protesting students. In the Assembly, Nurul Amin, then Chief Minister of East Pakistan, continued to oppose the demand for Bengali. '*Rashtra bhasha Bangla chai, Nurul Amin-er rokto chai*' (translated verbatim, 'We want Bengali as the national language, we want the blood of Nurul Amin'), was a popular slogan in East Bengal. The next day, many were injured and arrested. On 23 February, a memorial was erected at the spot where the students had been massacred. In 1963, this became a concrete memorial—the Shaheed Minar. This incident of police brutality sparked a new wave of protest movements against the Muslim League government, which continued until April 1952. Shaheed Dibash (Martyrs' Day) or Language Movement Day is observed as a national holiday in Bangladesh, on 21 February. Interestingly, the United Nations has now declared 21 February as the International Mother Language Day, highlighting the importance of language in a community and a nation.

THE LANGUAGE MOVEMENT TURNS POLITICAL

On 21 April 1952, Dhaka University re-opened, but tensions remained strong. The Bengal wing of the Awami League, the opposition party founded by Maulana Bhashani to counter the Muslim League and its policies, took the political struggle for the Bengali demand into its own hands. The Awami League was later joined by disgruntled leaders of the Muslim League, such as Huseyn Shaheed Suhrawardy and others. Suhrawardy soon became the leader of the All-Pakistan Awami League, with Sheikh Mujibur Rahman as its General Secretary. Later, the Awami League was prevented from contesting the provincial elections in West Pakistan in 1953, because the Muslim League government was preventing an election campaign of the Awami League candidates. Suhrawardy decided to do better in the upcoming elections in East Pakistan, to be held in 1954. Based on his proposal, the United Front (Jukto Front) was constituted in December 1953 and consisted of five Bengali opposition parties, of which, the two major ones were the Awami League and the Krishak Sramik Party of Fazlul Huq (founded in July 1953). Through an uneasy alliance, they managed to sign a 21-point charter, at the top of which was the demand for Bengali as a national language.

By taking up the language demand and other pressing problems of the Bengali population, the United Front swept the elections. They won 223 out of 237 seats and left only 10 seats for the Muslim League. The crushing defeat of the Muslim League in East Bengal weakened its stand in West Pakistan as well. So much so that later, in 1954, despite enjoying a majority in the Constituent Assembly of Pakistan, the Muslim League gave in to the pressure and resolved to grant official status to Bengali in the province of East Pakistan.

After a great deal of controversy over the language issue, the final demand from East Pakistan was that Bengali must be the official language and the medium of instruction in East Pakistan and for the central government, it would be one of the state languages along with Urdu. The East Bengal Legislative Assembly adopted a resolution recommending the recognition of Bengali as one of the state languages of Pakistan. The Language Movement continued until 1956, despite the combined strength of the West Pakistani politicians and bureaucrats resisting it.

While the Assembly was debating on the language issue, one of its members, Adel Uddin Ahmed, made an important amendment proposal, according to which Bengali was to be recognised as the second official language of Pakistan. Article 214(1) of the 1956 Constitution was accordingly re-worded to, 'The state languages of Pakistan shall be Urdu and Bengali' and was adopted unanimously by the Assembly on 16 February 1956. But the damage had already been done. The initial insistence that Urdu be made the national language on grounds of its alleged universality, and the fact that Bengali had been denied this honour, left scars that continued to fester, ultimately helping to pave the way for the secession of East Pakistan.

Notes

1. Source: http://www.londoni.co/index.php/24-history-of-bangladesh/1952-bhasha-andolon/204-bhasha-andolon-bangladesh-language-movement-1948-1952-dhirendranath-datta-stance-history-of-bangladesh.

2. Incidentally, his sons, Sohail Rahman and Salman Rahman, occupy prominent political and commercial positions in Bangladesh today, and they do so without any prejudice with regard to whichever government is in power.

3. Source: https://www.linkedin.com/pulse/east-pakistan-language-problem-bangladesh-abstracts-pathan.

4. *Dainik Azad*, 27 February 1948, p. 3.

5. *Jinnah: Speeches and Statements 1947-1948* (Karachi: Oxford University Press, 2000), p. 149; http://m-a-jinnah.blogspot.com/2010/04/national-consolidation-march-1948.html.

6. *Jinnah: Speeches and Statements 1947–1948* (Karachi: Oxford University Press, 2000), pp. 157–8; http://m-a-jinnah.blogspot.com/2010/04/students-role-in-nation-building-24th.html.

7. See events section of http://www.21stfebruary.info/ (the original URL containing the quote is not accessible: http://www.21stfebruary.info/event_21stFeb1952.htm).

8. Source: http://www.londoni.co/index.php/24-history-of-bangladesh/1952-bhasha-andolon/219-bhasha-andolon-bangladesh-language-movement-1948-1952-women-s-role-history-of-bangladesh.

3

Purba Pakistan
The United Bengal Plan and the Partition of Bengal

Indian history is replete with events—plans, plots, and negotiations—leading to the emergence of Pakistan and India, marking the end of British rule in the subcontinent. However, not all plans have been studied closely. In fact, one of these remained hidden for many years after Independence. It concerns British geo-strategic interests and the political initiative behind Partition and the creation of Pakistan. In 2005, a former civil servant and aid-de-camp to Lord Mountbatten, Narendra Singh Sarila, made interesting revelations based on research in newly disclosed documents in the British archives. He pointed out that it was US pressure on Britain since 1942, in favour of India's independence and the preservation of its unity, that forced British Prime Minister, Winston Churchill, to play the 'Pakistan card' and devise a plan whereby the British could retain a military presence in the subcontinent, after its withdrawal. Sarila writes:

> Once the British realised that the Indian nationalists, who would rule India after independence, would deny Britain military cooperation under a British Commonwealth defence umbrella, they settled for those willing to do so by using religion for the purpose. Their problem could be solved if Mohammad Ali Jinnah, the leader of the Muslim League party, would succeed in his plan to detach the northwest of India abutting Iran, Afghanistan and Sinkiang and establish a separate state there—Pakistan. The proposition was a realisable one,

as a working relationship had been established between the British authorities in India and Jinnah during the Second World War and he was willing to cooperate with Britain on defence matters if Pakistan was created.[1]

Another plan that never came to fruition was that for a united Bengal. While Lord Mountbatten had clear instructions regarding the western part of India, including assigning Indians with the responsibility of carrying out Partition, he did not have any such instructions regarding the Muslim majority areas in East Bengal. There, he was free to decide depending on the situation. There are indications that Mountbatten, alongside Jinnah, considered a Three Nation Theory—a fact studiously ignored by historians of both India and Pakistan. The third nation would have been an undivided Bengal.

Long before the Lahore Resolution of 1940, questions were raised regarding the economic viability of a divided Bengal. According to Sir Reginald Coupland, a British historian who had come to India with the Cabinet Mission in 1942, an East Bengal deprived of Calcutta would not be able to survive economically, or exist as a detached and backward province of Pakistan.[2] His judgement was based on the Partition of Bengal (1905–11), which had resulted in a fierce movement for reunification. By the end of the Second World War, Britain was in a precarious economic situation and eager to leave India. It wanted a quick withdrawal and saw partition as the best way achieve this. On 20 February 1947, Prime Minister Clement Attlee announced, for the first time, that 'it was the definite intention' of the British to leave India by June 1948, even if it meant transferring power in some areas 'to existing provincial governments'. This was the first sign that Britain was quite all right with dividing the subcontinent according to the wishes of the Muslim League, and Pakistan became a possibility. After this announcement, the Indian National Congress started rethinking its previous stance of refusal. Believing that Pakistan was not a viable option and would soon collapse, Congress agreed to partition.

That was when the idea of a 'United Bengal'—the third independent unit—was developed and subsequently expressed in public for the first time, at a press conference held in Delhi, on 27 April 1947. Huseyn Shaheed Suhrawardy, a Bengali Muslim leader, called upon the British to recognise 'an independent, undivided and sovereign Bengal in a divided India, as a separate dominion.'[3]

The logic of this proposal did not escape the British. As a result, Mountbatten's original plan, drawn up in May 1947, was amended with an option for a third dominion by the name of the United States of Bengal. According to Collins and Lapierre, in the plan that Mountbatten had sent to London for approval, he had inserted a clause that would allow 65 million Hindus and Muslims in Bengal to join into one viable country, with Calcutta as the capital.

> Despite its division into two religious communities, Bengal, even more than the Punjab, was a distinct entity. Whether Hindus or Moslems, Bengalis sprang from the same racial stock, spoke the same language, shared the same culture. They sat on the floor in a certain Bengali manner, ordered the sentences they spoke in a peculiar Bengali cadence, each rising to a final crescendo, celebrated their own Bengali New Year on 15 April. Its poets, like Tagore, were regarded with pride by all Bengalis.
>
> They were the descendants of a culture whose roots went back in time to the pre-Christian era when a Buddhist civilization flourished in Bengal. Obliged to renounce their Buddhist faith by a Hindu dynasty in the first centuries after Christ, the Bengalis of the east greeted the arrival of Mohummed's warriors along their frontier as a release from Hindu oppression and eagerly embraced Islam. Since then, Bengal had been divided into religious halves, Moslems to the east, Hindus to the west.[4]

Purba Pakistan—Early Bengali Visions about Pakistan

The latest research in the field of Bengali Muslim aspirations about the future of their province and the nation, include Neilesh Bose's research on the early ideas of a united Bengal, called 'Purba Pakistan' as part of the idea of Pakistan.[5] This idea had been developed by journalists and academics on the pages of Bengali literary journals like *Azad*, *Mohammadi*, and *Saogat*, since the 1920s. More definite contours were given to this idea by the East Pakistan Renaissance Society, founded in 1942, in the wake of the Lahore Resolution. One of its founding members, Abul Kalam Shamsuddin, declared, 'We understood the call to Pakistan to be not just a political one, but one inspired by and based on literary and cultural strength'.[6] The idea developed by this circle included a full-fledged Bengali Pakistan having its own unique elements of culture, based on the original idea of the Lahore Resolution—of a Pakistan consisting of multiple internal parts—thus countering Congress's idea of a unified Indian nation and state.

Another Bengali writer Mujibur Rahman Khan, in his 1942 book titled *Pakistan*,[7] provides a concise explanation of the intellectual idea of a Bengali Pakistan. He says that in a centralised state based on the colonial model, the minorities would always be disenfranchised and sidelined.

In order to prove the Bengali cultural separateness and excellence, groups were formed to explore and record local forms of music and literature, such as the *punthis*, which were hand-written texts on religion and folklore.[8] The results of the research were displayed in cultural fairs and festivals that helped spread an awareness of Bengali culture.

In September 1944, Mujibur Rahman Khan published a booklet containing a map and delimitation of the proposed Purba Pakistan. It included all of Eastern Bengal, Assam, Sylhet, and Calcutta and excluded Burdwan and a small portion of Murshidabad. The argument in favour of including Calcutta in East Pakistan was that if the non-Bengali Hindu migrants (Marwaris) were excluded, Muslims would form a small majority in city.[9]

It is apparent that Bengali writers were advocating the creation of two separate Pakistans—one Purba and one Western and a Bengal divided on religious lines. It shows that the idea of Pakistan developed by West Pakistani politicians of the Muslim League, was adjusted to Bengali circumstances by integrating into with Bengali cultural, literary, and language traditions. A united Pakistan, with a culture that was not rooted in local tradition—as was the case after August 1947—was never an option for Bengali Muslims.

THE UNITED BENGAL PLAN

Another short-lived proposition, in relation to the idea of a United Bengal, surfaced in the months prior to the announcement of Partition. It was based on the idea that Bengal, despite its religious divide, had a united culture and an integrated economy and that these would suffer if the province was partitioned. This outlook gained momentum after the British announced, in late February 1947, that they would exit India in a couple of months. Visionary Bengali nationalists, such as Huseyn Shaheed Suhrawardy, Abul Hashim, Chaudhury Mohammad Ali, and A.K. Fazlul Huq of the Muslim League, sought to amend proposals for Partition based on the two-nation theory, with the demand for a united and independent state of Bengal as a third nation. A second Hindu group, consisting of Kiran Shankar Roy and Sarat Chandra Bose—two leftist nationalists of the Indian National Congress—also supported this idea. After Suhrawardy had presented his plan for a united and independent Bengal on 27 April 1947, Hashim issued a similar statement in Calcutta, on 29 April. Interestingly, the ideological vision for a 'Greater Bengal' included the regions of Assam and some Muslim-majority districts of Bihar.

In order to win over political support for this plan, Suhrawardy held talks with the Governor of Bengal, Frederick Burrows, the head of the Muslim League, M.A. Jinnah and the Viceroy of India, Lord Mountbatten, at various points. Burrows supported the idea because he felt that it would be unfair to divide Bengal so that Calcutta and all the revenues would go to one half, while the other half would be left empty-handed, despite having contributed to the prosperity of the city. Jinnah, who relied in all matters concerning Bengal, on the advice of Mirza Abul Hassan Ispahani, a close confidante whose family had business interests in Bengal, agreed to the United Bengal scheme. Jinnah is on record to have said, 'If Bengal remains united,...I should be delighted. What is the use of Bengal without Calcutta[?]; they had much better to remain united and independent; I am sure that they would be on friendly terms with us'.[10] Jinnah tried to persuade Viceroy Mountbatten not to destroy the unity of Bengal and Punjab, which had national characteristics and a common way of life and 'where the Hindus have stronger feelings as Bengalis or Punjabis than they have as members of the Congress.'[11] According to Stanley Wolpert, Jinnah had told Mountbatten that he would have been delighted if the proposal to create a separate, sovereign Bengal was accepted. The main fear was that a divided Bengal, without Calcutta, would be economically deprived. Without the inclusion of Calcutta, East Bengal would be moth-eaten. This was based on the assumption that such a state would be on friendly terms with Pakistan and support its inclusion in the British Commonwealth. Obviously, Jinnah tried to keep Calcutta with Pakistan for the sake of East Pakistan, or else he would have agreed to Bengal's independence rather than opt for the kind of partition that happened later. There was, clearly, a flexibility in Jinnah's idea of what constituted a nation state. It can therefore be assumed that perhaps it was the Congress, along with Jawaharlal Nehru and V.J. Patel, who insisted on a partition that created a unit in East Bengal, which—deprived of Calcutta –was not economically viable.

The Sarat Bose and Kiran Shankar groups of the Bengal Provincial Congress Committee supported the United Bengal plan within the Bengal faction of the Congress. From the beginning of May 1947, both groups grew closer to each other. They met Gandhi with their proposals during the latter's visit to Calcutta and sought his suggestions. Finally, a tentative agreement was reached at a meeting, held on 20 May 1947, among Bengali leaders in Calcutta, who were

in favour of a united and independent Bengal. The terms of agreement
were as follows:

1. Bengal would be a Free State. The Free State of Bengal would
   decide its relations with the rest of India.
2. The Constitution of the Free State of Bengal would provide for
   election to the Bengal Legislature on the basis of a joint electorate
   and adult franchise, with reservation of seats proportionate to the
   population among Hindus and Muslims. The seats set aside for
   Hindus and Scheduled Caste Hindus would be distributed amongst
   them in proportion to their respective population, or in such
   manner as may be agreed among them. The constituencies would
   be multiple constituencies and the votes would be distributive and
   not cumulative. A candidate who got the majority of the votes of
   his own community cast during the elections and 25 per cent of the
   votes of the other communities so cast, would be declared elected. If
   no candidate satisfied these conditions, that candidate who got the
   largest number of votes of his own community would be elected.
3. On the announcement by His Majesty's Government that the
   proposal of the Free State of Bengal had been accepted and that
   Bengal would not be partitioned, the present Bengal Ministry
   would be dissolved. A new interim Ministry consisting of an equal
   number of Muslims and Hindus (including Scheduled Caste
   Hindus) but excluding the Chief Minister would be formed. In
   this Ministry, Chief Minister would be a Muslim and the Home
   Minister a Hindu.
4. Pending the final emergence of a Legislature and a Ministry under
   the new constitutions, Hindus (including Scheduled Caste Hindus)
   and Muslims would have an equal share in the Services, including
   military and police. The Services would be manned by Bengalis.
5. A Constituent Assembly composed of 30 persons, 16 Muslims and
   14 non-Muslims, would be elected by Muslim and non-Muslim
   members of the Legislature respectively, excluding Europeans.[12]

However, it was the Congress and the Hindu Mahasabha that
sought the partition of these provinces on communal lines. When
Mountbatten shared this plan with Nehru, the Indian leader was

horrified. The vision of India that emerged from the pages was a nightmare to him; it was an India divided not just into two, but into several pieces. He was opposed to this plan, which he felt would exacerbate India's fissiparous tendencies on the lines of ethnicity, culture, and language, creating a mosaic of smaller hostile states. Nehru was adamantly against such a development and thus against a United Bengal. He felt that this would substantially weaken the argument for a united Indian state with a strong centre as he visualised it. He also feared that if the idea gained support, other regions of India would clamour for separation on ethnic or religious grounds. Even today, clamour for separation can still be heard in various parts of India. The deprived states of Northeast India, known as the Seven Sisters, have been enduring insurgency and separatist movements for decades.

Actually, Suhrawardy had also envisaged a loose confederation of Bengali states, separate and independent from India. This would have been a viable option, considering the fact that the Seven Sisters have hardly any affinity with India—evident from the ongoing civil war and demand for greater autonomy. The leaders of Bengal were well aware of the economic advantages of a separate state that encompassed both Calcutta and Assam. According to Stanley Wolpert, had Viceroy Mountbatten followed the advice of these Bengali leaders, as well as that of Jinnah, rather than listening only to Nehru, a consolidated United Bengal may have emerged, with Calcutta as its capital, instead of the far weaker Bangladesh, which was born violently from Pakistani's eastern-half, a quarter of a century later.

From various historical accounts and recent analyses by Indian columnist M.J. Akbar, it is evident that Suhrawardy and A.K. Fazlul Huq were the main proponents of a United Bengal. Akbar, as he is prone to do, sees a malevolent purpose behind Jinnah's support for the plan of the Bengali leaders. According to M.B.I. Munshi's *The India Doctrine*, Akbar imputes that Jinnah did not mind the idea of an independent Bengal because it meant that Gandhi and Nehru would lose yet another part of India. Jinnah supposedly told

Suhrawardy that he would prefer the Balkanisation of India and that after he got Pakistan in the northwest, Suhrawardy could keep his Bengal; but there is no evidence to support this theory. Never in his lifetime had Suhrawardy ever mentioned such a plan to anyone. Akbar maybe a gifted writer, particularly apt at creating fiction from fact. His account must be taken with more than just a pinch of salt, as it is more of a hagiography of Nehru, a sort of nominal Muslim apology for partition.

The Muslims of Bengal understood the advantages of having a separate state, which would explain the terms of the Lahore Resolution moved by A.K. Fazlul Huq, the Chief Minister of Bengal, at the 27th Session of the All India Muslim League, on 23 March 1940. The Lahore Resolution categorically stated that geographically contiguous units are demarcated into regions, which should be so constituted, with such territorial adjustments as may be necessary, whereby the Muslim-majority areas are grouped to constitute autonomous and sovereign states.

However, the Hindu Bengalis under the influence of the nationalist Hindu Mahasabha and Congress led by Nehru and Patel, were vehemently opposed to the plan devised by Suhrawardy and others, for a united and sovereign Bengal. They wanted the maximum territory for India, while ensuring that Pakistan remained as weak as possible. With the Hindus insisting on the partitioning of Bengal, the Lahore Resolution was modified in 1946 and the concept of Pakistan was born.

To quote Begum Shaista Suhrawardy Ikramullah:

Bengal was the largest Muslim majority area and at the same time, it was backward, poverty-stricken and disorganized. Just before the election [in 1945], floor-crossing of the Muslims had become a scandal. This was to be no more. Shaheed Bhai, ably helped by Mr Abul Hashim, had organized the Muslims of Bengal in such a manner that they voted almost to a man for the Muslim League. Shaheed Bhai toured every district, town and village of the province,

speaking to the people in simple words, explaining the objectives of
the Muslim League and the reasons why they should vote for it.[13]

Ikramullah writes about the 1946 Resolution, which officially
amended the 1940 Resolution:

> Sayings of the Quaid, and slogans of the Muslim League were written
> on large white letters on green bands. Surrounding the *pandal* was the
> Quaid's definitions of what made us, the Muslims, a nation.
>   The writing said:

> > We are a nation of a hundred million, and what is more we are a nation
> > with our own distinctive culture and civilisation, language and literature,
> > art and architecture, names and nomenclature, sense of value and
> > proportion, legal laws and moral codes, customs and calendars, history and
> > traditions, aptitudes and ambitions—in short, we have our own distinctive
> > outlook on life and of life. By all canons of international laws, we are
> > a nation.

> The next morning was most important, for at 11.00…Shaheed Bhai
> was to present the resolution for Pakistan. The previous resolution of
> 23 March 1940 had been presented by Fazlul Haq and it was the right
> and privilege of Bengal, the largest Muslim majority province, to do
> so again. This time it was presented by Shaheed Bhai.
>   The resolution presented by Shaheed categorically and emphatically
> stated the demand for Pakistan. It said:

> > Whereas the Muslims are convinced that with a view to saving Muslim
> > India from the domination of the Hindus and in order to afford them full
> > scope to develop themselves according to their genius, it is necessary to
> > constitute a sovereign independent state comprising Bengal and Assam in
> > the North East Zone, and the Punjab, North West Frontier Province, Sind
> > and Balochistan in the North West Zone.[14]

The passing of this resolution by the newly elected Muslim
members of the Indian Legislature, gave weight to the Muslim League's
demand for Pakistan and to Jinnah's claim that there were not two,
but three parties to the settlement of the Indian question—the British,

the Congress, and the All India Muslim League. Jinnah could now argue from a position of strength. Pakistan was no longer a dream of a few ideologues or students; it was the demand of the majority of the Muslim politicians of the majority and minority provinces of India.

PARTITIONING BENGAL

Unfortunately, neither the United Bengal plan that was boycotted by Congress and the Hindu Mahasabha, nor the idea of Purba Pakistan as a separate state, became a reality. Against all better reasoning, Bengal was divided due to uncompromising attitudes within Congress and the negligence of the British. The manner in which the partition of Bengal was administrated, became a disaster not only for East Bengal, but Pakistan as well.

While there were a host of factors exacerbating the economic and cultural frictions between East and West Pakistan, these were compounded by political problems, starting with the partition of Bengal. Bengali Muslims reluctantly accepted it, while some opposed it outright. This was symbolised by Suhrawardy's last-ditch effort for a United Bengal. But an independent India, without Bengal and Calcutta in particular, was unacceptable to Congress. The Congress Working Committee announced, as early as 8 March 1947, that in the event that India was partitioned, it would have to entail the division of Punjab and Bengal. This resolve made the division of Bengal inevitable and views based on the insights of Bengalis had little chance.

Mountbatten announced his plan at a press conference on 3 June 1947; the date of independence was to be the night of 14/15 August 1947. For the partition of Bengal, the plan's main points were as follows: Hindus and Muslims in the Bengal Legislative Assembly would meet and vote on the issue of partition. If a simple majority of either group wanted partition, then the province would be divided.[15] Therefore, on 20 June 1947, three sets of polls took place in the Bengal Legislative Assembly.

1. A joint session of the House was convened, comprising all members of the Assembly. Voting then took place for or against a united Bengal joining India. The joint session of the House voted 126 against and 90 votes for joining the Indian Constituent Assembly.

2. A separate session of the members of the Muslim-majority areas of Bengal passed a motion by 106 to 35 votes, against the partitioning of Bengal and instead opted for the joining of an undivided Bengal to the new Constituent Assembly of Pakistan.

3. A separate session comprising members of the non-Muslim-majority areas of Bengal voted 58 to 21 in favour of partition of the province.[16]

The structure of this ballot was unusual and deliberately so. The dice was loaded to ensure that a united Bengal did not go to Pakistan, as that would have meant that the Seven Sisters[17] become part of Pakistan. It also reveals a lesser-known truth: the voting arrangement showed that the representatives of Muslim constituencies never voted in favour of partition of their province—only the Hindus did. The Muslim members, representing East Bengal, voted against the partition of Bengal.[18] The united Assembly voted in favour of the partition of India, while the Hindu members voted for the partition of Bengal. With the virulent Congress propaganda and the deliberately staged riots in Calcutta, in 1946, the Hindus of the province were scared to live under a Muslim majority East Pakistan, particularly since they resented the partition of their province. This, at least partly explains the strong unity between Muslims and Hindu Bengalis and their later problems adjusting to Pakistan under West Pakistani rule.

The British chose to ignore these legitimate demands. Instead, the Radcliffe Commission awarded not only Calcutta, but also the Muslim majority district of Nadia, to India. Nadia district would have allowed East Pakistan access to Assam and the Seven Sisters that remained with India. Thus, 6,000 square miles of territory, with a population of 3.5 million Muslims, remained in India, deprived of being a part of an economically viable East Pakistan.

Ayesha Jalal argues that it was the intransigence and selfishness of the Congress leaders that led to partition in 1947.[19] Jinnah would have supported a United Bengal, but Congress and the Hindu Mahasabha insisted against it. As Governor Burrow gloomily predicted, 'Bengal will be sacrificed on the altar of Nehru's All-India outlook.'[20] While nobody could foresee the violence and devastation that partition would cause, early signs of resistance were disregarded in favour of a narrow outlook and power politics by the Nehru-led Congress that wished for a unified and centralised India, containing the maximum territory and an unviable Pakistan that would soon collapse and fall back onto India's lap. That did not happen, but Partition turned out to be fatal for both countries. The break-up of Pakistan, though inevitable, brought about untold plight for the East Bengali Muslims; it was also economically detrimental for Bangladesh and only served to damage the identity of the newly truncated Pakistan.

Notes

1. Narendra Singh Sarila, *The Shadow of the Great Game: The Untold Story of India's Partition* (HarperCollins Publishers India, 2005), pp. 9–10.

2. R. Coupland, *The Indian Problem: Report on the Constitutional Problem in India* (London: Oxford University Press, 1942), p. 89; https://archive.org/stream/indianproblemrep009634mbp#page/n625/mode/2up/search/bengal+calcutta, p. 627.

3. Bidyut Chakrabarty, 'An Alternative to Partition: the United Bengal Scheme', *South Asia: Journal of South Asian Studies*, 2003, 193–212, 26:2, p. 195, doi. org/10.1080/085640032000089744.

4. Larry Collins & Dominique Lapierre, *Freedom at Midnight: How Britain Gave Away an Empire* (New York: Simon & Schuster, 1975), p. 135.

5. Neilesh Bose, 'Purba Pakistan Zindabad: Bengali Visions of Pakistan, 1940–1947', *Modern Asian Studies* 48, 1 (January 2014): pp. 1–36.

6. Abul Kalam Shamsuddin, *Atit Diner Smriti* (*Memories of Old Days*) (Dhaka: Bangla Academy, 1994), pp. 359–60.

7. *Pakistan* was published in 1942 by the Mohammadi Press on Lower Circular Road. As mentioned in Neilesh Bose, ibid., p. 10.

8. Muhammad Husain, *East Pakistan: A Cultural Survey* (Karachi: Pakistan P.E.N. Centre, 1955).

9. Mujibur Rahman Khan, *Eastern Pakistan: Its Population, Delimitation, and Economics* (Calcutta: East Pakistan Renaissance Society, 1944) as cited in Neilesh Bose, ibid., 15.

10. Nicholas Mansergh and Penderel Moon (eds.), *Constitutional Relations between Britain and India: The Transfer of Power 1942–7. Vol. X: The Mountbatten Viceroyalty: Formulation of a Plan, 22 March–30 May 1947*, pp. 451–2.

11. Ibid., p. 852.

12. Banglapedia—the National Encyclopedia of Bangladesh, http://en.banglapedia. org/index.php?title=United_Independent_Bengal_Movement.

13. Begum Shaista Suhrawardy Ikramullah, *Huseyn Suhrawardy—A Biography* (Karachi: Oxford University Press, 1991), p. 47.

14. Ibid., p. 48.

15. This was quite a strange stipulation. Actually, the Act already decided in favour of partition and the formation of East Pakistan. One wonders why this kind of voting was considered necessary.

16. Mohammad Abu Tayyub Khan, 'Saga of Bengal Partition', *Journal of History and Social Sciences* 2, (1) (January to June 2011).

17. Meghalaya, Arunachal Pradesh, Nagaland, Tripura, Assam, Manipur, and Mizoram.

18. Joya Chatterji, 'The Fashioning of a Frontier: The Radcliffe Line and Bengal's Border Landscape 1947–52', *Modern Asian Studies* 33, 1 (1999), p. 186.

19. Ayesha Jalal, *The Sole Spokesman: Jinnah the Muslim League and the Demand for Pakistan*, p. 280.

20. Burrows to Mountbatten, 28 May, *Transfer of Power*, Vol. X, p. 1025.

4

Economic Disparity and Delayed Development of East Pakistan

From an economic viewpoint, the partition of Bengal was a disaster. During the 200 years of British rule, the province had developed as an integrated economic zone, in which East Bengal had largely retained its characteristic as an agricultural hinterland, while the political, industrial and educational centres were situated in West Bengal—in and around Calcutta. Partition first separated the hinterland from its industrial and organisational base, in West Bengal and Assam, and left it without factories, a port, and trading lines. In the 1930s, when reviewing the possibility of partitioning British India, Sir Reginald Coupland had expressed the opinion that severing the Muslim majority areas of East Bengal from Calcutta would make them economically unsustainable, since all trade and supply lines would be cut. In that sense, East Bengal was at more of a disadvantage compared to, for instance, West Punjab, which retained its capital, Lahore, after Partition. The canal colonies developed in western Punjab between 1885 and 1940, brought about an agricultural revolution, as arid subsistence farming was replaced by the commercialised production of wheat, cotton, and sugar.

Official estimates claim that by 1951, about 800,000 people from the surrounding areas of India migrated to East Pakistan—most of them educated Muslims from urban backgrounds, in search of employment. Meanwhile, about 2.5 million people, mostly Hindus, left East Bengal for West Bengal, in India. Some had been landowners who left their property behind when they became concerned about their future under Muslim rule. They took away their money and their business capabilities, which turned out to be a major setback for East Bengal's economy. Their exit changed the structure of society in East Bengal as no large agricultural estates were left and political aspirants hailing from the middle-class were on the rise. With the Hindu landowners gone, middle-class Hindus started to feel the wrath of the Muslim peasants, which led to a new outflow of population from East Bengal.

The newcomers in East Bengal were mostly Urdu-speaking Muslims from Bihar and other Indian provinces, who were educated and came in search of new opportunities, mainly in the cities, thus challenging the livelihood of the Bengali urban middle- and lower middle-classes. The migrations also served to destabilise the economy in a major way. This had started before partition, when Hindu–Muslim riots were shaking Calcutta, Noakhali, and Bihar and causing Muslims to flee the mess. Partition then created a new wave of refugees in search of jobs and business opportunities in the newly created state. It created political fault-lines between the Urdu-speaking Biharis and the economically disadvantaged Bengalis who had been left behind. It is important to keep in mind that despite a constant gradual outflow of Hindus from East Pakistan, about 10 million of them stayed behind—many more than, for instance, in Punjab.

Partition deprived East Bengal of over one hundred jute and cotton processing and manufacturing industries situated in and around Calcutta and access of the Calcutta harbour and airfields. Replacement of these losses should have been a priority of the newly founded state but this was not the case. East Bengal remained a largely rural society, where 80 per cent of the population found a livelihood in agricultural work.

For East Bengalis, independence brought in its wake a severe food crisis that had started at the beginning of 1947 and was intensified by the chaos and disorder of Partition. East Bengal, comprising mainly of the Ganges delta, was densely populated and prone to food scarcity caused by flooding since the early twentieth century.

The last severe famine had occurred in 1943, during the Second World War. An estimated 2.1 to 3 million people had died at that time, from starvation, malaria and other diseases, aggravated by malnutrition, population displacement, unhygienic conditions, and a lack of adequate health care. Millions were impoverished as the crisis overwhelmed society and large segments of the economy. Partition aggravated the already volatile situation because East Bengal was now surrounded almost completely by India. This left East Bengalis with little prospects for finding new agricultural land, markets for their produce, or help elsewhere. The food crisis became critical by March 1948, when it reached the previously surplus-producing areas of East Bengal, such as Sylhet.[1] The government's failure to effectively handle the situation—prevent hoarding and smuggling, install an effective distribution system and transfer stocks of rice from warehouses in a timely manner—created a sense of disillusionment among East Pakistanis.

Given the rural state of East Pakistan's economy, land was the main source of income for most Bengalis but the vast majority of landholdings were too small to feed the owners and create funds for land improvement. Over 50 per cent of all farms were smaller than one hectare, while almost 90 per cent of all landholdings were smaller than three hectares,[2] making them too small to be tilled efficiently using machinery. East Bengalis pinned their hopes on the land that had once belonged to the Hindus and which, after Partition, had become evacuee property under the state but most of that land was appropriated by few influential landowning families and by Muslim Leaguers who pushed shady claims on the land and were allotted it. It only made matters worse. About 20 per cent of the rural population had no access to any land and thus depended on daily wage labour for an income. This policy, linked with the fact that the population growth was an astonishing 3 per cent per annum, created a situation where a 3 per cent growth in agricultural production would not lead to an improvement in the food crisis, but would be 'eaten up' by new-born babies. The actual growth rate, during the years, lay below the 3 per cent mark, which means a growing population was not able to feed itself and there was a need for food imports. The small size of landholdings and the poverty of East Bengali peasants prevented them from profiting from the Green Revolution of the 1960s. In West Pakistan, it was mainly Punjabi landowners who could avail opportunities such as government loans for the construction of tube wells, the purchase of tractors, and an improvement in yields through the use of chemical fertilisers and hybrid wheat and rice. No such support was provided in East Bengal.

The task of industrialisation and structural change in East Pakistan lay mainly with the government, as members of society did not have the funds or the expertise to initiate the process on their own. The Pakistani government, however, failed to do so. Government institutions, dominated by West Pakistanis, made East Pakistan its dependency. In 1947, East Bengal was the world's largest producer of raw jute, however, after Partition, all processing industries were located in West Bengal and therefore out of reach for jute producers. Additionally, the Pakistan government banned trade with India, leaving East Bengal with the options of either smuggling raw jute to India, or finding new buyers in the international market—both of which only incurred losses. It was a while before jute mills were established in East Bengal—the most famous among them being the Adamjee Jute Mill in Narayanganj, which started producing in 1955.[3]

Until 1958, the process of industrialisation progressed at a slow pace, gaining speed after the first military coup by General Ayub Khan. He pursued an ambitious economic and social development programme, for which he relied on Western economic theories and input. In other words, private capital was encouraged, by incentives and loans, to build industry. Given that, there was no moneyed class of capitalists among the Bengalis to invest in the industries and industrialisation remained largely a West Pakistani development. The economist Mahbub ul Haq and Ayub Khan's Harvard Advisory Group were in charge of policy outlines, which were fixed on achieving economic growth first and foremost. Haq, who was Chief of the Planning Commission at that time, expressed his view that Pakistan, being an underdeveloped country, must accept growth as its philosophy and shelve any ideas of equitable distribution and a welfare state. He was of the opinion that only developed states could afford such 'luxuries'.[4] This economic philosophy kick-started a decade of high growth in Pakistan in the 1960s and the country was viewed by the West as a model developing economy. The price Pakistan had to pay was the disparity in income, with a large part of the newly gained wealth concentrated in few hands, growing poverty in the case of the majority of Bengalis, and a widening gap between East and West Pakistan. The lopsided manner of economic development can be judged from the fact that by the late 1960s, 66 per cent of Pakistan's industrial wealth and 87 per cent of the banking and insurance industries, were controlled by 22 families. That none of these families was Bengali cannot solely be attributed to the market-dominating position of West Pakistanis. There was a lack of a flair for entrepreneurship among Bengalis in general; and it would develop only much later, after the creation of Bangladesh, when they were provided with the opportunities to develop entrepreneurial skills.

Apart from the cultural bias that might have played a role, only those sectors and regions were invested in, that would yield the maximum profit in the minimum period of time—East Bengal was not one of them. During the three Five-Year Plans, public investment in East Bengal was always below that in West Pakistan, while private investment in the eastern part was only 22 per cent throughout the period. In addition to this, the government exploited East Bengal's export sector. While much of the foreign exchange earnings (43 per cent) were created by the eastern part through jute export, the money earned was not flowing back into East Bengal and was utilised mainly in West Pakistan. Both Mahbub ul Haq and Ayub Khan acknowledged this. The latter admitted that roughly 2 per cent of East Pakistan's regional income in the pre-plan period and about one per cent during the plan were taken away by West Pakistan.[5] However, this was only half of the truth. There was also economic exploitation through open market rates of foreign exchange. The foreign exchange that the jute growers earned was surrendered to the government in return for Pakistani rupees at the official rate. As the rupee was overvalued by 50 per cent, it meant that for each dollar a Bengali agricultural worker received 4.25 rupees, while the dollar was actually worth 8.61 rupees.[6] Such an imbalance was highlighted by the fact that the federal capital, Karachi, which consisted of all the institutions that were receiving a huge chunk of the government investment, was situated in West Pakistan. The banking sector was located in West Pakistan, which meant that it was much more difficult for East Pakistan to obtain financing for industries. Moreover, the government retained the bulk of the budget for West Pakistan.

Such an economic policy put the eastern half of the country at a disadvantage, giving rise to widespread poverty. When East Pakistan complained about this, the Planning Commission would retort, 'We cannot distribute poverty. Growth is vital before income distribution can improve it.'[7] This attitude could have been changed even at the last minute, when disparity and discontent had reached a disquieting level. G.W. Choudhury recalls:

> The National Economic Council met under Yahya's chairmanship on February 3, 1970. Even the debate in the 'nominated cabinet' reflected the widening gap between the ministers and the economic experts belonging to the two wings of the country. Sometimes the debate was acrimonious; there were few voices that could approach this grave issue with proper appreciation and a broad perspective. While the Bengali ministers, aided and supported by the Bengali bureaucrats, were urging a big push for the development of East Pakistan, the West Pakistani ministers, aided by top officials of the planning commission who were mostly non-Bengalis, presented the same old arguments against a substantial redirection of resources and development expenditure to East Pakistan—such as lack of absorbing capacity, inadequacy of administrative machinery and the difficulty of measuring actual regional disparity, and so forth. It was a pity that, even at this stage, they could not understand properly the depth of the Bengalis' feelings on the question of economic disparity.[8]

Despite Yahya's attempts at finding a solution by directing commission members in the next plan to reduce disparity, it could not be done. Reviewing the draft plan for the year 1970–1, the Bengali economists stated:

> Our analysis indicates that despite the formal commitment of the Government of Pakistan to reduce disparity, the extent of disparity in *per capita* income between East and West Pakistan has widened at an increasing rate over the past decade and the commitment was only honoured in the breach.[9]

The West Pakistani economists in their report stated:

> The phenomenon (regional disparity) was inherited at the time of partition. The disparity has progressively worsened during the last two decades and it is now as high as 38 per cent. The removal of this disparity between East and West Pakistan is an important national objective…. But it is obvious that the disparities cannot be removed overnight.[10]

The Annual Development Plan 1970–1 was to be finalised during the meeting of the National Economic Council on 2 June 1970. Under the guidance of M.M. Ahmed, the Vice-Chairman of the Planning Commission, the Fourth Five-Year Plan was approved.

When the allocations for the Annual Development Plan 1970–1 became known, they were criticised by the Bengali cabinet ministers as insufficient. Choudhury recalls:

> The allocations for East Pakistan under the annual plan for 1970–1 were neither adequate nor in accordance with the supreme objective of removing the regional disparity. Yet Yahya allowed the Planning Commission to go ahead with its proposals, notwithstanding the strong notes of dissent from the three Bengali ministers. This was a big shock for my two colleagues and myself.[11]

At the end of the debate and after the Bengali cabinet ministers had written a combined resignation letter to Yahya, the allocations for the Annual Development Plan 1970–1 were changed. But even that turned out to be too little, too late.

According to the Harvard School of Economics—which largely influenced Pakistan's economic policy—economic inequality and the concentration of wealth in the hands of a select few was the natural order of things. The social and political implications of this policy seem to have been conveniently ignored, or never fully understood. While East Pakistan did suffer from setbacks that cannot be blamed on the government—such as the unfavourable plan for partition and the high density of the population—a concerned government would, nevertheless, have gone to great lengths to improve conditions in that disadvantaged part of the country. The focus should have been on flood protection and soil improving measures, a population control programme, and priority investment but West Pakistanis, who dominated the government, did not show compassion or even fairness and treated the eastern part of the country as an 'interior colony' of sorts. According to Choudhury, East Pakistan did not get a fair share in various sectors of the economy, such as revenue expenditure, development expenditure, utilisation of foreign aid, or foreign exchange. In fact, its share was most unsatisfactory and unjust.[12]

The blame for a misguided economic policy in East Pakistan does not rest on the government alone. In those years, Western economic theory, dominated by the Harvard School, favoured aid-induced development. Pakistan had joined the Western security block and came under the influence of Western aid policies that were believed to promote and accelerate economic growth. Pakistan being a Western ally became the recipient of economic aid, a smaller part of which was spent in East Pakistan. Thus, in 1953, a village, agricultural and industrial development programme was initiated, aiming to make the eastern delta a 'laboratory' for experiments in rural development and local government.[13] Despite a history of dismal failure on the part of cooperatives in this part of the world, the newly founded Comilla Academy of Rural Development, financed by American aid, tried to square the circle and develop a rural cooperative economy by changing people's attitudes—without much success. Other goals included family planning, the development of irrigation networks, and the distribution of electricity.

Next, in 1958, came the so-called Public Works Programme (a US development aid project) initiated by John F. Kennedy that aimed to utilise the food surplus produced by the US to influence policies in developing countries and gain political mileage. It was called the Food for Peace Programme and meant that the US would provide food worth US$621 million to Pakistan, which would be paid for in rupees. The money would be put into a US-counterpart fund in Pakistan, out of which development projects would be financed and the rest would be used for the expenditures of the US Embassy in Pakistan. Initially, the programme was meant to be used to finance the Indus Replacement Works in West Pakistan. The Planning Commission and the Harvard Advisory Group proposed that East Pakistan should also come under the programme, seeing that it was food deficient. Thus, it was attached to the Pakistan Academy for Rural Development in Comilla.

The first project was limited to flood control and proved successful. Later, the programme was extended to all of East Pakistan. When the focus of the work shifted from flood control to road construction, there proved to be a lack of connectivity between new and existing roads, and the location of local markets. As such, no real economic impact was achieved, though the reports of the Harvard Group stated otherwise. The jobs created during the project involved road-construction and earthwork. No real increase in purchasing power or a reduction in poverty were witnessed.[14]

The planned industrialisation needed electricity, which was scarce throughout the country. Pakistani economic planners persuaded foreign aid providers to finance a huge hydroelectric project in the Chittagong Hills. The project brought thousands of Bengali workers to the region and upset the local ethnic balance. The huge lake that was created in the process, submerged many villages and forests and 40 per cent of the agricultural land in the area. Over a hundred thousand locals were displaced, almost none of the affected people received any compensation, nor did the project generate employment for them. They had to find refuge elsewhere and many of them moved to Burma and India, where they were barely tolerated and faced hardship.[15]

Those years saw the establishment of a policy that relied on foreign aid and foreign ideas more than on the mobilisation of indigenous people and resources. The lack of success of the various projects added to the frustration of the East Bengali population and did little to improve conditions. East Bengal was an underdeveloped area to begin with and even the most promising economic policy would probably not have brought it to par with West Pakistan. But the major complaints of the Bengalis were in regards to the deprivation of a good share in investment by the central government and the injustice regarding the handling of foreign exchange created from jute exports. It led to the formulation of the Six-Point demand of the Awami League and, as a consequence, to the break-up of Pakistan.

Notes

1. Badruddin Umar, *The Emergence of Bangladesh: Class Struggles in East Pakistan (1947–1958)* (Karachi: Oxford University Press, 2006), p. 22.
2. Willem van Schendel, *A History of Bangladesh* (Cambridge: Cambridge University Press, 2009), p. 139.
3. Ibid., p. 140.
4. Syed Humayun, *Sheikh Mujib's 6-point Formula: An Analytical Study of the Breakup of Pakistan* (Karachi: Royal Book Company 1995), p. 162.
5. Ibid., p. 166.
6. Ibid., pp. 167–8.
7. Ibid., p. 163.
8. G.W. Choudhury, *The Last Days of United Pakistan* (Karachi: Oxford University Press, 1993), p. 61.
9. *Report of the Panel of Economists on the Fourth Five-Year Plan (1970–75)*, Planning Commission, Government of Pakistan, May 1970, p. 11, as cited in G.W. Choudhury, p. 62.
10. *Report of the Panel of Economists on the Fourth Five-Year Plan (1970–75)*, pp. 104–6, as cited in G.W. Choudhury, p. 62.

11. Ibid., p. 64.
12. Ibid., p. 65.
13. Van Schendel, *A History of Bangladesh*, pp. 145–7.
14. Badruddin Umar, *The Emergence of Bangladesh: Volume 2: The Rise of Bengali Nationalism (1958–1971)* (Karachi: Oxford University Press, 2006), pp. 29–37.
15. Van Schendel, ibid., pp. 149–50.

5

Political Differences between East and West Pakistan

COLONIAL LEGACY

According to the Indian Independence Act of 1947, Pakistan was to be ruled under a parliamentary democracy based on the Westminster model—another colonial heritage. This created problems for the newly constituted state. In a democracy, the majority rules. With the population of East Pakistan larger than that of West Pakistan, the former would have had a majority of the seats (54 per cent) in the Parliament (according to the 1961 census, the population of East Pakistan was 50,853,721 and that of West Pakistan, 42,987,261). East Pakistan consisted mainly of a Bengali population, with a minor non-Bengali tribal population in the north and southeast and migrant Biharis forming a minority. This meant that parliamentarians from East Pakistan would have been united based on their common ethnicity, while the representatives of West Pakistan would have had to divide its share of seats (46 per cent) between its ethnically diverse provinces.

The fact that Bengalis would dominate Pakistani politics came as a shock to the prospective rulers of the country. It was totally unacceptable to the Punjabi and Muhajir political elite that dominated the Muslim League and was aspiring to dominate the government at the centre. The Muslim League had won Pakistan mainly with the support of the Muslims from Muslim-minority provinces of British India, such as the United Provinces, the Central Provinces, Bihar and

Bombay (now Mumbai). The Muslim Leaguers who had relocated from India to West Pakistan, were called Muhajirs and comprised no more than 5 per cent of Pakistani population. Punjabis, meanwhile, comprised around 60 per cent of the West Pakistani population; they were economically and politically powerful and not ready to concede to, or even share power with the Bengalis of East Pakistan, whom they regarded as culturally inferior.

Difference of Social Structure

Another factor that divided the rulers of East and West Pakistan was the question of land reform. Hindus who had left East Pakistan to become refugees in India, had mostly been *zamindars*, absentee landlords, and moneylenders who had exploited their mostly Muslim peasants and the local communities. Their exodus was welcomed by most of the East Bengali population. The land they left behind was distributed, or taken over by the State. The East Bengal Assembly, in 1950, voted for a land reform, to put an end to feudalism by abolishing permanent settlement and absentee landlordism, imposing ceilings on land-holdings and thus making sure that no new holdings were able to crop up. Such action was impossible in West Pakistan, where the Muslim League and the political elite were dominated by landlords. The feudal mind-set was, and is, vehemently against any such land reform that would result in the destruction of feudal landholdings and the patron-client relations that hold agricultural workers hostage to their employers. The very fact that local bodies are not allowed to function in Pakistan today, is evidence of a continuation of the feudal mind-set, which promotes a defaced version of democracy. How can you have democracy at the macro-level, while giving only lip service at the micro-level? Thus, the two parts of Pakistan had very different ideas for developing a common political vision; the inherited system of democracy was ill suited to successfully ruling a new country that had a diverse social structure.

Unlike Punjab and Sindh, Bengal did not have a strong feudal upper class, but a vast lower-middle class and agricultural workers. Most of the politicians came from this lower-middle class background and had no stakes in feudal landholdings. This was why socialism and communism were prevalent in the politics of East Bengal prior to Partition. In the nineteenth century, Bengal had been the theatre of the revolutionary Faraizi Movement that had declared 'Jihad' against British rulers as well as Hindu landlords. Though the movement failed to achieve its aims, it left a deep mark on the life and thinking of the lower class Bengali Muslims. 'Their gifts to them were a spirit of revolt, readiness to suffer for a cause, realisation of the value of social and religious reforms, radicalism and the ability to challenge established authority.'[1]

The fact that East Bengali society was mainly rural and lacked a strong Muslim feudal elite, also contributed to the different way in which Islam was practiced in East Pakistan; it was what we call 'popular Islam', characterised by a joint heritage and understanding with Hindus, Hindu mysticism, and religious culture. The more literalist Deobandi style of Islam did not suit most of the Bengali people; it alienated them and this explains the popularity of a man like Maulana Bhashani, who, despite his education at Deoband, was professing an inclusive model of society for East Bengal. At a council session of the Muslim Awami League in 1955, he proposed that the word 'Muslim' be dropped from the party's name. And in his welcoming speech to the Kagmari Conference, held from 6–10 February 1957, at Kagmari, in Tangail district, he pushed aside Jinnah's two-nation theory, insisting that while it was a country with a Muslim majority, Pakistan was 'for Hindus, Buddhists, Christians, adivasis and other small nationalities alike'.[2] This stand divided Bhashani and his movement from the Muslim League and the Pakistan ideology as professed by the government. Other Bengali politicians of a middle class background, like A.K. Fazlul Huq and later, Sheikh Mujibur Rahman, also leaned towards political programmes that catered to the labourers and lower-middle class, rather than the elite. Their attitude was deeply resented by West Pakistani leaders and gave them cause for grave apprehensions.

DEMOCRACY AND FEUDALISM

One of the central themes of democracy is that every vote is accepted as having equal weight, that all citizens are considered equal before the law and have equal access to the legislative processes. Equality and freedom are identified as important characteristics of democracy. Restrictions rooted in irrationality cannot apply to anyone seeking to become a representative on the strength of a free voting process. The freedom of the citizens is secured by legitimised rights and liberties and protected by a constitution governed by the rule of law.

MIT economist Daron Acemoglu and Harvard political scientist James A. Robinson argue that the key differentiator between countries is 'institutions.' Nations thrive when they develop 'inclusive' political and economic institutions, and they fail when those institutions become 'extractive' and concentrate power and opportunity in the hands of only a few.[3] Unfortunately, in Pakistan, the institutions the government is supposed to preserve have instead been systematically attacked to purposely erode the ability and the credibility of these institutions. According to Acemoglu and Robinson, 'Inclusive economic institutions…are more conducive to economic growth than extractive economic institutions that are structured to extract resources from the many by the few….'[4]

CONSTITUTIONAL CONSEQUENCES

The partition of Bengal and the power structure in Pakistan remained an 'apple of discord' in the deliberations in the Constituent Assembly, which was tasked with developing and agreeing upon the first Constitution of Pakistan. Several drafts were under discussion. Interests clashed on the status of the Bengali language and the question of power distribution between the eastern and western parts of Pakistan. This was the reason for the long delay in the drafting and finalisation of the new Constitution, which happened as late as 1956. The Bengali members of the Constituent Assembly were of the view that the original Lahore Resolution provided a confederal solution, given the concerns of East and West Pakistan and the considerable geographical distance between them, but the West Pakistanis rejected this. Whether the electorate would be separate or joint was another point of contention, with Muslim League insisting on a separate electorate as a 'historic asset' of the fight for Pakistan and the Awami League arguing in favour of a joint electorate.

The Parliament delayed the development of the first Constitution and devised the tools of One Unit and parity. This meant that the provinces of West Pakistan were pooled into a single unit. Between East and West Pakistan, a parity of representation was established; it denied the Bengali population their inherent majority rights—another glaring negation of the one-man one-vote concept. The ultimate tragedy was that East Pakistan had never claimed the right to rule at the centre; all it had ever demanded was to be treated fairly and at par with the other provinces, and was denied even this.

Fearing the Bengali majority, West Pakistani politicians created a political stalemate that opened space for manipulation of the political process by the bureaucracy, which was well organised and efficient in those days. Those in charge of the civil service deliberately looked for a growing role for the army, on the premise that the military would keep the quarrelling politicians in line. The succession of Governor General Khawaja Nazimuddin, after the assassination of Prime Minister Liaquat Ali Khan, was against all the rules, since he had to first resign as governor general to take up this position. The dismissal of subsequent prime ministers and the ruthless dissolution of the Constituent Assembly at the will of powerful men, undermined political institution-building in Pakistan, weakened the bond between the two parts of the country and paved the way for military intervention and ultimately, the break-up of Pakistan.

With Karachi being chosen as the capital of Pakistan, East Pakistan was already put on the back seat. In addition to this, the headquarters of the Pakistan Army, which was the source of a major power bastion, in which Bengalis had hardly any representation, was also situated in West Pakistan, as were the headquarters of the Pakistan Air Force and the Pakistan Navy. West Pakistanis dominated the country's government, administration, and military. Bengalis were so underrepresented that even within their own provincial government, the senior administrative posts were occupied by West Pakistanis and non-Bengali Urdu speakers—mostly Biharis and UP-ites, belonging to the ruling Muslim League. Also included were a small number of Urdu speaking Bengalis. This, over the time, became a matter of great resentment for Bengalis. The situation was compounded by the language policy.

East Pakistani Parties and Politicians

The Muslim League had never been a strong party in united Bengal, or East Bengal, before 1947, despite its formation in Dhaka in 1906.[5] Tariq Mahmud, a former student of Dhaka University, wrote:

> As I reflect back, I feel that Bengal had never been a part of the mainstream subcontinent or the Indian land mass. Its rich, alluvial and deltaic character always marked this area with a sense of exclusiveness. Had there been no colonial sharing under the British, it may well have been yet another Muslim country on the fringes of Southeast Asia. This distinctiveness also ran through its political streams. The Pakistan movement did push this exclusivism into the background for a while, but an average literate Muslim Bengali in that part was clear in his mind that his religion separated him from Hindu Bengalis, hence the quest for Pakistan, while his language and culture distinguished him from fellow West Pakistanis, all the more reason for complete regional autonomy.[6]

Even before Partition, East Bengal had a separate set of political parties and politicians that did not subscribe to the Muslim epithet of the Muslim League. One lower-middle class leader who inherited this legacy and came to play an important role in the politics of East Bengal, was Abdul Hamid Khan Bhashani. He was born in 1880 at Dhanpara village in Sirajganj district. Despite his training at the Deoband Madrasah in the early twentieth century, he never became a typical *mullah*. His association with Maulana Mahmud Hasan (Shaykh al-Hind) and other thinkers of early political Islam at Deoband inspired Bhashani to represent the rights of the rural/ urban poor and fight against British imperialism and indigenous feudalism. Bhashani's ideology of *Rabubiyat*[7] preaches the undivided equality of all people, whatever their caste, nationality, or religion. It advocates the abolition of private ownership based on religion, 'Man is only a custodian, whereas Allah holds ownership over all properties that exist. Thus, the state should abolish all private ownership, and should distribute things in equal proportions, on the basis of need.'[8] For him politics and religion were intertwined. In a speech at the 1957 Kagmari Conference favouring regional autonomy, he threatened, prophetically, that if East Bengal were not granted autonomy, the people would ultimately say '*Assalamu Alaikum*' (goodbye) to Pakistan.[9]

Another political leader of East Bengal was A.K. Fazlul Huq (1873–1962), popularly known as Sher-e-Bangla, who had launched a party of his own by the name of Krishak Praja Party (Popular Peasant Party), in 1936. Coming from a middle class background, he was interested in promoting the interests of middle and lower-middle class people. Initially, his party had both Muslim and Hindu members, which set it apart from the Muslim League and was the reason why his alliance with the latter was terminated at that time. After the 1937 elections though, he was compelled to form a coalition with the Muslim League which gave him the opportunity to become the Chief Minister of Bengal—an act of sheer expediency. Huq went down in history for having moved the Lahore Resolution in 1940, thus supporting the Muslim League's idea of Pakistan. In 1941, Jinnah made the Muslim League withdraw from the coalition when Fazlul Huq refused to resign from the Viceroy's National Defence Council.[10] Huq formed a new government in Bengal, this time in coalition with the Hindu Mahasabha, Congress (Bose group), and the Scheduled Castes. This shows that his alliance with the Muslim League was not based on shared ideas, but political expediency. He was then excluded from the League and until 1943, was struggling to settle his relationship with Jinnah, with little success. In 1943, he was forced to resign by the British Governor of Bengal and only then was the League able to form a government there.

The most well-known Bengali politician—and one who was not of middle-class background—was Huseyn Shaheed Suhrawardy. Born in 1892, in Midnapur, he hailed from an illustrious Bengali family of Suhrawardy, who trace their descent to the first Caliph. He read law and political science at Oxford and upon his return to Calcutta, entered the legal profession and joined the Muslim League. He was part of the provincial government of Bengal in 1943, when a famine broke out and millions of Bengalis perished. This strained his relationship with Chief Minister Nazimuddin and he contested the 1946 election against him and became the Chief Minister of Bengal.

In 1947, when partition came under discussion, he was leading the efforts for a united Bengal. The plan did not come to fruition and Bengal was divided. Suhrawardy, instead of moving to Pakistan, stayed on in Calcutta after 15 August, and together with Gandhi, tried to prevent Hindu–Muslim riots. He called for peace and shifted to Pakistan only in March 1949, but was not welcome there. Nazimuddin, by then the Governor General of Pakistan, forced him out of the Muslim League, after which he joined the Bengali opposition camp and became one of the founders of the Muslim Awami League in 1949. His tenure as Prime Minister of Pakistan, in 1956/7, was cut short due to growing critique against him and resistance within the government and in the Awami League, on the grounds of his pro-American and anti-Soviet policy that was, incidentally, rejected by Bhashani.

Disgruntled, Suhrawardy withdrew from politics and left Pakistan for Beirut, Lebanon, where he died in 1963. In any case, the vacuum he had left in his wake was soon filled by his devoted disciple, Sheikh Mujibur Rahman, a politician who represented a new generation in Bengal and in the Awami League.

These facts of history, though often forgotten, did make the relations between East and West Pakistan difficult and contributed to the souring of political ties. During the first Constituent Assembly session in September 1947, Begum Shaista Ikramullah's proposal for alternate meetings of the assembly in Karachi and Dhaka, to accommodate Bengali sensibilities, resulted in an early clash between East and West Pakistan. The proposal was not accepted. Prime Minister Liaquat Ali Khan had replied to Begum Ikramullah in mock horror, 'Women never understand practical difficulties'.[11] This, and the fact that all key positions in the Muslim League and in the administration of East Bengal, were taken by non-Bengali Urdu speakers, created a sense of inequality and persecution among East Bengali Muslims.

As we have seen, what became East Pakistan had an independent political history and trajectory. This became clear right from the very beginning, when the new state of Pakistan was less than five months old. On 4 January 1948, the East Pakistan Student League was founded as an opposition student's organisation under the leadership of the young and promising Sheikh Mujibur Rahman. This was followed on 23 June 1949, by a meeting of leaders and workers known to be supporters of Suhrawardy.

The discord over the national language issue brought the people of East Pakistan out onto the streets. The first wave of the Bengali Language Movement, in 1949–50 and the second, in 1952, consumed whatever sympathies had existed for West Pakistanis, among the intelligentsia and roused the masses. From thereon, the Language Movement received support from the Bengali political opposition, with the newly founded East Pakistan Muslim Awami League acting as a mobilising power.

The East Pakistani nationalists' break-up with the All Pakistan Muslim League, Pakistan's largest political party, and the establishment of the East Pakistan Awami Muslim League in June 1949, marked an important turning point. The gathering took place at Rose Garden.[12] The word 'Muslim' was dropped from Awami Muslim League to emphasise the secular nature of the party and woo Hindus into its fold. Bhashani was the first Chairman; Shamsul Huq the first Secretary; Sheikh Mujibur Rahman (interned in jail at the time) the first Joint Secretary; and Yar Mohammad the first Treasurer. The Awami League was the first Opposition Party in East Bengal (later renamed East Pakistan) and since its inception, championed the political rights of the Bengali people.

During the 1953 elections in West Pakistan, there was a strong bias against the political opposition of the All Pakistan Awami League and the government impeded its election campaign. Suhrawardy, by then the head of the Awami League, did not want a repetition of this in East Pakistan and devised a plan for a United Front or Jukto Front, of opposition parties in East Bengal, where the provincial elections were to take place in March 1954. In December 1953, he skilfully managed to bring into existence the United Front, a cluster of five opposition parties, the most important ones among them being the Awami League and Fazlul Huq's Krishak Sramik Party.

The opposition alliance formulated the Ekush Dafa, or 21-point charter, as their election manifesto. Among its pledges were the demand of making Bengali a state language, maximum autonomy for the province, reform in education, an independent judiciary, making and empowering the legislative assembly. The United Front's programme also demanded that the relation between East Bengal and West Pakistan be restructured on the basis of full regional autonomy; the programme identified three portfolios for the central government—defence, foreign affairs, and currency. As confidence building measures, the United Front's programme suggested that Pakistan's Naval Headquarters be relocated to East Bengal and that an arms manufacturing factory be built there. With this programme, the United Front swept the elections, rooting out the Muslim League in East Pakistan.

This came as a huge shock for the Pakistani ruling elite. The United Front won 227 out of 236 of Muslim seats, while the Communists won 5 seats and the Muslim League, which was the ruling party, won only 10 seats out of 309. This landslide victory revealed how estranged the Bengali population already was in 1954, owing to the failure of the Muslim League to deliver on the promises made during the campaign for Pakistan. A United Front government, with Fazlul Huq as Chief Minister, came into power on 3 April 1954. He drew up a cabinet containing many prominent activists; among them was Sheikh Mujibur Rahman, who served as commerce minister. The most important short-term development under this dispensation was the recognition of Bengali as an official language on 7 May 1954. Later that month, on 30 May, Governor General Ghulam Mohammad dismissed the elected government.

Left reeling with disbelief, the Muslim League could not concede defeat in the elections. The Centre was looking for an excuse to dismiss the United Front government and Fazlul Huq's controversial visit to Calcutta, from 4–8 May 1954, provided them with such an opportunity. At a reception, he is reported to have expressed the hope to remove the artificial barriers that had been created between the two Bengals. He further said that Bengalis are bound by common language and heritage. On another occasion, he is reported to have condemned the political division of the country.[13] Things became more estranged when *The New York Times* article, published on 23 May 1954, added fuel to the fire. It reported that Huq was trying to separate East Bengal from Pakistan. Suhrawardy wrote:

> With his [Fazlul Huq's] usual emotionalism and want of balance when in the presence of an audience, he made a speech at a meeting in Calcutta which was calculated to draw the acclaim and plaudits of his Hindu-India audience. The newspapers reported him stating that he could not understand the *raison d'etre* of Pakistan and would bend his

energies to bring the two parts of Bengal together. ...several meetings were held in East Bengal condemning him, including one presided over by Maulana Bhashani.[14]

The statements he issued during his Calcutta visit turned him into a controversial figure in Pakistan. This further deteriorated the uneasy relations that already existed between the Centre and the United Front's newly elected provincial government. Huq denied the charges of high treason that were brought forward against him, but no one listened.

One of the main challenges faced by the United Front government was the deteriorating law and order situation in East Bengal. In the last week of March 1954, a gruesome riot at the Karnaphuli Paper Mills left thirteen people dead and thirty-five injured. Throughout the government's brief stint in office, the province was gripped by industrial violence, including trouble in Dhaka Central Jail, which resulted in fifty injured, nineteen of whom were victims of police firing. The climax was reached with the outbreak of riots at the Adamjee Jute Mills, infamous for their sub-human working conditions; some 400 people were killed and many more wounded. The army had to be called in and the blame for this disturbance was placed on the provincial government's Communist allies. The Centre asked Fazlul Huq to round up the Communists who were allegedly wreaking havoc in Dhaka. This complicated the matter because Huq denied the Communists' involvement in the violence.

In a meeting in Karachi, Chief Minister Huq, denied the charge of high treason, but the Centre had made up its mind by then, to get rid of his ministry. Huq was declared a traitor, his cabinet dismissed on 29 May 1954, and Governor's rule imposed under Section 92-A of the Constitution. The charges brought forward by the Centre were that the ministry was unable to maintain law and order, failed to inspire confidence in the administration, and that Huq had conspired to disintegrate Pakistan. Iskandar Mirza was made the new Governor and he banned political activities and arrested United Front activists.

Sheikh Mujibur Rahman, A.K. Fazlul Huq, Yusuf Ali Chowdhury, and thirty-three members of parliament, along with number of workers, were arrested.

The United Front leadership resented the dismissal, declared it undemocratic and arbitrary, but appealed to the public to maintain peace, and promised to continue the struggle to vindicate their democratic rights. East Bengalis felt that there was a US hand in the dismissal of Fazlul Huq's ministry. The dismissal had followed the 19 April 1954, defence aid pact between Pakistan and the US and *The New York Times* report of 23 May. Demand for the independence of East Pakistan was heard from 1954 onwards, and the acceptance of Bengali as the second official language of Pakistan in 1956, made no difference.

In 1955, Prime Minister Mohammad Ali Bogra implemented the One Unit scheme, which merged the four western provinces into a single unit called West Pakistan, while East Bengal was renamed as East Pakistan. In September 1956, the Awami League formed a coalition with the Republican Party, to secure a majority in the new National Assembly of Pakistan. Suhrawardy, the Awami League President, became the Prime Minister of Pakistan. He pursued a reform agenda to reduce the long-standing economic disparity between East and West Pakistan, greater representation of Bengalis in the Pakistani civil and armed services and attempted to alleviate the food shortage in East Pakistan, albeit unsuccessfully, as he was he was removed three months after coming into office.

The period of military rule, from 1958 to 1962, brought with it some new developments. Realising the tension between East and West Pakistan, Field Marshal Ayub Khan acknowledged in his speech at Peshawar University in 1960, that such discontent could lead to disunity and eventually to the destruction of Pakistan. He started a series of measures in order to meet the expectations of East Pakistan. These included the bifurcation in 1962 of formerly central institutions, such as the Pakistan Railways, the Pakistan Industrial Development Corporation, and the Water and Power Development

Authority, creating an eastern and a western wing of each organisation. However, provincial autonomy was weakened in comparison to that which had existed in 1956. This was deliberate; as a soldier, Ayub considered provincial autonomy detrimental to Pakistan's capacity to defend itself and therefore, the administrative splitting of central organisations did not achieve its purpose.

Notes

1. K.K. Aziz, *The Murder of History: A Critique of History Textbooks Used in Pakistan* (Lahore: Sang-e-Meel Publications, 2015), p. 253.
2. Syed Abul Maksud, *Maulana Abdul Hamid Khan Bhasani* (Dhaka: Bangla Academy, 1994), p. 149, as cited in Peter Custers, 'Maulana Bhashani and the Transition to Secular Politics in East Bengal,' *The Indian Economic & Social History Review* 47, (2), (2010) pp. 231–59.
3. Daron Acemoglu and James A. Robinson, *Why Nations Fail: The Origins of Power, Prosperity, and Poverty* (London: Profile Books, 2012); Thomas L. Friedman, 'Why Nations Fail', Sunday Review, Op-Ed Columnist, *The New York Times*, 31 March 2012, https://www.nytimes.com/2012/04/01/opinion/sunday/friedman-why-nations-fail.html.
4. Ibid., pp. 429–30.
5. The Muslim League scheme had been developed by Nawab Sir Khawaja Salimullah, the Nawab of Dhaka, one of the few feudal landlords in East Bengal and an Urdu speaker hailing from Kashmir.
6. Tariq Mahmud, 'Remembering Dhaka', *The Express Tribune*, 16 December 2013; https://tribune.com.pk/story/645895/remembering-dhaka/.
7. Maulana Bhashani, 'Rabubiyater Bhumika' (April 1974), published in Syed Abul Maksud, ibid., p. 398. *See also*, Maulana Bhasani, *Rabubiater Bhumika* (*The Role of Rabubiyat*) (Santosh: Hukumate Rabbani Samiti Publications, 1974).
8. Maulana Bhashani in Syed Abul Maksud, ibid., p. 701.
9. *See*, Shah Ahmed Reza, *Bhashanir Kagmari Shammelan O Shayatshashoner Sangram* (Dhaka: Ganaprakashani, 1986), p. 51; Syed Abul Maksud, ibid., p. 126; Muhammad Samsul Haque, *Maulana Bhashanir Rajnoitik Jiban. Tatvalochona O Mulyayan* (Tangail, Bangladesh, 1987), p. 30 as cited in Peter Custers, ibid.
10. A.K. Fazlul Huq was not the only leader expelled for joining the Defence Council. Sir Sultan Ahmed and Begum Jahan Ara Shahnawaz were also expelled.
11. Begum Shaista Suhrawardy Ikramullah, *From Purdah to Parliament* (Karachi: Oxford University Press, 1998), p. 166.

12. Built in the late nineteenth century by a Hindu *zamindar*, Hrishikesh Das, Rose Garden is a prominent mansion and garden in Old Dhaka. The palace was bought by Khan Bahadur Kazi Abdur Rashid from Hrishikesh Das, in 1936 and renamed Rashid Manzil. Rashid left behind three sons and two daughters; his eldest son (Ikram Sehgal's cousin) Kazi Mohammed Bashir (Humayun Sahib) was the first mayor of Dhaka Municipal Corporation, after independence, in 1947. The place was known popularly as Humayun Shaheber Bari (Humayun's House) and continues to be referred to as such till date. Possibly because of the Suhrawardy connection (he was related to Bashir), when Bengali liberal and social democrats converged in Dhaka to form an alternative political force against the Muslim League in Pakistan, it became the birthplace of the Awami Muslim League.

13. Rizwan Malik, 'The Process of Constitution Making in Pakistan: 1947–56', *Pakistan Journal of History and Culture*, pp. 57–80, 22 (1), 2001, p. 75.

14. Mohammad H.R. Talukdar (ed.), *Memoirs of Huseyn Shaheed Suhrawardy: With a Brief Account of His Life and Work* (Karachi: Oxford University Press, 2009), p. 86.

6

The 1965 War, the Six-Point Movement, and Agartala

In March 1963, Pakistan's rapprochement with China in a border dispute[1] saw the start of a new era of Sino–Pakistan relations. It inevitably strengthened the regime of General Ayub Khan, who had by then lost much of his initial support. The regime, emboldened, attempted to find a military solution to the Kashmir conflict that had been looming since 1947. Group Captain (retd.) S.M. Hali described the situation as follows:

> By 1965, Ayub had lost a lot of political ground he had gained on first deposing Iskander Mirza as President on 27 October, 1958. Perhaps he felt that by becoming the liberator of Kashmir he would redeem himself in the eyes of the people, or through such [a] venture he hoped to unite the people.[2]

Civilians too had vested interests in such a venture. According to General K.M. Arif:

> At that time, the policy-making in the country was highly personalised. The institutions were weak and by-passed. Pakistan's Foreign Office, with Mr Aziz Ahmed as the Foreign Secretary and Mr Z.A. Bhutto as the Foreign Minister, called the martial tunes. It had miscalculated that despite 'Operation Gibraltar', the fighting was likely to remain confined inside the disputed state of Jammu and Kashmir. The Foreign Office is on record to have assessed that India was not in a position to risk a general war with Pakistan…for inexplicable reasons, the General Headquarters based its operational plan in Kashmir on this wishful

logic. The misplaced ego, the high ambition and the naive approach of a selected few, plunged the country into an armed conflict. The outcome of the war, or the lack of it, eclipsed Ayub's position.[3]

Commenting on the ill-fated Kargil debacle, I had recalled:

> While Akhtar Malik was a brilliant tactician with impeccable motivation, both Bhutto and Aziz Ahmed were embarked on a 'heads I win, tails you lose' option. If the Operation Gibraltar succeeded, they would get the credit, if it didn't, the discredit and the damage would be to the account of the armed forces, a sure way of bringing them to heel as they did manage to do later.[4]

The 1965 Pakistan–India war (6–23 September) was the 'unexpected' aftermath of two botched operations of the Pakistan Army. In early August, Operation Gibraltar sent a force of *c.* 6,000 men, subdivided into nine groups and camouflaged as *mujahideen*, into Indian-held Kashmir (IHK). Their mission was warfare in the enemy's rear, including harassing enemy communications, distributing weapons among Kashmiris with a view to provoke an armed insurrection, leading to a national uprising against Indian rule in Kashmir. For that, the necessary groundwork, i.e. contact and coordination of support with Kashmiris in Azad Kashmir and in IHK, had been missing, logistic planning was weak or unavailable, and personnel were sent into IHK inadequately equipped with food supplies, shoes, and other items. Under these circumstances, instead of receiving help from the local Kashmiris, most were handed over to Indian troops and the cat was out of the bag before the mission could be accomplished.[5] When the Indians realised what was going on, they started attacking the infiltrators and conquering Azad Kashmir territory such as Haji Pir Pass, so that GHQ would fear the fall of Muzaffarabad. To pre-empt that, Operation Grand Slam was put into effect on 1 September 1965. It aimed to take Akhnur, a lightly defended area in IHK and should have distracted attention from Muzaffarabad. But like Gibraltar, Grand Slam failed, this time due to a change of command in the operation, while it was in progress. It created a delay that gave the Indians the time they needed to reinforce Akhnur and thus prevent it from falling to the Pakistan Army.

For reasons unimaginable today, GHQ and Ayub Khan had masterminded the entire adventure, believing that Indians would retaliate to the attack only in Kashmir, across the ceasefire line of 1948. They never anticipated an attack across the international India–Pakistan border. What's more, many people seem to think that Operation Grand Slam was the *raison d'être* for the Indians attacking Pakistan on 6 September 1965, when in fact it was Operation Gibraltar that convinced the Indians to prepare for an all-out war. Operation Grand Slam commenced at the end of August and extended into the beginning of September. To engage in an outright offensive on the scale that the Indians deployed against Pakistan in September, the planning and logistics had to start much earlier. This has been confirmed in the writings of many Indian Generals who took part in the offensive. That the Indian Army was able to mobilise undetected, so close to the border, was a massive failure on the part of Pakistani intelligence and by extension, the country's General Staff.[6]

In addition, on 3 September, an Indian dispatch rider carrying comprehensive orders for the Indian attack was captured by a patrol of Special Service Group (SSG) personnel. The information about an imminent attack was forwarded to the GHQ, where it was dismissed as deception![7] When, on 6 September, a massive Indian offensive was launched on Lahore and Sialkot, the military command and the Foreign Office of Pakistan were taken by surprise. Neither President Ayub, nor the Commander-in-Chief, General Musa Khan, were prepared for a full-scale war with India—a testament to a lack of professional acumen. Bold officers, such as Colonel Syed Ghaffar Mehdi, who, at that time, was commanding the elite SSG force, told General Akhtar Malik that Operation Gibraltar would be a non-starter. In an interview with Hali, Mehdi said, 'Initially, I was pressurised to withdraw my observations and go along with the plan. When I did not budge, I was relieved of my command and told to destroy all copies of my correspondence with GHQ on the subject.'[8] He preserved a copy of his objections at the SSG headquarters. He added, 'Neither the C-in-C Army nor the General Staff had the guts to stand up to the President and tell him that his advisers in the Ministry of Foreign Affairs supported by GOC 12 Division, Akhtar Malik, were taking him on a long ride.'[9] Mehdi's bluntness damaged his military career and he retired as a Colonel. But even after being deposed of his command of the SSG on 31 August 1965 and posted as Colonel Staff 15 Division, he convinced his GOC to move 15 Division troops to cover Sialkot's flank, otherwise, the Indians would have been astride the Grand Trunk Road between Lahore and Gujranwala, before last light, on 6 September.

To put it bluntly, the Indian Army had the superior leadership, but did not have the young officers or troops required to execute its brilliant plans. Pakistan may have had the proverbial morons in its senior command, but luckily, had the young officers and troops to diffuse the Indian advance. Despite blunders by those at the helm of the decision-making process in Pakistan, it was able to halt the advance of a force far superior to its own. It is for this very reason that Pakistan claimed to have won the war of 1965. The Pakistan Air Force had hit most of India's forward bases by the late afternoon of 7 September— the first day of the war. The war may not have been a victory for Pakistan in the traditional sense, but it certainly was a morale-booster and gave the country the upper hand, psychologically.[10]

We seldom eulogise our real heroes and are impressed only by those who talk of bravery instead of actually displaying it. Writer Charles Edward Montague famously said, 'War hath no fury like a non-combatant'. Many unsung heroes fought and died for this nation in the seven decades of its existence. The sound of a bullet is a great equaliser—it distinguishes the men from the boys. Those who have smelt cordite during battle (as opposed to those who do so on the firing ranges and who have never heard a shot being fired in anger, but can talk a good talk, convincingly) are a different breed altogether.

Yet the main loser in 1965 was Pakistan and if the lessons of this war had been learnt, another military disaster—Kargil 1999— could have been avoided. The 'unmitigated disaster', as Hali calls it, alienated East Pakistanis, despite the fact that unity in West Pakistan was 'never greater than in the period of 1965 war.'[11] Mian Arshad Hussain, a former Foreign Minister of Pakistan (April 1968–April 1969) made the following statement in *The Pakistan Times* in 1977, 'In my opinion, the 1965 war bred the 1971 war and is thus an important contributory cause of the latter and the tragic events that have followed the conflict.'[12] Moreover, General Nawabzada Sher Ali Khan Pataudi is quoted as having said, 'The war lasted 17 days, starting from 6 September, 1965, but in those 17 days a few final nails in the coffin of a united Pakistan have been driven.'[13]

The war, though only for seventeen days long, should not have happened, however, once Operation Gibraltar was launched, it became inevitable. A brilliant but childish plan, Operation Gibraltar was great in theory, but disastrous in planning and timing. It is inconceivable how the senior army officers miscalculated the possibility of an Indian attack across the international border, once Pakistani troops were committed in IHK. Yet the high command in the GHQ did just that. The army demonstrated a duality in its command; after all, why we were being rushed out of the Pakistan Military Academy post-haste except as potential cannon fodder for a war that was imminent? Yet one-third of the army was on annual leave/furlough and nobody was making any moves to recall it. When the late Brigadier Aftab Ahmed Khan (later Lt. Gen.), moved his troops into the forward defended localities on the approaches defending Lahore, the Indian Army was taken by surprise. Indian intelligence had confirmed that the forward defended localities along the border were unoccupied.

The war ended when the United Nations mandated a ceasefire in late September and the US and Soviet Union supported peace talks conducted in Tashkent, Uzbekistan, in January 1966. Moderated by Russian Premier, Alexei Kosygin, General Ayub and Z.A. Bhutto from the Pakistani side, and Indian premier Lal Bahadur Shastri, negotiated a peace treaty that Indian and Pakistani forces would pull back to their pre-conflict positions, that both countries would pledge not to interfere in each other's internal affairs in future, and that diplomatic relations would be restored. The Tashkent Agreement was widely unpopular in Pakistan, causing major political unrest against Ayub's regime in both parts of the country, though the unrest in East Pakistan was greater.

The worst breakdown occurred in Dhaka and the port cities of Chittagong and Khulna. 'A' company of 2 EB was sent under Major (later Lt. Gen.) H.M. Ershad, in 'aid of civil power', to Khulna. I was sent ahead with a jeep and wireless set as liaison with the Deputy Commissioner, Mr Idrees (father of second lieutenant A.S.M. Nasim—later Lt. Gen. and COAS of the Bangladesh Army) and DIG (later IG) A.K.M. Habibur Rahman. I was then sent poste-haste from Khulna barges with 'B' Company to Dhaka, where the disturbances were centred around Dhaka University. Even though I had not attended this institution, most of the members of the Dhaka University Central Students Union had been close friends of mine during my college days in Dhaka. It was unreal to be facing them with rifles as they were gathered in a mob in front of the university library. Thank God, their stone pelting on the police ceased when we came on the scene and we did not have to resort to any violence.

East Pakistan's predicament during the 1965 war was quite different from that of West Pakistan. During the war that took place entirely in West Pakistan, East Bengal became completely isolated from the rest of the country due to a halt in airline services across the country and was left to its own fate, without military defence and security, while the Pakistani rulers were busy defending the frontiers of West Pakistan. Although neither India nor Pakistan could really claim a victory in that war, it became a vital concern for the Bengalis that they were being defended by an army that was stationed mainly in West Pakistan. What was especially rankling was the strategic nonsense espoused by some armchair military experts, who postulated that the defence of the east lay in the west. On these grounds, they justified that the forces defending East Pakistan be limited to only one division, three brigades, a PAF squadron, and a small sub-unit of the navy. East Pakistanis, who paid their share of military expenditure, but received little in return, resented this farce. The experience of 1965 showed them that the Pakistan Army was too far away to defend them effectively. When Zulfikar Ali Bhutto, then Foreign Minister, remarked in a speech that East Pakistan had been protected from a possible Indian invasion on the eastern side by China, it created a considerable consternation on the Chinese side, who did not think they were responsible for the defence of East Pakistan. Now, the Bengalis earnestly started to question their belonging to Pakistan.

Soon after the end of the war, Sheikh Mujibur Rahman raised the historic Six-Point demand, a charter for political, economic, fiscal, and military emancipation from the perceived exploitative Pakistani state system. It carried the demands of the people of East Bengal, for self-determination, self-defence, and economic emancipation. The Six Points announced in March 1966, were:

1. Pakistan shall be a federal state. There shall be a parliamentary government formed by a legislature, elected on the basis of universal adult franchise.

2. The federating units, or provinces, shall deal with all affairs except foreign relations and defence.

3. There shall be two separate but easily convertible currencies for the two wings of Pakistan. Alternatively, there may by a single currency, with the provision that the Federal Bank shall take adequate measures to stop the siphoning off from East Pakistan to West Pakistan.

4. The federating units, or provinces, shall reserve the right to levy taxes. The central government, of course, shall have some share of the tax proceeds.

5. Separate accounts shall be maintained for the foreign exchange earnings of the two wings. The foreign exchange earned from foreign trade shall be under the control of the respective wings.

The federating units shall be independent in conducting trades with foreign countries.

6. The federating provinces shall be able to raise para-militia or para-military forces for their own defences.

Almost all Bengalis believed that these Six Points were the key to gaining control of their own resources. The rulers of West Pakistan, however, saw the programme as being at the heart of all the problems between both wings.

THE SIX POINTS—AN ANALYSIS

The first point was fairly simple and logical in a democratic environment. It required a federal and parliamentary form of government, with elections to the legislature held on the basis of universal adult franchise. The one-man one-vote principle had been denied for twenty-five years on the basis of a contrived formula of parity and a separate electorate.

The function of the federal government was limited in the second point, to defence and foreign affairs. By implication, this meant the provinces would control the remaining portfolios. Provincial autonomy is the most enduring guarantee of a strong federation for a state that comprises ethnic and cultural diversity, and is geographically divided. It was Jinnah's preferred model for an independent India of the future, one that he had advocated from 1929—when he commented on the Nehru Report in his Fourteen Points—until 1946, when he supported the idea of an independent Pakistan, consisting of only one unit.

According to the third point, there were to be either two different currencies, or one, in the event of which two separate federal banks were to prevent the flight of capital from one region to the other, subject to certain safeguards, such as establishing a federal reserve system with regional federal reserve banks. This point provided for either a common currency with some limitations on it, or 'two separate but freely convertible currencies' for East and West Pakistan. The proposal for separate currencies made critics suspects that Bengalis were asking for a confederation.

The fourth point concerned fiscal policy—the federal government was to be provided funds in accordance with appropriate constitutional provisions, to ensure that the federal government's revenue requirements were met consistently. The demand was based on past experience of the federating units not being allocated their due share of the national resources. The federal government was encroaching on provincial turf in utter disregard for a Constitution that had been mutilated beyond recognition. It controlled all local and provincial taxes, including octroi and doled this out in 'charity' to the provinces, from what little was left after its profligate expenses, mostly on mega projects and defence.

The fifth point required separate foreign exchange earnings accounts for each federating unit and entitling the federating units to independently negotiate foreign assistance and trade, and meet the foreign exchange requirement of the federal government 'in accordance with procedure laid down in the Constitution.' Provinces were required to pay usurious interest (about 20 per cent) for foreign assistance received by the federal government at concessional terms. The fifth point, therefore, intended to deny unjustified income that the federal government earned by the process of relending foreign loans to the foreign lender.

The last and sixth point concerned the creation of parity of military forces stationed in East Pakistan and/or a paramilitary force for the security of each federating unit. This point was a direct result of the experiences of Bengalis during the 1965 war. The demand for relocation of the Naval HQ to East Pakistan seems a logical point as well. In any case, the decision to shift it instead to Islamabad—far away from the sea—lacked logic.

The Six Points for autonomy looked more and more like a roadmap whereby East Pakistan could get hold of the total control over its foreign trade, exchange earnings, as well as government revenues and expenditures. They were expressions of the experiences so far made by the Bengalis with united Pakistan and secondly, an expression of the specific geographical, political, and economic distance that existed between the two wings since 1947. Besides, the wording of the Six Points and probably the philosophy behind it had seen changes over time. The first version was developed, not by Mujib, but by Tajuddin Ahmed, the party's Secretary General at the time.[14] The opportunity for a united stance by the Bengali opposition came during the visit of President Ayub to Dhaka, in late January 1966, and his invitation to listen to the Bengali demands during a round table meeting. Mujib persuaded the other Bengali leaders to agree to a common charter of demands to present to Ayub. He further stressed that the charter should include a number of specific points defining the quantum of autonomy that the Bengalis considered essential to secure their interest. Though nothing specific came out of that meeting, from thereon, the Six Points summarised and represented the demands of the Bengali opposition, headed by the Awami League. The wording may have been slightly revised a year later, in February 1969, for another meeting with Ayub Khan and then again a year later, in 1970, when it was made the election manifesto.

A point worth noting was the fact that if the military rulers believed these demands to be detrimental to the interest of the federation, they should have disallowed electioneering on any one or all points. After all, the regime had empowered itself by promulgating the Legal Framework Order to replace the 1962 Constitution and imposed a large number of restrictions on what the political parties could or could not do.

Justice A.R. Cornelius, a retired Chief Justice of Pakistan, who served as a constitutional expert in General Yahya's military regime, had this to say to the Hamoodur Rehman Commission:

He (Yahya Khan) was familiar with them (the Six Points) and he used to talk about them from time to time, but he never asked for an analysis. In my own mind, I think that about four of them were quite easily acceptable and I think I said in a meeting of the cabinet that it would be easily possible to amend the Constitution so as to give effect to most of the six points and that would perhaps ease the political situation.[15]

The observations of the Hamoodur Rehman Commission do confirm the hypothesis that Ayub and after, him Yahya, maintained an off-hand attitude towards the Six Points and perhaps did not have any intention of considering them in earnest—at least not before the elections. On the contrary, immediately after its inauguration, Ayub Khan declared the Six-Point programme as 'secessionist' and its author was named the enemy number one of Pakistan. Ayub also threatened to use brute force to suppress this charter of demands, but Mujib and the Awami League remained undaunted by such threats. Mujib started a three-month-long mass contact programme that took him to every nook and corner of East Pakistan. He was arrested eight times in the first three months of the Six-Point movement. By then, he had also been made the President of the Awami League. He was finally thrown into jail on 8 May 1966. After that, a general strike was observed all over East Pakistan, in support of the Six-Point programme and for the release of Mujib, during which police firing in Tejgaon, Tongi, and Narayanganj, killed several people,[16] this was followed by large-scale arrests of Awami League leaders and followers throughout the country. All measures taken by the Ayub regime to suppress the dissent in East Pakistan, proved counter-productive.

THE SIX-POINT DILEMMA

So, was Mujib a secessionist bent on dividing Pakistan, or was he willing to negotiate? The Agartala Conspiracy case and the all-out support that was provided by India to the Mukti Bahini in 1971 went a long way in damaging the credibility of Mujib and that of his party in the eyes of West Pakistan. In the international arena, he was seen as the founding father of Bangladesh. Although, in the final analysis secession brought independence but cost the separated state of Bangladesh priceless resources—both in terms of human and material. Because of India's involvement in East Pakistan, the governments of Saudi Arabia and China were quite critical of Mujib and recognised Bangladesh's independence only after his death.

One of the biggest dilemmas of the Six-Point demand was how a dialogue could take place when it was perceived to pose a threat to a united Pakistan. While the majority of the Bengali population in East Pakistan was fully supportive of the demand for such far-reaching regional autonomy, the Muslim masses in rural East Pakistan, perhaps failed to understand that the Six-Point plan could mean a confederation between two—more or less—independent countries, i.e. the end of united Pakistan as it existed.

While Mujib did agree to modify the Six Points and make them more flexible, this could have happened only in the course of a negotiation between West and East Pakistani leaders. With Ayub and the military rejecting any such negotiation, or a rethinking of the existing Pakistan project, no modification could take place and as a result, the Six Points caused more estrangement between East and West. In addition, there were people within the Awami League who had hardened views on the Six Points. At the end of the day, Mujib and the Awami League fought the election campaign and won the election based on the old wording of the Six Points. Because of the heavy mandate, with only two seats going to another party he and his party became, in a way, prisoners of their own programme.

Before the elections, Mujib kept on insisting that his Six Points stood for the integrity of Pakistan. However, after 1971, he tried to create the impression that Bangladesh had always been his intention. Safdar Mahmood has documented some of Mujib's statements that provide an insight into his later pronouncements. On one occasion, in 1974, Mujib is reported to have said:

The final issue had come before the party in 1966, when the party declared its Six Points programme... A clear path was charted out before the people; it was a path of different kind where Bengalis had to break the bondage of Pakistan.[17]

Mujib also confessed in a TV interview with David Frost that he had been 'working for Bangladesh since 1948'. But all these statements should be looked at as an afterthought to justify the turn that history had taken. It cannot be ignored that the Awami League negotiated with Yahya Khan and western political leaders from 13 to 23 March 1971, about a joint constitution and had almost reached an agreement.

There is another problem that Mujib had. It seems that instead of aiming to become Prime Minister of Pakistan and being power-savvy, he was rather wary of that coveted position given the hostile relations between the two wings, with Bhutto scheming, the bureaucrats caballing against him, and in view of the compromises that he would have to make in that position. According to Sultan M. Khan, a former Foreign Secretary of Pakistan, Mujib would 'rather be the founding father of Bangladesh than the prime minister of Pakistan'.[18] Dr Aftab Ahmed, a renowned intellectual, recalls:

> I was Joint Secretary of the Central Ministry of Information in Dhaka, I met Sheikh Mujibur Rahman for the first time at one of the British Deputy High Commissioner's parties soon after the Martial Law of 1969. I was introduced to him by Mr S.G.M. Badruddin, the then editor of the *Morning News*, Dhaka. During the course of conversation, Mr Badruddin said to Mujib that as a disciple of Mr Suhrawardy, he had to rise to the occasion and play his role. Folding his hands in an apologetic manner, Mujib replied: 'Budruddin Bhai, Suhrawardy Sahib was a great man. He was an all-India leader of the Muslims, and later an All-Pakistan leader. I am a very small man, I can only be a Bangladesh leader'.[19]

After the Awami League had swept the polls in December 1970, Mujib is reported to have said to many people, including S.G.M. Badruddin, 'Do you think I can run this country on the basis of the numerical strength of my party in the National Assembly, with the

Punjabi army and Punjabi bureaucracy still around?'[20] While there is no doubt that Mujib was wary of becoming Prime Minister, it is highly unlikely that he would have declined the position if it was the only way to keep Pakistan united.

Things changed fundamentally when the convening of the newly elected assembly was delayed and then postponed indefinitely, thus denying the Awami League the electoral victory. In early February 1971, as a reaction to the reluctance to convene the newly elected parliament, Mujib actively considered the possibility of a declaration of independence in a meeting with party leaders held behind closed doors. Hossain was asked to prepare a draft declaration of independence that was handed over to Mujib around 10 February.[21]

The fallout of the 1965 war and the unpopular Tashkent agreement gave rise to discontent in both wings of the country. An alliance of political parties was founded whose main demand was the end of military rule as well as the One Unit scheme. Ayub Khan, who felt his power was dwindling, tried to appease the political parties from both wings by convening a Round Table Conference in Rawalpindi, in 1969, to negotiate their demands. East Pakistanis insisted that Mujib be released from jail and attend the conference as the representative of East Pakistan. Grudgingly, this was conceded to and the conference took place from 10 to 13 March 1969, in Rawalpindi. Misreading the situation, Ayub refused both demands—the Six Points of the Awami League, as well as the dissolution of One Unit. The conference ended without any understanding, and on 24 March, Ayub resigned, and handed over power to Commander-in-Chief, General Yahya Khan, while reportedly saying, 'I cannot preside over the disintegration of my country'. Yahya declared Martial Law, dissolved the National Assembly and abrogated the 1962 Constitution. In November, he announced the dissolution of the One Unit in West Pakistan and elections for October 1970.

In retrospect, Mujib's Six Points could have served as a wake-up call to understand the resentment that was brewing over the years among the Bengali populace, against political, economic, and fiscal arrangements devised by the military and bureaucratic elite of the western wing. A pragmatic diagnosis at that point, appreciating the failure of the political system that had been engineered for a decade by the military and civil bureaucracy, might have resulted in a different course of history for what was once a united country. But like so many opportunities, it was lost through a reactionary war and short-term political gains.

AGARTALA CONSPIRACY CASE

The Six-Point movement launched by the Awami League, the East Pakistani student organisations, and opposition parties, made the Ayub regime feel the heat. It drew up schemes to counter Mujib's popularity among Bengalis.

In January 1968, thirty-five 'conspirators' were indicted in the Agartala Conspiracy Case for working with India to bring about the secession of East Pakistan. The name was derived from the meeting of some of the accused with Indian Intelligence Bureau officials at Agartala, in India's Tripura State. The person behind the meeting was Lieutenant Commander Moazzam Hussain. After receiving training in the British Royal Navy in 1950, Moazzam was commissioned into the Pakistan Navy. Promoted in 1967 to the rank of lieutenant commander, after being appointed chief engineer in the Chittagong Naval Base in 1966, he is considered to be the first Bengali national to think that an independent Bangladesh could only be achieved by an armed uprising.

Being in the navy, such overt activities were not possible for him or his colleagues without being discovered. Moreover, Moazzam calculated that such dissent only within the armed forces could not trigger a full-fledged movement. Help was required from a political leader of some standing, who had the support of the public. Such a leader could organise the people and give a call for an uprising as and when the time was ripe. On contacting leaders of several political parties, he was frustrated to find that almost all refused to back his scheme, as they were more concerned about their own safety and well-being if the Pakistan authorities came to know of their plans. The only exception was Mujib, who agreed with Moazzam's views but wanted to keep a low profile. Asked to come to Islamabad in November 1967 for a conference, Moazzam learnt that it was just a ruse; Pakistani intelligence had come to know of his involvement in organising an armed uprising to gain independence from Pakistan. Using a pseudonym, he managed to return to Dhaka on 7 December 1967 and hid in his younger brother's house. Two days later, Inter-Services Intelligence (ISI) operatives raided the house and arrested Moazzam.

In January 1968, Pakistan's Home Department announced that it had uncovered a plot to destabilise Pakistan and break the eastern wing through an armed revolt and had arrested eight people. Prominent among those arrested was Mujib and it was widely believed that he was the brain behind the Agartala plan. Bangladeshi history likes to project this as true, but in fact the main architect was Moazzam. Both were arrested on 18 January 1968, released on 9 May, only to be re-arrested later. Among the thirty-five political personalities and senior government officials tried under civil law, were:

1. A.B. Khurshid
2. A.K.M. Shamsul Haque
3. A.N.M. Nuruzzaman (captain)
4. Abdul Jalil (sergeant)
5. Abdul Latif Majumdar (master warrant officer)
6. Abdur Rauf (lieutenant)
7. Abdur Razzaque (subedar)
8. Abdus Samad (corporal)
9. Ahmed Fazlur Rahman (CSP)
10. Ali Reza
11. Azizul Haq (havildar)
12. Benedict Dias
13. Bibhuti Bhushan Chowdhury (alias Manik Chowdhury)
14. Bidhan Krishna Sen
15. Dalil Uddin (former havildar)
16. Khan Mohammad Shamsur Rahman (CSP)
17. Khondkar Nazmul Huda (captain)
18. Khurshid Uddeen Ahmed (captain)
19. M. Rahman (lieutenant)
20. Mahbub Uddin Chowdhury
21. Mahfiz Ullah (flight sergeant)
22. Mahfuzul Bari

23. Md. Abdur Razzaque (former flight sergeant)
24. Md. Fazlul Haq (flight sergeant)
25. Mohammad Abdul Muttalib (captain, 21 Baluch Regiment)
26. Mujibur Rahman (former clerk)
27. Mujibur Rahman (steward, navy)
28. Nur Mohammad
29. Ruhul Quddus (CSP)
30. Shamsul Alam
31. Shamsul Haq (sergeant)
32. Shawkat Ali (captain)
33. Sultanuddin Ahmed
34. Tajul Islam (former subedar)
35. Zahurul Haq (sergeant)

Overall, nearly 1,500 Bengalis were arrested in connection with the plot, in 1967.

Moazzam was the number one accused; however, a decision was taken to kill two birds with one stone. Mujib was implicated as the number one accused, while Moazzam's name was shifted to the number two spot. This move turned out to be a blessing in disguise for Mujib, because when the trial commenced, he became a hero overnight. Since many of the accused involved military personnel, Pakistan at first decided to try them by court-martial. However, a civil trial was preferred in order to implicate the politicians ahead of the 1970 elections, as well as to provide publicity of the trials. The charge sheet of 100 paragraphs presented before the tribunal included 227 witnesses and 7 approvers. The accused were moved from Dhaka Central Jail to the secure environment of the Dhaka Cantonment.

Not only did many refuse to believe the facts about the case, the general perception was that Mujib's political participation was being manufactured along with the military connection, as a conspiracy by the government against East Pakistan's movement for political autonomy. This gained more credence, since the government was keen to prove that Mujib was an Indian agent and a separatist. Mass movements were organised mostly in East Pakistan; they demanded an immediate withdrawal of the case and the release of all prisoners.

On the morning of 15 February 1969, Sergeant Zahurul Haq was shot and killed by a guard in his jail cell. On hearing this news, a furious mob set fire to the State Guest House and other government buildings. As the chief government lawyer was in residence there, some of the case files and the evidence was burnt as a result of arson. In the face of the mass movement, the government withdrew the Agartala Conspiracy Case on 22 February 1969 and the accused were released the following day. At the grand reception held for the accused at the Race Course Maidan, Sheikh Mujib was given the famous title of 'Bangabandhu'.

One of the ironies of the Agartala Case is that Moazzam never thought very highly of Mujib, nor was he convinced that the Awami League could deliver. He found Mujib vacillating on the question of Bangladesh's independence and believed that he had no qualms about sticking to the autonomy demand within the federal structure of Pakistan. Mujib, meanwhile, never liked Moazzam's candour and straightforwardness. Within the armed forces, little was known about Moazzam. Some of us were shocked to learn that Captain Nuruzzaman, whom we knew and admired as an officer, was among the accused. When he was arrested, he was serving in the ISI and we found it difficult to believe that he could have been involved in the conspiracy.

Almost all of the accused pleaded innocence, they maintained this even among friends in private conversations. It was only after 16 December 1971, once they were safely out of Pakistan's reach, that they proudly announced their involvement in plotting the break-up of Pakistan. I came to know first-hand, many details about the case from my sister Shahnaz's father-in-law, Abdus Salam Khan[22] who despite being the President of the Pakistan Democratic Party, was chosen by Mujib as his chief defence lawyer in the Agartala Case.

Much later, in 2010, Mujib's daughter, Sheikh Hasina, admitted that her father had made plans to break away from Pakistan.[23] On the anniversary of the withdrawal of the Agartala Case, on 22 February 2011, the surviving conspirator and Deputy Speaker of the Parliament, Shawkat Ali, confessed to the House on a point of order that the charges read out to them in 1968 were accurate. He stated that a

Shangram Parishad (Action Committee) had been formed under Mujib for the secession of East Pakistan. Another parliamentarian, Tofail Ahmed, added that had the case not been filed, the plot would have culminated in the secession of East Pakistan without bloodshed.[24]

By the time of his release, Mujib had become a hero in the eyes of the Bengali people and the undisputed leader of the Bengali Opposition. His famous Six-Point programme became the rallying point for the political opposition of East Pakistan.

Notes

1. China ceded over 1,942 square kilometres to Pakistan and the latter recognised Chinese sovereignty over hundreds of square kilometres of land in Northern Kashmir and Ladakh.
2. S.M. Hali, 'Operation Gibraltar—An Unmitigated Disaster?' *Defence Journal*, Vol. 15, No. 2, September 2011, p. 11.
3. K.M. Arif, 'How Pakistan Blundered into War,' *Dawn*, 6 September 1990.
4. Ikram Sehgal, 'Gibraltar-2', editorial, *Defence Journal*, October 1999.
5. Hali, p. 9.
6. Extract from Ikram Sehgal, 'Days to Remember', *The News International*, 6 September 2011.
7. Hali, p. 23.
8. Ibid., p. 15.
9. Ibid., p. 16.
10. 'Nur Khan reminisces '65 war', *Dawn*, Karachi, 6 September 2005.
11. Hali, p. 11.
12. *The Pakistan Times*, 23 October 1977.
13. Hali, p. 33.
14. Kamal Hossain, *Bangladesh: Quest for Freedom and Justice* (Karachi: Oxford University Press, 2013), p. 17.
15. *The Report of the Hamoodur Rehman Commission of Inquiry into the 1971 War* (As Declassified by the Government of Pakistan) (Lahore: Vanguard Books, 2001), p. 72.
16. The Bangladesh Awami League official site, 'The 6-point Programme: 'Magna Carta' of Bangalees', Saturday, 31 August 2013, http://my.albd.org/index.php/en/party/history/23-history/116-the-6-point-programme-magna-carta-of-bangalees.
17. Safdar Mahmood, *Pakistan Divided* (Lahore: Ferozsons Ltd., 1984), p. 72.
18. Sultan Muhammad Khan, *Memories and Reflections of a Pakistani Diplomat*, 2nd edition (Karachi: Paramount Books Pvt Ltd., 2006), p. 288.

19. Dr Aftab Ahmed, 'Regrets to Bangladesh', *Dawn*, Friday, 3 August 2002, hartford-hwp.com/archives/52/003.html.
20. Ibid.
21. Hossain, p. 72.
22. Abdus Salam Khan (1906–72) was a lawyer, politician, and writer. A distant maternal uncle, former leader of the Awami League.
23. 'War plans made as early as '69: Hasina,' 7 March 2010; https://bdnews24.com/bangladesh/2010/03/07/war-plans-made-as-early-as-69-hasina.
24. 'Agartala conspiracy case was not false,' bdnews24.com, Wednesday, 23 February 2011; https://web.archive.org/web/20120319055449/http://www.bdnews24.com/details.php?id=188118&cid=2.

7

Towards Open Confrontation

In order to fully understand the background behind the 'change of guard' from General Ayub Khan, to General Yahya Khan and the latter's subsequent political position, we need to refer to the inside story as told by a person close to the events, the professor of political science and bureaucrat, Golam Wahed Choudhury. Having been a member of Yahya's administration and a close confidante, his description and analysis of the period in his book, *The Last Days of United Pakistan*, is valuable. Interestingly, John Richard Sisson and Leo E. Rose corroborate the same events in a much shorter description in their book titled, *War and Secession: Pakistan, India, and the Creation of Bangladesh*.

It becomes increasingly clear from Choudhury's writing that the main difference between the Ayub and Yahya regimes was that the former tried to install a civilian regime under his de facto military leadership with a civilian government designed to function without parties, through a system of Basic Democracies. Ayub's argument had been that democracy did not suit Pakistan's situation. This idea prevented him from being able to successfully relate to and negotiate with political party representatives—especially those in East Pakistan. Choudhury writes, 'As for the East–West Pakistan relationship on which the viability of a united Pakistan depended, Ayub's understanding was extremely limited.'[1] His political set-up of indirect elections did not work. His economic policy created a sharp concentration of wealth in the hand of a few West Pakistanis and left East Bengalis poor and frustrated. His regime got itself increasingly into trouble after the 1966 Tashkent Agreement, and politicians such as Bhutto, who had at one time supported and even guided him, now left him out in the cold. After Zulfikar Ali Bhutto left the Cabinet, he founded the Pakistan Peoples Party (PPP) and used it skilfully to bring himself into power.

By 1968, not only was East Pakistan up in arms, rallying for the Six Points, and the dismissal of the Agartala case, but political parties and movements in West Pakistan also demanded a return to democracy, elections, and the end of One Unit. In addition, Ayub's health failed and rumours had it he might not survive, so much so that the GHQ was making contingency arrangements. According to the 1962 Constitution, if the President was incapacitated, the Speaker of the Assembly would assume presidential duties. Since the Speaker, Abdul Jabbar Khan, was a Bengali this was not acceptable to the GHQ. According to Choudhury, 'The battle for succession within the military junta began: the generals, air-marshals and admirals were "jockeying and jostling" with each other to take the President's place; the constitutional arrangement was put aside.... Soon it became evident that Yahya was the strongest contender....'[2]

Anti-Ayub protests had by then turned violent in both East and West Pakistan and it was feared that the country would end up in turmoil. Under the pressure of the political parties led by the newly founded PPP in West Pakistan and the Awami League under Mujib, Ayub asked the army to bail out his regime and suppress the opposition movement. But the GHQ was reluctant. The generals, in a series of meetings in February 1969, advised him to talk to the politicians, help himself and not rely on the armed forces. Against all expectations, Ayub recovered, though slowly, and resumed his work. But poor health coincided with the political weakness of his regime. He tried to overcome his reluctance and started talks with the politicians, but neither in February 1968, nor a year later, did his Round Table Conferences (RTCs) make any headway. The RTC of February 1969, was boycotted by Bhutto and Bhashani, with Mujib as the only major politician attending. Though Ayub conceded to the demand for a parliamentary form of government and not a presidential regime, the negotiations failed, as did a round of secret meetings and talks between Mujib and Yahya.

The President's position had become untenable and the situation in the country deteriorated fast. Tired also and frustrated, he sought for an escape. In a meeting between him and Yahya, Ayub asked his Commander-in-Chief to impose Martial Law as a solution to the country's ills.[3] Yahya agreed that Martial Law was now the only possible solution, but he also demanded that Ayub should first sack the provincial governors, dissolve the provincial assemblies and abrogate his constitution. This amounted to a handing over of power to Yahya and the GHQ, which an ailing and politically weakened Ayub finally agreed to do. Thus, on 25 March 1969, Ayub Khan's rule came to an end.

There is considerable evidence to suggest that the military under the Commander-in-Chief, General Yahya Khan, deliberately allowed the situation to slide out of control so as to bring the Ayub regime to an end. In any case, the new regime under Yahya was, from the very beginning, a purely military one, with the GHQ sometimes more in charge than even Yahya himself. It was designed to prepare for the return to civilian rule as soon as possible. While there was no adverse reaction in East Bengal to the takeover by Yahya—perhaps because the Bengalis had had enough of Ayub—the imposition of Martial Law came as something of a shock to many in the eastern wing. What kept emotions under control was Yahya's promise, made on 26 March 1969, the day after his take-over, that power would be transferred to the elected representatives, elections would be held on an adult franchise, the system of Basic Democracies would be done away with, and that the future constitution would be framed by the elected representatives. The promise of fast elections and return to civilian rule brought the opposition movement to a halt. In addition, Yahya allowed political parties to function despite the presence of Martial Law and the dissolution of the assemblies. This made it possible for him to talk to the political leaders and consult them on the details of political arrangements. Obviously, he had no such apprehensions as Ayub had had about talking to politicians in order to arrive at a compromise and he felt that in order to be successful, his rule needed legitimisation.

This readiness to talk to politicians included Mujib, because Yahya understood that the real problem was East Pakistan, the Awami League, and the constitutional problem hidden in the Six Points. Therefore, in order to address that problem, he needed to regain the trust of Mujib and his party that had been lost when Huseyn Shaheed Suhrawardy was removed as Prime Minister in 1957. At first, Yahya talked quietly to different leaders including Mujib, Bhutto, and Bhashani, in the months from April to November 1969. Choudhury, who was privy to the talks, describes the situation as follows:

> …Yahya was, no doubt, sincere and Mujib gradually became convinced of the sincerity of his pledge, but Yahya was never [the] master of his own house as Ayub had been. He never had more than a limited hold over the army generals who in fact constituted the ruling junta between March 1969 and December 1971....[4]

The bottom line though, was a united Pakistan. 'Any threat to break-up the country was to be met with effectively, on that there was no difference of opinion'.[5] About the talks with Bhutto at that time, Choudhury reveals:

> Bhutto, the dapper and aristocratic leader in West Pakistan, was busy building his political base in West Pakistan as well as cultivating links with various members of the military junta. Like Bhashani, he had hardly any constructive suggestion or plan for solving the constitutional dilemma.[6]

It took Yahya until November 1969, eight months, to study the opinions of the different political leaders and inquire about their 'red lines'. In order to manage the transition and meet the expectations of the politicians and Pakistani people, Yahya's focus had to be on constitutional settlement, to organise power to quieten civilian demands, keep the country united, and find a place of political influence for the military in the new set-up. Among the many issues faced by him upon taking over the reins of governance, the most important were:

- The dissolution of One Unit and the restoration of the West Pakistani provinces of Punjab, Sindh, NWFP, and Balochistan;
- The problem relating to parity between East and West Pakistan and restoration of the principle of 'one man one vote';
- The preparations for elections based on adult franchise;
- Whether the relationship between the Centre and the provinces should be determined before the elections, or be left to the new Constituent Assembly to take up;
- The economic disparity between the two wings.

From his deliberations, it seemed that Yahya was sympathetic to the genuine grievances of the people of East Pakistan. He strongly felt that they were getting a raw deal. In his own words, 'They were fully justified in being dissatisfied with this state of affairs'. The need to rectify that situation was reflected in his address to the nation on 28 November 1969, '...the requirement would appear to be maximum autonomy to the two wings of Pakistan, as long as it does not impair with the national integrity and solidarity of the country'. Yahya appeared to be sincere about resolving the problem in East Pakistan, handing over power to the elected representatives and most importantly, doing so in a manner acceptable in a democratic system, provided the integrity and solidarity of the country was not affected. In order to address the constitutional problem, he announced that he would develop a 'legal framework', within which, after the elections, the elected representatives would be called upon to develop a new constitution. Here, we can observe how narrow a line he was walking. On the one hand, he wanted to give a free hand to the elected representatives, while on the other, he laid down limits to their freedom in order to secure the unity of the country. The whole thing seemed to amount to a 'squaring of the circle'.

Mujib, during those months, declared himself and his party to be ready to negotiate the Six Points.

> He told Yahya and Ahsan [Admiral S.M. Ahsan the Governor of East Pakistan], that his six points were not 'the Koran or the Bible' and the plan was negotiable. One morning in the autumn of 1969, he [Mujib] told me, pointing at the photo of Suhrawardy…'How could I think of destroying Pakistan, being a disciple of this great leader?'[7]

At that time, it seemed that the problem was manageable. The vast majority of the East Bengali Muslims were not asking for secession; but they did demand that they get their legitimate share in national affairs, and it was the failure to tackle this vital problem that ultimately led to the tragic developments of 1971.

In November 1969, the matter looked quite positive and Yahya, in his speech, acknowledged the right of the people to demand constitutional, financial, and economic autonomy in the decision-making process. This was, if not an answer to all problems, a first step in the right direction. Yahya's speech, though received favourably by many civilians and the military, was criticised by Bhutto and some unnamed generals in the GHQ. They were worried that too much autonomy would weaken the central government to the extent that ruling Pakistan would be difficult for a future Prime Minister. Bhutto saw himself occupying that position and wanted it to be a powerful one.

Caught between a rock and a hard place, Yahya tried to square the circle by issuing the Legal Framework Order (LFO) on 28 March 1970. The LFO that had been developed during close negotiations with the 'inner circle' of the GHQ and Yahya's constitutional committee consisted of five main points. It aimed at forming a parliamentary type of democracy, based on the principles of Islamic ideology. It would have democratic institutions guaranteeing fundamental rights to citizens and provide for free and fair elections. It demanded that the territorial integrity of Pakistan was preserved and last but not least, provided for a maximum of autonomy for the provinces, with the constraint that the federal government would still have adequate power to discharge its responsibilities. The LFO consisted of a preamble, twenty-seven articles, and two schemes. It envisioned one federal and five provincial parliaments elected on the basis of adult franchise and an independent judiciary to enforce the fundamental rights of the citizens and the laws of the country. Furthermore, the LFO demanded that the elected representatives develop the new constitution within 120 days of the formation of the new assembly and required that Yahya 'authenticate the constitution'.

While the 120-day limit was justified by the fact that it had taken nine years for the first Constitution to come into being, there was a need for Yahya to approve of an 'emergency exit', should the new Constitution violate the 'red lines'. Though this latter point was criticised by the parties as a retreat from the announced principles of 28 November, it was grudgingly accepted as a compromise.

The real bone of contention was the structure of the federation. Based on their experience of twenty-three years in Pakistan, the East Pakistanis, led by the Awami League, had already in 1966 formulated their demands in the Six Points, for a loose federation with maximum autonomy for all the provinces. This was seen as the biggest challenge to the political forces in West Pakistan. While Yahya seems to have been quite confident at this point that the Bengali majority in the parliament, based on their population, would be contained by political divisions within East Pakistan, he still wanted to make sure that he would have a veto on the Constitution once the election was over. For that, he inserted Article 25 in the LFO, which ordained that he would have to authenticate any Constitution drafted by the Parliament, or else it would be invalid.

The manner in which Yahya handled the political situation showed the difficulties that he was facing. On the one hand, the demand for civilian rule and the dissolution of the One Unit scheme that had been installed mainly to neutralise the Bengali majority, could not be resisted any longer. On the other hand, the danger of West Pakistan losing power to East Pakistan was a major concern of the military and West Pakistani politicians. But the missing political power and autonomy of East Pakistan was one of the main grievances that had been maintained by the eastern part of the country over the years. The LFO contained seeds of controversy between the two parts of Pakistan. The Awami League considered the 120-day deadline for the formulation of the Constitution as a pressure tactic against East Pakistan.

Yahya, having promised the transfer of power to the elected representatives, initiated moves towards this end. From 1 January 1970, he waved all remaining restrictions to political activities like demonstrations and corner meetings and lifted limitations on press freedom. Justice Abdus Sattar was appointed as the first Chief Election Commissioner of Pakistan, with a three-member Election Commission whose first task was to enrol as voters all citizens of Pakistan who were 21 years and older, on 1 October 1969. At the conclusion of this exercise, the number of registered voters in the country was as follows:

East Pakistan	31,211,220
West Pakistan	25,730,280
Total	56,941,500

Most importantly, Yahya decreed that it was only fair that the parity of representation in the National Assembly, between the East Wing and the West Wing, would be based on the population of each wing and that the previous model that had existed under the 1956 and 1962 Constitutions, would end. Based on the voters registered by the Election Commission, seats were divided as follows:

East Pakistan	162 seats	plus seven reserved for women
West Pakistan	138 seats	plus six for women

The date for the first-ever general election in Pakistan was set for 5 October 1970. The election campaign was one of the longest in the country's history, lasting for almost a full year. With all restrictions removed, the Awami League conducted its campaign under the Six Points programme and '*Joy Bangla*' cries became a common feature. On 1 July 1970, Yahya dissolved One Unit and the four West Pakistani provinces were restored—a central demand of the Western political parties that found support in the Awami League as well.

The election campaign displayed the sharp differences between the two leading political parties, the Awami League and the PPP. On the one hand, Bhutto campaigned in the western wing on a nationalist and pseudo-leftist platform. Despite the fact that he hailed from a prominent Sindhi landowning family and agricultural workers on his land were kept in abject poverty under the feudal system. The slogan of his party was, 'Islam is our Faith, Democracy is our Policy, Socialism is our Economy.' Bhutto said that the PPP would provide '*roti, kapra, aur makaan*' (bread, clothing, and shelter) to all and promised a 'hundred years of war against India'. While the West Pakistani campaign, which showed a religious edge, was centred on Bhutto's drive for power and was decorated with slogans on poverty, in East Bengal it was the autonomy question that took centre-stage. The Awami League popularised its Six Points more and more during the campaign and claimed that it was only because of the eastern wing's products that the western wing had prospered, and that the former was not getting its due share. It demanded maximum autonomy for East Pakistan, complaining about the exploitation of its resources by the federal government.

The Six Points, however, also advocated that Bengal was in fact a 'colony' of the western wing of the country. This obvious difference in outlook created the impression that the western wing did not support the autonomy demand, which was not entirely true. Nevertheless, it was yet another reason why the radical Awami League leaders, who were ready to break the country, were gaining influence within the party during the election campaign.

In speeches made during the earlier phase of the campaign, Mujib claimed that united Pakistan was his goal. Later, however, voices were heard preaching secession openly. As the election campaign became heated, the mood changed and slogans of Bengali nationalism and independence increased. Instead of countering this, the PPP concentrated more on Bhutto's creation of Islamic socialism while using Islam and anti-Indian feelings as a political rallying point. And to make matters worse, the PPP shut down its branch in East Pakistan—a move that was taken as a sign that the PPP only represented the western side, leaving East Pakistan to the Awami League. Pakistani intelligence services tasked with monitoring the undercurrents of the situation as it developed, obviously missed this development. How else could they have reported to Yahya that the forthcoming election would produce a split vote, so that no danger of a single majority party was to be expected?

It became evident in election campaign the Awami League would gain a majority in the East, with the PPP that was quite popular in the western part leaving the field open to political opponents. That did not necessarily mean a move towards separation, but it was a dangerous development nevertheless. The issues that were raised in the two wings in the run-up to the elections stood at such a contrast, that it seemed almost impossible that the two parties and their leaders would pull together in one political direction.

India, watching the developments closely, decided it was a good time to make existing problems even worse. G.W. Choudhury reports that All-India Radio, from its station in Calcutta, was broadcasting a programme every evening about 'This side and that side of the same Bengal', thus creating the (false) impression that East Bengal had more in common with West Bengal than with West Pakistan. If that were the case, why did Congress not agree to a United Bengal in 1947? It was a clear provocation. There were other reports also about Indian money and arms finding their way into East Pakistan, to ensure the success of the Awami League in the elections and for an eventual confrontation with the Pakistan Army in a secessionist war. India had been unable to digest Partition; therefore, dismembering Pakistan and thus proving it wrong, was its long-term policy.

General elections for the National Assembly were set for 5 October 1970, the idea being that by then the annual monsoon would have subsided and communication lines would be functional. According to Yahya's plan, the newly elected National Assembly was obliged within 120 days to draw up a new Constitution, which would meet those demands. That was of course a very short period of time for developing a consensus between the two parts of the country on how the future political set-up of Pakistan should be designed. For instance, the Six Points demanded that all powers of taxation rest with the federating units, but the West Pakistani political forces and the military were reluctant to allow such a degree of autonomy and made it clear that the federal government would require its own independent powers of taxation, well beyond those contemplated by the Awami League.

Yahya was well aware that if the demands of the Awami League were granted, it would considerably weaken West Pakistan's grip over the eastern part, but he nevertheless seems to have been ready to concede that much. The question of autonomy continued to be the main problem; West Pakistani politicians were eager to insert a clause into the constitutional proposal, demanding two-thirds, or at least 60 per cent majority, for constitutional changes that would have neutralised the East Pakistani majority in the Parliament. According to G. W. Choudhury, who was privy to the deliberations, the 60 per cent clause would have been a knockout criterion for Mujib and that is why Yahya dropped it at the last minute. He writes, 'Mujib, the subsequent founder of Bangladesh, was paradoxically the last hope for a united Pakistan—provided he could be persuaded to modify his six points. I carefully examined the substance of the Yahya–Mujib and Mujib–Ahsan talks in 1969–70 and can vouch that Mujib repeatedly assured that he would modify his six points once the elections were over.'[8]

By the summer of 1970, the seeds of trouble had been sown and were clearly visible to those who cared to look. Yet Yahya's genuine attempt at restructuring the political system of Pakistan into a loose federation, may have been the only way to keep the country united.

And while the geo-political features of the region were not conducive to the creation a centralised nation state, learning from history and reverting to a loose federation with maximum autonomy could have saved the project of a united Pakistan. But the odds were stacked against this idea—and more so from August onwards.

Notes

1. G.W. Choudhury, *The Last Days of United Pakistan* (Karachi: Oxford University Press, 1993), p. 42.
2. Ibid., p. 28.
3. Ibid., p. 40.
4. Ibid., p. 75.
5. Ibid., p. 76.
6. Ibid., p. 77.
7. Ibid., p. 85.
8. Ibid., pp. 91–2.

8

First General Election in Pakistan
December 1970

In 1970, a string of natural disasters hit East Bengal that brought the election campaign to a grinding halt and cast a shadow over the outcome of the first and last general election in a united Pakistan. It seems in hindsight that even nature had conspired against a united Pakistan.

It all started in August and September 1970, when the monsoon resulted in severe flooding in large parts of the country. Many places were inaccessible and voters were unable to reach polling stations. Flooding was not new to East Pakistan and the region has always been prone to it; much of East Bengal lies on a river plain and delta of the Ganges and Brahmaputra rivers, at a low elevation above sea level—at some places, only one meter. While floods occur almost every year in the region, the monsoon of 1970 had brought with it heavier than usual rains, so that a territory of 115,000 square miles was flooded and 30 million people—nearly half of East Pakistan's population—affected. Rapidly rising floodwater brought death and destruction and locals were forced to evacuate their homes in boats and makeshift rafts. In Dhaka, the provincial capital, with a population of 750,000, river water entered the streets, flooding houses in many parts of the city; roads and railway lines were destroyed. It took three weeks for the water to recede, yet areas continued to remain inaccessible by road or railway and food supplies had been destroyed.

The Pakistan Army was called in for emergency relief operations. Pakistan Air Force planes flew in about 45 tonnes of supplies, which were distributed by army helicopters to camps, housing thousands of people evacuated from stricken areas. The helicopters dropped supplies of rice and medicine in the worst hit areas, while speedboats were used to ferry supplies. Immediately after the news of flooding reached President Yahya Khan, he flew into Dhaka to inspect the damage personally. He drove, walked, and waded round Dhaka and visited the Sarafatganj Community Centre, to see for himself the vaccination campaign being carried out there. The President also visited two relief camps in the city, and the severely flooded areas of Mohammadpur, Gandaria, and Sadarghat.[1]

There does not seem to have been much critique of West Pakistan and the Pakistan Army helping to tackle the disaster. Even a Bangladeshi website reports that Yahya visited 'all the camps primarily located in the local schools and temporary shelters. He distributed clothes, blankets, wheat, rice, and other ready-made food items. Yahya became a popular figure outright to the poor people. Everyone chanted "Yahya Zindabad". Days later, a cross-section of the same people chanted anti-Yahya slogans when the Awami League launched campaign meetings in various parts of Dhaka and other districts that were inundated with flood water.'[2] It seems that the occasion was used by the Awami League—still in election campaign mode—to gain political leverage.

Due to the unprecedented flood in East Pakistan, the election dates had to be changed. After an emergency cabinet meeting in Dhaka on 8 August 1970, the President postponed the general election scheduled for 5 October by two months.

On 12 November, however, another disaster hit the country—one that was far worse. A tropical cyclone and tsunami swept through the coastal areas of East Pakistan. Referred to as Bhola, the cyclone was the deadliest one to have been recorded in the region. While the estimated loss of lives during the summer floods was approximately a hundred people, an estimated number of 500,000 people lost their lives when Bhola struck, primarily because it washed away the low-lying islands and areas of the Ganges Delta. The storm surge devastated many offshore islands, wiping out villages and destroying crops throughout the region. It made landfall on the East Pakistan coastline during the evening of 12 November, around the same time as the local high tide. Once on land, the system began to weaken, but was still categorised as a cyclonic storm on 13 November.

Despite the fact that there had been a disaster warning by the East Pakistani authorities, most people were not able to reach fortified structures and did not take the warning seriously because of the frequency of such alarms. Some Pakistani observers blamed the Meteorological Department for failing to notify the coastal areas of the impending storm and alleged that the weather bulletin did not provide an indication of the severity of the storm and consequently, 'confused people.'[3] The department is also said to have failed to comment on the expected tidal bore, so that the people on shore and ships at sea did not take adequate precautions.

The death toll in the densely populated areas was high—thirteen islands off the East Pakistani coast lost almost their entire population. The airports at Chittagong and Cox's Bazar were submerged for several hours and runways damaged, thus impeding air travel. US Consul General, Archer Blood, described the scene as he witnessed it from a low-flying helicopter, 'There are still thousands of bodies of cattle and hundreds of bodies of people strewn on beaches and countryside. Fifty miles down, the eastern coastline of Bhola and then up the same island, about two miles inland, the situation is appalling.'[4] Over 3.6 million people were directly affected by the cyclone, and the total damage from the storm was estimated at US$86.4 million.

Most of the homes in the affected areas were destroyed and people lost their businesses. Fisher-folk either lost their lives or their fishing boats, peasants their harvests, the villages their food supplies. For three months, the population continued to live on food hand-outs and the provision of drinking water. Meg Blood, the wife of Archer Blood, went out to deliver emergency supplies in villages. She recalled, 'People were up in trees holding their children, and the trees were swept clean away…. The homes were mostly thatch, on the water, and they were the first to go, to be swept away.[5]

The international response to the disaster was overwhelming, with helicopters coming in for rescue operations, and the provision of food and tents, all at short notice. The most important need was that of helicopters, because the affected areas could not be reached via road and for immediate relief, goods needed to be airdropped. On 18 November, the Chief Secretary of East Pakistan phoned Archer Blood to say that relief efforts had come to a standstill in the absence of helicopters. *The Pakistan Observer* ran the headline 'Foreign Relief Goods Remain Dumped in Dhaka: No Airdropping Yet.' On 22 November, the US government sent a 'Helicopter Roundup'— detailing that helicopters were either in operation or on their way to East Pakistan:

A. Ten U.S. Four [*sic*] Army 'helicopters here: four more now scheduled [to] arrive November 23. Two USAID Nepal small helicopters here.
B. Ten UK helicopters. Two of these are small and already here (arrived November 20). Rest due November 24.
C. Five German helicopters due during course of [the] week of November 23.
D. Three French helicopters expected [in] East Pakistan [on] November 23.
E. Four Pakistani military helicopters one of which small. Pakistani helicopters were all in East Pakistan at [the] time [of] disaster: originally, only one was in working condition. All now operating.[6]

The British had airlifted from Singapore, forty troops, one dozen land rovers, and two Sioux helicopters—too small to carry relief goods. The eight larger UK helicopters arrived off Patuakhali, on the mini-carrier, Intrepid, which also brought one company of Royal Engineers, one company of riflemen, and equipment such as bulldozers. According to US government calculations, 'the total number of helicopters made available for disaster relief finally reached

General Yahya Khan

Zulfikar Ali Bhutto

Huseyn Shaheed Suhrawardy

Sheikh Mujibur Rahman

Kazi Bashir (Humayun),
cousin of Ikram Sehgal

Gen. M. A. G. Osmany

J. A. Rahim

Abdus Salam Khan

Lt. Gen. Sahabzada Yaqub Khan

Lt. Col. (later Brig.)
Mohammad Taj

Maj. (later Brig.) Jaffar Khan

Brig. (retd.) Mujahid Alam,
Principal, Lawrence College,
Ghora Gali, Murree

Lt. Gen. Ali Kuli Khan HI (M)

Col. Salman Ahmed

Maj. (later Lt. Gen.) Lehrasab Khan
HI (M), SJ, SBt

Lt. Col. (later Lt. Gen.)
Imtiaz Waraich HI (M), SJ

Officers of 2 EB in 1967. Ikram Sehgal is second from right.

Dinajpur Cricket Team in 1963. Ikram Sehgal is 5th from right and Shamsher Mobin Chaudhry (future foreign minister of Bangladesh) is sitting 2nd from left.

Gen. Yahya Khan and his wife at a rest house in Sylhet when he was GOC 14 Div. in 1963. Author's father, Lt. Col. Abdul Majeed Sehgal, is in uniform and the author is leaning against a pillar with a rifle.

Last Eid of United Pakistan in 1970 in Baitul Muharram Jame Masjid, Dhaka. From right to left Brig. (later Maj. Gen.) Ishaq, MS to President; President Gen. Yahya Khan; Maj. Gen. Ghulam Omar, National Security Advisor to the President; and the author's father Lt. Col. (retd.) Abdul Majeed Sehgal.

Ikram Sehgal as a Lieutenant in
Infantry School, Quetta,
during training.

Ikram Sehgal as Captain,
Army Aviation.

Ikram Sehgal with General Agha Mohammad Yahya Khan.

Standing next to an Alouette-3 in Azad Kashmir.

On the tarmac with an Alouette-3 in Dhaka.

Meeting the NCOs of 2 EB in Dhaka Cantonment in 2008. The Commandant of East Bengal Regimental Centre (EBRC) had specially flown in from Chittagong for the visit.

Meeting the NCOs of 2 EB in Dhaka Cantonment.

Visiting 2 EB NCO's Mess in Dhaka Cantonment in 2008 where the author's photographs were on display as 'We Remember'.

CO 2 EB, Lt. Col. Abu Jahid Siddiqui, presenting Ikram Sehgal with his father Lt. Col. Abdul Majeed Sehgal's photograph duly signed by all the then serving officers of the unit.

Group photograph alongwith author's younger daughter Nefer Sehgal with the officers of 2 EB in Dhaka Cantonment in 2008.

Standing in front of 'Sehgal Company' barrack in Malir Cantonment in 2008 alongwith the then CO 4 Sindh 2009 Lt. Col. (later Brig.) Muhammad Shahid Jawad Khan.

Ikram Sehgal meeting the JCOs of 4 Sindh in 2012 in Malir Cantonment.

When the author visited Comd 5 Corps Lt. Gen. Naveed Mukhtar in Karachi in 2015, Delta Company 4 Sindh was guarding the Corps HQ. The men of Delta Company quickly got the Corps Intelligence Section to write the sign 'Sehgal Coy'.

Ikram Sehgal getting a red-carpet welcome by CO 4 Sindh Lt. Col. Rashid Bashir in 2015 in Malir Cantonment.

Inspecting the Quarter Guard of 4 Sindh alongwith CO 4 Sindh Lt. Col. Rashid Bashir in Malir Cantonment in 2016.

Ikram Sehgal with some friends, among them Amir Zia, on a visit to 'Sehgal Company' barracks in Malir Cantonment.

Attending the funeral of US Marine Master Sergeant Frank Adair in California in April 2017.

thirty-eight, which included later arrivals from Iran, Saudi Arabia, and the Soviet Union. The Soviet helicopters were among the last to arrive and the last to leave.[7]

One of the major problems was the number of human dead bodies, as well as those of cattle, that remained unburied for many days and constituted a major health hazard. One American military Colonel, a Vietnam War veteran, said that this scene was far worse than anything he had ever seen.[8] It was a matter of political importance that British soldiers were reported to have buried the bodies, instead of Pakistani soldiers.

> The Hamood-ur-Rahman Commission was told that Pakistani soldiers refused to handle Bengali dead bodies. Witnesses reported to have seen a large number of dead bodies lying unburied. A cynical comment one heard at the time was that the Bengalis did not want the dead buried so as to attract greater sympathy. The fact is that the survivors were too few and even they were not equal to the task...[having] gone hungry for days and lost many members of their families. There was a glaring contrast in the manner in which the world rushed to provide succour to the Bengalis as against the passivity of the Islamabad government.[9]

The US government made an independent assessment of the organisation, performance, and capability of the official disaster relief effort by Pakistan. It stated that Pakistan was simply not in a position 'Either physically or psychologically', to deal with a disaster of such scope. It was not even equipped to handle the distribution of the large-scale foreign assistance. The Pakistani military did not make the effort of which it was capable at that time. In addition, there is the failure of Yahya and his cabinet to display 'more heart', which embittered the East Pakistanis. Yahya's dismissive attitude had greatly contributed towards this. However, after an initial delay, military and civilian relief efforts picked up momentum. The efforts of East Pakistan Governor, Admiral S.M. Ahsan, in particular have been mentioned in Blood's report. Ahsan personally took part in the relief effort, supervising airport operations, and expediting the shipment and distribution of relief goods.

But regardless of their achievement, perceptions remained different. The Pakistani government and army were severely criticised for their perceived delayed handling of the relief operations following the cyclone, both by local political leaders in East Pakistan and in the international media. In his memoirs, Blood declared:

> President Yahya had stopped in Dhaka on November 16 en route back from China, where he had a very successful visit, winning a commitment for larger amounts of military assistance. It was reported, and widely believed in East Pakistan, that he had celebrated heavily on his flight back and had spent his one day in East Pakistan in something of an alcoholic daze. His aerial reconnaissance was not by helicopter but in a plane flying at 3,000 feet. Back at the Dacca airport, before returning to Islamabad, Yahya made a few comments indicating his sorrow but, according to some press accounts, was heard to say, 'It didn't look so bad.'[10]

Syed Shahid Husain recalls in his memoirs, 'Ironically, Yahya was in Dhaka on that fateful day, but went back to West Pakistan without knowing what had really happened.'[11] This negligence on the part of General Yahya made Bengali alienation all but complete. Gary Bass writes, 'Even the Nixon administration secretly admitted that Pakistan's government had flubbed it.'[12] After severe critique in the media Yahya, went back for a second, short visit to East Pakistan to superficially take command of the relief operation but this did not stem the tide.

The first relief effort by West Pakistanis was seen in the affected areas, ten days after the tragedy. The Pakistan Army showed up eventually, but there were reports that soldiers did not appear to be committed. This situation made East Pakistanis feel abandoned once again and reinforced their resentments. The Awami League, on the other hand, took this opportunity to prove its worth, by organising relief work and sending its cadres into the field. Its cause was further strengthened because West Pakistani politicians were perceived as callously indifferent to the Bengali victims of the November cyclone and slow to come to their aid.

Based on Archer Blood's records, one can spell out yet another result of the cyclone and its aftermath. He reports that Bengalis in general and Mujib in particular, were impressed with international relief efforts and international attention and sympathy that the disaster had received. He observed that this reaction was mistaken by them as a sign of international sympathy for the Awami League and their cause of autonomy and, eventually, secession from West Pakistan, though this was not the case at that point in time. Furthermore, he observed that during the course of the natural disasters, the international media swarmed into East Pakistan and started reporting from there but as was often the case, the international community had already made up its mind about who to blame; this was a result of skilful Indian media propaganda supported by the Soviet Union and the socialist countries. There were huge media campaigns supporting the 'freedom struggle' of the East Bengalis. In the atmosphere of the Cold War' in those days, the role of West Pakistan as an associate of the US, was described by the socialist countries and the non-aligned movement as that of a coloniser and the Pakistan Army was blamed for refusing to help poor people in despair.

Natural disasters always wreak havoc wherever they strike and analysing the crisis from hindsight, one always sees room for improvement in the way in which matters are handled. Even Archer Blood, who was prejudiced in favour of the East Pakistanis, admitted in his memoirs:

> Often, however, their reporting seemed grossly unfair and even self-serving. For example, listen to the words of David Loshak, the South Asia correspondent for the *London Daily Telegraph* and a prime example of these know-it-alls from out of the West:
> 'The situation in Dhaka was extraordinary. The administration was paralyzed. Officials as hapless as the cyclone victims themselves gaped

open-mouthed at press conferences and left it to foreign journalists to put forward suggestion after suggestion for improving—or, more accurately, for initiating the relief efforts.'[13]

Pakistan's case in East Bengal was lost in the field of propaganda, among other places. This is true not only for the reporting on the cyclone, but for the disinformation spread during the civil war and the nefarious role of India in the matter.

The Awami League was at the forefront of helping establish a relief centre at its headquarters and in Dhaka University, along with the East Pakistan Student League. Mujib, taking advantage of the situation, castigated West Pakistani politicians who preached integration of the two wings, but who failed to even visit Pakistan to extend sympathy and succour to the survivors. He even went as far as to accuse West Pakistani leaders of cold-blooded murder saying that 'The textile millionaires have not given a yard of cloth for our shrouds.'[14] When General Yahya hastened back to Dhaka on 24 November to stem the tide of anti-Western rhetoric, it was too late. The precondition for secession had been put into place despite West Pakistani efforts to insist on maintaining the unity of the country.

While opposition parties asked for a further postponement of the elections, the Awami League strongly opposed this demand—not ready to give away the gain in popularity that they had made. Mujib, fearing the postponement of elections, played down the losses in a press conference, arguing that millions of Bengalis had already died in the struggle for their rights and more are ready to die if the elections would not take place.

In any case, Yahya resisted postponing the entire election and polls were to be held in only those areas worst-hit by the cyclone a few days later (17 constituencies). In an address to the nation on 3 December 1970, he said, 'Many doubts were expressed regarding the sincerity and intentions of this regime but despite this, we remained steadfast in our aim of bringing back democracy in our land'.[15] Blood remarked:

It could be argued that the Awami League would have won a resounding victory at the polls regardless of whether the Government of Pakistan's disaster relief record had been superb, so-so, or downright bad. True, but I doubt if the Awami League's margin of victory would have been as great as it was, had not the Awami League been able to exploit the widely shared view in East Pakistan that the Centre had once more clearly demonstrated its disregard for the East's needs.[16]

Between late November and early December, 1970, there were three more secret meetings between Yahya and Mujib, in which the latter provided reassurances that the country would not be broken up, even in the event of an Awami League victory and that the Six Points would be so modified as to keep the country together. From G.W. Choudhury's account, it seems that the two were honest in their intentions, but neither of them was fully independent in his respective decision-making. There were forces in the Awami League that did want a break-up of the country and there were forces in West Pakistan that would prefer a break-up rather than giving power to the Bengalis. At the same time, Yahya's resolve for a political solution may have been not too strong because, as mentioned earlier, he was informed by the secret services active in East Pakistan that a split vote was to be expected in the elections and not a singular victory of the Awami League. A split vote would undermine the singular pressure of the Six Points and could be used to neutralise them. This assessment, though, proved to be fatally inaccurate.

During the election, the parties contested the 300 seats of the National Assembly based on an adult franchise; East Pakistan was assigned 162 seats and the four West Pakistani provinces, 138 seats. The Awami League single-handedly won 160 out of 300 National Assembly seats, which made it the single majority party in the Pakistani Parliament that would be able to form a government without any coalition partner even though it did not win a single seat in any of the four western provinces.

The PPP captured only 83 seats out of 300, which made it the second-largest party in Parliament. Even this result came as a surprise, because having been founded only in 1967 such a success of the PPP and Bhutto had not been expected. The remaining 57 seats were taken by seven different West Pakistani parties. In NWFP and Balochistan, the National Awami Party (NAP) and Jamiat Ulema-e-Islam (JUI), respectively, got the majority, while neither of them, or the PPP, won a single seat in East Pakistan. This result already seemed to clearly cut the country into two. How could the Awami League rule a united Pakistan without a single seat of support in West Pakistan? Moreover, could the PPP expect to rule all Pakistan without a single seat from East Pakistan? The election result was a clear sign that a united Pakistan could not be ruled through a simple majority system.

The victory of PPP in West Pakistan roused the ambition of Bhutto, who anyway had given up on East Pakistan by closing down his party offices there. From thereon, he manoeuvred to carve out the maximum of power for himself, even if it meant undermining the unity of the country. In this endeavour, he could be sure of the support of Punjab and Sindh and immediately after the announcement of the election results, he started courting the parties of NWPF and Balochistan for support. His excellent contacts with some of the generals in the Pakistan Army enabled him to garner considerable military backing. Nevertheless, to state that the PPP became the majority party in West Pakistan, as is often done, is not entirely accurate. Bhutto and his party only represented the population-strong provinces of Sindh and Punjab. In Balochistan and the NWFP, he had little or no representation.

> It was argued that since the Awami League had no representation from
> 'West Pakistan' therefore it had no legitimate right to rule over the
> whole of Pakistan. Following this line of thought, Mr Bhutto had no
> representation in Balochistan and a nominal one in the NWFP. Then,
> how did his party form governments in both these provinces? This is
> a question awaiting an answer for a long time.[17]

The first general election in Pakistan, held twenty-three years after its creation, was testament to the fact that a democracy could not be established merely by the stroke of the pen, or an LFO. While the then chief election commissioner described the election as free and fair in his report, this claim has been contradicted by other reports of intervention by the Pakistan Army, present in East Bengal. Syed Shahid Husain touches on the subject in his book.[18] The Awami League, on the other hand, also 'helped' itself to victory. To quote Lt. Col. (later Brigadier) Mohammad Taj, SJ & Bar, from the transcript of his audio recording:

> I was General Staff Officer I [GSO-I] Intelligence in HQ 14 Division Dhaka, since 1969. The situation in East Pakistan was extremely bad when I landed there and it continued deteriorating ever since. Every day that passed East Pakistan was being driven into an uncertain situation and it was politically motivated, the elections of 1970, [that] aggravated the situation. Sheikh Mujib was the leader of Awami League, the only majority party in East Pakistan and during the elections Awami League personnel stopped other party members [from going] anywhere near [the] polling stations. I disagree with those who say that the polling was fair, because people were not allowed to go to the polling stations. However the result of the polling was in favour of Mujib and his Awami League—only two seats were lost by them. The Awami League emerged as the majority party in East Pakistan.[19]

One can assume that despite the attempts to manipulate the election, the will of the voters was fairly visible in the election results. The split result expected in the vote in East Bengal did not bear fruit, especially after the main opposition party to the Awami League, the Maulana Bhashani-led National Awami Party, decided to boycott the elections. Mujib's party managed to win 167 out of the 169 seats assigned to East Bengal and 74.9 per cent of the votes polled in East Pakistan. One of the two other seats went to Nurul Amin, a former Muslim League member who was then the head of the Pakistan Democratic Party and one to Raja Tridiv Roy, the Chakma Chief who contested as an independent candidate.[20] This result was a clear vote by the Bengalis in favour of the Six-Point programme of the Awami League, which had been the focus of their campaign. The Awami League did not contest a single seat in West Pakistan and did not even fight an election campaign there. This was another sign that the division of the country was in the making.

For Yahya, the sweeping victory of Awami League came as a rude surprise. Yahya had obviously believed the reports of the intelligence agencies that had predicted a split vote in East Bengal. Now, the terms of negotiations with Mujib had changed fundamentally: he was the victor and the people's choice for Prime Minister. The Six Points were the basis of his electoral victory, which made changing them after the elections close to impossible. Whether the vote was a sign that the public was in favour of secession or just greater autonomy, is a matter of debate. Choudhury argues that the illiterate majority of Bengalis could not have understood whether the Six Points referred to secession, or autonomy. Moreover, Mujib, in his election speeches in 1970, never made mention of a separate state. Voices that as early as the summer of 1970 had demanded that Mujib not be allowed to contest the elections under the Six Points without a proper definition of what autonomy would mean, were proven right. The negotiations that could have achieved this clarity had been frowned upon by the West Pakistani establishment and had therefore failed.

When reflecting on the course of events that led our country to an overwhelming electoral victory of the Awami League and further towards civil war, natural disasters had played a decisive part. The inadequate dealing by the government and army with the devastation of the cyclone not only contributed to Awami League's victory but also shaped the perceptions of East Bengalis after the election during the rehabilitation phase of the relief effort.

The political impact of the cyclone ... that slightly less than five per cent of the East Pakistan population were directly affected by the disaster, which was confined to the coastal fringes and the offshore islands. The rest of the people gained their impressions of the destruction and loss of life, and the relief effort, from the local newspapers, primarily those in the Bengali language, and, in the case of those living in Dacca and south of Dacca, from their own observations of activity or inactivity.

There was much that was easily observable. The sky over Dacca and southern East Pakistan was full of unprecedented numbers of helicopters and cargo planes coming from all over the world. The airports at Dacca and Chittagong were operating at maximum capacity. Men in strange foreign military uniforms were a common sight in Dacca and around the base camps set up near the disaster area to accommodate the various helicopter contingents. And a host of foreign newsmen and TV crews made known their presence noisily and demandingly. Inactivity could be just as noticeable particularly if one lived near a military cantonment. The press began to comment on the sight of bored soldiers, weeding flower plots on their bases or the absence of any unusual vehicular movement from Army installations.

...East Pakistanis in private have expressed dismay for inexplicable (as they see it) absence of visible contributions by primarily West Pak-based military to relief effort, sole exception being locally-based Army helicopter and PAF C-134 transport which have been pressed into relief operations. Where, they asked, are the helicopters which are based in West Pakistan? Why, when foreign nations are so visibly helping out, is no major assistance apparently forthcoming from their brethren in West Pakistan?[21]

Notes

1. 'Devastating summer floods of 1970', http://www.londoni.co/index.php/25-history-of-bangladesh/1970-bhola-cyclone/312-bhola-cyclone-1970-august-monsoon-flood-cyclone-frequency-pre-bhola-history-of-bangladesh.

2. Bangladesh Genocide Archive, 'The Legal Frame-Work Order—A Discussion on the Liberation War of Bangladesh,' 3 March 2008, http://www.genocide bangladesh.org/the-legal-frame-work-order-a-discussion-on-the-liberation-war-of-bangladesh/

3. Archer Blood, *The Cruel Birth of Bangladesh: Memoirs of an American Diplomat* (Dhaka: The University Press Limited 2002; third edition 2006), p. 76.

4. Ibid., p. 98.

5. Gary J. Bass, *The Blood Telegram: India's Secret War in East Pakistan* (Penguin Random House India Pvt Ltd., 2013), p. 23.
6. Blood, ibid., p. 82.
7. Ibid., p. 83.
8. Ibid., p. 99.
9. Syed Shahid Husain, *What was Once East Pakistan* (Karachi: Oxford University Press, 2010), p. 16.
10. Blood, p. 77.
11. Husain, p. 16.
12. Bass, p. 23
13. Blood, pp. 89–90.
14. Blood, p. 116.
15. Choudhury, p. 126.
16. Blood, p. 121.
17. Abdul Khalique Junejo, 'Evaporating Governance: The Facts', *Dawn*, 1 November 2017, https://www.dawn.com/news/1367519/evaporating-governance-the-facts.
18. Husain, pp. 27–34.
19. Interview with Brigadier Mohammad Taj, February 2017, Islamabad.
20. Hossain, p. 65.
21. Blood, pp. 113–14.

9

Election Aftermath

The results of the first general elections came as a surprise to not only the military, but Mujibur Rahman and Zulfikar Ali Bhutto as well because neither had expected a sweeping victory. In East Pakistan, the Awami League had a straight win, owing to the boycott of the elections by Maulana Bhashani's party. In West Pakistan, the rhetoric of poverty alleviation that inspired widespread support as well as the support for the military did the trick. G.W. Choudhury records that after the announcement of the results, hectic activity began in Islamabad, in which the implications of the new situation were assessed. While a split vote would have compelled the parties and their leaders to negotiate a compromise in order to form a government, the winning of an absolute majority by the Awami League made compromise difficult for Mujib to justify to his party workers and the Bengali public.

Before the elections, Mujib had been prepared to adjust the formulation of his Six Points to make them acceptable to coalition partners and the LFO, but now it seemed unnecessary to yield to pressure and demands. On the contrary, budging on the Six Points now could endanger the integrity of the party and undermine Mujib's grip on it. Since the Agartala conspiracy, a radical group of 'hawks' had cropped up within the Awami League who were less interested in keeping Pakistan united, let alone compromise for its sake. Their voice grew stronger now, with the electoral victory.

Bhutto, who had displayed ambitions for power at the national level, felt encouraged by his party's victory, despite the fact that it won only 81 seats out of 300. Nevertheless, these figures meant the

PPP was the second-largest party in the country and the largest in West Pakistan. He now insisted on a share of political power at the Centre and not ready to sit in the opposition and be content with provincial politics. In a speech on 24 December 1970, Bhutto said, 'People voted for [the] P.P.P. in great majority in West Pakistan and for Awami League in East Pakistan. Both these parties have to share responsibilities of the country as the majority parties.'[1] By saying this he made his 81 seats equal to the 160 seats of Mujib and put his foot firmly in the door to power.

But there was a personal side to Bhutto's quest for power.

He saw himself as the rightful "heir to the throne" after Ayub's regency. It was he who had led the movement that had unseated the "king" and who had guided a mass movement for the restoration of representative institutions; it must thus be he who would exercise ultimate executive authority. One of the president's senior ministers observed to Yahya just after the elections that if Bhutto did not assume power within a year he would literally go mad.[2]

That was why he could not wait.[3] As a result of Bhutto's unmitigated push for power, his personal relationship with Mujib—which had never been a good one to begin with, owing to differences in background—would suffer further.

By mid-December, the battle-lines had been drawn. With Mujib, declaring the elections 'a referendum on the Six Points' and Bhutto desperate to seize power, things began to look very different from the way they had before the elections. In response to Bhutto's suggestion power had to be shared with the PPP since it was the majority party in West Pakistan, Mujib pointed out in his Ramna Course speech on 3 January 1971, that the Awami League was the majority party in the whole country and not just East Pakistan, and that there were no two majority parties. He added that he would take responsibility for the whole country under a constitution that would be based on the Six Points and that no one could stop that.[4]

It was important now to ensure that any draft of a new constitution would fulfil the requirements of the Awami League, the PPP, and the LFO, because it was quite clear to all that the 120-day deadline to finalise a Constitution was too short a period, given the complexity of the situation. Thus, major preparatory work had to be done beforehand. Choudhury submitted on 11 December 1970, a draft to Yahya that conceded to almost all of the Six Points. The only exceptions were granting East Pakistan the right to negotiate foreign loans and aid on its own and the demand that the federal government control only three portfolios (the draft retained five or six unspecified portfolios with the Centre).[5] Kamal Hossain, advisor to Mujib, writes, 'According to our assessments in late December, it seemed that Yahya would make his own independent and preliminary attempt to negotiate with the Awami League to press for modification of the Six Point formula, so as to secure the interests of the ruling elite and of the army.'[6]

The situation appeared to be very different from Mujib's point of view. He and his party had won the elections on the Six Points and now he had to be careful to uphold these. During a mammoth meeting on 3 January 1971, he announced that the Six Points were now the property of the people and that he had no authority to compromise on them. Yahya was thus anxious to start talks with Mujib and Bhutto. He first invited Mujib in his capacity as future Prime Minister of Pakistan to come to the capital, but Mujib declined and asked that Yahya come to Dhaka instead.

In the middle of January, Yahya travelled to Dhaka and met with Mujib to discuss the Six Points and the draft Constitution he had prepared. According to Choudhury, a disappointed Yahya complained that 'Mujib has let me down. Those who warned me against him were right; I was wrong in trusting this person.'[7] The unexpected margin of victory had shocked Yahya, who became wary of Mujib's intentions, losing much of the trust he had placed in him. In the two meetings held between them, Mujib explained to Yahya how he planned to ensure that the Six Points complied with the LFO and with Yahya's draft. Despite Yahya's apprehensions, the talks seem to have gone sufficiently well. 'At the end of his stay, Yahya referred to Sheikh Mujib as the next prime minister of Pakistan, adding that his job was finished, that he was preparing to leave office, and that the transfer of power would occur soon.'[8] Accompanying Yahya, General S.G.M.M. Peerzada was less optimistic; he had separate meetings with Hossain and others and warned that West Pakistan—meaning Bhutto—would have to be carried along.

Yahya naturally felt frustrated and his visit ended inconclusively, despite some positive indicators. From Dhaka, he went straight to Larkana, where he met Bhutto on 17–18 January 1971. There are not many details available about this meeting, but there cannot be any doubt that a strategy was being discussed about how to deal with the situation. We have Choudhury's contemporary account of it and Sisson and Rose collected memories about the Larkana meeting years later. The third account is that of Pakistan's Foreign Secretary, Sultan Muhammad Khan.[9] Choudhury mentions that a hunting party had assembled in Bhutto's Larkana home that included Yahya, General Peerzada, and General Abdul Hamid Khan, all of whom 'enjoyed Bhutto's hospitality, and in the course of rather colourful social evenings a new and most sinister alliance seems to have developed between the military junta and Bhutto.'[10] Bhutto's own version of the event is this, 'We discussed with the President the implications of the Six Points and expressed our serious misgivings about them. We nevertheless assured him that we were determined to make every effort for a viable compromise....'[11]

Sisson and Rose mention Mustafa Khar and Mumtaz Bhutto among those present at Larkana. But it seems most of the substantial meetings took place between Bhutto and Yahya in private and that others were informed about them later. Bhutto displayed extreme displeasure at Yahya's calling Mujib 'the first prime minister of Pakistan', which he said was not for Yahya to determine, but for the National Assembly. Bhutto seemed to imply that this step of Yahya pre-empted his efforts to create a majority for himself among the elected representatives. Yahya replied that it was not he, but the election result, that had given Mujib the majority and that in any case an understanding between Bhutto and Mujib was needed if Bhutto did not want to sit in the Opposition.[12]

Sultan Muhammad Khan writes:

> Yahya Khan went to Dhaka to talk to Mujib and on his departure made a public statement that he had just met the future prime minister of Pakistan. On his return, he promptly visited Larkana to meet Bhutto. From sketchy accounts of this meeting, which are supported by subsequent events, Bhutto succeeded in convincing Yahya Khan that Mujib as prime minister would be a disaster for Pakistan. He would abandon Kashmir, reduce military expenditure, raise an East Pakistan militia, transfer the capital to Dhaka and generally dictate terms to West Pakistan, a prospect very unpalatable to the armed forces, the bureaucrats, the industrialists and the feudal landowners, in short the establishment, which has always ruled Pakistan. From then on, Bhutto frequently met Yahya Khan and the more they met, the greater were suspicions in East Pakistan....
>
> With a clear majority enjoyed by Mujib in the Assembly Bhutto suspected that he would be completely bypassed and all that he could see for himself was the role of the leader of opposition, without any hope of ever coming into power. If that was what democracy meant, it was not acceptable to him.[13]

The varying accounts of the Larkana meeting all seem to agree about the fact that Bhutto rejected whatever consent had been achieved between Yahya and Mujib in Dhaka, and the Generals Peerzada and Hamid, who belonged to Bhutto's inner circle, supported him instead of Yahya. This set the stage for the weeks and months to come. Mujib, on hearing about this, started regarding Bhutto as an enemy and a representative of the hawkish elements of the GHQ, which certainly did not help the situation. After this, when someone suggested to Mujib that he could make Bhutto deputy prime minister and foreign minister, Mujib was reported to be ready to make him 'agricultural minister', but never trust him with the foreign office.[14] In order to gain time for his plans to obtain a share in political power, Bhutto demanded that Yahya delay the convening of the National Assembly. Though Yahya remained non-committal at this point, Bhutto would keep working on this issue.

As a result of the Larkana meeting, Bhutto went to Dhaka on 27 January 1971, for three days, where he held several rounds of talks with Mujib and other Awami League leaders. According to Hossain, the PPP delegation, instead of discussing the details of the Six-Point-programme, launched into an abstract discussion on the meaning of socialism[15] and how a strong Centre was prerequisite to it. Such behaviour suggests that Bhutto was not interested in a breakthrough. According to Bhutto's version of the talks, 'Mujib's strategy was to bring the National Assembly to session without loss of time in order to give legal sanction to his Six Points.'[16] While the quote that is ascribed to him—'*idhar hum, udhar tum*'—shows that Bhutto was ready to sacrifice the unity of Pakistan for his prime ministership, its authenticity has come into question.[17] The negotiations ended inconclusively and Bhutto returned to West Pakistan 'in order to evaluate the discussion' for which they needed at least a month—until the end of February—after which the delegation would return to Dhaka. The delaying tactic to convene the National Assembly and hand over power even two months after the election was apparent and it angered the Bengalis.

On 1 February 1971, an event occurred that had far-reaching consequences. On 30 January 1971, Indian Airlines Fokker F27 Friendship aircraft named Ganga—flying from Srinagar to Jammu—was hijacked by two Kashmiri separatists, Hashim Qureshi and his cousin, Ashraf Qureshi. They belonged to the Jammu and Kashmir Liberation Front (JKLF). It was flown to Lahore, where the passengers and crew were released and the aircraft burnt on 1 February 1971. Ganga was one of the oldest aircraft in the Indian Airlines fleet and had been withdrawn from service, before being re-inducted only days before the hijacking.

In an article in *The Friday Times* on 11 April 2003, Khalid Hassan wrote about the Ganga episode as he was present at Lahore airport when the incident occurred. Incidentally, Bhutto too was at the airport, having arrived from Dhaka. He took advantage of the situation by giving the hijackers a welcome for heroes. As the Ganga passengers anxiously killed their time in a nearby hotel, India and Pakistan negotiated their release, as well as that of the aircraft. The hijackers had demanded the release of some two dozen jailed members of JKLF by the Indians and political asylum in Pakistan. Hassan recalls that initially, there had been no bar on Pakistani journalists walking across the tarmac and talking to the two hijackers, but then all of a sudden, their access was blocked. In a dramatic turn of events, Pakistani security agencies set the Ganga airplane on fire. No one was allowed to go close to it, not even the West Pakistan Chief Secretary, Afzal Agha, who happened to be a Kashmiri from Srinagar. Both Hashim and Ashraf were arrested, tried, and sentenced by a special court on charges of being 'Indian agents'. The passengers of the hijacked plane were later driven by bus over the border and into India.[18]

It was later revealed in a blog post that the entire plot had been planned by RAW:

> The hijacker, Hashim was a RAW agent, an ex-BSF officer. The travellers were all Indian services personnel or their family members. As expected, Pakistan was not aware of the hijack operation. The drama reached its crescendo when Hashim contacted Lahore air base seeking permission to land the hijacked plane on Pakistan soil. It was never difficult for Hashim and Ashraf to convince the then foreign minister and future prime minister of Pakistan, Zulfikar Ali Bhutto. The strong case of seeking world attention to the Kashmir problem was evident. It was perceived to be a blow to India, which was already interfering [in] East Pakistan (now Bangladesh). Bhutto himself welcomed Hashim at Lahore [and gave him credibility]. However, under pressure from India, all the passengers were released and the aircraft was destroyed. Pakistan realized this soon [about the existence

of the plot] and arrested Hashim and [Ashraf]. Hashim was given a
13-year jail term by [a] Pakistan court. RAW has always maintained
a diplomatic stand on this chapter. It has neither denied nor accepted
the fact that the hijack was planned.[19]

While Bhutto was socialising with the hijackers and trying to use
the incident to his favour, the Awami League responded differently. It
deplored the incident and suspected that the government would used
it to delay the convening of the National Assembly. Mujib detested
the fact that he had not been informed about the details leading to
the burning of the aircraft.

Indian intentions became clear on 4 February 1971, when India
unilaterally suspended Pakistani aircrafts' right to fly over Indian
Territory. This meant that the connection between West and East
Pakistan was made much more difficult, as now all flights had to
take the route via Sri Lanka. In case of an unrest in East Pakistan, it
meant that military personnel and supplies would take much longer
to reach Dhaka and any operation would be much more expensive
for the Pakistani government. India had been watching the growing
dissent between the two wings and saw a promising opportunity
to make things difficult for Pakistan. This cancelling of overflight
rights played a decisive role during Operation Searchlight and the
war that followed. It proved a major handicap for supplies of men
and materials to reach East Pakistan in time.

The unsuccessful talks with Bhutto in late January, his aggressive
public posturing and the inability to agree on a date for the meeting
of the National Assembly, led to heightened tensions between the
two halves of the country. Awami Leaguers felt that their election
victory was disregarded and that attempts were underway to undo
it. The prevailing aggression reduced any chances of successful talks
and created a polarised political environment. In early February,
the Awami League leadership began considering the possibility of
declaring independence, in a secret meeting. Hossain recalls:

I was asked to draw up a draft declaration of independence, which I did under Tajuddin Ahmed's close guidance. The text used as a precedent, was the American Declaration of Independence which recited the injustices perpetrated by the British Crown to justify the act of declaring independence. Closeted with Tajuddin Bhai in my chambers in Sharif Mansions for over two days, I typed the draft declaration myself, given its absolutely confidential nature. We duly prepared the draft and handed it over to Bangabandhu around 10 February.[20]

On 13 February 1971, Yahya finally announced 3 March as the date when the National Assembly would meet in Dhaka. Mujib and his colleagues welcomed the news, tensions eased and they started working on a draft constitution. But here, Yahya had reckoned without his host. Two days later, on 15 February, Bhutto announced that he and his party would not attend the opening because of the missing understanding regarding the Six Points. The PPP showed no readiness to accept the election outcome despite the fact that Bhutto's attempts to cobble a coalition in West Pakistan to contest Mujib's majority en bloc had seen little success. Much more time was needed to reach any such an agreement. Instead, Bhutto started coordinating his policy for power with the army generals.

Perhaps Bhutto had never been interested in a compromise with Mujib, who, in the event of an agreement, would have been the next Prime Minister of Pakistan, leaving only a secondary position for Bhutto. The GHQ and especially the hawks therein, had also lost whatever little hope they might have had in Yahya's efforts for an agreement with Mujib. Their pressure on Yahya, who had never been entirely free in his political conduct, grew, and a result of this was the dissolution of the civilian cabinet. The military was clearing the way for action.

In an important meeting on 20 February 1971, Yahya declared that 'Mujib was not behaving and needed to be sorted out'. Options for action to be taken against Mujib and the Awami Leaguers were

presented and discussed. Choudhury reports that in mid-February, '…
the army junta met formally in Rawalpindi…to discuss the political
situation. It was at this meeting that the junta decided to challenge
Mujib if he persisted in his uncompromising attitude, but significantly
it ignored Bhutto's provocative speeches.'[21]

Two days later, a meeting between Generals Yahya, Hamid,
Peerzada, Yaqub and Admiral Ahsan took place, where Yahya
announced that he would now postpone the meeting of the National
Assembly to give more time to the politicians to resolve their
differences. Ahsan cautioned that the reaction in East Pakistan to
such an act would be instantly hostile and public order would be
disturbed. The attendees did not know the situation in East Pakistan
as Admiral Ahsan did, who had been Governor of East Pakistan since
1969. They called his views 'alarmist'.[22] Yahya insisted that he would
announce the postponement on 1 March and tasked Ahsan to prepare
Mujib 24 hours in advance. The next day again, a delegation tried to
convince Yahya that postponement was a bad idea, but Yahya is on
record to have said that he could be convinced 'but that they should
just try and convince Bhutto.'[23] This seems to indicate that it was
Bhutto more than Yahya, who was pressing for postponement with
the help of his GHQ crew.

On 25 February 1971, Governor Ahsan and Maj. Gen. Rao Farman
Ali Khan, in charge of civil affairs in Martial Law Administration of
East Pakistan, went to Karachi in a last-ditch effort to convey to
Bhutto their fears for public unrest and civil war in East Pakistan.
Bhutto was not convinced, he downplayed the fears of civil war and
insisted on his boycott of the National Assembly meeting.[24]

After this, Yahya finally decided to announce the postponement
of the meeting on 1 March 1971. He asked Choudhury to write a
draft of the announcement, which is reprinted in full in Choudhury's
The Last Days of United Pakistan and was formulated very carefully,
citing the 'deadlock' between the principal parties as the reason for
the postponement. The East Pakistani public was assured that the
postponement was only by two to three weeks, until the impasse

was overcome. He writes, 'I personally handed over the draft of the statement at Islamabad airport as Yahya was leaving for Karachi. He subsequently gave it to Peerzada, who, in alliance with Bhutto, torpedoed it.'[25] Peerzada struck out the passage on the two-to-three-week limit, which made the postponement seem indefinite. Choudhury records that though he has no documentary evidence, he later 'heard from the personal staff of the President...that Yahya was most reluctant to sign the statement prepared by Peerzada in collusion with Bhutto.'[26]

The Awami League did not know of these developments. Mujib, during those days, kept meeting and talking to visiting representatives of West Pakistani parties, such as Maulana Mufti Mahmud and Maulana Hazarvi of the Jamiat Ulema-e-Islam. He tried to convince them to attend the National Assembly's opening, assuring them of his readiness to talk about the Six Points. The leaders of the smaller West Pakistan parties were convinced of Mujib's sincerity to accommodate alternate viewpoints.[27]

Ahsan returned to Dhaka empty-handed and communication came to a halt during the last days of February, between Rawalpindi and Dhaka. Until 28 February 1971, there had been hope that the National Assembly would meet on 3 March, but Bhutto's Lahore speech on 28 February dashed all of it. It was in this speech that he 'threatened personal as well as public harm if he were denied control of the political situation.' He threatened his party members that he would break the legs of the person who would dare to go to Dhaka. 'He told the other Assembly members that they had better go on a 'one-way ticket'.[28]

Thus, on the night of 28 February 1971, Governor Ahsan went to meet Mujib, as per his orders, and inform him about the postponement that would be announced next day by Yahya. Mujib was frustrated and said that the authorities were bent on destroying not only him but Pakistan. Ahsan, deeply worried and frustrated, tried to contact Yahya in Rawalpindi to tender his resignation, but he was not available. Later that evening, Ahsan received a telegram notifying him that he had been relieved of his duties as Governor and that he was being replaced by Lt. Gen. Sahabzada Yaqub Khan.

During the political negotiations, the military junta was making contingency plans to meet any unrest or uprising in East Pakistan. Syed Ali Zia Jaffery writes:

> The stalemate had irked General Yahya so much that he was convinced that something else will have to be done to meet the ever-dangerous milieus. General Yaqub updated the plans of Operation Blitz, which was made on 11th December, 1970, just 4 days after the elections. This operation was kept top secret and was ostensibly developed to counter the impending threat.[29]

Maj. Gen. Khadim Hussain Raja reports in his memoirs:

> ...during January and early February 1971, General Yahya had visualized the possibility of a military crackdown.... He, therefore, prepared a plan called Operation Blitz, which was cleared with the headquarters of the Chief Martial Law Administrator and a copy provided to the GHQ.... Operation Blitz meant the suspension of all political activity in the country [East Pakistan] and a reversion to Martial Law rule. This meant that the armed forces...would be permitted to move against defiant political leaders and to take them into protective custody.[30]

On 26 February, General Yaqub convened a Martial Law conference in Dhaka, where the commanders in East Pakistan were informed that on 1 March 1971, Yahya would announce the indefinite postponement of the National Assembly planned for 3 March. The army was instructed to put into place Operation Blitz in the event that any unrest broke out after that announcement. According to Raja's memoirs, 'General Yaqub directed that we be ready to put Operation Blitz into action at short notice. I was also informed that 57 Brigade, ex 16 Division at Quetta, was already on the move to Karachi from where it would be ready to fly into Dhaka at a given codeword.'[31] But Raja reminds us that the reinforcements could not carry their weapons with them and this limited their usefulness. This information by army officers involved in the events of early 1971 shows that although Yahya felt betrayed by Mujib, he had not given up hope of a negotiated solution. However, he left his options open for a military operation.

There is a good chance that hawkish forces in the army had been pressing for a military solution even before February. Yahya, having failed in his negotiations with Mujib, finally relented. It proved fatal for the future of Pakistan. Admiral Ahsan, it seems had sensed the impossibility of a military solution and tried to persuade Yahya not to postpone the National Assembly session. Yahya did not agree and relieved Ahsan of his governorship, installing General Yaqub for a brief period, until General Tikka Khan arrived in Dhaka on 7 March 1971.

In hindsight, it seems that Blitz was the GHQ's first option—one that had been delayed for too long and should have been implemented earlier if it was to have any chance of success. The Hamoodur Rehman Commission Report confirms that the decision to postpone the Assembly had already been taken on 22 February, in the Corps Commander Conference in Rawalpindi. The army was instructed to put Operation Blitz into place in case of unrest.

Besides, it underestimated the vulnerability of the situation in East Pakistan and, therefore, had a limited programme. Arresting the politicians would not have tackled the popular unrest that was going to break out upon Mujib's arrest but probably even before. The operation would also have prevented a political solution and for this reason, was postponed until there was no hope for reconciliation. Thus, it was not the army that kept a contingency plan ready, but the refusal of Bhutto to reconcile and share power with Mujib, that escalated the situation.

By the end of February 1971, Pakistan's military dismissed any notions of a political solution to the crisis that had evolved in the wake of the 1970 December general election. Yahya failed in his negotiations with Mujib and civilian political forces headed by Bhutto were disinterested in a deal with Mujib for their own reasons. Bhutto's refusal to attend the National Assembly session in Dhaka and insistence that Yahya not allow power to end up in East Bengali hands, made Bhutto and the military strange bedfellows.

Notes

1. *Dawn*, Karachi, 25 December 1970 as cited in G.W. Choudhury, *The Last Days of United Pakistan* (Karachi: Oxford University Press, 1993), p. 146.
2. Richard Sisson and Leo E. Rose, *War and Secession: Pakistan, India, and the Creation of Bangladesh* (Karachi: Oxford University Press, 1992), p. 57.
3. Ibid., p. 58.
4. Ibid., p. 62.
5. Choudhury, pp. 141–2.
6. Kamal Hossain, *Bangladesh: Quest for Freedom and Justice* (Karachi: Oxford University Press, 2013), p. 66.
7. Choudhury, p. 149.
8. Sisson & Rose, p. 63.
9. Sultan Muhammad Khan, *Memories and Reflections of a Pakistani Diplomat* (Karachi: Paramount Books Pvt Ltd., 2006).
10. Choudhury, p. 152.
11. Zulfikar Ali Bhutto, *The Great Tragedy* (Karachi: Pakistan Peoples Party, 1971), p. 20, http://sanipanhwar.com/The per cent20Great per cent20Treadegy per cent20by per cent20Zulfikar per cent20Ali per cent20Bhutto per cent20 per cent20—per cent20August per cent2020, per cent201971.pdf.
12. Sisson & Rose, p. 67.
13. Sultan M. Khan, p. 288.
14. Choudhury, p. 154.
15. Hossain, p. 68.
16. Bhutto, p. 22.
17. 'Idhar hum, udhar tum: Abbas Athar remembered', *The Express Tribune*, Pakistan, 8 May 2013, https://tribune.com.pk/story/545869/idhar-hum-udhar-tum-abbas-athar-remembered/.
18. Arjimand Hussain Talib, 'Hijack that Changed History,' 14 March 2015, Greater Kashmir, http://www.greaterkashmir.com/news/gk-magazine/hijack-that-changed-history/163118.html.
19. Shrikant Iyer, 'How India won the 1971 War against Pakistan—Read this Smart Plot,' 11 November 2015, http://pippingcoffee.blogspot.com/2015/11/how-india-won-1971-war-against-pakistan.html.
20. Hossain, p. 72.
21. Choudhury p. 154.
22. Sisson & Rose, p. 85.

23. Ibid.
24. Ibid.
25. Choudhury, p. 157.
26. Ibid., p. 158.
27. Sisson & Rose, p. 86.
28. Ibid., pp. 88–9. This quote has been reiterated by people who have listened to Bhutto's speech. The version that is published by the PPP under Bhutto.org has been smoothened over in this regard.
29. Syed Ali Zia Jaffery, 'A Leaf from History: India and the Breakup of Pakistan,' Setting the Record Straight, pp. 85–6, *Stratagem* bi-monthly magazine, May 2017, Issue 11, pp. 80–9, http://www.stratagem.pk/setting-the-record-straight/ leaf-history-india-breakup-pakistan/.
30. Maj. Gen. Khadim Hussain Raja, *A Stranger in My Own Country: East Pakistan 1969–1971* (Karachi: Oxford University Press, 2012), pp. 41–2.
31. Ibid., p. 42.

10

Outrage in March 1971

The announcement of 1 March started a new phase in the political crisis in East Pakistan. At 1:05 p.m., the text of a statement ascribed to President Yahya Khan was read out over the radio. The bottom line was that it had been decided to delay the summoning of the National Assembly to a later, unspecified date. That sounded like an indefinite postponement and a refusal to transfer power and as a result, emotions soured. The reason given for the delay was that an 'accepted consensus on the main provisions of the future constitution had not been arrived at by the political leaders.' It is unclear how a missing consensus on the main provisions of the Constitution would be a valid reason for postponement, after all, constitution making and legislation is one of the foremost tasks of any parliament.

Yahya, the West Pakistani politicians, and Bhutto were afraid that an Awami League dominated parliament would frame a Constitution and introduce a confederal system of government. Such a scenario would not suit them and would put an end to Yahya's dreams of being President in the new set up. Prior to Yahya's announcement, new political developments had started to become apparent since early February. With only one functional international airport, troop movements in East Pakistan were quite visible. Due to a shortage of military units of purely West Pakistani origin, units of non-Bengali origin were flown in from West Pakistan to augment the Pakistan Army's Eastern Command contingent in East Pakistan. The idea was to keep the Bengali units at bay, as there were doubts regarding their loyalty towards a united Pakistan.[1]

GHQ consultations on Operation Blitz were somehow leaking out. Maj. Gen. (retd.) Khadim Hussain Raja records that Mujibur Rahman and the Awami League high command, were reliably informed about the planned cancellation of the National Assembly meeting on 28 February, and thus had time to plan their reaction.[2] That was why he gave formal orders on 27 February, to be prepared to put Operation Blitz into action at a short notice and on a given code word.[3]

Kamal Hossain remembers things differently:

> The entire Constitution Drafting Committee of the Awami League was assembled at the party office to finalise the draft Constitution Bill. We were still working under a March 1 deadline, and had very nearly completed our work when one of the party workers came in to report that an important radio broadcast was to be made at 1 p.m. We stopped working when Bangabandhu and the other party leaders joined us as the time of the broadcast approached. A radio set was brought in to enable us to hear the broadcast. There was a hushed silence and the atmosphere was tense.[4]

Hossain contends that the Working Committee of the party was not informed about the announcement beforehand. But that is either untrue, or there is a possibility that the information was only provided to Mujib, who kept it under wraps so as to use the shock to his advantage and incite a protest movement.

Hossain's story is also in sharp contrast to what has been recorded by Sisson and Rose:

> On the evening of 28 February, following the president's directive of a few days earlier, Ahsan called Mujib and Tajuddin to the Governor's House to inform them that Yahya was going to announce the postponement of the National Assembly in his address to the nation the following day. Ahsan tried to assure them that it would be only for a short time, but Mujib was not to be mollified. He said that the authorities were bent on destroying not only him but also Pakistan. Tajuddin observed that this confirmed their darkest suspicions that

West Pakistan would never hand over power to a party from the East. After the formal meeting, Mujib asked Ahsan if they could meet briefly in private. He pleaded that a new date for the convening of the Assembly be given in the president's speech announcing the postponement. Mujib would then have some flexibility and would be able to control the reaction to the announcement. Otherwise he could not.

After the Awami League leaders had left, Ahsan and Generals Yaqub and Farman Ali discussed what was to be done. Between 9 and 10 p.m. they tried to reach Yahya by telephone. The president's personal staff officer in Rawalpindi suggested the governor call the him in Karachi, where Ahsan spoke with Maj. Gen. Ghulam Umar, the head of the National Security Council. Umar informed him that the president was 'otherwise indisposed,' but that he would relay the message expressing the concern of the officers in the east. Ahsan then spoke with General Hamid, the army chief of staff, in Sialkot, in the Punjab, urging him to inform the president of the gravity of the situation. Hamid replied that he was not conversant with political matters but that he would try to get in touch with Yahya. The governor then drafted and sent a telex to Yahya in Karachi, which concluded: 'I beg you even at this late hour to give a new date for the summoning of the Assembly and not to postpone it sine die, otherwise…we will have reached the point of no return.

Then, at 10:30 p.m., Ahsan received a telegram informing him that he was being relieved of his duties as Governor of East Pakistan and being replaced by Yaqub.[5]

Despite all preparations, Operation Blitz was not launched in view of the massive wave of protest in the province. According to Raja,

In view of the situation that had developed province-wide, on 1 March 1971, I had quick consultations with my senior staff and some commanders available in Dhaka regarding the feasibility of Operation Blitz in the prevailing circumstances. Each one of them was of the opinion that it would be sheer 'lunacy' to attempt the operation at that time.[6]

Raja says that the officers were counting on a political solution. In hindsight, it seems increasingly likely that the only successful military solution would have been one launched prior to 1 March. Brigadier (retd.) Zahid Alam Khan writes, 'Everyone who served in East Pakistan in March 1971 was of the opinion that East Pakistan was lost due to the lack of action immediately following the announcement of the postponement of the meeting of the National Assembly.'[7] Yahya's announcement achieved exactly what had been predicted and what should have been avoided if the unity of the country was a priority. It made the Bengalis feel that despite their electoral victory and majority in parliament, the 'ruling minority' of West Pakistan was not going to allow power to be taken away from it. The postponement was taken as a breach of trust. 'There was no doubt that a decisive moment had been reached in our history,' as Hossain put it.[8] After twenty-three years of growing resentment, the Bengali population was furious at this attempt to snatch this victory away from it.

Over and above that, the message underlying Yahya's words was that the ruling minority would reserve the power to veto the compilation of the Constitution. Until and unless there was an acceptance of the West Pakistani position to retain control, the Assembly session would not be convened. This was distasteful to the Bengalis of East Pakistan. They felt cheated. It just took only one decision for the mood of the entire nation to change drastically. The collective outrage in Pakistan's eastern wing was felt across the board.

As the people listened to the radio broadcast, the mood grew darker by the minute. The statement was brief, but its effect was to be stronger and longer-lasting than the authorities could conceive. The contagion spread like lightning throughout East Pakistan. From the zenith of elation, the people plummeted to the nadir of despair, which soon turned into a volatile anger with government employees walking out of the secretariat and other government offices in protest. The employees of banks, insurance companies, and other commercial organisations followed suit. Students thronged the streets in spontaneous demonstration, shouting slogans of '*Joy Bangla!*'

('Victory to Bengal!') and '*Bir Bengali osthro dhoro, Bangladesh shadhin koro!*' ('Brave Bengalis take up arms, liberate Bangladesh!') Hundreds of East Pakistanis joined the students and came out into the streets of Dhaka, protesting loudly, shouting nationalist slogans, and demanding independence. There was a unity of action to be seen well beyond Dhaka, in all the cities of East Pakistan, and well beyond the political reach of Awami League.

Brigadier (retd.) Zahid Alam Khan thinks that the reaction to the announcement was pre-planned and not spontaneous:

> …the reaction was immediate and seemed planned. In Comilla there was a total strike, shops, offices, banks, everything closed down. From the battalion, a party had gone to collect the pay from the National Bank and since all the units in Comilla were collecting their pay, there was [a] long queue. As soon as the announcement was made the bank closed and our party had to return without the pay.[9]

If that was the case then Operation Blitz should have been started before the announcement, or parallel to it, so as to prevent a coordinated movement of Bengalis. However, the seriousness of the situation was never recognised and events took their own course.

In fact, I experienced the mood in Dhaka and Comilla first hand, the same day. Undertaking a sortie to Comilla at about 11 a.m. on the morning of 1 March 1971, I deliberately flew low over Dhaka Stadium, where a cricket match between the Commonwealth Cricket Team and Pakistan was being played. Thousands of spectators in a holiday mood waved back from the stadium. Three hours or so later, as I landed back, I could see Brigadier (later Lt. Gen.) Jahanzeb Arbab, Commander 57 Brigade and his Brigade Major, Major (later Brigadier) Jafar Khan (known to me as Jeff[10]) at the helipad in Dhaka Cantonment. Major (later Lt. Col.) Patrick Tierney instructed me to take Brigadier Arbab and Jeff on an aerial reconnaissance of Dhaka and Narayanganj immediately after refuelling. With Jeff sitting next to me, and Brigadier Arbab on his left, I took off from the helipad with a full load of fuel. Ominously, the Alouette-3 sank a bit in the depression beyond the barbed wire. Brigadier Arbab ordered me to head towards Narayanganj.

On my way back from Comilla, I had approached the helipad from the east, to avoid the birds over the city in the afternoon. Within a minute, I was crossing the city centre; all around, one could see fires, roadblocks, and people gathering by the numbers. The *shamianas* (canopy; marquee) in Dhaka Stadium were on fire— my sister Shahnaz's house, close to Baitul Mukarram and the stadium was a marker for me. The scene of bliss that had existed a few hours earlier was no more. Instinctively, I decided to gain altitude. Totally bewildered, I asked Jeff what had happened and still remember his reply, 'Hell has broken loose, the president has postponed the National Assembly session.'

The situation in the industrial and river port town of Narayanganj was the same as in Dhaka—vehicles and tires were being torched at numerous roadblocks. Circling low over Dhaka to get a good idea of the troubled spots, the entire city seemed engulfed in columns of smoke. On some rooftops around Dhaka Stadium, I could see people had taken refuge. When I was dropping off Brigadier Arbab and Jeff at the helipad, Jeff leaned over to me, patted me on the shoulder and said, 'Ikram, go get them!' Without waiting for permission from my flight commander, I headed back over Dhaka City with only my crew chief. Some people were heli-lifted from the centre of the pitch in the stadium, where they had been hiding. I evacuated others from adjacent rooftops, like that of the DIT Building, Purbani Hotel, and one was even lifted from the roof of Gulistan Cinema. Ferrying them to the Governor's House in batches of three and four, I was amazed that my rotors did not hit a wire, or any other obstacle.

Low on fuel, I flew back towards Dhaka Airport, Kurmitola. What I saw at Farm Gate, near the old airport, was shocking. A Dodge truck of the Pakistan Army had been besieged by a mob. One could see that at least two of the occupants were either injured, or dead, but the rest were keeping the attackers at bay by firing at them. Very deliberately,

I auto-rotated downwards on the crowd. Seeing the Alouette-3 falling out of the sky, the crowd dispersed. After we landed on the road and discovered that none of the soldiers were dead, my crew chief helped all the five soldiers, including those injured, into the helicopter. I flew the injured straight to Combined Military Hospital, Dhaka, before returning to our own helipad. Along with the Commander Eastern Command, Lt. Gen. Yaqub Khan, and Maj. Gen. Khadim Hussain Raja, General Officer Commanding 14 Division, and many other officers, Jeff was still waiting for me at the helipad with a hot mug of tea, when I returned drenched in sweat. I have never forgotten his approving smile, embrace and pat on the back, 'Good boy, proud of you!' To me, Jeff was always very special.

Sheikh Mujibur Rahman, upon hearing the broadcast, directed all Awami League members of parliament to assemble at Hotel Purbani at 3 p.m., where the future course of action was to be decided upon. Hossain recalls, 'It was clear that there was only one course of action for the Bengalis—of defiance. Thus, the threat of confrontation was now imminent.'[11] There was an uncertainty as to when the military onslaught would begin and whether it would start that very day, according to him.

> By the time I reached Purbani Hotel, militant processions were seen advancing towards the hotel from different directions. The militancy of the processions was evident from the fact that almost everyone carried a bamboo or stick in his or her hand and shouted slogans for 'independence'. Women, too, showed that they were ready to face the risks and joined the marchers.[12]
>
> In order to meet problems as they arose, further directives were issued on 4 March. These directives now had to be in the form of positive instructions. Not only did we ask people to refrain from doing certain things, but specifically directed them to take certain actions or carry out functions in accordance with the guidelines issued by the Awami League. This was the first step towards the Awami League assuming the functions of a *de facto* government in the eastern wing. Thus, on 4 March, specific directives were issued that government and

non-government offices, where employees had not as yet been paid their salaries, should function between 2.30 p.m. and 4.30 p.m. for the purpose of disbursing salaries only. Banks were directed to function within these hours, and only for cash transactions of salary cheques not exceeding 1500 rupees.[13]

Mujib addressed a rally once again, on 3 March, but this time his tone was more conciliatory. In view of the furious reactions in East Pakistan, some damage control seems to have been considered. A message arrived from Islamabad in the evening of 3 March that a Round Table Conference was to be convened by Yahya in Dhaka, on 10 March. However, this was not considered by Mujib and his circle as an adequate response coming out of West Pakistan, because it had been ordained single-handedly. As such, the protests continued to aggravate the law-and-order situation.

Clearly, the ruling minority was not prepared to concede victory to the victorious Bengali majority. The western wing believed it had the military clout to suppress the agitation. As for the Bengalis, they had the consolidated unity of 75 million people, armed with a staunch resolution not to submit any more to the domination by the rulers in West Pakistan. They were ready to pay a heavy price in response to what they perceived as their democratic rights. Many telephone exchanges were attacked throughout the province and forced to close down. A new 'Bangla Desh' anthem was played in compliance with instructions from the Awami League. Mujib announced the launching of a civil disobedience movement throughout the province, 'for the realisation of the rights of the people of Bangla Desh'.

The Non-Cooperation Movement turned out to be very effective, but soon turned violent. West Pakistanis and people sympathetic to West Pakistan, like the Biharis, came increasingly under attack. The outbreak of violence made West Pakistani students in Dhaka University and business families such as the Bawanis and Ispahanis scramble to leave the country. Long queues were reported at the airports and in front of ticket offices, of people trying to leave as soon as possible. While waiting for a flight, they took refuge in the Defence Colony of Dhaka, according to Raja.[14] The situation of the army grew increasingly precarious after the contractors responsible for supplying fresh food to the army and the cantonments, joined the strike and food scarcity became commonplace. The cantonments in Dhaka and other cities, came under siege; shops closed, milk, eggs, vegetable hawkers stopped selling, petrol and meat were not available and everyone became dependent on whatever food supplies they had in stock. However, this lasted for only a few days and the vendors resumed their work, as they had no other market. 'The de facto position was that all organs of the East Pakistan government reported to Sheikh Mujib's headquarter for instructions,'[15] explains Raja.

General Yaqub Khan, who had resigned from his post as Martial Law Administrator, had to stay on until a replacement arrived, but the public perception about his resignation weakened the army's chain of command. The Awami League published a press release calling the proposed Round Table Conference on 10 March a 'cruel joke'. People in East Pakistan waited in anticipation for Mujib's announcement on 7 March. They expected him to declare independence.

Meanwhile, the West Pakistani troops present in East Pakistan were trying to get a grip on the situation. During a meeting of the martial law administrators in Rawalpindi in February, General Yaqub had been told that two divisions were in reserve near Karachi, ready to be airlifted in case of an emergency, which was another hint that a military solution or 'plan B' had been on the cards long before March 1971. At the time, Yaqub felt that this would not be needed, but by early March, things had changed and he asked for reinforcements to be sent immediately. Indian restrictions on overflying their territory made sending reinforcements difficult. Men could be sent by air but equipment often had to be left behind and shipped to Chittagong.

In the eyes of the GHQ, it was inconceivable that the postponement of the National Assembly session alone could have triggered such a violent response in East Pakistan. The physical and mental distance from the events in East Pakistan obviously resulted in a different understanding of the situation and the leading army generals in Dhaka grew increasingly frustrated. The resignations of Admiral Ahsan and General Yaqub were a result of this. Naming General Tikka Khan—who already had a reputation as a ruthless warrior lacking in diplomatic skills—as Yaqub's replacement, was a definite step towards aggravating the situation in East Pakistan.

Accounts of the carnage in East Pakistan vary, depending on the narrator. Military personnel were, all of a sudden, subjected to abuse and intimidation after having dominated the region for nearly twenty-five years. It would be an understatement to say that they wanted to get even. Cooped up in cantonments and medium- to small-sized outposts across East Pakistan, they grew increasingly furious at the atrocities against defenceless non-Bengalis and their inability to assist them. In some stray cases, soldiers did venture out to bring the victims of violence to safety. Nevertheless, there was simmering anger and a deep resentment that they could do nothing about it.

At about 4 a.m. on 4 March, the operator asked me to stay on the line while he put me through to the Commander Eastern Command, Lt. Gen. Sahabzada Yaqub Khan. This by itself was unusual. In the months that I had qualified as a VIP Pilot, all instructions came mostly through my flight commander, or through the Colonel General Staff, Colonel Akbar, occasionally from his staff officers, or from Captain Mazhar, his Bengali ADC. The commander said that there were disturbing reports coming from Chittagong, of rioting and arson near Chittagong Railway Station. He said the roads through the Tiger Pass from the Chittagong Cricket Stadium—where the army units in aid to civil power were temporarily located—were blocked and an independent confirmation was not available. He asked if I could fly out immediately and do an aerial survey.

Informing my flight commander about the mission, by 6 a.m. I was flying along the railway line close to the area. Even though there was an early morning ground mist, not unusual for Chittagong Port, one could see columns of smoke. In another twenty minutes, it became apparent that large parts of Feroz Shah Colony and T&T

Colony (also called Wireless Colony) had been burnt. Hardly any building was left unscathed. As I descended, I could see blackened bodies. While it is impossible to give an accurate figure as to how many non-Bengalis, mostly from Bihar, were killed there, it must have been in the hundreds. I passed on my eyewitness account to Dhaka Air Traffic Control (ATC), to be conveyed to Colonel Akbar in Eastern Command. Badly shaken and in need of refuelling, I flew to the Chittagong Cricket Stadium next to the Rest House and the Chittagong Club.

That was where 8 EB was located and since some of the personnel had come from 2 EB (particularly from No. 6 Platoon, B Company), they mobbed me as soon as I got out of the helicopter. I chatted with them while my crew chief got the Alouette-3 refuelled with a hand pump. In the meantime, Brigadier Majumdar of the East Bengal Regimental Centre (EBRC) and Lt. Col. Rashid Janjua, Commanding Officer 8 EB, also came to speak to me, along with Major Ziaur Rahman, second-in-command 8 EB, and Captain Ahmed Din—two officers who had been posted with nearly a company-plus from 2 EB to 8 EB on its raising. They did not seem to comprehend the tragedy that had taken place a few miles away, hours earlier. Captain Ahmed Din took me aside and said Colonel Janjua wanted to take a column for their relief but the Commandant EBRC decided that shooting their way through would result in too many casualties.

In the meantime, an agitated Captain Rafique Islam (a friend of mine), from East Pakistan Rifles came and met us. From his tone and demeanour, it was clear that he sympathised with the people protesting in the streets. Contrary to all claims post-March 25, Major Zia showed no such inclination or emotion! In fact, the only other army officer who showed any emotion was the staff officer accompanying Brigadier Majumdar, Captain (later Maj. Gen.) Amin Ahmed Chaudhry. Despite his easy-going manner, he was agitated and excited about what was happening. After refuelling, I flew back to Dhaka, taking a swing over Nasirabad Housing Society, where some of my relatives lived.

Violence continued unabated throughout the province. At Jessore, a train coming from Khulna was derailed and the passengers were forced out and killed. Cases of stabbings and the burning of houses continued in Chittagong. The telephone exchange in the Khalispur and Daulatpur areas of Khulna was attacked and a number of employees brutally killed. While telecommunications between East and West Pakistan remained suspended, the province was cut off from the outside world, as employees stopped sending and receiving messages on the orders of the Awami League. A total of 341 prisoners escaped in a jail-break at the Central Prison in Dhaka, while seven prisoners were killed. The escaping convicts paraded the streets of Dhaka, shouting threatening slogans. The scene was one of complete lawlessness and dystopia.[16]

In those early days of March, I got involved with the situation in yet another way. On the morning of 5 March, while on a mission to Sylhet and Srimangal, I got a message from the tower asking me to come to the flight headquarters. There I was told that Colonel General Staff Eastern Command, Colonel Akbar wanted me at Eastern Command immediately. On reaching his office, I was told to stand by for an important call from Rawalpindi. Before long, Maj. Gen. Ghulam Umar, National Security Advisor (NSA), called and said, 'Ikram, the chief wants to speak to you. You are not to repeat his instructions to anyone.' Shortly thereafter General Yahya Khan came on the line, and said 'Chand, go to Mujib through "Muchh" (meaning Colonel M.A.G. Osmany) and tell him I am coming to Dhaka and am ready to discuss anything openly and without any reservations. But tell him clearly that if he declares independence, then I will do everything in my power and go to any lengths to keep the country intact. Get me his reply.'

I was uniquely qualified for the task given to me by Yahya. He was a good friend of my father, Lt. Abdul Majeed Sehgal, and very fond of me since my childhood days. Colonel Osmany, the father of the East Bengal Regiment, treated Salman, the son of Brigadier Mohammad Ahmed, who had commanded 1 E Band myself, as his two 'tiger cubs' who had grown into full-fledged 'tigers'. While Yahya was adamant on my joining the army and as GOC 14 Division had ensured that I did, Colonel Osmany wanted me to join the Junior Tigers (2 EB), since I belonged to the second generation. Therefore, by some unique coincidence, there I was right in the middle of two individuals who would be among the principle autocrats in the civil war in East Pakistan.

Yahya also knew that my sister, Shahnaz, was married at that time to Omar Hayat Khan, the son of Abdus Salam Khan, a distant maternal uncle of Mujib and President of the Pakistan Democratic Party (Nawabzada Nasrullah Khan's colleague). Abdus Salam was Mujib's chief defence counsel during the Agartala case trial.

I arranged for a car immediately, went to Colonel Osmany's house in Bonani, and requested that he arrange to take me to Mujib's house so that I could convey the message. Since I had done this routine a couple of times before, Osmany said we would go once he had gotten Mujib's approval, but it would most likely be late in the evening. When we reached Mujib's house, I waited in the lounge while Osmany went in alone to see him. After some time both came out and Mujib greeted me affably. He asked, 'What's happening?' and I replied 'Who knows more than you do?' At this he laughed and said 'tell me what Yahya wants.' I repeated verbatim what the President had said. He kept staring at me and then asked me smilingly in Bengali '*Tum amaki marey de bay na ki?*' ('Will you kill me?') He left out 'on Yahya's order'. I did not reply immediately, then said 'yes'. On this, Mujib stared at me but remained silent. After a few moments, he got up and without a word, left the room. Osmany followed him. When he returned, Osmany was quite agitated. He berated me all the way back to his home in Bonani. I told him that Yahya was my commander-in-chief and that if given an order, I would have little choice but to follow it. I told Osmany that what I had said to Mujib would have been the instinctive reply of any soldier. In hindsight, I must admit I was wrong, the reply may have been instinctively blurted out but it was very immature of me. It also exceeded the President's instructions, which were not to discuss or volunteer anything, I was simply to be a conduit. I should have just stayed silent as ordered. My silence would have conveyed the message.

On 7 March 1971, Mujib addressed the much-awaited public meeting at the Race Course ground in Dhaka. But to the disappointment of many Bengalis, the expected declaration of independence did not come. Instead, he formulated four demands that would have to be fulfilled before the Awami League would be ready to attend any National Assembly meeting. Those demands were: (1) the immediate withdrawal of Martial Law; (2) the withdrawal of the army to the barracks; (3) an inquiry into the army killings in East Pakistan; and (4) the immediate transfer of power to the elected representatives (all before the National Assembly meeting). Hossain, in his memoirs, explains why Mujib stopped short of declaring independence at that point:

> Unilateral declaration of independence would mean directly engaging the full force of the military. Not only would they have used this as a pretext for applying force, but they would hit out with everything they had in order to impose their will. Could an unarmed population absorb the shock of such an onslaught and emerge victorious? What would the reaction of the outside world be? Would governments come forward to recognise an independent Bangladesh?[17]

Brigadier Mohammad Taj, SJ & Bar, another eyewitness of the events, recalls:

> The President of Pakistan was always kept informed about the reaction in East Pakistan to the situation. He was requested by the Commander Eastern Command to hold the National Assembly session as early as possible. However, this was not done. On 1 March, against the advice of the Commander Eastern Command, the President of Pakistan declared that the National Assembly session would be postponed for an indefinite period. This announcement resulted in [a] general reaction that was aggressive, with people coming out and agitating

against this decision. On this, the Governor East Pakistan, Admiral Ahsan resigned. When General Yahya refused to come to Dhaka, the Commander Eastern Command, General Sahibzada Yaqub, who had taken over as Acting Governor, also decided to resign. General Tikka was appointed to replace him. He landed in East Pakistan on 5 March 1971. On 7 March, Mujib decided to hold a public protest meeting at Ramna Racecourse against the decision to postpone the National Assembly session. The people generally thought that he was going to unilaterally declare independence of Bangladesh. However, he did not do that, but placed new demands before the government and those were the acceptance of his six points, holding of the National Assembly session in Dhaka and so on. This public meeting was attended, in my estimation, by more than 200,000 people.[18]

It would be a gross understatement to describe the rally at Ramna Race Course on 7 March as a large one—it was huge. Mujib was in his element and gave a masterful demonstration of his oratory skills. He displayed to the crowd his toughest public stand against the western wing and the firm commitment of his party to the emancipation of the Bengali people. He declared that he would not attend the National Assembly for which now a new date had been envisaged on 25 March, unless the four demands were met by the Martial Law authorities. He also enumerated additional points or principles that were to be translated into a series of directives to guide the continuing Non-Cooperation Movement.

During his speech of 7 March, Mujib recounted events, both recent and historical, going back to the early days of Pakistan, that were examples of calculated efforts by West Pakistanis to deprive the Bengalis of the right to govern. The Awami League's choice of a date for the first meeting of the National Assembly had been 15 February, but that of the PPP had been 3 March; the latter date was chosen. The Awami League had given public assurances to all parties on 24 and 27 February, that any and all suggestions concerning the drafting of the Constitution would be heard and that those judged 'just and reasonable' would be accepted. However, on 28 February, Bhutto had threatened West Pakistan politicians with dire consequences if they attended the inaugural session of parliament in Dhaka.

By this, Mujib observed, the session had actually been rendered impossible. Another detail Mujib referred to in his speech was that the current decision to set a new date for the Assembly was a continuation of this pattern; the date of 25 March had been set without seeking the advice of Mujib and the Awami League and had been announced after a five-hour meeting between President Yahya and Bhutto. The decision to hold a ten-party conference had also been made without explicitly seeking his counsel and the President, who had indicated that Mujib had pledged to attend the meeting, had misled the public. In fact, Mujib exclaimed, he had merely invited the President to come to Dhaka to see the situation for himself and understand the need for immediate corrective action. He also recounted the dismissal of governments in the 1950s, when West Pakistani interests had been threatened by the assertion of Bengalis' political power. Because of what Mujib called the current military build-up in East Pakistan, it appeared that 'political confrontation was soon to be followed by military confrontation, if the majority did not submit to the dictation of the minority.' Towards the end of his speech, using the evocative symbols that were increasingly becoming the norm among Pakistani leaders as they addressed their supporters, Mujib declared emotionally, 'If the ruling coteries seek to frustrate these aspirations, the people are ready for a long and sustained struggle for their emancipation. We pledge to lead this struggle and ultimately, to attain for the people their cherished goal of emancipation for which so many martyrs have shed their blood and made the supreme sacrifice of their lives.'[19] According to Sisson and Rose, 'If there had been any question about the authority accorded [to] the Awami League by the Bengali public before 7 March, there certainly was none thereafter.'[20]

Announcing his plans for a parallel government, Mujib formally issued a number of directives. These included a weeklong programme for continuing the so-called non-violent, non-cooperation movement, the initiation of a no-tax campaign, the closure of all government and semi-government educational institutions, and courts of law. Detailed directives were issued to radio, television, and newspapers, on the pattern of the Awami League coverage, failing which, 'Bengalis working in these establishments shall not cooperate'. One directive ordered that 'banks shall not effect remittances to the western wing, either through the State Bank, or otherwise'. Another directive specifically laid down that a Sangram Parishad (Revolutionary Council) was to be organised in each union council, *mohallah*, *thana*, sub-division and district 'under the leadership of the local Awami League units'. On 8 March 1971, the party organised meetings and violent processions in which anti-Pakistan slogans were chanted, throughout the province. In Dhaka, weapons and ammunition were collected forcibly from licence-holders.

Check posts were set up in various parts of Dhaka, 'To stop the flight of wealth from Bangla Desh.' Money and belongings of those 'searched by these volunteers, were confiscated in the name of "Bangla Desh".' Writing in the *Daily Telegraph* on 9 March 1971, its correspondent, Kenneth Clarke, argued, 'Dhaka collapsed into complete lawlessness on Sunday night [7 March 1971], as Sheikh Mujib took the province to the edge of secession. Terming his movement one of independence, the Sheikh, leader of the Awami League, laid down conditions for cooperating in National Assembly which cannot be met by President Khan.' The paper also noted Sheikh Mujib's directive that 'liberation committees be formed under Awami League leaders in all villages'.

The Awami League announced that, 'There shall be no operation of (bank) lockers and that no cooperation was to be extended by port authorities, except as indicated in Sheikh Mujib's directives.' On the night of 11–12 March, a jail-break was reported in Barisal, Bogra. Police opened fire, killing two and injuring eighteen prisoners. Cyclostyled and hand-written leaflets on behalf of these 'Liberation Fronts' and para-military organisations were clandestinely circulated, aimed at inciting racial hatred and violence.[21]

The considerations of Mujib and his party at this point, seem to have been tactical rather than strategic. It was clear that they wanted complete control in East Pakistan, but not necessarily at the Centre, keeping in mind Mujib's fear that Bengalis might kill him if he went to West Pakistan as Prime Minister. On the other hand, it also had become clear that the hawks in the army would not allow power at the Centre to be diminished. In his speech on the eve of 7 March, Yahya had made a declaration on his own behalf, saying, 'Finally, let me make it absolutely clear that no matter what happens, as long as I am in command of the Pakistan Armed Forces, I will ensure complete and absolute integrity of Pakistan.'[22]

The army high command had opted to replace the resigned General Yaqub with General Tikka Khan, a hawk among generals known for his uncompromising and even cruel attitude in handling military tasks. This was a clear and unambiguous message to the Awami League. General Tikka arrived in Dhaka on 7 March, taking over as Commander Eastern Command immediately, but the Bengali chief justice refused to take his oath as Governor. Mujib, at this point, seems to have been disturbed by the looming confrontation. General Khadim, who was the de facto general after Yaqub's resignation, reports that Mujib sent messengers asking that he be taken into protective custody as he was under a great deal of pressure from extremists and student leaders within his party.[23]

Lt. Col. (later Brigadier) Mohammad Taj, SJ & Bar, recalls that by March, the situation in East Pakistan had turned fatal; Dhaka cantonment was denied rations, the maximum amount of funds that could be withdrawn from a bank was limited to 8,000 rupees and soldiers were abused and humiliated every time they went into town. 'However, we took command and remained calm and quiet and accepted all that was going on,' he says, adding that a number of Biharis and West Pakistanis were killed in that month. Even the ladies were not spared and were insulted and mocked; women and children were among those killed. While Yahya eventually did go to East Pakistan on 15 March, Bhutto did not go with him, arriving

later, on 19 March, with members of his team and was made to stay
in Intercontinental Hotel. The next day, he met Yahya at the President
House. Some West Pakistani political leaders who were not part of
the PPP also came to East Pakistan.[24]

In this unstable atmosphere, the Awami League seems to have
preferred a loose federal, or even a confederational arrangement, with
a weak central government. For this reason, instead of going ahead
and declaring independence, Mujib, on 7 March, only went so far
to say, 'Our struggle now is for independence, our struggle now is
for freedom.' He called upon his followers not to do anything that
might precipitate the already explosive situation. He vowed to seek
the cooperation of the army for the maintenance of law and order
and insisted that Pakistan must remain united and demanded that
the immediate termination of Martial Law and the transfer of power
to the elected representatives be put into effect.

By 7 March, the fate of a united Pakistan had been sealed by the
machinations of Bhutto and the war mongering of the GHQ, but
the declaration of independence had not yet been made. However,
the option of a somewhat united country, although slight, did exist.

Notes

1. Ikram Sehgal, *Escape from Oblivion: The Story of a Pakistani Prisoner of War in India* (Karachi: Oxford University Press, 2012), p. 3.
2. Raja, *A Stranger in My Own Country*, p. 50.
3. Ibid., p. 47.
4. Hossain, p. 79.
5. Sisson & Rose, pp. 89–90.
6. Raja, pp. 51–2.
7. Z.A. Khan, *The Way It Was: Inside the Pakistan Army* (Karachi: Dynavis Pvt. Ltd., 1998), p. 271.
8. Hossain, p. 80.
9. Khan, *The Way It Was*, p. 259.
10. Jeff belonged to Lawrence College, Ghora Gali, where I was the youngest in the house of which he was the head (Peake House) in 1957. In a few months, he left for Pakistan Military Academy, along with Brigadier Asmat Beg. My

heroes and role models also included Brigadier Rao Abid Hameed, Major Sabir Kamal Shaheed, Major Farooq Adam Khan (who later succeeded Jeff as Head of House in Ghora Gali) and the late Colonel Mahmud Nawaz. Coming under the influence of another Gallian colleague of his in the National Accountability Bureau, a confirmed scoundrel and drunkard, my boyhood hero Farooq Adam Khan became a disappointment.

11. Hossain, p. 81.
12. Ibid.
13. Ibid., pp. 85–6.
14. Raja, p. 55.
15. Ibid., p. 57.
16. White Paper on the Crisis in East Pakistan, Government of Pakistan, 5 August 1971, select chapters, p. 7.
17. Hossain, p. 87.
18. Interview with Brigadier Mohammad Taj, February 2017, Islamabad.
19. Sisson & Rose, p. 101.
20. Ibid.
21. White Paper on the Crisis in East Pakistan, Government of Pakistan, 5 August 1971, select chapters, pp. 8–9.
22. Ibid., p. 99.
23. Raja, p. 60.
24. Interview with Brigadier Mohammad Taj, February 2017, Islamabad.

11

A Deadly Polarisation

The Yahya regime failed to open a dialogue with Mujib, despite the fact that he had not declared independence in his 7 March 1971 speech, as was expected. This was further complicated by the change in Eastern Command, with Lt. Gen. Tikka Khan taking over on 7 March. Having no experience whatsoever of the East Pakistani political climate, Tikka Khan was expected to be the military commander and from 6 April onwards, the Governor of East Pakistan, while suspecting a possible mutiny among his troops. His capacity had been stretched ever since he was promoted beyond the rank of lieutenant colonel. As martial law administrator, he did not have the support of the civil administration and faced a situation in which secession seemed imminent.

His takeover marked a point of no return. The situation in Dhaka and the province as a whole was deteriorating by the day. The mind-set of the majority of Bengalis had by now lost faith in the western wing. While being palpable, the polarisation was deadly. Sartaj Aziz noted in his diary on 7 March 1971, that 'All hopes of saving Pakistan as one country are now dead. The separation of East and West Pakistan is now inevitable. The only question is how soon and how tortuous this process is going to be.'[1]

Sartaj Aziz had seen the danger of a split long before it occurred, but was unable to stem the tide. Many, especially those at the helm of affairs, did not realise this fact. Among them were General Yahya Khan, the GHQ and several West Pakistani politicians. And the worst impediment of all was the 'pointman'—General Tikka—selected to contain the East Pakistani public. If the right and insightful commander had been in charge of the country, the loss of thousands of lives and properties could have been avoided. But even sheer military power was not enough to keep Pakistan united.

Yahya had announced on the eve of 7 March that the new date for convening the Assembly would now be 25 March. But he had done so single-handedly, without consulting any of the politicians in either East or West Pakistan and therefore the announcement did not provide a respite. The leaders of the smaller parties took the initiative and planned a meeting in Lahore, for 13 March, to find a workable solution and avert the brewing crisis. Representatives of the Council and Convention of the Muslim League and the religious parties—the Jamaat-e-Islami, JUP, and JUI—accepted the four new demands made by Mujib in his 7 March speech and the new date for convening the constituent session of parliament announced by Yahya.

With Zulfikar Ali Bhutto and his party members missing at the meeting, it was obvious that Bhutto had his own plans, thus setting him and his party apart from any reconciliatory attempts. He intended to prevent the other parties of West Pakistan from manipulating themselves into the power structure. Before the convening of the new parliament, he had insisted that the basics of a new Constitution would have to be settled beforehand, between him, the army, and Mujib. That idea was rejected by the participants of the conference, who argued that, 'compromises insisted upon and arrived at outside the floor of the house and concealed from the scrutiny and vigilance of the people can have no relevance to constitutional settlement…'.[2] Moreover, the parties asked President Yahya to proceed to Dhaka to remove all misunderstandings, doubts, and suspicions in frank and cordial talks with Mujib.

The Lahore meeting of 13 March thus was a tacit support for Mujib and his Awami League and an indirect critique of Bhutto's plans for holding talks behind closed doors and Yahya's refusal to go to Dhaka and meet Mujib personally. It also accepted and understood Mujib's refusal to participate in the all-parties conference proposed by

Bhutto, where each party would be represented by one leader, thus putting the Awami League in a minority position.

Since the announcement of the election results in January, Bhutto had been working on strategies to undo the Awami League majority and despite having won only 87 seats in a 300-seat house, manoeuvred to get himself into the seat of power. This had undermined all trust between Mujib and Bhutto and, as a result, between East and West Pakistan, to the extent that any talks between the two leaders would have invited the ire of the Bengali public. Consequently, for the Awami League, talks could be held only with the government and the smaller political parties of West Pakistan.

On 14 March 1971, Wali Khan of the National Awami Party flew to Dhaka with Ghaus Bux Bizenjo and met Mujib. Bizenjo asked Mujib whether he wanted to declare independence and the latter commented on the irony in the fact that those who had sided with Congress during Partition were asking a staunch Muslim Leaguer like him about dividing Pakistan.[3] On the other hand, Bhutto, in a speech on 14 March, announced that if there were to be a transfer of power before the framing of the Constitution, it would have to be to the Awami League in the East and the PPP in the West. This, along with the *idhar hum udhar tum* remark commonly ascribed to him, illustrates that Bhutto was among those who caused the break-up of Pakistan.[4] His speech was severely criticised by politicians of East and West Pakistan—though not by the military—and it set the ball rolling in a specific direction. Bhutto later tried to deny what he had said and blamed the media, but it proved too little too late and was not true. The President's arrival in Dhaka on 15 March did little to prevent the slide into chaos.

Superseding all previous directives, Mujib announced a new 'programme of action, commencing from 15 March 1971'. Meanwhile reports kept pouring in from several areas that people were being subjected to brutal treatment on racial and political grounds, as part of the 'search' operation at various Awami League check posts in Dhaka. Four members of the Shawadhin Bangla Kendriya Chhatra

Sangram Parishad (Independent Bengal's Central Students Action Committee) admitted that 'some armed miscreants using vehicles were still raiding different houses and collecting money forcibly in the name of Sangram Parishad.' In Comilla, armed mobs surrounded and attacked an army field unit at Feni. The BBC reported, 'Sheikh Mujibur Rahman made a statement urging civilian defence workers to defy the army order to return to work. He also issued more than thirty directives aimed at tightening control of the region; they included orders that taxes should be paid to his regime rather than the central government. Writing in *The Guardian* on 16 March 1971, the correspondent Martin Adeney described the meeting of one of the Awami League action committees, 'They were discussing their next step in what they already regard as independent East Bengal—Bangladesh.' *The Statesman*, an Indian daily, reported on 16 March 1971, that Mujib said he was assuming control of Bangladesh and that the 'president will be our guest'. Observers in Dhaka interpreted this as a clear sign that East Pakistan considers itself a separate territory from West Pakistan.[5]

The Awami League had virtually taken over the administration of East Pakistan and anything that needed to be done required its approval first. The civil disobedience moment now morphed into a parallel government with the armed forces remaining under virtual siege in their cantonments and outposts. New forces were joining the resistance as well. On 9 March, Bhashani had made his goodbye speech to Pakistan, at the Paltan Maidan and asked his red brigades to work towards independence. The movement took on violent proportions after the 7 March speech. The violence was directed against the representatives of West Pakistani civilians, Biharis, and Pakistan Army personnel and installations. The so-called Biharis were the target of easy aggression as they were civilians and unarmed. The leading industrial families of East Pakistan such as the Ispahanis and Adamjees also belonged to this group. Realising the imminent danger, they were busy during that time transferring their money and other assets out of the country.

By mid-March, Awami League supporters set up check-points on the approaches to Dhaka airport, in order to search fugitives to West Pakistan to see that they were not taking large sums of money or jewellery with them. While it is suspected that much larger sums were transferred from East Pakistan through the banks, this was not possible until the situation was restored to a degree of normalcy, at the start of 15 April 1971. Nobody has ever really investigated how West Pakistanis emptied out their bank accounts. In any case, it did leave Bangladesh short of money and other assets by the end of the year.

During this time, the movement of troops from West Pakistan into East Pakistan continued. It was hampered in no small degree by the Indian ban of overflights for Pakistani aircraft in the wake of the alleged hijack of Ganga, an Indian passenger jet. This made Pakistani flights much longer, having to travel first to Colombo for refuelling and thus slowing down the process of troop mobilisation. Another consequence of this was that most troops arrived with light weapons. This was a logistical miracle on the part of PIA in very adverse circumstances and must be counted as one of the great successes. It was only possible due to the complete cooperation of the Sri Lankan government. All the aircraft refuelled in Colombo on the way out and again on the way back from Dhaka, because fuel supplies were limited in East Pakistan. Most of the military and civilian supplies, including food, had to be shipped into East Pakistan and this turned out to be a problem because of the refusal of the Bengali labourers in Chittagong to offload the ships. Ships were laid up in Chittagong for weeks waiting to be unloaded.

There were other problems as well for the army. Suppressing the upheaval in East Pakistan was the only solution offered by the GHQ. This meant violence, death, and destruction within one's own country and was unacceptable to some in the military high command in East Pakistan. Admiral Ahsan, who tried to dispute the orders coming from the GHQ, had been the first casualty. He was relieved of his post. The second loss was that of Lt. Gen. Yaqub Khan, who also refused to accept the usefulness of a military option. He had already resigned from his post, which brought him close to court martial. Others were critical, but never voiced their views openly. In order to make sure the military solution received full acceptance, hardliners like Lt. Gen. Tikka Khan and careerists like the newly promoted Lt. Gen. A.A.K. Niazi, were sent into East Pakistan. While they could not avoid the inevitable, they did well to enhance the losses and misery for civilians and soldiers in East and West alike.

The Non-Cooperation Movement was not relenting and Bengali activism grew more pronounced. Troops were told to act with restraint, but this order could not always be followed. There was a rising level of violence, especially in Dhaka and the civil administration of East Pakistan had virtually collapsed. Confined to the cantonments as per the orders, the sense of uncertainty reflected in the mood of the troops. The Bengali troops were suspected to be simmering with possible rebellion and their loyalty was doubted by General Officer Commanding 14 Division, Major General Khadim Hussain Raja, even though the regular troops of the East Bengal Regiment gave no such indication. General Khadim writes, 'The most disturbing aspect of the overall situation was that the Bengali troops were seething with revolt, and widespread mutiny seemed to be in the offing.'[6] He concedes, however, that after visiting all the units, 'There were no significant cases of proof of insubordination or mutiny before 25 March.'[7]

Mujib, meanwhile, was making his own arrangements. He appointed Colonel Osmany as Commander of the Revolutionary Forces. Colonel (later General) Osmany was a Bengali officer of the Pakistan Army, who had been commissioned in the British Indian Army in 1940 and after the foundation of Pakistan, opted to join its army. Throughout his career, he tried to increase the number of Bengalis in the armed forces and create additional Bengali regiments. He retired in 1967, disappointed and frustrated. He joined the Awami League in 1970, winning a seat in Parliament in the December 1970 election. He acted as military advisor to the party's leadership and raised the Mukti Bahini together with a few other retired Bengali-origin officers of army, starting from March 1971.

Members of the Awami League, including the student wing, had been armed and trained for quite a while. Their activities would be acid responses to the wrongs that were done to Bengali civilians by the Pakistan Army. In the words of Maj. Gen. Hakeem Arshad Qureshi:

> The murder of army personnel, caught in ones and twos, became an everyday occurrence. In our area we lost Lt. Abbas of 29 Cavalry, a West Pakistani. With an escort of Bengali soldiers, he had ventured out of the unit lines to buy fresh vegetables for the troops. The escort was 'rushed' by the militants, the officer was killed, weapons were 'confiscated' and the Bengali members of the guard sent back unharmed.[8]
>
> Lurid stories started making the rounds, of Biharis being massacred, of West Pakistani army officers lured from their homes and exterminated in cold blood by the Bengali 'comrades' of the East Bengal Regiment (EBR), of the public humiliation, molestation, and execution of officers and junior commissioned officers (JCOs) of EPR and their families. [While not a single non-Bengali belonging to EBR was killed, or suffered in any way before 26 March.] All ranks became apprehensive. The psychological state of the men in uniform could not have been termed normal. The prevalent atmosphere had badly affected everyone, especially those with women and children in tow. It provoked varied responses from different individuals: some acted beyond the bounds of human courage, others attempted to eliminate any potential threat to their security, while some gave up hope and wanted to surrender without a fight.[9]

With the Non-Cooperation Movement spreading throughout East Pakistan, more and more people and parts of the administration were affected. They either ceased to operate, or kept activity to a minimum. At this juncture, a message arrived from Yahya that he would be visiting Dhaka shortly, with a solution that would satisfy the East Bengalis. Messengers arrived from Rawalpindi to find out if Mujib was ready to see Yahya. After Mujib had expressed his willingness to negotiate, Yahya arrived in Dhaka on 15 March, accompanied by General Abdul Hamid Khan and others. The first briefing they got from their generals in Dhaka seems to have come as a shock to them. Nobody in West Pakistan had imagined the degree to which relations had deteriorated on the ground. Major General Hakeem Arshad Qureshi sheds light on the circumstances at the time:

> In mid-March, 1971, we were visited by the General Officer Commanding (GOC) 14 Division, General Khadim Hussain Raja. In his address to the garrison officers, he told us that the government was earnestly trying to bring the political parties together with a view to arriving at a negotiated solution to the ongoing situation. [The] Use of force, he said, was out of [the] question. We assumed that the policy statement was aimed at the Bengali officers, as the prevailing conditions, to our inexperienced minds with limited information, precluded any political settlement without the re-establishment of some modicum of order and the writ of law.
>
> After the lecture, over a cup of tea, we questioned the GOC closely, out of earshot of our Bengali 'comrades'. He reiterated his earlier statement, and assured us that a political settlement, without use of force, was state policy. What that settlement was to be, no one asked the GOC. Why the political parties needed the Martial Law Administration to help them to bring about the dawn of civil rule, i.e., their rule, was also not explained. Was the referee playing foul to keep the contestants for power in perpetual confrontation to serve his own interests? Or was it that the Awami League, being the majority party, refused to share power with others and the rulers did not approve of it? Or was it that antecedents of the Awami League were suspect and the rulers had realized it rather late in the day?
>
> We were lulled into inactivity. We started hoping for the best without making ourselves ready for the worst.[10]

The meeting gave the officers stationed in the province an opportunity to speak out. They briefly but poignantly expressed their concern regarding a military solution to the crisis. The first one to speak on this matter did so with vehemence. He spoke forcefully, with an eloquence unusual in military councils. He argued that military efforts to suppress the Bengalis would be an 'act of madness'. Instead of restoring public tranquillity, such action would cause deep and permanent hostility toward both the army and West Pakistan that no amount of negotiations could erase. Nor would it resolve the prevailing conflict. It would merely create new and more intractable ones. General Farman Ali, who had previously expressed similar sentiments to the President, strongly backed this position. He observed that military action would not only make a political solution more improbable, but would further disrupt an already fragile economy and severely interrupt inter-regional trade. The distrust within the Pakistan Army towards Bengali soldiers, officers and units who had not shown any signs of rebellion, was, in my view, a fatal blunder. It was another nail in the coffin of a united Pakistan.

Analysing the situation in his diary, Sartaj Aziz writes on 7 March:

> The real trouble is that we have no real national leader in the country today. Yahya was trying to act above the parties, but in this crisis Mujib has relegated his position to a pro-western leader, to make the cleavage between East and West Pakistan almost complete. Mujib, of course, has been working for separation without taking the responsibility for it. I have the feeling even Bhutto has been trying for separation, since that is the only way he can get power to rule West Pakistan immediately and effectively.[11]

Apart from some longstanding difficulties that could have been overcome with time and effort, the crisis between East and West Pakistan was created mainly by big egos and the lust for power among individuals who failed to uphold the national interest of the country. It is an important lesson that Pakistan today must learn from, in order to avoid a repetition of the same mistakes.

Notes

1. Anwar Dil (comp.), *Hunger, Poverty and Development: Life and Work of Sartaj Aziz* (Lahore: Ferozons Pvt. Ltd., 2000), p. 503.
2. *Dawn*, 14 March 1971, as cited in Sisson & Rose, p. 103.
3. Yasser Latif Hamdani, 'Partition of Pakistan 1971,' *The Criterion*, 14 January 2016, Vol. 10, No. 2, http://www.criterion-quarterly.com/partition-of-pakistan-1971-2/.
4. *Dawn*, 15 March 1971.
5. White Paper on the Crisis in East Pakistan, Government of Pakistan, 5 August 1971, selected chapters, p. 11.
6. Raja, *A Stranger in My Own Country*, pp. 67–8.
7. Ibid., pp. 68–9.
8. Major General Hakeem Arshad Qureshi, *The 1971 Indo-Pak War: A Soldier's Narrative* (Karachi: Oxford University Press, 2002), pp. 16–17.
9. Ibid., pp. 17–18.
10. Ibid., p. 22.
11. Anwar Dil (comp.), *Hunger, Poverty and Development*, p. 504.

12

The Stalemate

East is East, and West is West,
and never the twain shall meet

– RUDYARD KIPLING, *The Ballad of East and West*, 1889

On 15 March, President Yahya Khan and his team arrived in Dhaka and on the following day, met with Mujibur Rahman and his team. The first complaint against Yahya was that he had taken the decision to postpone the meeting of the National Assembly singlehandedly, without consulting Mujib, the prime-minister-in-waiting. According to the memoirs of Kamal Hossain, the Awami League saw this as a decisive step that should not have been taken in the manner it had been and was particularly hurt by Bhutto's role in it. At the meeting on 16 March, Mujib reiterated the demands he had made in his 7 March speech—the immediate transfer of power to the elected representatives and an end to Martial Law. The next day, the two met again, this time in the presence of their legal advisers to discuss the details of how a Constitution could be developed. Mujib, according to Hossain, proposed that the elected members of East Pakistan draw-up specific points of their interest that would be part of the Constitution for the eastern wing, while the elected members of West Pakistan would draw points for the Constitution of the western wing. Thereafter, they could sit together and draft a Constitution for Pakistan.[1]

All reports on the fateful negotiations between 16 and 22 March reveal that, despite the deteriorated state of affairs, there were efforts of give-and-take from both sides. The question was, how much was each side was willing to give and where would the red lines be drawn?

There was readiness on both sides to reach a compromise. General Farman remembers, for instance, that while reviewing the situation after the first meeting with Mujib on 16 March, Yahya remarked, 'The father of the nation [Jinnah] was not averse to the idea of two Pakistans. Who am I to oppose such an idea?'[2] With this attitude, considerable progress was made in the negotiations that took place on two levels. Yahya and Mujib agreed that negotiations should proceed along two tracks. Firstly, the provisions, both substantive and procedural, to be included in the constitutional arrangement, would be discussed by negotiating teams representing the Awami League and the government, and these provisions would be prepared as a 'draft proclamation.' Secondly, Yahya and Mujib would continue their deliberations on the transfer of power and the formation of an interim government.

After the private meeting between the two, the President was joined by two senior military aides, while Mujib was joined by Tajuddin Ahmed, Kamal Hossain, and Syed Nazrul Islam, to discuss the agenda and procedures for negotiating the interim constitution. They agreed on the following: (1) the lifting of Martial Law; (2) the continuance of Yahya as President during the interim phase; (3) the creation of two constituent committees, one each for East and West Pakistan, to resolve provincial issues; and (4) the drafting of a Constitution in the National Assembly, sitting as one body after the regional committees had completed the preliminary work. They also agreed that the negotiating teams would work out the details of implementation and that they would decide upon the powers to be exercised by the Centre and the provinces during the interim period. Each side was to study these matters before meeting again on 19 March 1971.[3]

Despite the seemingly positive developments during negotiations, Yahya kept his double-standard tactic of a parallel military option alive. Either that or General Tikka Khan was not on the same page as the President. General Khadim reports that Tikka Khan informed him on 17 March 1971, that the negotiations with Mujib were 'not proceeding well', and the President, therefore, wanted the army to be ready for military action and ordered the preparation of a plan accordingly. Was he double-crossing the attempts for a political settlement? On 18 March 1971, General Khadim and General Farman spent their day preparing Operation Searchlight, keeping it a secret from the Bengali officers. In the evening, the plan was presented to Yahya and his team and was approved of without discussion.[4] It seems a distinct possibility that Tikka Khan, one of the hardliners in the team, was pushing the military option in the name of Yahya, despite the progress made in negotiations, and Yahya did little to prevent it.

By 18 March, a military 'plan B' was in place that favoured the hawks within the army. It seems that this double-edged strategy had been followed from the outset, with the military option always present. It could be interpreted as dishonesty on the part of the West Pakistani delegation. It can be assumed that the talks were held by Yahya to buy the time needed to provide the Pakistan Army in East Pakistan with the details of the real plan. But the reports of people who were close to the negotiations tell another story. Both sides seem to have been serious in their attempts for a successful settlement, at least at the Yahya–Mujib level, while the hardliners on both sides could be contained during the early days, despite the violence outside the negotiation rooms.

Hostilities against the army were on the rise in East Pakistan. On 19 March, an army vehicle returning from Mymensingh was ambushed by a crowd at a level crossing in Dhaka and all six occupants, along with their weapons, were whisked away. On 20 March, locals attacked Pakistani Army trucks moving through a village outside Dhaka and there was an exchange of fire. Bengalis, meanwhile, refused to offload goods from MS *Swat*, a West Pakistani ship bringing in supplies consisting mainly of military assets, to East Pakistan. When Yahya complained about these incidents, Mujib insisted that negotiations were ongoing and therefore the army was expected to stay in the barracks. On the same day, the press that was largely under the control of the Awami League, reported that an agreement had been reached on a compromise constitutional formula that included most of the Six Points. Hong Kong's *The Far Eastern Economic Review*, reported on 20 March 1971, that, 'While President Yahya Khan was pondering his next move in the West Wing, Sheikh Mujib in his Dhaka house adorned with traditional Bengali symbolism told me, "This is the final round". Asked what he meant, he answered with the slogan he has hurled at adoring crowds a thousand times: "*Joy Swadhin Bangla*"—Long live Independent Bengal.'

In Dinajpur, Awami League members led a violent procession carrying the effigy of Yahya with an arrow in its chest. Reports were received of Indian arms in some of the tea gardens in Sylhet. Pakistan Day was renamed 'Resistance Day' and Pakistani flags were replaced by the new Bangladesh flags atop public and private buildings in Dhaka and other towns of East Pakistan.' March-pasts and parades were held by paramilitary liberation fronts and ex-servicemen. Residents of Mirpur and various other areas insisted on flying the Pakistan flag and refused to hoist the Bangladesh flag. Mujib took the salute at an armed march-past at his residence, where the Bangladesh flag was ceremonially unfurled. Student groups kidnapped West Pakistani businessmen and demanded ransom. Armed crowds brick-batted/ attacked and harassed outgoing passengers near Farmgate, on the way to Dhaka airport.[5]

A third meeting between Yahya and Mujib took place on the morning of 19 March 1971. It began with Justice Alvin Robert Cornelius presenting his argument on the illegality of the lifting of Martial Law. He did this in a manner that the Awami League found condescending. Cornelius proposed that the removal of Martial Law before the adoption of a Constitution would leave the country in a legal void since all governmental authority was derived from the proclamation of Martial Law on 25 March 1969. At that time, the Constitution had been abrogated and the office of the President had been created under the supreme authority of Martial Law, which was also the basis for the proclamation of constitutional procedure and the promulgation of the Legal Framework Order (LFO). The lifting of Martial Law would therefore also abolish the presidency and the other basic laws, under which the country was being governed and from which existing institutions derived their legitimacy. A member of the Awami League team interrupted Cornelius and expressed his surprise and dismay that this should be an issue at this stage of the negotiations, inasmuch as the President had already explicitly committed himself to the lifting of Martial Law—a fact Yahya obviously had not mentioned to Cornelius.

During the negotiations, both parties expressed their disillusionment concerning the recent turn of events. A commission had been set up to carry out an inquiry into the actions of the police and army earlier that month that had cost the lives of dozens of Bengali civilians. On 18 March 1971, Tikka Khan, the Martial Law Administrator in East Pakistan, had appointed this commission of inquiry to be headed by a judge of the High Court of East Pakistan nominated by the Chief Justice and to include four additional members, selected from the civil service, the police, the army and the East Pakistan Rifles. The army would nominate its own representative, and the chief secretary of the East Pakistan government would select the other three. This commission would report to Tikka Khan, but its impartiality seems to have been doubted by the Awami League. In a climate of mistrust and suspicion, it became impossible to arrive at a compromise that had to be based on mutual trust. Despite all this, the talks did not stop just yet.

In their negotiations, Yahya and Mujib chiefly focused on the agenda for the talks between the negotiating teams and on the composition of an interim government. Each side put forward changes in the agenda. Mujib indicated that the Awami League now wanted provisions included in the draft proclamation that would grant full legislative powers to the civilian governments at both the national and provincial levels upon the transfer of power. Yahya indicated that this could be discussed, even though it had not been agreed upon as part of the original agenda. He asserted that while the transfer of power appeared possible, his Constitutional Advisor, Justice Cornelius, had said that there was a serious question regarding the legality of a complete abrogation of Martial Law before the meeting of the National Assembly and the promulgation of a new Constitution. The matter, therefore, had to be placed on the agenda and reopened for discussion.

The two leaders also continued their discussions about the form of an interim government. After this meeting, Mujib informed a senior military officer that he and Yahya had tentatively agreed on the formation of a national government composed of eleven ministers. Six of these, including the Prime Minister, were to come from East Pakistan, and five (three from the PPP and two from Wali Khan's National Awami Party) were to come from West Pakistan. It was an unexpected breakthrough in the talks and Mujib, on the evening of 19 March, in a telephone conversation with General Farman, expressed his satisfaction with the results. Farman writes:

> He [Mujib] told me that they had arrived at an agreement and the president would issue a proclamation, which would contain the outline of arrangements for the transfer of power. He also stated that he was to be prime minister, with five ministers each from West and East Pakistan. I asked whether he was satisfied with the arrangement. He said yes and asked for prayers for his success.[6]

Based on the 19 March agreement, Yahya's team, on 20 March, prepared a draft of the proclamation. Mujib and Yahya met again on 21 March, with all their constitutional experts. A draft proclamation affecting an immediate transfer of power was tabled; it provided for the formation of provincial and central cabinets from among the elected representatives. G.W. Choudhury claims to have seen the full text of this proclamation in May 1971, though it was never made public and is not presented fully in the White Paper published by the Government of Pakistan.[7]

The Awami League and Mujib, in all appearances, seemed to have been interested in a peaceful political solution to the crisis in East Pakistan as Mujib's positive evaluation of the situation indicates. Choudhury writes:

Colonel Hasan told me how, while Yahya was making concession after concession to make Mujib agreeable to a political settlement, the junta warned him of the 'dire consequences' of 'weakening' the national Government. There has always been a tendency among the Pakistani Army generals to believe that they alone could protect the *Izzat* [honour] and *Ghairat* [self-respect] of the nation.[8]

This impression is in conflict with Hossain's version of events. The latter describes in detail the change that had taken place around this time in Mujib's attitude and the reasons for it. Seeing the precarious situation in the streets, Mujib decided to change the constitutional proposal insofar to now demand transfer of power only in East Pakistan and not in the Centre. He was refraining from taking over as Prime Minister of Pakistan, because that would have brought him in the environs of Islamabad and he feared the hostility of Rawalpindi and having to compromise the Six Points. By this time, Bengali students and people in the streets of Dhaka and other towns in East Pakistan had obviously opted for separation. Mujib did not want to lose the sympathy of the public and whatever his personal trepidations may have been, was swept forward by the wave of sentiment. There was no looking back, no scope for compromise any more.

The presidential team prepared a draft document the same day, incorporating the items put forth by the Awami League with which they felt comfortable and including a provision for presidential emergency powers, since the authority of Martial Law was to be removed. The principle elements of the draft proclamation were as follows:

1. Martial law would be ended, effective with the administration of the oath of office to provincial cabinets;
2. The Provisional Constitutional Order of 4 April 1969 would serve as the fundamental law until a new constitution became effective;
3. Yahya would continue as president during the interim period;

4. The president would exercise power as authorized by the Provisional Constitutional Order and the 1962 Constitution;

5. A central cabinet would be selected from among the representatives of East and West Pakistan;

6. The National Assembly was to function as prescribed under the 1962 Constitution, except for 'limitations and modifications to be agreed upon with respect to the Province of East Pakistan';

7. The functions of the provincial assemblies would be the same as under the 1962 Constitution, again with exceptions made for East Pakistan;

8. Provincial governors would be appointed by the president in consultation with the leaders of parliamentary groups of the provinces and were to hold office during his pleasure, while a cabinet of ministers was to be appointed with a chief minister at its head to 'aid and advise the Governor in the exercise of his functions';

9. Within seven days of the creation of the provincial governments, two constitutional committees would be established—one in Dhaka and one in Islamabad—for the purpose of 'formulating special provisions and requirements of each province of Pakistan to be incorporated in the constitution to be framed by the National Assembly,' which would be convened by the president after the committees had completed their work; and

10. 'Whenever it is made to appear to the President on a report from the Governor of a Province or otherwise, that a situation has arisen in which the Government of the Province cannot be carried on, the President may by Proclamation assume to himself all or any of the functions of the executive government of the Province.'[9]

By 21 March, both sides had covered a long way in five days, proving that the negotiations were undoubtedly serious. Some of the West Pakistani leaders of minority parties had reached Dhaka and were informed about the negotiations. Among the first party leaders to arrive, on the evening of 19 March, had been Mian Mumtaz Daultana and Shaukat Hayat Khan of the Council Muslim League and Maulana Mufti Mahmud of the Jamiat Ulema-e-Islam. Wali Khan and Ghaus Bux Bizenjo of the National Awami Party (Wali Khan) had already been in Dhaka since 13 March. Qayyum Khan, leader of the Muslim League (Qayyum) and Maulana Shah Ahmed Noorani of the Jamiat Ulema-e-Pakistan arrived on 23 March.

Trouble arrived on 21 March in the shape of Bhutto, who landed in Dhaka in the afternoon of that day despite having refused to go to Dhaka before. Having heard the rumours of a settlement between Mujib and Yahya, he was worried that he may be left out of developments. He saw the President the same evening and was briefed about the state of affairs. Bhutto was not going to be relegated to the background as an observer-in-waiting. He refused to be a mere pawn in the game of chess and was determined to have his say and exert his pressure. For that, his presence on the scene was necessary and therefore he came to East Pakistan in person. His intervention proved not only to be significant, but decisive in the events that unfolded.

In Bhutto's own language, the position on his arrival was as follows:

At 7.30 that evening I met President Yahya Khan, at President House. The President informed me of the series of meetings he had held with Sheikh Mujibur Rahman from the 16th to the 20th. In view of the headway made, Sheikh Mujibur Rahman had addressed a press conference on the 18th in which he said that progress had been achieved. As a result, the experts of the Awami League and of the President also held discussions on the proposed constitutional arrangements. The President proceeded to inform me about the proposal made by the Awami League leader.'[10]

The salient features of Sheikh Mujib's proposals were:

- Martial Law to be withdrawn immediately and power transferred to the five provinces without affecting a similar transfer in the central government.

- The President was to continue running the central government as was being done at the time, or with the assistance of advisers not drawn from the peoples' representatives.
- The National Assembly be divided, *ab initio*, into two committees (East and West Pakistan) comprising the elected representatives of each province. The committees would prepare their separate reports within a stipulated period and submit their proposals to the National Assembly. It would then be the task of the National Assembly to discuss and debate the proposals of both the committees and find out ways and means of living together.
- Under an interim arrangement—an amended form of the 1962 Constitution—East Pakistan would be given autonomy based on the Six Points. The provinces of West Pakistan would have powers as provided in the 1962 Constitution, but would be free to work out their quantum of autonomy according to a procedure accepted by all, and subject to the President's approval.
- The entire scheme was to be published as a Presidential Proclamation.[11]

Sartaj Aziz records in his diary that he was summoned on 20 March to accompany M.M. Ahmed as member of an economic team to Dhaka, in order to discuss and fix the economic implications of the Presidential Proclamation that was planned to be made public on, or after, 23 March. He arrived in Dhaka the next day. When driven to the President's House on 22 March, where the negotiations were taking place, he was struck by the situation in the streets. 'The drive from the cantonment to the President's House was a painful experience,' he recalls. 'To have to travel in one's own country with a military escort through tense, hostile crowds can hardly be otherwise.'[12] He was shown the draft proclamation and made some additional points, two of which were accepted.

On the evening of 22 March, the draft was shown to Bhutto and his team. According to Sartaj Aziz, Bhutto had accepted the substance of the agreement between Yahya and Mujib, making three suggestions to it 'that looked sensible, and I slept with a great sense of relief and expectation. Now that the substance of the proposals had been accepted by both [the] Awami League and [the] PPP, adjustments to agree and finalise the draft itself should not be difficult.'[13]

But efforts were to come to a halt that very same day. When, on the evening of 23 March, the Awami League team returned to resume discussions, they learned that Yahya had not been in the President's House the entire day. While 23 March was traditionally celebrated as Pakistan Day, the Awami League had now declared it Resistance Day. Instead of the Pakistan flag on that day, the Bangladesh flag was seen everywhere, excluding only the cantonments. The resistance movement in the streets reached its peak on that day—a clear sign that the streets of East Pakistan overruled the progress that had been made behind closed doors in the President's House.

The mood in East Pakistan at the time, particularly among the students, was that the people's movement should not be compromised and that the Awami League should not, for the sake of power, compromise any of its demands. Taking power at the Centre could well be projected as such a compromise and the student leaders were vehement on this point. They watched the progress of events closely, ready to erupt at the slightest sign of a compromise. To them, it would be tantamount to betrayal. They were agitated, restless and their defiance was reaching a crescendo. In pragmatic terms too, taking power at the Centre, in the absence of a Constitution, would have exposed the Awami League to the risk of being ineffective and thus being discredited even before a Constitution could be framed.

According to Sartaj Aziz, 'The meeting on the evening of 23 March was eventless and inconclusive. M.M. [Ahmed], Law Minister and Peerzada exchanged views on all the points, but in the end, we could not gather whether Peerzada was ready to accept the Awami League draft...or would insist on the president's draft.'[14] Discussions on

24 March also remained inconclusive. M.M. Ahmed and his team were told to return to Karachi the next day—the time for negotiations was up.

Lt. Col. (later Brigadier) Mohammad Taj recalls:

> The subsequent meeting between the negotiating teams ultimately yielded a historic irony: the issues that had prompted postponement of the National Assembly, were resolved before it would have met. [The] Agreement was reached on the provisions of the draft proclamation that involved the Six Points. Two days prior to the date initially set for the convening of the National Assembly, there was consensus in this respect. The crucial differences concerning those items of the draft encompassed the four demands that had surfaced as a consequence of the postponement. The opposition to these arrangements, primarily over the terms of the lifting of martial law and the transfer of power, came from the PPP and several senior army officers. The PPP feared exclusion from power; the military feared ethnic division in its ranks and an unsympathetic government beholden to a hostile public.[15]

The draft by the Awami League called for lifting the Martial Law, but on different terms. The government had proposed its abrogation on the day provincial cabinets took office, while the Awami League proposed that Martial Law be revoked in a province when its Governor took the oath and no later than seven days after the Presidential Proclamation was made. The Awami League's proposal would thus make the withdrawal of Martial Law effective immediately, inasmuch as the government could not leave the province without any political authority at all. The government's draft had allowed the continuation of Martial Law through a provision that provincial ministries need not be appointed under certain conditions. The Awami League draft also included the abolition of all Martial Law regulations and orders, as well as of the Provisional Constitutional Order. The new Presidential Proclamation would serve as the source of constitutional authority in the interim period, with the administration conducted as closely as possible in accordance with the 1962 Constitution.

Both drafts maintained that Yahya would continue as President in the interim period. According to the Awami League draft, he would also be the Commander-in-Chief of the army and the supreme commander of all armed forces until a new head of state was selected under the new Constitution. This draft also proposed that the President be assisted by his personally appointed advisors, rather than by a cabinet composed of representatives from the political parties of the various provinces, as suggested in the government draft.[16]

There was considerable consternation within the government team, regarding three provisions in the Awami League draft. One was of particular concern, due to both substance and its timing. Each of these provisions held important symbolic meaning for the members of the government team, and probably for the Awami League as well.

First, the teams had agreed that members of the National Assembly would meet in two constituent committees for the purpose of formulating special provisions and requirements of each province of Pakistan, after which, they would convene as the National Assembly to draft a national Constitution. In its draft, the Awami League had substituted 'Constituent Convention' with 'Constituent Committees', though their purpose was unchanged.

The second provision concerned the nature of the oath under which members of the National Assembly were to be sworn into office. The government's oath emphasised sovereignty and its obligation to the state, but the Awami League's version emphasised its obligation to the Constitution.

The third and biggest point of contention is described by Sisson and Rose:

Each of these changes became magnified in the judgment of the government team as a consequence of a third and final change. At what appeared to be the end of the discussions, a member of the Awami League team indicated that he had been instructed by Mujib to change 'Federation of Pakistan' to 'Confederation of Pakistan.' At this suggestion, one distinguished member of the government team temporarily lost his usually calm demeanor. Jumping from his seat, he exclaimed that a confederation was in essence an agreement between two sovereign states, and that such an arrangement had not even been intimated, much less discussed, before. He said that the word 'Union'—if the Awami League was so intent upon using the Indian constitution as a model—was acceptable, but that 'Confederation' was inimical to the welfare of the Pakistani state and was completely out of the question. Another member of the government team observed, however, that the Awami League could amend its own draft in any way that it saw fit and that the government team then had the prerogative of either agreeing or disagreeing.[17]

After going through the document, the President held meetings with the military commanders present, Maj. Gen. A.O. Mitha and others. It was more or less clear that the West Pakistanis would never agree to a confederation. The East Pakistanis stuck to their demands and any semblance of a compromise began to diminish.

In retrospect, Rudyard Kipling's words seem all too poignant and precise in context of the tumultuous days of 1971. The negotiations had been complex and demanding, but undeniably sincere. There was no dearth of effort. Both sides had bargained, some compromises were made, but neither side relented wholly to the other's satisfaction. Despite the good intentions, a truce was not on the cards. Confederation was regarded as a break-up of Pakistan—it clearly crossed the red lines of the military.

What were the East Pakistanis thinking at that juncture? According to Kamal Hossain,

As the Awami League team drove into [the] President's House at 11.30 that morning with Bangladesh flags on their cars, the hostile reaction of the military officers at President's House was all too visible. When the Awami League team entered, they were told that M.M. Ahmed and some other financial experts had been brought over by the government to examine the implications of the financial and economic provisions. Indeed, M.M. Ahmed started by saying that he thought that the Six Points scheme could be given effect with some minor practical adaptations. Peerzada proposed that M.M. Ahmed sit with the Awami League's financial experts, and mentioned the name of Nurul Islam. The Awami League's financial experts, ... had been meeting daily at Nurul Islam's house; in fact, the financial and economic provisions in the Awami League's revised draft had been vetted by them. The Awami League team did not, however, wish to accept this proposal for a separate meeting between financial experts as it was seen as a time-killing manoeuvre. The Awami League team had begun to sense that Yahya's advisers were trying to prolong discussions on each clause; this was clearly seen as a dilatory tactic. At the evening sitting, M.M. Ahmed produced a number of written slips by way of amendments and insertions to the draft. M.M. Ahmed even showed some flexibility in respect of foreign trade and aid. He said foreign trade could be left with the eastern wing without any difficulty. About aid, he said the difficulty could be overcome if foreign policy aspects were left with the Centre. About the reconstruction of the State Bank, he said this also could be done and that, in the interim period, the Dhaka branch of the State Bank could function as the Reserve Bank of Bangladesh. There could also be a bifurcation of the foreign exchange account— the earnings generated by exports from the eastern wing could be maintained in an account with the Dhaka branch. Bifurcation of tax collection presented a more complex problem, and it was agreed that the Awami League team would present a memorandum on how to deal with this matter in the interim phase.[18]

On 23 March, there was another round of negotiations in the President's House, but it seems to have been a ploy to buy time. Hossain reports that they had sensed that Yahya's advisors were trying to prolong negotiations, while the President himself had spent the entire day in the cantonment, in a meeting with generals. On 24 March, another meeting took place where Mujib proposed that the new structure be named the 'Confederation of Pakistan'. This proposal was rejected vehemently by the government team. Predictably, no agreement was reached. They had come up against a wall once again.

The events of the day made a deep impact on representatives from West Pakistan. They were all the more convinced that the East

Pakistanis were not committed to a negotiated solution that would be acceptable to the West. The army strongly believed this too.

Meanwhile, the people had taken to the streets in full fervour. There were demonstrations and processions everywhere. The agitating students demanded independence and called for armed resistance. They paraded the streets, marching in military formation with the Bangladesh flag held high. The Pakistan flag was trampled underfoot and was only hoisted in military installations. On the eve of Resistance Day, Radio Pakistan in Dhaka started to refer to itself as Radio Dhaka. The Dhaka television station ceased to broadcast the events of that day due to alleged military harassment.

The army's high command was concerned about a meeting of ex-servicemen. Maj. Gen. M.U. Majid and Col. M.A.G. Osmany, both now retired, addressed this meeting. The two called for the support of the Bangladesh movement and led a procession to Mujib's Dhanmandi residence, to seek his blessings. A student militia group, the Joi Bangla Brigade, staged a parade at Paltan Maidan where four student leaders of Chhatra League, the Awami League-student front, hoisted the Bangladesh flag and saluted it. After doing so, they too proceeded to Dhanmandi.

Militant student and labour groups circulated handwritten pamphlets and cyclostyled posters in various parts of the province, inciting people to violence.

The National Liberation Movement of East Bengal is on. Spread this wildfire to every place. Patriotic and revolutionary people, take up arms. Resist and liquidate the enemy troops. Defend the [free] areas through armed resistance... People, get armed with the available weapons to stop the inroads of the enemy, cut off the roads, bridges, rail links, etc in those areas which are not in their control. Keep ready hand bombs and Molotov cocktails in every house. If we have to surrender, or we are directly attacked by the enemy, we will have to resort to a bloody war of resistance. Please keep in mind that the national liberation of East Bengal is only possible through armed struggle which will be of long duration. Hence, without guerrilla war tactics, we shall not be able to resist the enemy. Be ready to protect the freed areas at any price. The long struggle of liberation of East Bengal is not at its end. It is just the beginning. To weaken us, the enemy may impose economic blockade. The victory of East Bengal is inevitable. We have torn off the shackles of Pakistani colonialism. Independent East Bengal-Zindabad.[19]

The proverbial last straw was perhaps the arrival at the President's House of the Awami League team flying the Bangladesh flag, on 23 March. This was felt to be a slap in the face of the authorities. The military personnel in particular took this as a deliberate insult at a time when negotiations were still on for a political solution. They felt as if the gauntlet had been throw. Maj. Gen. Hakeem Arshad Qureshi writes, 'It is easier to crush an insurgency, a rebellion, in its conspiratorial stage/infancy than when it is a full-fledged ongoing movement, well entrenched in the minds and emotions of a population.'[20]

From 24 March onwards, the initiative had been taken over by the military. Generals Khadim and Farman travelled by helicopter to personally pass on to commanders outside Dhaka, the instructions for Operation Searchlight, the military operation devised by them on 17 and 18 March. When President Yahya met West Pakistani politicians on the evening of 23 March, they made some suggestions regarding the negotiations, but Yahya replied that it was too late.[21] Hossain remembers the news coming in of the army having moved to unload MV *Swat* in Chittagong and rumours of a military operation. He recalls, 'In the evening [of 24], the reading of all clauses and schedules of the draft was concluded. I asked Peerzada, with a note of urgency, as to when the draft could be finalised. ...When I suggested that a time be fixed for the following day, Peerzada again intervened to say that this could be done over the telephone....'[22] But the next day was 25 March and the phone call never came.

The Pakistan Army had dispatched its troops to offload MS *Swat*. On their way to Chittagong, people were blocking the roads leading to the port. Military clashes were reported from several places, including Rangpur. It was clear that the time for negotiations had run out. Yahya quietly left Dhaka on the evening of 25 March, prior to the start of military action. The Pakistan Army launched Operation Searchlight at midnight on 25 March, in an attempt to achieve what was, arguably, unachievable through military action. This was the beginning of the end.

The end of Jinnah's Pakistan thus arrived some twenty-three years after its inception. But the break-up did not only mean the end of the state as it had been created in 1947, but also the end of the two-nation theory that had been developed in order to justify the creation of Pakistan. The country was a testament to the fact that the finest experiment of nationhood in its time had resulted in a tragedy.

Nations are built first and foremost on geographical grounds. It is an integrative process that must unite different ethnic, religious, cultural, and economic entities into a community of equals. There must be a unity of purpose and equity among the constituent units. A superficial national identity is easy to create by appealing to emotions, waving flags and singing songs, but such an identity exists only on the surface. Real identity can only be developed under secure fundamental principles—the sharing of resources, equal opportunities, and respect for different beliefs and traditions. This had been neglected with regard to East Pakistan from the very beginning and the bill for that was presented in 1971.

Notes

1. Hossain, p. 92.
2. Rao Farman Ali Khan, *How Pakistan Got Divided* (Karachi: Oxford University Press, 2017), p. 88.
3. Sisson & Rose, p. 114.
4. Siddiq Salik, *Witness to Surrender* (Karachi: Oxford University Press, 1977), Appendix 3.
5. White Paper on Crisis in East Pakistan, Government of Pakistan, 5 August 1971, selected chapters, p. 13.
6. Rao Farman Ali Khan, p. 90.

7. G.W. Choudhury, p. 166.

8. Fazal Muqueem Khan, *The Story of the Pakistan Army* (Karachi: Oxford University Press, 1963), p. 63 as cited in G.W. Choudhury, p. 167.

9. Sisson & Rose, pp. 118–19.

10. Zulfikar Ali Bhutto, *The Great Tragedy* (Karachi: Pakistan Peoples Party, 1971), http://sanipanhwar.com/The per cent20Great per cent20Treadegy per cent20by per cent20Zulfikar per cent20Ali per cent20Bhutto per cent20 per cent20—per cent20August per cent2020, per cent201971.pdf, p. 36.

11. Ibid.

12. Anwar Dil (comp.), *Hunger, Poverty and Development*, p. 506.

13. Ibid.

14. Ibid., p. 508.

15. Interview with Brigadier Mohammad Taj, February 2017, Islamabad.

16. Sisson & Rose, pp. 118–19.

17. Sisson & Rose, p. 127.

18. Hossain, pp. 100–101.

19. White Paper on the Crisis in East Pakistan, Government of Pakistan, 5 August 1971, selected chapters, p. 14.

20. Qureshi, p. 31.

21. Sisson & Rose, p. 130.

22. Hossain, p. 102.

13

Operation Searchlight Phase-I

During the negotiations of March 1971, it was widely felt that they would eventually lead to a positive outcome. But this was not meant to be, largely due to the sentiments of extremists on both sides. The plan for military action to restore the writ of the central authority in East Pakistan was unanimous, finalised by the local military commanders in the week before 25 March. Though inevitable, only its timing came as a surprise. Two irreconcilable forces were working within the negotiations; on the East Pakistan/Bengali side it was the Awami League, a pro-secession group within it, and the support of the Bengali masses, while on the West Pakistani and government side, it was the military hierarchy, which acted on the belief that the military option was necessary to keep the country united.

According to Sisson and Rose:

> The military further noted that the cost of inaction and continuing the political negotiations would be great, first in the slide toward anarchy in the east and second in the alienation of the population in West Pakistan. The costs of military action would be relatively small, and it would have the positive consequence of "cleaning the political stables" in the east, while at the same time, creating conditions that would be more conducive to a lasting political solution the military and western political parties could live with. Military action was thus seen as the only means of halting the continuing political crisis and as essential as well to avoid loss of control over the East Pakistani military units.[1]

Maj. Gen. Hakeem Arshad Qureshi describes the military position:

> Here were two people, armed to the teeth and suspicious of each other, one apprehensive but reluctant to initiate measures to re-establish the writ of law because of inadequacy of resources, the other rebellious by nature, aroused to fever pitch by a parochial leadership, emboldened by the inaction of authority, and poised to strike the first blow for Bengali nationalism. Yet neither was sure of his purpose, or confident of his success, but both kept their fingers on the trigger, waiting for something to happen. Apparently, in our case, it was fear of failure that forced us into inaction—a sure recipe for ultimate disaster.
>
> To avoid an armed conflict and a bloodbath, it was necessary that those Bengalis bearing weapons as part of various units were disarmed without a firefight. It was necessary that this act of defanging took place simultaneously. If that was not possible, however, because of inadequacy of strength, at least a coordinated action in tandem against major concentrations of EPR, EBR, and police, needed to be initiated. Had we been able to pull off this basic requirement of peace, the history of the break-up of Pakistan might never have been written.[2]

Operation Searchlight was launched on the night of 25 March, in order to re-establish the Pakistani hold over the administration of East Pakistan and destroy the centres of resistance in the population. While open and armed rebellion had not yet broken out, sporadic clashes between the Bengali population and the army had been a recurring feature since the beginning of March and the Non-Cooperation Movement of the Awami League, initiated on the first of that month, brought political power in East Pakistan safely under Awami League control. Scott Butcher, a young political officer of the US Consul General (USCG) in Dhaka, remembers a wave of civil disobedience, with outraged crowds in the streets and a number of clashes with Pakistani authorities. The next day, Bengalis launched a general strike, in the storied tradition of mass mobilizations against the British Empire,' he recalls. 'This showed the generals who really ran Pakistan....' Butcher was impressed with the military's restraint, which he found remarkable. 'They were be spat upon, harassed and hassled by locals, but behaving quite well under the circumstances,' he says.[3]

Operation Searchlight was meant to achieve several aims, according to Sisson and Rose:

> While there were differences of opinion within the general officer corps on how to handle the military operation, there was consensus on the objectives to be achieved and the strategy to be employed in what was called "Operation Searchlight." The objectives were to neutralize the political power of the Awami League and to reestablish public order. First, the top leadership of the party had to be captured. The second priority was to neutralize its more radical elements, in particular student leaders and…various cultural organizations that advocated a Bengali renaissance. Several residential halls at the University of Dhaka would need to be cleared of students and checked for arms that were believed to be there in preparation for rebellion. Leaders were to be taken peacefully if possible, but if armed resistance was offered, troops were to respond with force.
>
> Third, the Bengali armed force had to be disarmed and neutralized. The army assumed that the East Bengal Regiment, the East Pakistan Rifles, the Ansars, and the police would all turn against the military authorities. Finally, the operation called for the establishment of control over all communications media. After taking over the large urban areas, the army was to restore order in the remainder of the province in four phases: (1) [by] clearing all major border towns and sealing routes of infiltration; (2) opening essential river, road, and rail communications; (3) clearing all major towns in the interior and coastal areas; and (4) combing out rebels and infiltrators from the whole of the province.[4]

While the last meetings between Yahya and the Awami League team were still going on, the launch of the operation was finalised. The success of it largely depended on a simultaneous start in all arenas of action and carrying it out according to plan. Lt. Col. Taj recalls:

GOC 14 Division, Maj. Gen. Khadim Hussain Raja, briefed his brigade commanders at various places in Comilla and Jessore, as well as Commander 57 Brigade located in Dhaka. They also decided that I, as G1 Intelligence, will take over the command of two battalions, that is 18 Punjab and 32 Punjab, from [the] previous CO and clear Dhaka of all militants by dawn, 26 March... So a plan was made and the brigade commander and other forces were briefed, the troops earmarked for Dhaka operations were two battalions, 31 Cavalry... to look after Dhanmondi, which was a civilised area without much problem [trouble]. The operation was to start only after the capture or arrest of Mujib. He was eventually arrested by commandos by 1 a.m. and brought to the cantonment, after which clearance was given to start the operations in Dhaka.[5]

Mujib's arrest rendered the rebellion leaderless. Being a non-violent person with little inclination towards heroism, Mujib had ordered the Awami League leadership to disperse in Dhaka's old town as soon as the military made its move and to cross the river to avoid arrest. On the night of 25/26 March, he waited for the military in his house; different sources report that he had no desire to run and if need be would have surrendered himself to the army. He believed in the power of the people's verdict and that, according to him, had to be acknowledged. He thought himself to have done nothing wrong. Under explicit orders from Yahya, he was not to be harmed. Mujib was in a difficult situation. According to General Lehrasab, Mujib told him in November 1970 that 'If I go as prime minister to Islamabad, Bengalis will kill me; if I stay as Chief Minister of Bengal the army will kill me.' Therefore, he quietly waited for his arrest.

After a couple of days in confinement, he was flown to West Pakistan, where a trial was instituted against him in Faisalabad. Brigadier (retd.) Z.A. Khan (then a lieutenant colonel commanding the SSG), who took Mujib into custody, describes how the password that he had been given in order to be allowed passage through the airport area had not been forwarded to the necessary persons, as a result of which the party heading out for Mujib was denied passage at the airport. He also recalls how the roadblocks by the Awami League prevented a part of the party to even reach Mujib's house on time and how, after he had been arrested, nobody seemed to have thought about where he would be detained. Another, rather shameful detail, is that a junior member of the arresting party was allowed to slap Mujib—an act that demonstrated the emotional attitude of the army towards Bengalis.[6] What is shocking is that in his account, Z.A. Khan, who was in charge of the arrest, was quite brutal and treated the entire incident as a matter of routine.

On the night of 25 March, at 11 p.m., Z.A. Khan led his commandos from Dhaka airfield, past the MNA hostel on the road to Mohammadpur. Vehicles without lights carrying the commandos, belonged to the Signal Corps, they followed his jeep, which had its headlights on. About a quarter of a mile from Dhanmondi, the road was blocked with trucks and other vehicles turned. When the soldiers fired rocket launchers, Colonel Z.A. Khan had to walk from man to man to make them stop. To create a gap in the roadblock, a five-ton vehicle with a winch pushed aside some of the now burning vehicles and created the gap needed.

Z.A. Khan recalls:

> We walked down the Mohammadpur-Dhanmondi road to the street on which Sheikh Mujib's house was located and turned right on the lane between the house and the lake. Captain Humayun's group entered the house adjacent to Sheikh Mujib's house, ran across the compound and jumped over the wall into Sheikh Mujib's house. Fire was opened, some people in the compound ran out of the gate, one man was killed. The East Pakistan Police guard[s] outside the house got into their 180-pounder tent, lifted the tent by its poles and ran into the lake. Sheikh Mujib's compound perimeter was secured. It was pitch dark—Mujib's house and the adjacent houses had no lights.
>
> While I was instructing Captain Saeed on how to sort out the vehicles, there was a shot, then the sound of a grenade exploding, followed by a burst from a sub-machine gun, I thought that someone had killed Sheikh Mujib. I ran back to the house and upstairs and

there I found a very shaken Sheikh Mujib outside the door of the room that had been closed. I asked Sheikh Mujib to accompany me, he asked me if he could say goodbye to his family and I told him to go ahead. He…came out quickly and we walked to where the vehicles were. Captain Saeed had still not managed to turn them around, I sent a radio message to inform the Eastern Command that we had got Sheikh Mujib.

Sheikh Mujib then told me that he had forgotten his pipe, I walked back with him and he collected his pipe. By this time Sheikh Mujib was confident that we would not harm him and he told me that we had only to call him and he would have come on his own, I told him that we wanted to show him that he could be arrested. When we got back, Captain Saeed had the vehicles lined up, Sheikh Mujib was put in the middle troop-carrying vehicle and we started back to the cantonment.[7]

On the same night, Major Ziaur Rahman, second-in-command of the East Bengal Regiment based in Chittagong, had declared the independence of East Pakistan, after killing the West Pakistani commanding officer.[8] Kamal Hossain says that the leadership of the party had received the order on 25 March to disperse to the Old Town of Dhaka and cross the river to move into the countryside as soon as the military moved in to avoid arrest. Because of the curfew that made movement difficult in Dhaka, Hossain was delayed in the city and was arrested on 3 April, detained, and later flown to West Pakistan where he was kept for nine months in Haripur Central Jail.[9] Nevertheless, the majority of the Awami League leaders escaped detention and found refuge in India. The military's 'Searchlight' was too dim and weak and thus failed to achieve its objective.

'SEARCHLIGHT' IN DHAKA UNIVERSITY

One centre of Bengali resistance and the Bengali students' movement was Dhaka University. That was why the operation paid special attention to the campus and the dormitories located therein. Classes had been suspended since the beginning of March and most of the students—out of fear of the violence to come—had returned to their homes. Meanwhile, the militant Bengali students holed up in the hostels, had been joined by other students and volunteers from Dhaka and the surrounding areas. 'The university areas harboured most of the armed dissidents and had become a stronghold of the rebellious students, professors and other intellectuals,' according to General Matinuddin.[10] Thus, one major part of the action on 25 and 26 March was centred on Dhaka University campus. Supported by tanks and artillery, the 18 Punjab Regiment, under the command of Lt. Col. Basharat Sultan, was responsible for securing a campus that was offering tough resistance.

The two main hostels targeted were Jagannath Hall, the hostel of Hindu students, and Iqbal Hall. Despite statements that Rokeya Women's Hostel was also targeted in the action, Sarmila Bose has found no eyewitness to support this claim. The women's hostel had been vacated long before, as classes had ended in early March and due to the worsening security situation in Dhaka. Nevertheless, Matinuddin reports that some students were still there.[11]

The headquarters of EPR Peelkhana and the Rajarbagh Police Lines were attacked with overwhelming force. The Bengali soldiers and police officers responded when fired upon, and the force used seemed to be far greater than was needed. To civilians, even a rifle company's firepower can be overwhelming. Colonel Taj recalls:

I was given command of the force consisting of 32 Punjab and 18 Punjab, on the night of 24 March. President Yahya flew back on 25 March, just before the operation started. Bhutto stayed back in the Intercontinental Hotel with a number of reporters who came from various countries. I had earmarked one rifle company for Iqbal Hall (Dhaka University)—this was considered the concentration of Mukti Bahini force. Jagganath Hall and also some police stations were to be taken over in the first phase; moreover, the TV station, and police lines in Rajarbagh had to be cleared. By morning of 26 March, we had cleared Iqbal Hall, Jagganath Hall, and the nearby police stations.

The only resistance came from Rajarbagh... where I personally went with a company of 32 Punjab and cleared the area. By 8 o'clock in the morning, Dhaka was completely under control. Some of the senior officers came and visited us in Rajarbagh, where the ammunition dump was on fire; we controlled the fire and met the senior officers.[12]

As the army approached, some students fought back but most did not appear to be using the weapons or training that they had been equipped with. The two hostels were the centre of resistance and this was where the most casualties were incurred. A professor of the university, Nurul Ula, was reportedly able to film executions by the Pakistan Army, of captured and unarmed students, including the injured ones. Sarmila Bose reports that this footage is not available in Bangladesh and she could only see a short sequence of it in a BBC report. While the number of dead differ radically depending on the source, rumours of mass graves dug by soldiers that night, in order to hide the dead bodies, have not been investigated by Bangladeshi authorities. If a graveyard was found and excavated, there would have been an idea of the real number of people killed.

Not only students, but male faculty members residing on the campus were killed as well—all at random though, as no specific guidelines seem to have been followed. The fact that the Hindu faculty was singled out and shot shows the suspicion that was engrained in the army as to the reasons for the revolt in East Bengal. The military suspected the Hindus, Indians, and communists to be behind the trouble—a reflection of the longstanding prejudice prevailing in West Pakistan in general. The official number of casualties on the Bengali side was 66 dead, 31 injured, while 4 soldiers were also reported to have been killed. Various independent sources claim that 500 people had been killed that night.[13] However, there is little evidence to support these figures.

The lack of an investigation into the atrocities of 25–26 March and the negligent attitude of the Bangladeshi state and society is a shocking fact portrayed by Sarmila Bose. It is testament to the fact that the history of the crisis lacks objectivity and is a politicised version of how the ruling elite would like to present the past.

In her book, Bose provides the eyewitness accounts of those who were present on campus on that day, including the faculty members. According to these, the Bangladeshi version of events, that the Pakistan Army was attacking unarmed Bengali students, was not true. On the contrary, the university was a violent nest of support for Mujib and weapons had been smuggled onto campus and collected there over time. Training with these weapons was carried out on a regular basis and student leaders made violent speeches, threatening the government. She writes, 'The reality is that there were weapons, and training, and no matter how unequal the fire-power, a few Bengalis apparently did put up a fight. The "victim" story denies them their true role while undermining the credibility of the narrative as a whole, as it is contradicted by Bengali eye-witness accounts...'.[14]

Third on the 'to do' list was the disarming and neutralising of Bengali armed forces because of the doubts that West Pakistani officers were having with regard to their loyalty. One example was Colonel Taj who said in his recorded interview:

One thing I want to say about [the] Joydebpur operation which I have not covered so far. The brigade commander, Brigadier Arbab, went to Joydebpur on 19 March, to visit 2 EB. It had one company and the intelligence headquarter. He had his lunch, but while coming back he found that a number of barricades on the road had come up and even trucks were placed on railway tracks. He tried to clear it and faced lot of problems... as a mob had collected armed with *lathis* and weapons and anything else they could lay their hands on. It was a problem for the brigade commander to return safely. He asked for reinforcements which somehow could not be supplied, so he had to open fire with his own guards he had taken from other units, cleared the barricades and came back to Dhaka. This was an unfortunate incident, but it made it clear to those who mattered that Bengali troops in East Pakistan are not obeying [the] orders that they should have obeyed and it was obvious now that the army, particularly the Bengali troops in East

Pakistan, will not support any operation that is being taken. Later on, this was proved to be true; non-Bengali elements of 2 EB, led by one of the officers, came and joined us in Dhaka and stayed with 32 Punjab during the operation in East Pakistan. This was [a] most unfortunate incident where the Bengali troops defected and used their weapons against their West Pakistani comrades in uniform. It was here that one was almost clear that unless the events were controlled physically, the situation may get worse, which ultimately happened.[15]

The perception prevailing in West Pakistan was that there had been a spontaneous mutiny by the units of the East Bengal Regiment, after the Dhaka crackdown of 25 March. But this proved inaccurate. There is compelling eyewitness account provided by General Lehrasab (at that time a major and senior major in the unit), who was involved in the disarming exercise. He recalls:

On 29 March, Commanding Officer [CO], Colonel Reza ul Jalil, visited the unit in the camp and I briefed him about our training plan after this break. He inspected the camp, met officers and men and appreciated the level of proficiency that they had achieved during last one month or so. After having met JCOs and men, we came back to the officers' living area for a cup of tea. While we were having tea, I received a telephone call from Major [later Lt. Gen.] Muhammad Shafiq, Brigade Major [BM], 107 Brigade at Jessore. He asked me to bring the unit back to the unit lines at Jessore by tomorrow morning. I informed the CO that the BM was on the line and wished to talk to him. Both had a brief conversation during which [the] CO repeatedly asked the BM about the future role of the battalion. I felt at that point in time the fear of the CO that our unit may be disarmed once it arrives at Jessore, because some of the Bengal Regiment units had already been disarmed and some of them had defected. It was a very uncomfortable situation, particularly for the commanding officer of a well-trained unit which had so far shown no signs of discontentment. Since the CO was invited for a dinner at the brigade commander's house, he left after having had tea. He asked me to move the unit back to the lines and start marching as early as possible.

I decided to move the convoy of vehicles under the command of a Subedar to reach the unit lines during daylight, along with four West Pakistani non-commissioned officers. Hurriedly, the evening meal was prepared and served to the troops before sunset and the battalion started moving back on foot to the cantonment, immediately after last light. It was a very tense situation because nobody was sure as to what the battalion would likely be employed for. An indication was given by the Brigade Headquarter that 1 EB would likely be deployed on Benapole road, about 10 kilometres from Jessore. I was leading the move back at full pace and we reached unit lines at about 1:00 am. I could feel the tense atmosphere when Subedar Major Azeem received us.

The troops felt relieved after a very intensive training period and interacted with the rear-party in the unit lines. After depositing the weapons in the unit *kotes* [armouries], the troops had a cup of tea together which was arranged by the rear-party. After taking tea, I gave my jeep to bachelor officers and sent them to the officers' mess. Meanwhile, I could see JCOs [junior commissioned officers] whispering in small groups at different places in the veranda of [the] adjacent barracks. Suddenly, I saw the Commanding Officer, Colonel Reza ul Jalil, in his car, going towards his house. Subedar Major Azeem, who was standing next to me, told me that the CO had gone for a dinner at the residence of the brigade major. Meanwhile, my jeep returned from the officers' mess and I informed my senior JCO of the company, Subedar Abdul Majid, to call me from the house if [the] CO asks for me in the morning, before 9 o'clock. I told him that I will be coming to the office at 9 o'clock. I left for my house in the jeep and reached home to see that all officers' families were awake in our neighbourhood and were expecting that [the] 1 EB arrival may trigger trouble in the cantonment where West and East Pakistan families were living in the same area. When I reached home, my wife, who was the only West Pakistani lady living alone there with two children, felt very relieved and happy to see me…she informed me that the families were very worried on hearing the news that 1 EB had arrived in the cantonment. I consoled her and we went to sleep after spending little time with our children since I was quite exhausted after having footed 20 miles of distance up to the Jessore Cantonment.

I, with my family, was fast asleep in my house on the morning of 30 March, when I heard the noise of firing from the direction of 1 EB and some bullets hit the ventilator of my house. Between this residential area of officers and the unit lines of 1 EB, there was only one big ground and a school building. Next to 1 EB unit lines there was, under construction, a building of CMH [Combined Military Hospital] Jessore. The main frame of this building was ready and it was the first major double-story building in the cantonment. I immediately got up and moved out of my house in the direction of 1 EB; they had already picked up arms and fighting had commenced. The brigade commander advised me to return to my house and stay inside… I came back to my house and informed my wife of the prevailing situation.

It was later revealed that the brigade commander, during the dinner on the night of 29–30 March, had persuaded Colonel Reza ul Jalil to disarm 1 EB, to which he had agreed reluctantly. The brigade commander assured the CO that 1 EB, after disarming, will be allowed to continue normal activities in the unit lines and the commander will safeguard all families and troops of 1 EB. It was decided that the brigade commander would arrive at the 1 EB CO's office at 7 o'clock in the morning of 30 March, to receive the keys of the unit *kotes* and magazines. The brigade commander, as scheduled, arrived in the CO's office, but the keys of the *kotes* and magazines were not there. After a while, the subedar major of the unit brought the keys and handed them over to Reza ul Jalil with tears rolling down his cheeks. The brigade commander consoled the CO and the subedar major, by assuring them that the unit will be taken good care of by him and they will continue to perform normal duties.

It was a tense environment and the brigade commander left the office of the CO and departed for the brigade headquarter. As per plan, the CO of 25 Baloch, Lt. Col. J.J. Din, who had arrived with the brigade commander and was sitting with CO 1 EB, was to walk back and reach the quarter guard area of 1 EB. When one of his companies, the only company available in the cantonment that day, was to reach the quarter guard, [they were to] overpower and disarm the personnel of 1 EB on quarter guard-duty, and post 25 Baloch guards, duly armed, for the protection of *kotes* and magazines. When

Lt. Col. J.J. Din arrived near the quarter guard, his company was not yet inside and this delay had a disastrous effect on the disarming plan. Meanwhile, the CO of 1 EB, lost control of the situation and all troops, in whatever dress or state they were in, rushed to the *kotes* and magazines, shouting slogans that they will not surrender their arms and fight back. They broke the locks of the *kotes* and magazines, took out the arms and ammunition and started firing in the direction of the cantonment, the family areas and a workshop nearby, where the 25 Baloch Company had arrived. It was within the first fifteen minutes that the major of the artillery unit, who was about to conduct the artillery fire on the lines of 1 EB, was hit and wounded. Luckily, one battery of artillery, which was about to leave for Kushtia, deployed itself along the unit lines and engaged 1 EB effectively. The artillery fire saved the day for the rest of the cantonment and 1 EB troops did not come out of their lines to engage sensitive areas in the cantonment.

By 30 March, a refugee camp had been established in the cantonment school, to accommodate civilian Pashtuns who had assembled there from different areas of the interior of East Pakistan, who were basically involved in different business activities. There were about 600 people who were residing in this school. The brigade commander ordered for [the] arming of all those civilians and the administrative units as well for the defence of the cantonment.

The CO 1 EB, Lt. Col. Reza ul Jalil, remained in contact with [the] brigade commander on telephone, who asked him to control the situation, stop the firing, and achieve the surrender of arms. On that day, there were five West Pakistani Officers in 1 EB. The CO, in spite of repeated efforts, could not exercise control over his unit—at one stage, he decided to defect with the unit. The brigade commander, meanwhile, decided to attack the unit lines of 1 EB at 3 p.m., to push them out and secure the parameter defences of the cantonment. This attack commenced by artillery firing and the CO 1 EB asked for the jeep and ordered everyone to get out of the cantonment, making use of the advantage of being located on the perimeter of the cantonment. The West Pakistani officers got around the jeep of the CO and asked him to give clear orders to them for accompanying the unit, which was already defecting. On this, the CO came out of the jeep and decided to surrender, along with all West Pakistani officers, some JCOs, and men. They quickly arranged a white flag and all of them marched into attacking troops with [the] white flag and surrendered. They were, all in all, about forty men. The 1 EB escaped from the unit lines and ran away towards the Indian border. The day ended with the restoration of the perimeter defence and all families who had gone barefoot to the CO's mess, reverted to their houses after sunset. It was a painful day, loaded with insecurity, tragic in consequence, but ended with a ray of hope for temporary survival. What the dawn of 31 March had in store for this garrison, nobody knew.[16]

The decision to disarm loyal units is a particularly unfortunate chapter of the events that transpired in 1971, because prior to 25 March, no mutiny or insurrection had occurred to support such suspicions. It was, therefore, a Catch-22 situation. Under General Tikka's command, any military action to re-establish civil authority in East Pakistan was bound to be ruthless and enhance the doubts of Bengali officers and soldiers. Nevertheless, many remained loyal and more would have done so, if trusted.

There were rumours of an impending revolt by 2 EB Regiment. Up to and including 12 March, I had been flying the Commander Eastern Command, GOC 14 Division and a number of other senior officers, to various cantonments in East Pakistan. I visited 2 EB at Joydebpur, 8 EB and the EBRC in Chittagong, 4 EB at Comilla, 3 EB at Rangpur/Saidpur and 1 EB at Jessore. I knew almost everyone in the regiment—Bengalis and non-Bengalis. While I did find tension among the officers and the men, it was not different to similar propaganda which [was] taking place in 18 and 32 Punjab in Dhaka, 29 Cavalry at Rangpur, etc., because of the political situation. Not at a single place I saw gave even a hint of an impending revolt. As had been expected, Lt. Gen. Tikka Khan's brutal crackdown on the civilian uprising during the Operation Searchlight, won him the epithet 'Butcher of Bengal' among Bengalis.

The civil war in East Pakistan in March, April, and May, was fought with extreme cruelty on both sides. On the side of the Pakistan

Army, this persisted in areas and units in which their commanders failed to enforce strict discipline, while the officers of Mukti Bahini generally failed to control their personnel. However, most of those who indulged in rape, torture, and murder, were not even Mukti Bahini. While the Pakistan Army was not trained for military action against its own people and thus lost focus in difficult situations, mob mentality prevailed among the civilian elements of the rebels. As has been aptly shown by Yasmin Saikia in her book,[17] keeping humanity alive in an inhuman situation is a high order that cannot always be maintained.

A large number of Bengali members of the EBR, EPR, police and other paramilitary forces, were expected to mutiny. It came as no surprise in the face of stories of the army's atrocities against the civilian Bengali population and the latter's strong sense of identity. The spark finally came in the form of military action, when the EBR units and the Bengali elements of EPR, were required to hand over their weapons to the West Pakistanis. As was expected, they refused to do so and when faced with a military confrontation, rebelled, and fought their way into the lap of the enemy-turned-protector, India.[18]

Many of them ended up deserting the military after killing West Pakistani officers and went on to join the Mukti Bahini—Bangladesh Liberation Army. One example cited by General Matinuddin, was that of the Bengali Major, Khaled Mosharraf, who was the Brigade Major of 57 Brigade in Dhaka and had been sent away from the main arena (probably to prevent him from mutinying) by being posted as second-in-command 4 EB. Minus a rear-party consisting mostly of headquarter troops and families, 4 EB was moved to Brahmanbaria, for internal security duties under their West Pakistani CO, Lt. Col. Khizar Hayat.

Once Khalid had information about the rear-party of 4 EB and Bengali SSG personnel of other units being executed in cold blood by West Pakistani elements in Comilla, he refused orders to come back and put his CO and some other West Pakistan officers under arrest. He formed a rebel group in Brahmanbaria, consisting of 4 EB, EPR, police and other personnel. Later he contacted Major Shafiulla of 2 EB and concentrated his unit along with 2 EB, in and around Teliapara Tea Estate, in Sylhet district. Many Bengalis did not revolt and stayed loyal. 'All Bengali officers of the 23 Field Regiment, artillery, at Saidpur, remained steadfast in their loyalty.'[19] Other examples can also be quoted. The decision to secure units by disarming them, therefore, turned out to be a major folly. It was done despite Maj. Gen. Hakeem Arshad Qureshi's clarification that no written orders to disarm EBR, or EPR, were given and that this was left to the discretion of the local commander.[20]

On the night of 25–26 March, 22 Baloch Regiment simultaneously attacked the EPR's base at Peelkhana (to the west of Dhaka University), the Rajarbagh Police Line, the Gazipur ammunition factory and the arms depot at Rajendrapur. Fierce resistance was encountered and US Consul General Archer Blood reported heavy firing from those areas. Maj. Gen. Khadim Raja reports, 'less than ten casualties on both sides,'[21] but he might be playing the numbers down. According to Sarmila Bose, 'The disarming of Bengali police and army personnel turned into a bloodbath in many places, with casualties on both sides, and many Bengali personnel escaped with their arms, to return to fight another day.'[22] However, rumours about the incumbent disarmament seem to have been afloat.

Before 25 March, Bengali officers and men located in East Pakistan, comprised about 4,500 regulars in six battalions of the EBR (10 EB being a National Service Battalion), 1500 in EBRC at Nutanpara, Chittagong, 12,000 to 15,000 EPR personnel, and about 45,000 Bengali police officers. They were numerically superior to the West Pakistanis, even if they were not as well organised. There were enough indicators of an imminent military operation; changing the CO 2 EB (Lt. Col. Masudul Hasan Khan) with CO 32 Punjab (albeit another Bengali officer, Lt. Col. Raquib), only confirmed the Bengalis' worst suspicions.

On the other hand, Brigadier Mazumdar, Commandant EBRC, sent Captain Amin Ahmed Chaudhry (later major general in the

Bangladesh Army) to India before 25 March. Brigadier General B.C. Pande of the Border Security Force sent him by air to New Delhi to meet the Indian Prime Minister, Indira Gandhi. Even though the army did not know this, there were suspicions about Mazumdar's loyalty and he was brought to Dhaka on the pretext that he was needed to calm 2 EB at Joydebpur, which had grown restive after the removal of its CO.

Maj. Gen. Khadim Hussain Raja and many others among West Pakistanis in the army felt that the number of Bengali units in East Pakistan was inordinate. An attempt to balance these numbers was made in March 1971, after the election. But a year earlier, in 1970, the GHQ had ordered the raising of three purely Bengali units. In hindsight, it seems to have acted out of a sense of premonition. We should have remembered our history; after the insurrection of 1857, the Indian Army was reorganised by the British. The composition of regiments was modified to create sub-units with distinct ethnic, religious, and linguistic identities, generating healthy rivalry and intense professional competition and enabling the government to keep a tag on 'belly-aching' and any rebellious trends. All units of the Pakistan Army should have been integrated along the lines of the British re-organisation of the Indian Army post-1857.[23]

On 26 March, after killing the CO and other West Pakistani officers, 8 EB momentarily captured Chittagong city, isolating it from the cantonment. With half the personnel at the naval base in Chittagong being Bengali, securing Chittagong harbour was essential for the survival of the Pakistan military. Securing Comilla Cantonment, the 53 Brigade HQ and 24 FF were tasked to retake Chittagong. Delayed by demolished bridges, it took them until the end of March to recapture the city.

My entanglement in the situation in East Pakistan arose because of my dual identity/nationality—West Pakistani from my father's side and Bengali from my mother's. I was less than three years old when my father was posted to East Pakistan, to raise 2 EB, in 1949. I had grown up practically in the unit and considered myself a member of it long before officially joining in 1965. I almost gave up my country and my life for my unit and certainly gave up my career for it. I reached Dhaka on 27 March 1971, on posting to Logistic Flight, Eastern Command and was on 'joining time' when I heard that my unit, 2 EB, in Joydebpur, had revolted on 28 March. I decided with my heart rather than with my head and chose to go and see my unit, to find out for myself. One could never believe that the personnel had killed their West Pakistani officers. When I arrived in Bhairab Bazar on 31 March, my romantic notions that the glory and honour of the regiment must come first, were turned upside down. Despite this, I can never forget the vociferous adulation I was given by the unit on my arrival. This part of Operation Searchlight remains especially fateful and painful for many who were in East Pakistan in those days.

Propaganda Warfare

The aim of Operation Searchlight, one which was not spelt out officially, was to conceal the character and severity of the operation from the West Pakistani population and the international community. Pakistani authorities understood that a military crackdown would not go down well internationally or in the western wing. If West Pakistanis had known the full truth about the protests and the military's response, a wave of sympathy would have been generated, undermining law and order in West Pakistan as well. With regard to the international community, Pakistan tried to play down the precarious situation. It also tried to counter India's propaganda war, in which India blamed Pakistan for what was happening in its eastern wing. Even though the electronic media at that time was relatively underdeveloped and its reach limited, propaganda has been an influential means of warfare globally, throughout the twentieth century. Regarding Pakistan though, this instrument of war was handled clumsily by the Pakistan government and the army. And it would not be an overstatement to say that Pakistan lost the propaganda war as well.

From the very beginning, Pakistan had decided to take a defensive stand instead of an offensive one. In order to hide the Operation Searchlight from the West Pakistani and international public and in order to complicate communication between the East Bengalis, all internal and external communication was closed down from the outset. Few international journalists managed to escape deportation. Among them was Simon Dring of *The Daily Telegraph*, who avoided being rounded-up by hiding on the roof of the Intercontinental Hotel and then later went around Dhaka dispatching first reports on the operation. The reports of those journalists, who managed to escape, became even more one-sided and took an explicitly anti-Pakistani tinge. Dring's accounts of the army's raid of Dhaka University published under the title 'How Dhaka Paid for a United Pakistan' on 30 March 1971, recorded the events of the night of 25–26 March:

> Led by the American-supplied M-24 World War II tanks, one column of troops sped to Dhaka University shortly after midnight. Troops took over the British Council library (situated within the campus) and used it as a fire base from which to shell nearby dormitory areas. Caught completely by surprise, some 200 students were killed in Iqbal Hall, headquarters of the militant anti-government students' union, I was told. Two days later, bodies were still smouldering in burnt out rooms, others were scattered outside, more floated in a nearby lake.... At another hall, reportedly, soldiers buried the dead in a hastily dug mass grave which was then bull-dozed over by tanks.[24]

Another journalist escaping deportation was Arnold Zeitlin, who also brought information on the fury of the military crackdown to the international community. Then, the Pakistan Army started Operation Misinformation, by playing down reports about atrocities and hiding the extent of the death and destruction that had been unleashed by it.[25] Colonel Taj recalls:

> After (the operation) I went to the Intercontinental Hotel, where Bhutto and press reporters were staying, I met Bhutto and his words

were, "You have saved Pakistan today" and I replied, "Sir, time will only decide." The press reporters requested…that they want to go around Dhaka and see what had happened last night and how many casualties were there. I told them that as per information as given to me by my senior commander, thirty people were killed in Iqbal Hall, along with one or two ladies in Jagannath—in all about thirty-two were killed. About Rajarbagh, I did not know how many policemen were killed…[other than that] there is now peace in Dhaka and that I had no objection in their going and visiting around Dhaka. However I said I had to inform my superiors, which I did and was told by DG ISPR that he will look after this affair of taking the press reporters to town…so I was quite happy. Later, I was told that the press reporters were taken, by whom I do not know, probably he meant by members of ISPR team to the airport, their camera films were exposed and they were sent back to Karachi. But after landing at Karachi, they took a flight for London, came to Calcutta and back again to Dhaka.[26]

Dealing with the media clearly seems to have been a weak area in the Pakistan Army and no coordinated policy appears to have been in place. The result was that exaggerated reports created anti-Pakistani sentiment across the globe.

Such reports reinforced the West's belief that East Pakistan was fighting a 'war of liberation from West Pakistani suppression'. The idea that any country faced with secessionist movements would fight against secession and has a right to do so, was hardly opportune in those days. Sympathies roused by reports like those of Archer Blood and journalists defying deportation, contributed to that. This contributed to force multiplying the adverse Indian propaganda.

The former Soviet Union, siding with India in this affair, made sure that Eastern Europe too would harbour anti-West Pakistan sentiment. China would not take sides in this case and the official US policy would, once again, avoid official comment and indirectly support to West Pakistan as a recourse for West Pakistan's efforts enabling a US–China meeting for President Richard Nixon.

The misinformation plan worked out, as far as the main West Pakistani public was concerned. People in West Pakistan remained more or less unaware of the severity of the situation and were in shock when the country finally broke up. It took many years for West Pakistan and the Pakistan Army to come to terms with the outcome of their actions and carry out an appraisal of mistakes that had been made—a process that remains incomplete to date. In fact, no serious efforts have been made to learn from the crisis.

There is no doubt that overwhelming force was used to break through the numerous barricades and overpower any opposition. It is difficult to search out the truth when the two opposing sides have totally different numbers when it comes to casualties. At the time of the conflict, biased versions were used by both sides to gain public sympathy, which was further complicated by India attempting to portray its own version of events. The truth got lost somewhere in between. The casualties suffered by the Pakistan Army were far higher than reported, while those on the Bengali side were far lower.

Colonel Taj, a major player in Operation Searchlight, also sees it this way:

Later, 18 Punjab was sent to town to clear any pockets remaining and then they had their own operations under the directions of Tiwana, or [the] HQ responsible for Dhaka operation. I must further say that Dhaka remained peaceful and that I personally did not find anything anywhere wrong during the period of military action. I was also the sub-martial law administrator of Dhaka and while some peaceful agitations, once or twice were seen on the roads…no untoward incident in Dhaka was reported to me. Once, I was told that there was some concentration of militants across Dhaka, so we went there, but did not find anybody except peaceful citizens in a mosque, to whom I [I suggested that they] go back to their homes as there was nothing to fear as long as they remained peaceful. The report about militants was a false report, but the troops were sent to ensure there was nobody there and it remained peaceful. Various allegations were made about the operation, the allegation about killings at the university, television and radio stations, were baseless except for what I have mentioned above and nobody else was killed....[27]

Notes

1. Sisson & Rose, pp. 156–7.
2. Qureshi, p. 30.
3. Bass, *The Blood Telegram*, pp. 28–9.
4. Sisson & Rose, pp. 157–8.
5. Interview with Brigadier Mohammad Taj, February 2017, Islamabad.
6. Z.A. Khan, *The Way It Was: Inside the Pakistan Army* (Karachi: Dynavis Pvt. Ltd., 1998), pp. 266–9.
7. Khan, *The Way It Was*, p. 269.
8. Choudhury, p. 186.
9. Hossain, pp. 105–109.
10. Matinuddin, *Tragedy of Errors*, p. 249.
11. Ibid.
12. Interview with Brigadier Mohammad Taj, February 2017, Islamabad.
13. Matinuddin, p. 250.
14. Sarmila Bose, *Dead Reckoning: Memories of the 1971 Bangladesh War* (Karachi: Oxford University Press), p. 52.
15. Interview with Brigadier Mohammad Taj, February 2017, Islamabad.
16. Interview with General Lehrasab.
17. Yasmin Saikia, *Women, War, and the Making of Bangladesh: Remembering 1971* (Durham, NC: Duke University Press, 2011).
18. Matinuddin, p. 225.
19. Ibid., p. 226.
20. Qureshi, p. 33.
21. Raja, p. 82.
22. Bose, *Dead Reckoning*, p. 50.
23. Qureshi, p. 20.
24. *Daily Telegraph*, London, and *Washington Post*, 30 March 1971 as cited in Choudhury, p. 185.
25. Blood, p. 199.
26. Interview with Brigadier Mohammad Taj, February 2017, Islamabad.
27. Ibid.

14

Winning the Battle but Losing the War—I

The Pakistan Army spent April and May 1971, mopping up operations and trying to secure military victory. Having controlled the major cities of Dhaka and Chittagong in the first phase of Operation Searchlight, the army consolidated its central authority in those cities that had cantonments, or where army units or sub-units were physically present. They succeeded in re-establishing control over most of East Pakistan by the end of April 1971, but not before incurring considerable collateral damage among military men and civilians.

Thousands of civilians, some of them armed, gathered to side with the Bengali troops that had revolted and mutinied. The disarming of 3 EB in Rangpur became a bloody affair, with many casualties on both sides. 'Action' in Dinajpur and Saidpur, during the night of 25–26 March, was only partly successful. The disarming in Pabna and Kushtia was botched, resulting in the massacre of many non-Bengalis.

There is evidence that Operation Searchlight was accompanied by severe atrocities against unarmed Hindu civilians who were in no way connected to the Awami League, or the ongoing insurgency. One such example is the attack on Shankharipara, described in Bose's book.[1] Shankhari Bazar was one of the oldest *mohallas* in Old Dhaka. It stretches along a narrow lane (Shankharipara), lined with thin slices of richly decorated brick buildings that had been built mostly during the late Mughal or colonial period. As many as twenty temples dotted the street. It was traditionally home to the Hindu *shankha* (conch shell) business. Bose had visited the location and talked to people who had been there during the night of 25 March, when a police post in the area was attacked and during the next day, when the army entered the *mohalla*.

The survivors report that the army was killing adult men, while leaving women and children unharmed. The number of victims remains uncertain; Anthony Mascarenhas claims in his book[2] that 8,000 people were killed, is inaccurate as there were not that many people living there. There are other reports of army men searching for male Hindus in villages outside Dhaka and executing them. The reason behind the army's hatred of Hindus is documented in the memories of army personnel who served in East Pakistan at that time.

One example is Maj. Gen. Hakeem Arshad Qureshi's book, in which he expresses his opinion that it was because of the Hindus that Bengali Muslims were prevented from identifying with their Muslim heritage and, consequently, with Pakistan. That is why the Hindus, according to him, were the cause of the trouble in East Pakistan.

> On their part, the Hindus (including over five million in East Pakistan), having appreciated the binding force of the Two Nation Theory and understood the terrible ill will against them that was a result of the communal riots which preceded and followed Partition, selected the plank of common language and culture to bring the communities together. This was essential in subverting the Muslim mind and de-linking it from the rich Islamic heritage preserved in Urdu literature.[3]

This is, of course, an easy way to avoid an impartial analysis of the history and situation in East Pakistan and put the blame for secession on the Bengali Hindus. Gary Bass, in his analysis of Archer Blood's documents, notices that even though the Bengali Muslims overwhelmingly supported the Awami League, the West Pakistanis seemed to blame Bengali nationalism and secessionism on the Hindus. Blood later called the excessive killing of Hindus 'criminally insane' and without any military benefit.[4] He seems to have concentrated on gathering incidents of anti-Hindu atrocities, of how the Pakistan Army would move into a village, ask where the Hindus lived and then kill the men among them. It is remarkable though that he said that there was little evidence of the killing of Hindu women and children.[5]

The fighting between the Pakistan Army and rebel groups resulted in the loss of many lives, but most of the killing was not a result of military action. Once the idea of independence took hold among armed Bengalis, their frenzy took over all other considerations. Bengali civilians suspected of helping, or cooperating with the Awami League, or Mukti Bahini, were killed without trial or the collection of proper evidence. Mukti Bahini and armed Bengalis are on record to have butchered Bihari families—all of them civilians.

In the jute factories in Khulna, the civilians carried out the killings. The workers of the Crescent Jute Mill and People's Jute Mill were mostly Bengalis and Biharis. Bengalis in those mills had already been organised under the local leadership of the Awami League, since early March. When the situation became tense after the launch of Operation Searchlight, both groups organised peace committees to patrol the mills and the surrounding areas. But on 28 March, armed rebels arrived, the situation got out of hand and a terrible slaughter took place. The army arrived later to find hundreds of bodies floating in the river; they found a slaughterhouse and instruments of execution. The real number of dead could not be ascertained, but Sarmila Bose thinks it may have been over a thousand. In her interviews with surviving Biharis, it is clear that by killing Bengalis in the army's presence, they were taking revenge for the atrocities committed against them.[6]

In some places, like Joydebpur, Gazipur, and Mymensingh, it was the West Pakistani officers and their families who were the victims. Bose has documented the events based on the descriptions found in the log of Brigadier Karimullah of the Ordnance Factory, in Gazipur. When the Pakistan Army arrived on 29 March, it turned out that the 2 EB stationed at Gazipur had rebelled the day before and the entire battalion was gone, having taken with it all the weapons and ammunition. Almost all the West Pakistani officers, personnel, and their families had been killed. The *Far Eastern Economic Review* reported on 24 April 1971, 'When the EPR mutinied, their first reaction was to wipe out the non-Bengalis in their own ranks. Some 40 per cent of the ten-to-fifteen-thousand strong EPR consisted of West Pakistanis, including most of the officers. One cart-load of bodies was dumped by EPR men one night across the border, near the Indian checkpoint town of Haridaspur.'[7]

The same happened in Mymensingh. Though not a formal cantonment, the EBR and EPR stationed in that town mutinied on 27 March and killed their West Pakistani colleagues, including their families. The atrocities, according to a witness, started after the news of the crackdown in Dhaka reached them. It was reported that thousands gathered outside the cantonment to side with the Bengali troops and hundreds of West Pakistanis were butchered as a result.[8]

Large-scale excesses took place against non-Bengalis—mostly women and children—in isolated areas. Colonel Taj recalls:

Being a temporary Commander of 32 Punjab in Dhaka, I was ordered to go to Rajshahi and control the situation as there was pressure of militants on our units in Rajshahi. We left Dhaka on 8 April, a sea column was under a naval officer with troops of 18 Punjab. I was to go to Nagarbari, but 18 Punjab could not reach on time so we went up to Pabna, where we heard that the Commander Eastern Command, General Tikka had been replaced. We reached Rajshahi on 13 April and I went straight to the university and I was told that militants and East Pakistan Rifles personnel who had defected, plus East Bengal personnel, were present there.

When I went…there was nobody in the university area and the vice-chancellor told me that except for some West Pakistanis and some Biharis, who were literally confined to the barracks, there was no one else and that there were no militants. So he gave me a guide and I went to the barracks where they were staying and with great effort, we convinced them that we belonged to Pakistan Army and had come to rescue them. They said they were hungry and since [the] last two days, the children were without milk and were in bad shape. I arranged food for them and milk for [the] children and I told them to go back to their houses, which they probably did the next day. Rajshahi was under control and I contacted the troops already stationed there and sent them towards Bogra and I told them to go up about 10 miles or so and come back. 25 Punjab happened to be there, so they went up and down and cleared the area... they were out of their bunkers as soon as we reached and made contact with them.[9]

The Times reported on 6 April 1971, 'Thousands of helpless Muslim refugees who settled in Bengal at the time of partition, are reported to have been massacred by angry Bengalis in East Pakistan during the past week. The facts about the massacres were confirmed by Bihari Muslim refugees, who crossed the border into India this week, and by a young British technician who crossed the Indo-Pakistani frontier at Hilli today.'[10]

One of the most dreadful aspects of the conflict was the treatment meted out to East Pakistani women—both, Bengali and Bihari. The atrocities were not limited to the killing of women and children. Rape, sexual abuse, and torture were used as a means of warfare and revenge—by Pakistani soldiers, Bengalis, and Biharis.

In a society where women were viewed as mere objects and the property of their male family members, or husbands, their voices counted for little. This aspect of the 1971 tragedy has received scant attention. One important work which has tried to make up for the void on this topic, is Yasmin Saikia's book, *Women, War and the Making of Bangladesh*, in which she has collected the memories of many Bangladeshi women and given them a voice. The memories of rape, hunger, and dying children, have not been forgotten and there has been no attempt at rehabilitation in either Pakistan or in Bangladesh.

Highlighting the reasons for the violence against women by the different elements in East Pakistan in 1971, Saikia writes:

> Violence was a passionate outburst staged in intervals, as reaction to previous episodes. It happened between and within communities of people who knew each other and lived alongside each other... Violence was also carried out by outsiders—the Pakistan Army and the Indian Army.[11]

Pakistani soldiers committed violence to 'teach Bengalis a lesson' and against Bengali women to dishonour Bengali men, who had dared to fight against the army. The violence by the Bengalis is one of the lesser-known facts of the conflict because, as Saikia explains, 'People in Bangladesh were reluctant to talk about the violence committed by the Mukti Bahini or disparate Bengali groups and individuals.'[12]

Throughout history, in times of war, rape has often been used as a symbol of male domination and a tool to dishonour the enemy. Incidents of rape are usually brushed under the carpet as they tarnish the achievements of war and dishonour those involved.

The severity of the first phase of Operation Searchlight, under General Tikka Khan, who earned the name 'Butcher of Bengal' for his conduct, became evident despite the virtual information blockade in West Pakistan. Despite the brutality, it would be inaccurate to call it genocide.

In April, General Yahya recalled Tikka from Eastern Command. Lt. Gen. Niazi volunteered for the transfer to East Pakistan after Lt. Gen. Bahadur Sher Khan and two more generals refused postings in East Pakistan. General Niazi accepted without realising the risks involved. General Khadim Hussain Raja has recorded the first briefing that took place the day General Niazi took over.

> He [General Niazi] announced that he had assumed command with immediate effect. He gave out some routine instructions for the future, including that all officers were to wear a pistol when in uniform. There was a sprinkling of Bengali officers in the gathering. To our consternation, Niazi became abusive and started raving. Breaking into Urdu, he said: '*Main is haramzadi qaum ki nasal badal doon ga. Yeh mujhe kya samajhtey hain.*' ['They don't know me. I will change the race of this bastard nation.'] He threatened that he would let his soldiers loose on their womenfolk. There was pin-drop silence at these remarks. Officers looked at each other in silence, taken aback by his vulgarity. The meeting dispersed on this unhappy note, with sullen faces. The next morning, we were given sad news. A Bengali officer, Major Mushtaq, who had served under me in Jessore, went into a

bathroom at the Command Headquarters and shot himself in the head. He died instantaneously. A brilliant officer…and his memory will always live with me. It is a pity that he should have been the first casualty of Niazi's words and deeds.'[13]

Once the towns were relatively secure, the reconstruction of the civil administration and the police force began. Security organisations were created to help the army restore peace in East Pakistan and re-establish the administrative writ of the government. However, thanks to its propaganda machine, the federal government was deceived by its own success in quickly overwhelming disparate rebel forces. By late April, the feeling took root in West Pakistan that with the swift military victory, the writ of the government had been re-established. As a result of this, the political and constitutional problems that needed to be discussed urgently, did not get the attention that they should have been given.

Based on this erroneous judgement, the military hierarchy concluded that rushing into a political settlement of the East Pakistan question was unnecessary. Instead, it focused on dramatizing the role of India in the conflict, its physical incursions into East Pakistan, and the oppression of Bengali Muslims by Hindus.[14] Indian involvement was a proven fact even at this early stage by the presence of Pakistani 'prisoners of war' in Agartala jail and the very existence of a POW camp in Panagarh, West Bengal that contained a growing number of Pakistanis in April 1971.[15]

A political settlement was also delayed due to the impression that the Bengali uprising had been successfully extinguished and the government believed that it was in control. Again, for the possibility of avoiding a break-up was wasted. Contrary to numerous historical precedents, the military rulers were on a high and refused to comprehend that the East Bengali crisis was not to be solved militarily. Advisors that suggested a political solution were either sidelined or dismissed.[16]

After mid-April, a semblance of stability returned to the cities of East Pakistan. PIA resumed three flights between Dhaka and Karachi daily and international visitors were allowed into East Pakistan again. But Bengali resistance continued in the countryside and succeeded in disrupting transport and communication lines and riverine traffic between Dhaka, Chittagong, Barisal, and Khulna.[17] In towns, students did not return to schools and universities; shopkeepers did not reopen their businesses; and workers did not return to factories. A boycott of West Pakistani goods was announced through leaflets and spread through word of mouth. In fact, only Dhaka, Chittagong, and some other major towns saw a return to normalcy.

By the beginning of May, the Mukti Bahini had organised itself into a force to be reckoned with, far removed from the ragtag army that saluted General Osmany in Dhaka on 23 March. It started operating in the countryside and small towns. A newspaper called *Purbo Bangla* was issued and leaflets and Bengali radio transmissions from India kept the resistance going. A devastating World Bank report gave a damaging account of the ongoing resistance and insecurity in East Pakistan's countryside to the international public.[18]

When the crackdown had been imminent in March, Mujib had instructed the Awami League leadership to disperse in order to escape arrest. Most of the leadership successfully escaped arrest, went into hiding, and later managed to cross the border into India. During this time, the Indian Border Security Force (BSF) was organising the operations and logistics of the rebels. An exiled government of the Awami League formally took oath at Meherpur, in Kushtia district, on 17 April 1971, with Tajuddin Ahmed becoming the first Prime Minister and Syed Nazrul Islam the Acting President. This was an important step for seceding forces and gave new strength to those Awami League leaders who had by then decided to go their own separate way.

Mujibnagar—the site where the exiled government actually functioned from, was situated in Calcutta. From there, pro-independence propaganda was organised and coordinated, a radio station launched with Indian help and the recruitment of anti-Pakistani volunteers carried out. Reorganised by the Indian Army to become the military arm of the provisional government, the Mukti Bahini was the nucleus of what would become the Bangladesh Army.

Mukti Bahini, translates into 'freedom fighters', a guerrilla resistance movement formed by retired and deserting Bengali personnel of the Pakistan Army, as well retired Bengali civilians ready to join the civil war in East Pakistan against Pakistan's armed forces. Much of the military victory of the East Bengalis over the Pakistan Army is credited to this paramilitary force and a whole range of folklore has been created around it, not all of which is true. Its members may have been enthusiastic, committed and offered great deal of sacrifices, but they were no match to the Pakistan Army in the short-term. If the war had gone on longer than a year, they would have had the time to evolve into a major player.

In places as far away as East Germany, colourful reports of Mukti Bahini, a liberation force from a faraway place, caused much excitement among the youth. Songs admiring its bravery were sung in Bengali by young East Germans, who, for the most part, did not have a proper grasp of what was going on in East Pakistan, or even about the location of Pakistan and the polarisation created by the Cold War.

Formally, the Mukti Bahini was founded on 17 April 1971, in Mujibnagar, India, which consisted of a number of buildings—including the former offices of the deputy high commissioner of Pakistan—that had been set aside by the Indian government for the use of the East Bengali rebels. Army Colonel (retd.) M.A.G. Osmany headed the Mukti Bahini as its first Commander-in-Chief. Osmany had retired in February 1967 as Deputy Director, Military Operations (DDMO), GHQ Rawalpindi. He had been DDMO for several years and should have been promoted to the rank of brigadier, but his constant campaign for more East Bengal regiments did not go down well with the GHQ hierarchy. He never publicly displayed his frustration about being passed over, but it may have provoked his later engagement with the rebel forces that chose him unanimously as their leader, with the rank of a full general. Even before the formal foundation of the Mukti Bahini, he had raised the roots of a paramilitary force of the Awami League in Dhaka.

My relationship with Osmany was a special one. From the early days, in 2 EB, we were quite close and he was considered to be my godfather. In early April, I was in Bhairab Bazar with my home unit, Bravo Company 2 EB, after having utilised my ten days 'joining time' in a visit to my old unit. I found myself caught in the middle of the ongoing crisis, with old colleagues happy to see me while others wanting to harm me. I was lured intelligently towards the Indian border, with a message that Colonel Osmany was calling me for a meeting. When I learned that I had to cross the border into India, I refused and my men refused to go without me. Arrested by Major Khaled Mosharraf (later major general) I was sent to Agartala jail and on 25 April, transferred to Panagarh, the first POW camp on Indian soil, set up seven months before the war had officially started. In Agartala jail, I was attempting to plan an escape, but before I could come up with any definite ideas, I was transferred to Panagarh, where I spent the next three months until an escape plan was ready for execution. In my memory, Osmany remains connected to the fateful events of 5 April 1971 that changed the course of my life so fundamentally.

That Colonel Osmany and Mujib had grown closer, was evident in the fact that the former was in charge of the paramilitary parade that took place on 23 March 1971, in Dhaka—two days before the start of Operation Searchlight. It consisted of young nationalist Bengalis, committed to the cause of the Awami League and ready to sacrifice their lives while fighting the Pakistanis. They were organised into units of 500 each and a women's wing was raised as well. The military demonstration organised on 23 March, was meant as a warning to the Pakistan Army and government, that any military operation would not find the Bengalis unprepared. Despite such occasional preparations for self-defence, there was no centrally organised resistance within the Awami League, or the Bengali population, before March. The actions were whimsical and confined to individual cells that were not in coordination with each other.

From mid-April onwards, the leadership of the Mukti Bahini and its training centres were shifted to the Indian side of the border, though some of the rebels continued to operate undercover in East Pakistan, with the help of the Bengali civilian population. It was impossible for the army to control a border that stretched over 4,000 kilometres and almost surrounded East Pakistan. This resulted in a constant cross-border movement by the Mukti Bahinis, as they were known to the Pakistan Army.

On 4 April 1971, twelve pro-Pakistan Bengali political leaders, including Nurul Amin, Ghulam Azam, and Khwaja Khairuddin, met Tikka Khan and assured him of their cooperation in opposing the rebellion and reviving the writ of the government, while pleading for a political settlement of the crisis. During the meeting, ways and means of solving the administrative problems were discussed, to make everyday life of the citizens easier. After this meeting, the pro-Pakistan political leadership proposed the formation of a Citizen's Peace Committee, consisting of 140 members, to restore peace in different areas of the province. For that purpose, Khwaja Khairuddin called a meeting in Dhaka on 9 April 1971, which then led to the formation of Nagorik [Citizen's] Shanti [Peace] Committee.[19] The peace committees seem also to have recruited paramilitary *razakars* in some cases. The first recruits included ninety-six Jamaat-e-Islami (JI) party workers, who started training in an Ansar camp at Shahjahan Ali Road, in Khulna. Later, the Citizen's Peace Committee renamed itself the East Pakistan Central Peace Committee. A working committee was formed, consisting of twenty-one members. It appointed one or more liaison officers for the various police stations in Dhaka. On 17 April 1971, the members of the committee apprised Tikka Khan of the progress made by them in restoring confidence among the citizens. Representatives of the committee were deputed to the district and divisional headquarters across East Pakistan. According to the historian Azadur Rahman Chandan, the committee was the first organisation to be set up by local residents who collaborated with Pakistan. Its members were drawn from the political opposition— the Muslim League and the JI—who had lost the election, but nevertheless thought an independent Bangladesh was against Islam and used the opportunity to make political gains in the absence of the Awami League.[20]

By the end of April, the Pakistan Army had re-established the writ of the government, at least in the cities, and rebel forces withdrew to the rural areas, or to India. By that time, Indira Gandhi had given the Indian Army full responsibility for equipping the Bengali irregulars and training them for guerrilla warfare. With Bengali deserters from the Pakistan Army joining them in India, this training was imparted to them as well. A total strength of 70,000 Bengali dissidents, excluding the police, was available to the Indians. Out of this force, it did not take long for them to organise eight trained and fully equipped battalions.[21] Dozens of trainings took place in camps established on the Indian side of the border, often within view of the East Pakistani side. The Indian Army set up six training centres and unleashed an unlimited cash flow to induce young Bengali students and others from East Pakistan, to join and be trained. All of these six training centres, which encircled East Pakistan on the Indian side of the border, came under the command of brigadiers of the Indian Army. Training was put under the command of an Indian general; it took about three weeks for the recruits to finish the course. Over 5,000 men were trained in these camps within three months. About 600 to 800 Bengali officers are reported to have been trained at regular Indian Army institutions, such as the military academy in Dehra Dun. A naval wing of the Mukti Bahini was also trained in underwater operations and in August 1971, 300 of them were sent for underwater training to Cochin.

With the tacit help of India, the Mukti Bahini was reorganised into eleven sectors and conducted a massive guerrilla war against the Pakistan Army. Soon, another 70,000 young Bengali students, inspired by Bengali patriotism, joined these camps for a three-week crash course in the use of mortars, mines, machine-guns, and PRC 25 wireless sets for communication. A select force of 600 was formed into the naval wing of Mukti Bahini, trained in a camp in Plassey, West Bengal, by Indian special forces as 'frogmen', to plant explosives under ships and take-over boats, barrages, and launches plying in the rivers of East Pakistan.[22] On the ground, the reality of the Mukti Bahinis was very different. G.J. Bass, describes in his book the actions of the organisation as that of an ill-trained and ill-equipped force that would be sent in civilian clothes into East Pakistan, to attack the military, or blow up bridges and roads. The youngest of them were hardly more than ten or twelve years old—today, they would be referred to as child soldiers.

Shahudul Haque, Archer Blood's friend recalls:

'I was very disappointed at how scratchy it all was…. 'No money, no ammunition, no equipment, only dedicated soldiers to teach us.' There was nothing to eat but jackfruit… Sleeping on bamboo platforms, the guerrillas were nearly washed away by monsoon storms. After a few weeks, he got seriously ill, bleeding in his stool. With no doctors or medicine, he could only try the home remedy of coconut water, to no avail.

Another rebel remembered that…[c]onditions were still miserable, with the fighters in dire need of mosquito repellent, waterproof sheets against the pounding monsoon rains, and antivenom serum for snake bites. At best, they got one cake of soap a month.'[23]

For the most part, 2 EB, 4 EB, and 8 EB had remained intact during those fateful days. Most of 1 EB and 3 EB had also gotten away, but without their equipment and only with light arms. From this nucleus, other forces were revamped in September 1971, such as the K-Force, which took its letter from Khaled Mosharraf's name and consisted mainly of 4 EB. Consisting mostly of 8 EB, the Z-Force, meanwhile, took its name from its commander, Major Ziaur Rahman, and the S-Force (2 EB), as the nucleus, had Major Safiullah in command. Safiullah recalls, 'S-Force came into being with its headquarters established at Fatikchhara, on 1 October. 2 and 11 EB regiments were the only two battalions, initially.'[24]

According to General Matinuddin, the most colourful troops were those of Abdul Kader Siddique, who raised his own force and named it Kader Bahini.[25] A student from Tangail and an ardent follower of Mujib, Siddique claimed to have 5,000 under arms and controlled the terrain between Tangail and Dhaka—the area where, on 16 December, the Indian troops landed unopposed, which, in view of these facts, seems to explain the quick advance and subsequent victory of the Indian Army.

During the early phase of Operation Searchlight, in March and April, the Mukti Bahini operated close to the Indian border from the Indian side, supported initially till mid-April by BSF and then by the Indian Army. During the second phase, from May to July, it was bold enough to go back into East Pakistan in civilian clothes and with the help and support of locals, blew up bridges, blocked roads, and ambushed convoys of the Pakistan Army. The Mukti Bahinis penetrated deep into East Pakistan to carry out their subversion with the support of Indian soldiers disguised as Mukti Bahinis. Together they carried out ambushes of Pakistan Army units, destruction of bridges, and other infrastructure, thus disrupting communication lines. The third phase of the operation began in August. From this point onwards, Mukti Bahinis were supported by the Indian artillery fire from across the border and able to hold on to certain areas within East Pakistan, from where they were able to launch further attacks.[26]

The stupidity and egotistical behaviour of our military and political leaders in 1971, gave India a long-awaited opportunity to blatantly do what they had been attempting surreptitiously for years, namely to dismember the finest experiment of its kind in nationhood. Officers and men of EB, EPR, and the police, along with thousands of volunteers, crossed over to India and were reorganised and sent back—armed and trained. As a result of this, half of the country was lost, the process of nation-building interrupted and the army weakened.

Given the civil disobedience and military superiority of the organised resistance, Operation Searchlight was necessary as a pre-emptive strike, but it had been applied too late. Nevertheless, the Pakistan Army fought heroic battles in many places. That this outstanding military success in the battle would end in a defeat and unmitigated political disaster was inevitable. Has anyone really been held accountable for it?

Notes

1. Bose, *Dead Reckoning*, pp. 73–6.
2. Anthony Mascarenhas, *Bangladesh: A Legacy of Blood* (London: Hodder and Stoughton, 1986).
3. Qureshi, p. 29.
4. Bass, pp. 81–2.
5. Ibid., p. 83.
6. Bose, pp. 80–2.
7. White Paper on the Crisis in East Pakistan, Government of Pakistan, 5 August 1971, selected chapters, p. 18.
8. Ibid., p. 83.
9. Interview with Brigadier Mohammad Taj, February 2017, Islamabad.
10. White Paper on the Crisis in East Pakistan, Government of Pakistan, 5 August 1971, selected chapters, p. 17.
11. Yasmin Saikia, *Women, War, and the Making of Bangladesh: Remembering 1971* (Durham, NC: Duke University Press, 2011), pp. 56–7.
12. Ibid., p. 59.
13. Raja, pp. 97–8.
14. Sisson & Rose, p. 160.
15. Ikram Sehgal, *Escape from Oblivion: The Story of a Pakistani Prisoner of War in India* (Karachi: Oxford University Press, 2012).
16. Ibid., p. 166.
17. Blood, *The Cruel Birth of Bangladesh*, p. 292.
18. 'Excerpts from World Bank Group's Report on East Pakistan,' 13 July 1971, https://www.nytimes.com/1971/07/13/archives/excerpts-from-world-bank-groups-report-on-east-pakistan.html.
19. *The Daily Observer*, 'Wartime Crime Charges against Ghulam Azam,' 25 October 2014, http://www.observerbd.com/2014/10/25/50744.php.
20. Source: http://www.kalantor.net/wp-content/uploads/2013/10/Ekattorer-Ghatok-O-Dalalra-2nd-edition.pdf.

21. Matinuddin, *Tragedy of Errors*, p. 230.
22. Asif Haroon Raja, 'From East Pakistan to Bangladesh,' 16 December 2018, http://pakistanthinktank.org/tag/east-pakistan.
23. Bass, p. 187.
24. Maj. Gen. K.M. Safiullah, *Bangladesh at War*, 2nd ed. (Dhaka: Academic Publishers, 1995), p. 211.
25. Matinuddin, p. 234.
26. Junaid Ahmed, *Creation of Bangladesh: Myths Exploded* (Karachi: AJA Publishers, 2016), p. 200.

15

Accusations of Rape and Genocide

Undoubtedly, the civil war that broke out in 1971 and lasted for almost nine months, took many unaccountable lives, the number of which has never been satisfactorily established. Gruesome atrocities were committed and the portrayal of the extent of the damage is an unrealistic one, as is the accusation that it was solely the doing of the Pakistan Army.

The twentieth century has seen an extraordinary frequency in wars and violence committed during those wars, among them the two World Wars and the anticolonial wars of Korea and Vietnam. In the subcontinent, independence came at a high cost. Amid the atrocities, millions were killed and 17 million were displaced.

The global rise in conflict can be attributed to the development of sophisticated weaponry, including the nuclear bomb in the twentieth century and drones in the twenty-first. The urge of western powers to control large swathes of the world, their markets and natural resources, has led to frequent confrontations. Nationalism and the creation of nation states only added to the bloodshed and justified it in the name of defence.

The breakup of Pakistan had a lasting impact, both politically and socially, on two separate states that emerged from it. Until today, no real rehabilitation has taken place between Pakistan and Bangladesh and that is why Pakistan alone finds itself accused by Bangladesh and India, of having caused all the death and destruction in the war. So far, Pakistani academia, politicians, and the armed forces have little to counter this accusation effectively.

One of the main accusations made against the Pakistan Army by Bangladesh and India is that of systematic genocide—the killing of three million Bengalis and rape of two hundred thousand women, in the nine-month-long war. While there is no doubt that that war had taken a heavy toll on the East Pakistani population, the way these events have been depicted in the nationalist histories of Bangladesh, as well as in much of Indian history, is exaggerated and in need of further investigation and research. It is purely for political reasons, rather than of the quest for truth, that the Bangladeshi and Indian governments have been talking about the number of civilian victims of the war. Reports in the international media in 1971 relied largely on secondary sources.

After the end of the war, only limited efforts have been taken to ascertain the truth of the matter. It seems that Pakistan and its army have not yet recovered from the shock of losing half the country. As early as July 1972, the Hamoodur Rehman Commission, under Chief Justice Hamoodur Rehman, was constituted, to prepare a full and complete account of the circumstances surrounding the atrocities and 1971 war, including the circumstances under which the Commander, Eastern Command surrendered and the members of the armed forces of Pakistan under his command laid down their arms. The findings of the commission, collected in the report, were considered to be too upsetting and damaging for the already diminished image of the army, so the government decided to keep it secret. It took until 2000 for its contents to first leak out to the press and then finally be published—at least in part. Today, this report should be one of the sources in the investigation of war atrocities in East Pakistan.

However, research and critical analyses on the events of 1971 started about twenty years ago. Since then, and especially in connection with the fortieth anniversary of the 1971 war, many army officers and civilians—most of them politicians involved in the events on both sides—have published their memoirs and a new and more balanced picture is emerging. The forty odd years that have passed have been long enough to overcome the immediate horrors of what had happened and to gain perspective with the benefit of hindsight.

Despite a flood of publications in the field of academia, only three works stand out, as they challenge the Bangladeshi and Indian version of what happened in 1971.

1. M. Abdul Mu'min Chowdhury, *Behind the Myth of Three Million* (London: Hamidur Rahman, Al-Hilal Publishers Ltd, 1996).[1]
2. Sarmila Bose, *Dead Reckoning: Memories of the 1971 Bangladesh War* (London: C. Hurst & Co., 2011).
3. Yasmin Saikia, *Women, War, and the Making of Bangladesh: Remembering 1971* (Durham, NC: Duke University Press, 2011).

M. Abdul Mu'min Chowdhury, a native of Sylhet, a Bengali nationalist, was a teacher at Dhaka University and actively participated in the separatist cause. He left Bangladesh in 1973 for London and spoke out to tell his story of what went on during that war. He cites an extensive range of sources to show that what the Pakistani Army was carrying out in East Pakistan could not have produced the numbers of dead that are officially being claimed. He quotes sources to explain how this number was created and what political purpose it served.[2]

Sarmila Bose,[3] was born in Boston, Massachusetts, but grew up in Calcutta (now Kolkata), where she witnessed as a teenager the events of 1971. Later, she worked first as a journalist in India and is today an academic and senior research associate at the Centre for International Studies, in Oxford University. Her book, *Dead Reckoning* and an article titled, 'Losing the Victims,'[4] both attempt to check up on the veracity of the accusation of genocide and rape. Bose carried out an extensive research in Bangladesh and Pakistan and interviewed witnesses. She explains her methodology as follows, 'While studying the application of statistics in public policy at Harvard, I learned that the real challenge was to apply the neat models of theory in the real world of imperfect, incomplete or unreliable information.'[5]

Yasmin Saikia is the Hardt-Nickachos Chair in Peace Studies at the Centre for the Study of Religion and Conflict and a professor of history in the School of Historical, Philosophical and Religious Studies, in Arizona State University. Her book is based on interviews with people on both sides of conflict. She focuses on gender violence in the 1971 war and collected the stories of both the rape victims and the perpetrators. Saikia interviews 123 retired officers of the Pakistan Army, many of whom had realised that their participation in the war had resulted in 'a breakdown of the human condition'[6] and that the violence that they thought had been their 'duty' had resulted in their loss of humanity or '*insaniat*', as she calls it. The examples she narrates show that 'killing and violence are not natural impulses but they were learned, taught, and cultivated as duty within the institution of the army.'[7] She illustrates that West Pakistani soldiers were not the monsters they are made out to be, but soldiers who, in the middle of a civil war for which they were ill prepared, found it difficult to uphold humanitarian values.

Regrettably, there has been no attempt in Pakistani scholarship to carry out such a study. In a politically polarised academic world, the effort to revisit the events of 1971 and give them a different treatment has met with a controversial response. Bose has been criticised by various—mostly Indian and Bangladeshi—historians and academics for numerous inaccuracies and over-reliance on Pakistani military and government sources. They have accused her of a flawed and biased methodology, historical revisionism, and of downplaying war crimes. However, there are other evaluations, like the one in *The Guardian* that welcomed the book as a 'long overdue study of Bangladesh's war of independence' and suggests that Bose's work 'should provoke both fresh research and fresh thinking about a fateful turning point in the history of the subcontinent.'[8] In the ongoing debate, some quarters raise the question of why numbers matter so much when even a single civilian killed, or woman raped, is inexcusable. The answer to this quite simply is that numbers matter because they alone can determine whether the war was a genocide or not.

In contrast to Bose, Saikia's book was well received, has won numerous awards, and been the subject of an international speaking tour by the author, despite the fact that it adopts a methodology similar to that of Bose—of using the testimonies of both Bengalis and Pakistanis. Her lecture on the book was introduced at the University of Waterloo, in Canada, as follows:

> The "hidden" narratives of men and women of the 1971 war offer an entry point to reflect on the dilemma of sexual violence and memory in Bangladesh and Pakistan today. Men's personal recollections of the war experiences have not been entered into the official records of history and women's experiences of sexual violence being relegated to the margins as "lies" and/or "shame", discourage public engagement.[9]

Let us start by examining the allegation that the Pakistan Army committed genocide in East Pakistan by killing about three million Bengalis during the war. While there is no doubt, mass killings did take place in 1971 in East Pakistan and not all the bodies have yet been recovered, the number of the killed could not have been even close to three million. This number seems to have been mentioned by Sheikh Mujibur Rahman in a speech that he gave on arrival in Dhaka, from jail in Pakistan, in January 1972. Soon after the speech, several sources started contradicting this number as impossible. In a report published in *The Guardian*, in 1972, William Drummond wrote:

> This figure of three million deaths, which the Sheikh has repeated several times since he returned to Bangladesh in early January, has been carried uncritically in sections of the world press. Through repetition of such a claim gains a validity of its own and gradually evolves from assertion to fact needing no attribution. My judgment, based on numerous trips around Bangladesh and extensive discussions with many people at the village level as well as in the government, is that the three million deaths figure is an exaggeration so gross as to be absurd.[10]

Moreover, as Drummond pointed out in 1972, that bodily remains cannot clarify, unless scientifically demonstrated, whether the person was Bengali or non-Bengali, combatant or non-combatant, whether the death took place in 1971, and whether it was caused by the Pakistan Army.

M. Abdul Mu'min Chowdhury, in his book, quotes Oriana Fallaci's interview with Mujib in 1972, in which it was clear that he was aware of the falsity of the number, but for political reasons, insisted on sticking to it.[11] He asserts that in 1993, Colonel Akbar Hussain (a decorated 'Mukti Juddha' and a cabinet minister under both General Ziaur Rahman and Khaleda Zia) challenged the figure of three million in the National Assembly of Bangladesh.[12]

Two Indian generals, Field Marshal Sam Manekshaw and Lt. Gen. Jagjit Singh Aurora, the Commander-in-Chief of the Eastern Command of the Indian Army during the war of 1971, rejected the three million figure. Aurora, in a widely circulated video interview, said that 'All of us knew' that the Pakistan Army had brutally killed 'about a million people' and that Mujib, who 'was more an agitator and less an administrator', decided to 'make it more brutish', by saying that the Pakistan Army had killed three million Bengalis. He pointed out that Mujib's figure was 'absolutely impossible', because the Pakistan Army had 'simultaneously fought within the country and at the borders'.[13]

Even within Mujib's circle, there were doubts about the number. Reporting from the Noakhali district in March 1990, Abdul Muhaimin, a long-time friend of Mujib, and an Awami League member of the constituent assembly said:

As Member of the Constituent Assembly, I was entrusted with the responsibility of finding out the casualty figure for the whole of Noakhali district. After contacting different police stations and unions, the figure I had was less than seven thousand. Even after adding up the number of *razakars* killed, the total did not exceed seven-and-a-half thousand. At that time, Bangladesh had 19 districts. All these districts were not equally affected by the war and Noakhali was among the districts which had seen severe fighting. If the figure obtained from Noakhali was seen as the mean average for the rest of the districts, even then the total killed would not exceed more than one hundred [and] twenty-five thousand [125,000].[14]

Nevertheless, the three million figure has been repeated over and over again in academic and political circles. The reason for this, as explained by Abdul Mu'min Chowdhury, was, 'Recalling this "heinous" Pakistani crime with suave moral indignation was made into a national ritual. Not only the beaten Pakistan Army, but also [a] subverted Pakistan came to be portrayed as inherently evil and her dismemberment a triumph of civilized values over barbarism.'[15]

Such propaganda suited India, who had also been a major player in the events of 1971 and had believed that the creation of Pakistan was a terrible mistake—a fact only reinforced by the breakup of the country. India did all it could to help break Pakistan and pin the blame on its army. For instance, *The Times* reported on 1 December 1971, that 'There is substantial evidence to prove that, if not all, at least a major portion of Mukti Bahini consisted of Indian soldiers'. Former Indian premier, Morarji Desai, in an interview to Oriana Fallaci said that thousands of Indian regular soldiers disguised as Mukti Bahini were dispatched to East Pakistan from April to December 1971 about 5000 of them died.[16]

Putting all the blame for killings on the Pakistan Army was also a convenient instrument to divert attention from the atrocities committed by both the armed and civilian forces belonging to the Awami League, against those Bengalis that supported a united Pakistan and the ethnic minority of Biharis.

CHECKING THE NUMBERS

Mujib was aware that his claims lacked credibility. In fact, he did attempt to prove the validity of the figure he had cited, by instituting in January 1972, an inquiry committee to this end. Based on the information collected from Awami League members in different districts, the committee would calculate the number of deaths and submit its report by April 1972. However, the report submitted in April was unable to prove the exaggerated numbers and for this very reason, was never published. Abdul Mu'min Chowdhury mentions that a draft of the report that had leaked out showed an overall casualty figure of 56,743. He adds, 'When a copy of this draft report was shown to the prime minister, he lost his temper and threw it on the floor, saying in angry voice "I have declared three million dead, and your report could not come up with three score thousand! What report you have prepared? Keep your report to yourself. What I have said once shall prevail".'[17]

There is yet another source of information on the possible number of victims. In January 1972, Mujib announced a compensation scheme for the families of those who had been killed at the hands of the Pakistan Army and its collaborators. Under the scheme, every victim's family was promised two thousand Bangladeshi Taka as compensation. William Drummond wrote:

> According to Abdul Muhaimin, the Ministry of Finance, [of the] Government of Bangladesh, had informed him that only 72,000 claims were received. Of them, relatives of 50,000 victims had been awarded the declared sum of money. There had been many bogus claims, even some from the *razakars*, within those 72,000 applications.[18]

Even if we consider that some undeserving individuals may have been compensated and that some families had lost more than one member, the estimated number of people killed would never come close to even half a million—and it would include all killings, including those by the *razakars*, Indians, and the Awami League itself.

Sisson and Rose have also raised doubts over the number of people killed. While their research, carried out in the 1970s, focuses more on the international political implications of the events, they nevertheless express their critique:

India set the number of Pakistani atrocities at three million, and this is still the figure usually cited. We interviewed two Indian officials who had held responsible positions on the issue of Bangladesh in 1971. When questioned about the actual number of deaths in Bangladesh in 1971 attributable to the civil war, one replied "about 300,000." Then, when he received a disapproving glance from his colleague, he changed this to "300,000 to 500,000". …it is still impossible to get anything like reliable estimates as to (1) how many of these were "liberation fighters" killed in combat, (2) how many were Bihari Muslims and supporters of Pakistan killed by Bengali Muslims, and (3) how many were killed by Pakistani, Indian, or Mukti Bahini fire and bombing during the hostilities. One thing is clear—the atrocities did not go just one way, though Bengali Muslims and Hindus were certainly the main victims.[19]

Bose, meanwhile, deduces from this that at that time, no reliable accounting had been done and the officials were quoting numbers off the top of their heads, trying to keep them as high as possible, without being incredible.[20] To this day, there has been no effort by the Bangladeshi government to shed light on the matter. Instead, old numbers are recycled. Official institutions have not attempted to open up the mass graves mentioned in the media, to determine the number, or ethnicity, of the dead and the circumstances in which they were killed.

One such story that lacks ample evidence is the killing of Bengali intellectuals by the Pakistan Army in Dhaka, in December 1971. Bose reports that until today, Maj. Gen. Rao Farman Ali is held responsible for those killings, based on the evidence of some lists containing the names of the killed that are written in his handwriting. The reason behind these killings, it is alleged, was the intention to cripple the academia of the new country. Farman Ali and others were questioned about this by the Hamoodur Rehman Commission and denied the charge. In any case, a list written in General Farman's handwriting is a weak piece of evidence to substantiate the accusation that he ordered the executions.

Based on Bose's interviews with the families of the executed intellectuals, she established that all victims had been picked up from their homes by armed Al-Badr youths. Al-Badr, a pro-Pakistan group of Bengalis and Biharis, had been created by the Pakistan Army and it may very well have been the case that this organisation started acting on its own.[21] Mu'min Chowdhury cites the case of Zahir Raihan, a Bengali Marxist said to have been disillusioned with the Bangladeshi political leadership. Raihan did not believe that the intellectuals were murdered at the behest of the Pakistan Army (his elder brother, Shahidullah Kaiser, was among the victims). He is reported to have been in possession of incriminating photographs of questionable activities being conducted by the Awami League leaders in India. While gathering information about the December killings, he was kidnapped in Dhaka in broad daylight and was never seen again. There is no doubt, according to Chowdhury, that he was killed by either those who were at risk of being exposed, or did not want the truth behind the killings to be revealed.[22]

THE GENOCIDE CLAIM

Genocide is defined as the systematic elimination of all, or a significant part of a racial, ethnic, religious, cultural, or national group. The word had been coined in connection with the mass killings of Jews during the Second World War, in Nazi Germany. In 1946, the first session of the UN General Assembly adopted a resolution affirming that genocide was a crime under international law, but did not provide a legal definition of it. In 1948, it adopted the 'Convention on the Prevention and Punishment of the Crime of Genocide,' which defined the crime for the first time. Article 2 of the convention defines genocide as 'Acts committed with intent to destroy, in whole or in part, a national, ethnical, racial or religious group, as such.' William Rubinstein argues that the origin of twentieth century genocide can be traced to the collapse of the elite structure and normal modes of government in parts of Europe following the First World War.[23]

Later on, many more killings have been declared as genocides in retrospect, including the killing of Armenians in the Ottoman Empire, in 1915—a judgment that is heavily disputed. The Government of Bangladesh found it helpful to label all the killings during their war of independence (or secession), collectively, as genocide, holding the Pakistan Army responsible and absolving the Awami League and Mukti Bahini of any wrongdoing.

Bose analyses the problems that arise if the killings of 1971 are labelled genocide on the part of the army. She draws attention to the fact that Bengalis had never been targeted by the Pakistan Army as an ethic group, because many were firmly in favour of a united Pakistan, even if they may have been critical of certain policies of the central government and felt alienated by the treatment East Pakistan was receiving at the hands of West Pakistan. The army was fighting those Bengalis and others—in the shape of Awami League—who were trying to break away from Pakistan or were perceived to be doing so. No state in the world would submit to secessionist movements and demands without trying first to tackle them politically and then militarily. Therefore, Bengalis were not the target in 1971.

> As the instances in this study show, the Pakistan Army was clearly not killing all Bengalis, even in the worst instances of massacres such as those at Thanapara, Chuknagar and Boroitola. There appears to have been a pattern of targeting adult men while sparing women and children, starting with the military action in Dhaka University on 25–26 March through the duration of the conflict.[24]

Therefore, although the army did commit political killings while fighting a secessionist movement, it was by no means aiming to wipe out the entire Bengali community. The 'liberation literature' of Bangladesh repeats the accusation of genocide and by using terms like 'holocaust', draws parallels with the killings in Nazi Germany during the Second World War. This, again, is misleading. The killing of Jews in Germany was grounded in a racist theory and is, therefore, of an entirely different scale and dimension. It is sheer callousness to use such comparisons. To illustrate the impossibility of the genocide claim, Bose refers to another comparison. When the Pakistan Army came for Mujib on the night of 25–26 March 1971, it arrested and imprisoned him. When the Bangladesh Army came for him on 15 August 1975, they brutally killed him and his extended family.[25] In the face of the facts, the accusation of genocide is unfounded and should be repudiated politically.

The Dimension of Sexual Violence Against Women in 1971

Rape is often used in ethnic conflicts as a way for attackers to perpetuate their social control and redraw ethnic boundaries. Women are seen as the reproducers and caretakers of the community. In honour-based societies, women are the custodians of a family's honour and especially that of their male members. Therefore, if one group wants to control, defile and subdue another, it is often done by impregnating women of the other community. Sexual violence is also used to destabilise communities, reduce their self-esteem and sow the seeds of terror among its members. The Human Rights Commission, Amnesty International, and Médecins Sans Frontières/ Doctors Without Borders, have collected ample evidence for rape and sexual abuse of women in multiple conflict zones all over the world. From conflicts in Bosnia and Herzegovina, Peru, and Rwanda, girls and women have been singled out for rape, imprisonment, torture, and execution. Rape, identified by psychologists as the most intrusive of traumatic events, has been documented in many armed conflicts, including those in Cambodia, Cyprus, Haiti, Liberia, Somalia, and Uganda.

While the sexual abuse of women has a long history, it is only in the twentieth century that warring parties have used it systematically as a weapon. From Japanese rapes during the 1937 occupation of Nanking, to the rapes by US soldiers in Vietnam and Iraqi prisons, to systematic rapes during the Serbian war against Bosnian Muslims, the past century offers endless examples. International organisations have drawn attention of the world community to this development but it took the UNSC until 2008 to adopt UNSC Resolution 1820, which makes sexual abuse a punishable offence. The effectiveness of this UN resolution in reducing sexual violence and bringing its perpetrators to book remains to be seen.

Saikia argues in her book about women and war, that the idea of '*insaniyat*', or humanity, which has been ingrained in South Asian ethics through the Sufi/Bhakti traditions, was undermined in various wars, including those, for instance, in Afghanistan. It can be observed that there is an ongoing trend towards a higher level of violence in the post-conflict zones as well as in the societies of the aggressor army. We must take into account the anxieties of Germany, the UK, US, and Russia, who are all afraid of the impact that repatriated soldiers and irregulars (jihadis) would have on their societies at home. And we have the experience of our own society, in Pakistan, that has suffered immensely from the rising violence brought in by jihadis returning from Kashmir and Afghanistan.

The number of women believed to have been raped or sexually abused in 1971 by the Pakistan Army, is roughly between 200,000 to 400,000. Again, as in the case of the three million people believed to have been killed, there is no doubt that rape and sexual abuse did take place during the war of 1971, but here too it seems that the numbers have been grossly exaggerated for political reasons. Mu'min Chowdhury refers to a Bangladeshi publication by Abul Hasanat, which cites the evidence of an unnamed doctor from Australia, who had come on the invitation of the Bangladeshi government, to administer abortions to the victims of rape in 1972. The surgeon, who had purportedly spent six weeks in Dhaka, allegedly supported the number of 200,000 pregnancies that occurred as a result of about 400,000 rapes, and claimed that 'Between 150,000 and 170,000 of the 200,000 who fell pregnant, were aborted in highly undesirable but unavoidable conditions before we even knew the problem existed.'[26]

For an army of 34,000 men to rape on this scale in eight or nine months (while fighting an insurgency and an invasion by India), it would have meant that each would-be-perpetrator would have had to commit rape at an incredible rate.

> ...the Hamoodur Rehman Commission, set up by the civilian government of Pakistan after the war and headed by a Bengali judge, was dismissive of the Bangladeshi claims, stating: 'According to the Bangladesh authorities, the Pakistan Army was responsible for killing three million Bengalis and raping 200,000 East Pakistani women. It does not need any elaborate argument to see that these figures are obviously highly exaggerated. So much damage could not have been caused by the entire strength of the Pakistan Army then stationed in East Pakistan, even if it had nothing else to do. In fact, however, the army in East Pakistan was constantly engaged in fighting the Mukti Bahini, the Indian infiltrators, and later, the Indian army. It had also the task of running the civil administration, maintaining communications, and feeding 70 million people of East Pakistan. It is, therefore, clear that the figures mentioned by the Dacca authorities are altogether fantastic and fanciful.'
>
> On the rape allegations, the commission added, 'The falsity of Sheikh Mujibur Rahman's repeated allegation that the Pakistani troops had raped 2,00,000 Bengali girls in 1971 was borne out when the abortion team he had commissioned from Britain in early 1972 found that its workload involved the termination of only a hundred or more pregnancies'.[27]

This has been ascertained by recent inquiries into the matter of rape. There is no proof that rape was, at any point, a systematic policy in the Pakistan Army. On the contrary, Bose argues that Bangladeshi participants and eyewitnesses of 1971 described battles, raids, massacres, and executions, but told her that women were not harmed by the army in these events except by chance, in crossfire. The pattern that emerged was that the army targeted adult males while sparing women and children.[28] Rape and sexual abuse may have been a tactic adopted by non-military armed groups like the *razakars*, consisting of pro-Pakistan Bengalis and Biharis and of armed groups of the Awami League and Mukti Bahini.

Maj. Gen. A.O. Mitha, a senior Pakistani General present in East Pakistan in March and April 1971, wrote that during a visit to the military hospital in Chittagong,

> As I was walking down the ward, a Bengali officer who was wounded and under guard called out to me. I stopped and went to him, and he said that all he wanted to tell me was that he and his men had stripped women from West Pakistan, and after raping them, had made them dance in the nude; having done this, he was quite happy to die. I made no reply and walked on....[29]

After analysing all of her interviews, Bose expresses severe doubts over the credibility of the rape claims. One argument was that an illiterate woman was made to sign a report of rape that she was unable to read; other narratives included the possibility that women had consensual sex with men for gratification or without it.

During her year-long research in Bangladesh, Saikia recorded the scarcity, inaccessibility, and haphazard method of evidence collection on the subject of female experience during the war. It led her to the conclusion that to this day,

> ...women's experiences could not be integrated within the national story. There was no effort in the halls of history-making institutions to move beyond an established position of casual indifference to these women. The scattered archive contributed in creating forgetfulness... regarding the experiences of women, as well as common people and minorities.[30]

Saikia reports that even today, women refuse to talk about their experiences, not because they are ashamed, but because they fear that they will lose the respect of their families, husbands, and sons in a rigidly traditional and Islamic society. When Saikia tried to interview the former chairperson of the Women's Rehabilitation Committee, Rahman Sobhan, who headed the commission in 1972, she was refused.[31] Thus, silencing the voices of rape and sexual abuse seems to be the official policy of the government, which is preventing any meaningful rehabilitation of the problem and the victims involved.

When Saikia asked a prominent freedom fighter and decorated soldier if he had ever tried to save a woman from rape he replied,

> I did not join the Mukti Bahini to save women. I joined the liberation war to save my country...This talk about women and rape is okay to an extent. But the kind of history that should be written about the war is the glorious victory of the Bangladeshis against the Pakistanis. Rape happened in the war. But that is not something to tell the future generation.[32]

While a dialogue on the 1971 war and its implications may be absent in Pakistani politics and academia, a degree of soul-searching has been taking place among officers and soldiers who fought in East Pakistan. During Saikia's research, plain admittance on their part of the atrocities committed was still rare.

> Violence was not a tested experience for a vast number of officers and rank-and-file soldiers in the Pakistan Army... [T]he Pakistani soldiers were exposed to the realities of a people's unrest, which they initially thought was no more than a rebellion. Gradually, when it grew intense and the East Pakistani Bengalis responded with their own violence, the West Pakistanis reeled under its impact and were broken.[33]

There is a dire need to rethink and re-evaluate the post-colonial history of South Asia, if the future of the countries and the region is to be secured and brightened. Problems of today will be more easily resolved if the past is properly understood and there is forgiveness on the part of the people and governments involved.

A BRITISH JOURNALIST'S EFFORT TO CHALLENGE THE BANGLADESHI VERSION OF HISTORY

David Bergman is a British lawyer, human rights activist, and journalist, married to the Bangladeshi lawyer and writer, Sara Hossain, the daughter of Dr Kamal Hossain. He has been keeping a critical track of the proceedings of the International Criminal Tribunal established by the Awami League government in 2011, with the help of a blog in which he published his observations, critique and rejoinders, to the verdicts that would not be allowed to be aired in public, in Bangladesh. One of his central points of critique was the lack of evidence to support the officially-sanctioned narrative of the three million dead. Bergman was indicted and found guilty of contempt by a Bangladeshi court, for questioning the 1971 war's official death toll. The judges ruled that the blog written and published by him, since 2011, was unprofessional and had 'hurt the feelings of the nation'. A lawyer involved in the trial explained that according to the verdict, 'No one has the right to question the three million death toll in the 1971 independence war. It is a settled issue'.

In his post of 11 November 2011,[34] Bergman highlighted that Mujib was the source of the three million figure, but where did the latter get it from? During the nine months of war, from March to December 1971, Mujib had been detained in prison in West Pakistan and was released only after the war was over. Serajur Rahman, the former deputy head of the BBC Bengali service, had met and talked with Mujib on the latter's arrival in London from West Pakistan. He remembers that Mujib appeared disorientated and did not know what had been going on in Bangladesh during his absence. Rahman briefed him about the war and mentioned an approximate number of three hundred thousand people killed, which Mujib later may have translated into three million. According to Rahman, 'Whether he mistranslated "lakh" as "million" or his confused state of mind was responsible I don't know, but many Bangladeshis still believe a figure of three million is unrealistic and incredible.'[35]

Bergman traced the number back to an editorial in *Purbodesh*, a daily newspaper, on 23 December 1971, according to which, 'enemy occupation' had resulted in the deaths of 'about 3 million innocent people.' Subsequently, the Soviet newspaper, *Pravda*, also quoted this figure, after which, the number was widely circulated in the

Bangladesh media. Later, the Eastern News Agency [ENA], picked up the *Pravda* piece and published an article stating, 'The communist party newspaper, *Pravda*, has reported that over 30 lakh person[s] (3 million) were killed throughout Bangladesh by the Pakistan occupation forces, during the last nine months.' Thus, it seems as Bergman has shown in his research that the three million number was probably a translation error from three lakhs to three million and was later kept in place for political reasons.

The real problem, however, is that successive Bangladeshi governments have turned this number into official history and into a part of national mythology. Whoever questions the reality of this number is considered to be an enemy of Bangladesh. A second blunder was made when it was insisted that Pakistan, its army and their associates alone were responsible for the deaths and rapes of 1971. This has been made part of the official narrative as well. Pakistani and Bengali eyewitnesses and researchers, including Sisson, Rose, Bergman and others, have testified that there were more parties to the killings.

In later additions to this topic in his blog, Bergman draws attention to the fact that not all those who died in 1971 in East Bengal were Bengalis and not all were killed by the Pakistan Army, or its collaborators. According to him, the categories of the dead included civilians murdered by the Pakistan Army and its collaborators; civilians who died in Bangladesh from war-related diseases; civilians who died in Indian camps; Biharis killed by Mukti Bahini and Pakistani soldiers; and Mukti Bahini who died in battle, or were killed after being captured.

It becomes clear from Bergman's deliberations that, from the very beginning, the number of three million dead was spread by the media and later made the 'official number' by successive Bangladeshi governments. Neither the count conducted by the government in 1972, nor one that were carried out later, have ever supported such a high number. It is not possible today to quantify the exact number and it may not even be necessary. The pain of those who were killed, maimed, or lost family members, cannot be understood adequately by quantifying it. Bergman has correctly pointed out that even if, hypothetically speaking, 30,000 people had died, it would not have decreased the magnitude of the tragedy. The problem with 1971 is that official facts have been distorted and this will do little to heal wounds, or bring justice to the victims.

Notes

1. Some sources mention that it was first published in 1973.
2. Source: http://www.storyofbangladesh.com/ebooks/myth-of-3-million.html.
3. Grandniece of Subhas Chandra Bose, granddaughter of Sarat Chandra Bose, and sister of Sugata Bose.
4. Sarmila Bose, 'Losing the Victims: Problems of Using Women as Weapons in Recounting the Bangladesh War,' *Economic and Political Weekly* 48 (32) (22–28 Sep. 2007), pp. 3864–3871, http://www.politics.ox.ac.uk/materials/profile_materials/sbose-losing_the_victims-epw_v_42_no_38_2007.pdf.
5. Bose, *Dead Reckoning*, p. x.
6. Yasmina Saikia, *Women, War, and the Making of Bangladesh: Remembering 1971* (Durham, NC: Duke University Press, 2011), p. 216.
7. Ibid., p. 218.
8. Martin Woollacott, 'Dead Reckoning by Sarmila Bose – Review,' The Guardian, 1 July 2011, http://www.theguardian.com/books/2011/jul/01/dead-reckoning-sarmila-bose-review.
9. 'The Loss of History: Memory, Humanity and Peace after 1971' with Yasmin Saikia, Waterloo Events, 21 May 2014, https://uwaterloo.ca/events/events/loss-history-memory-humanity-and-peace-after-1971-yasmin.
10. William Drummond, 'The Missing Millions,' *The Guardian*, London, 6 June 1972 as cited in Bose p. 176.
11. Chowdhury, *Behind the Myth of Three Million*, p. 7.
12. Ibid., p. 5.
13. Ibid., p. 9.
14. Ibid., p. 21.
15. Ibid., p. 1.
16. Ibid., p. 17.
17. Ibid., p. 29.
18. William Drummond, 'The Missing Millions,' *The Guardian*, London, 6 June 1972 as cited in Chowdhury, *Behind the Myth of Three Million*, p. 29.
19. Sisson and Rose, p. 306.
20. Bose, p. 178.

21. Bose, p. 154.
22. Chowdhury, *Behind the Myth of Three Million*, p. 4, footnote 1.
23. William D. Rubinstein, *Genocide: A History* (London and New York: Routledge, 2004), p. 7.
24. Bose, pp. 181–2.
25. Bose, p. 183.
26. Chowdhury, *Behind the Myth of Three Million*, pp. 43–4.
27. Sarmila Bose, 'Losing the Victims,' p. 3865.
28. Ibid.
29. Major General A. O. Mitha, *Unlikely Beginnings: A Soldier's Life* (Karachi: Oxford University Press, 2003), p. 341.
30. Saikia, p. 75.
31. Ibid., p. 77.
32. Ibid., p. 79.
33. Ibid., pp. 222–23.
34. 'How many were killed in the 1971 war?' Bangladesh War Crimes Tribunal [blog], Friday, 11 November 2011, http://bangladeshwarcrimes.blogspot.com/2011/11/sayedee-indictment-analysis-1971-death.html.
35. Serajur Rahman, 'Mujib's Confusion on Bangladeshi Deaths,' *The Guardian*, Tuesday, 24 May 2011, https://www.theguardian.com/world/2011/may/24/mujib-confusion-on-bangladeshi-deaths. A letter written in response to Ian Jack's article titled, 'It's not the arithmetic of genocide that's important. It's that we pay attention,' *The Guardian*, Saturday, 21 May 2011, https://www.theguardian.com/commentisfree/2011/may/21/ian-jack-bangladesh-war-genocide.

16

Winning the Battle but
Losing the War—II

By late April or mid-May 1971, the Pakistani forces had defeated the Bengali resistance in the urban centres and occupied the entire province by June 1971. In the light of the prevailing circumstances, Brigadier Ghulam Jilani, Chief of Staff for General Niazi, reviewed the East Pakistan defence plan in June 1971. The plan's basic assumption was that East Pakistan's defence would lie in West Pakistan, i.e. East Pakistani forces had to hold out only until India was defeated in the West. Therefore, only the area around Dhaka, the so-called 'Dhaka Bowl', had to be defended, leaving the border areas and the forward line exposed. Leaving the plan unchanged turned out to be a grave mistake. It allowed the Mukti Bahini in June and July, to regroup across the border with Indian aid, through Operation Jackpot, that sent 2,000–5,000 guerrillas across the border in an unsuccessful Monsoon Offensive, which was defeated by the Pakistan Army.

By July 1971, the Pakistan Army had built up an intelligence network to track Mukti Bahini infiltration and counter it through ambush, artillery shelling, and minefields, along the border with India. COAS, General Abdul Hamid Khan, prohibited any provocations that might lead to Indian retaliation. Commander Eastern Command, Lt. Gen. Niazi, was convinced that his defence scheme would have contained India; however, this has been contradicted by many analysts and events that took place later in the year. His main plan remained unchanged until September 1971—Pakistani units were to fight a series of defensive battles before deploying to defend the Dhaka Bowl and that every inch of the province would not be defended. After his surrender, General Niazi admitted that 'The Mukti Bahinis had made him blind and deaf', by disturbing and cutting off his communication lines and insisted that without Indian support, they would not have been able to defeat the Pakistan Army.[1] While this may be true in the short-run, if the war had lasted any longer, they would have done so.

Maj. Gen. Safiullah, the first commander of the Bangladesh Army, recalls of the East Bengali troops, 'A new organisational concept started gaining ground as the war progressed. Guerrilla warfare continued to harass, weaken and bleed the enemy...by adopting hit and run actions, but it was not capable to gain, hold, or consolidate ground. Orders came in early July, to organise and train Z Force.'[2] The K and S forces followed.

Nevertheless, the belief that the defence of East Pakistan lies in the West, was ridiculous—militarily and politically. Moreover, it only reinforced the impression among Bengalis that in the event of war, being under-equipped and exposed to Indian incursion, East Pakistan and its population would be sacrificed. This sentiment had become increasingly prevalent since 1965, when only an infantry division was defending East Pakistan.

A similar strain existed between the Bengali rebel units and the Indian Army. The latter, like the Pakistan Army, believed that the Bengalis were not warriors. This school of thought may have had its roots in the colonial period, when the British labelled Bengalis as a non-martial people. As the civil war in East Pakistan escalated, so did the feud between Bengali rebels and the Indians. The Mukti Bahini resented the control of the Indians over them. An example of this is the rough relationship between the Indian General Aurora, and the Commander of Mukti Bahini, General M.A.G. Osmany, who objected to losing control over the units he had raised.

The refugee situation was also partly responsible for rising indignation and anti-Bengali feelings among the Indians. By the summer of 1971, 6.5 million East Bengali refugees are reported to have been housed in 593 refugee camps, in Indian states bordering

East Pakistan. Another two million spilling out of the camps were trying to find refuge in the rest of the state of West Bengal. West Bengal's chief minister wrote in June, that 'West Bengal today is deluged with millions of victims of Pakistani oppression.'[3] Only a month later, his government collapsed. For the remaining period of the drama going on in East Pakistan, West Bengal remained under Delhi's control.

After the end of Operation Searchlight, the first task for the military was to restore the public's confidence in law and order, through the reconstitution of the police force in place of the East Pakistan Rifles (EPR) and the establishment of other security services, including the East Pakistan Civil Affairs Force (EPCAF) and the Internal Security Force, to support the Pakistan Army and to stabilise the military victory. In April, the military government created EPCAF, mainly from non-Bengali elements of the former EPR and West Pakistanis— mainly Punjabis and some Biharis—in an attempt to get civilian life under control. Not only were Bengalis not recruited, they were viewed with suspicion and, on their part, did not volunteer to be recruited.

Recruitment progressed at a slow pace and the force is reported to have reached 10,000 by November 1971.[4] These units were supposed to provide internal security in those areas of East Pakistan that had been vacated by the Pakistan Army. Yet despite all efforts, the force never became fully functional, mainly because there was not enough equipment to arm it and no training was available at the time. The recruitment of police personnel in the province, to replace those who had deserted, was another matter that needed urgent attention. The army asked those former police personnel that had not run away to India, to come back into service. They planned to reinforce the police with temporary transfers from the force in West Pakistan. According to Sisson and Rose, some 5,000 West Pakistani police officers arrived in Dhaka by the end of May, for a six-month special duty. At the beginning of those six months they proved efficient, but by the end, they had come close to mutiny for not being paid on time, waiting in vain for travel allowance and not being provided with family housing.[5]

'In an effort to counter the increasingly effective guerrilla activity, in late summer, the Martial Law authorities also attempted to raise paramilitary forces of mujahids and razakars.'[6] The force raised to support the efforts of the Pakistan Army consisted of groups named Al-Shams, Razakars, and Al-Badr and proved controversial. It consisted mainly of non-Bengali so-called Biharis and anti-secession Bengalis. According to Sisson and Rose:

> The former [Mujahids] were organized in thirteen battalions and forty-seven independent companies, but never became an effective force, owing to the absence of trained officer personnel, inadequate facilities for training recruits, and limited availability of arms. In most instances, Mujahid units were attached to regular army units, both to amass firepower and to inhibit the dissolution of the former. The Razakars were created in an effort to concentrate support among religious youth to protect lines of communication, but in some instances this fostered conflict. Al-Shams was charged with protecting bridges in and around urban areas and was relatively lax in recruitment and control. Al-Badr was recruited from public schools and *madrassas* (religious schools) and was used for raids and "special operations".[7]

The force raised consisted mostly of young Biharis lacking military discipline, they committed atrocities against the Bengali civilian population in retaliation for what had happened to them and their families in March and April. This was counter-productive and unleashed a bloody cycle of revenge. The West Pakistani recruits brought into East Pakistan were received with suspicion and hostility by the Bengali population and, as a result, developed a 'cantonment mentality' in an increasingly hostile, alien surrounding. They were refused local support by Bengalis who claimed not to understand or speak Urdu. The newly formed administration and security services were often isolated and refused information and therefore could not act effectively.

The next task, after the completion of Operation Searchlight, was to regain civilian control over the administration of East Pakistan and re-establish the writ of the state. During the months before the launch of the operation, the administration had ceased to function as a result of the civil disobedience movement launched by the Awami League. With the imposition of Martial Law by General Ayub Khan in October 1958, the whole of Pakistan had come under military control. In East Pakistan, the post of chief minister was abolished and it now came under a governor supported by the military.

The leading civilians of Ayub's administration were replaced by high-profile military officers in Yahya's government, which came to power in 1969. When the civil disobedience movement started in March, the politicians of the Awami League appealed to the Bengali officers still serving in the administration to pledge their allegiance to their party. Gradually, starting from December 1970, those loyal to the Awami League started taking over the administration—a process that accelerated in March 1971. After the operation began, many of the Bengali officers fled the country and went to India, leading to a complete breakdown of the administration. By the end of April, the Pakistan Army had regained control over the majority of the cities, if not the towns and rural areas of East Pakistan. Thus, the next step was to create conditions for selecting a civilian cadre loyal to Pakistan.

All of these efforts, however, were only partially successful. While some government functions could be revived in Dhaka and other cities, most towns and all of the rural areas remained in a state of civil war. Nothing short of Martial Law would have worked in such a situation and it was finally imposed with brutal force. Though some basic administrative functions were re-established in the urban centres, it remained more or less ineffective. According to Kamal Matinuddin,

> Although all major towns were secured, the countryside was still under the control of the dissidents and the mobility of the army remained restricted and its security jeopardised. Radio and TV stations came, once again, under the control of the government, but clandestine radio stations operating from Indian territory continued to wage psychological warfare against Pakistan.... Except for resuming the

administration of the province, the long-term objectives of the operation could not be achieved as the border could not be sealed, conditions for selecting a civilian setup were only partially obtained and a new political arrangement accommodating the non-radical elements of the elected representatives proved to be only a showpiece.[8]

Thus, it was only by the end of May that the government started weighing its options on how to carry out the transfer of power in East Pakistan. The most promising proposal was rejected; it included accepting the election results of December 1970, releasing Mujib and announcing a general political amnesty that allowed all refugees to return to East Pakistan. But the very success of Operation Searchlight turned out to be a prelude to failure. The army thought that the military victory would have a lasting impact and therefore refused to take a conciliatory approach. It is highly likely that this rejected proposal would have been the best way forward for both parts of Pakistan.

The alternate option, although impractical, was favoured by the military. It involved a drastic change of the election results of December 1970, by scrutinising the elected representatives on the basis of their loyalty to Pakistan. This process was handled by Yahya himself and its results were announced in early August. Of the 160 elected Awami League representatives, 76 were disqualified on the grounds that they were traitors and their seats declared vacant. A total of 195 of the 228 elected members of the provincial parliament were disqualified for the same reason. Those allowed to sit in the parliament could only do so without any attachment to Awami League, which was banned from political life. The opposition parties that had lost the elections in East Bengal were happy with a solution that gave them a new chance to win a seat in the absence of the Awami League.

By-elections were announced on 25 September, for the period between 25 November and 9 December,[9] but they never took place due to the ongoing conflict during this period. Therefore, the path chosen by the Yahya regime proved be a gross misjudgement of the situation on the ground. Those in the military who had undiluted power in East Pakistan, were ill-suited for negotiations and political compromise. Yahya, recognising the strain that refugees put on India and on India–Pakistan relations, invited the refugees to return to Pakistan towards the end of May. This effort culminated in the presidential address of 28 June, in which he announced rehabilitation efforts for the returnees. But to his surprise, the outflow of refugees grew to unprecedented proportions, instead of diminishing.

In his speech, Yahya also indicated that there would neither be a new election, nor a return to the status quo. He repeated that the Awami League would remain banned and Mujib would not be pardoned for his treachery. Like his predecessor Ayub, Yahya installed a committee of experts that were to develop a draft Constitution. He 'advised' them to include a paragraph banning parties whose support-base was limited to a single province. He intended to bridge the gap between the two wings of Pakistan by encouraging cross-wing political coalitions, such as National Awami Party (NAP). Such a clause, if implemented, would have led to the ban of almost all the parties that had taken part in the 1970 election, including the PPP. In any case, all these plans and half-hearted attempts did not bring about any political solution. They were single-handed efforts that did not take into account the will of the Bengali people. The Pakistan government was also shutting its eyes to the fact that elections, or even by-elections, would not have been possible during this period of instability.

The refusal to recognise the Awami League as a force that could not be neutralised, was the biggest mistake made by the military government since March. Yahya was unable to see the signs and proceeded with Mujib's treason trial. The irony is that due to US pressure, Mujib's safety had already been guaranteed. Why then, was it so important to declare him a traitor? Yahya also went ahead with his effort to disqualify the Awami League members of parliament that he considered unreliable.

By August, time for a political solution had run out and the initiative in the East Pakistan crisis had moved out of Pakistan, to India and other international players. G.W. Choudhury recalls a visit in Pakistan in early September:

> The whole situation had changed since my previous visit in May–June. Yahya was like a man in a trance. The other members of the junta—Hamid, Gul Hasan, Omar…and even Peerzada, were in the deepest gloom. The chief of Inter-Services Intelligence (I.S.I.D.), Major-General Gillani…and his able predecessor, General Akbar, both told me about the imminent Indo-Pakistan war on Bangladesh and its grave implications.[10]

With increasing external involvement in the crisis, the threat of war between India and Pakistan became imminent. Yahya tried to mimic a political solution to the conflict internationally, but by then it was already too late. The unrelenting flow of East Bengali refugees into India put the Indian government in a position to threaten and take action against Pakistan. The international exposure of the plight of the refugees and the horrific accounts of what they had been through, led to the demonization of the Pakistan Army in the media. The Indians assiduously propagated this on the world stage, by inviting public figures like US Senator, Edward Kennedy, to visit refugee camps in West Bengal and express their anger and dismay at what they witnessed.

A major 'distraction' that diverted the Pakistan government's attention from a political settlement in East Pakistan, was its foreign policy initiative to mediate between China and the US on the request of US President Nixon. In July, US Secretary of State, Henry Kissinger, through the good offices of Pakistan, had finally managed to go to China after a long Cold War between the two countries. Pakistan, having sponsored this visit through its good relations with China, was overly confident that the effort would prompt the US to extend its support to West Pakistan's position in East Pakistan, politically and by providing military equipment. This turned out to be another gross misjudgement. In fact, in early April, the US had stopped the sale of military equipment to Pakistan, in view of the operation in East Pakistan. In July, American economic aid was also suspended. According to Sisson and Rose, military sales of the US to Pakistan, for the whole period up to December 1971, when an embargo was imposed, amounted to less than US$5 million and this included spare parts for weapons acquired in the 1960s.[11] In addition, US commitment in Vietnam did not allow them further military engagement in the Asia.

American support, therefore, remained more or less verbal. President Nixon is on record to have said that 'Nobody has occupied the White House who is friendlier to Pakistan than me'. If this was true, it did not apply to the State Department, or Congress. All Nixon could do for Pakistan was to refrain from open criticism while continuing to caution Yahya in private to look for political solutions instead of military ones. Those quiet reminders remained without success. The reason for this was that foreign policy was Yahya's exclusive domain during his rule; an independent foreign-policy-defining body in Pakistan did not exist in those years. According to Filippo Boni,

> As for the 1971 war, the NSC [National Security Council], although created in 1969, was not operational under General Yahya Khan, who instead centralized the decision-making process in his person and in a few military leaders, relegating the civilian cabinet and the NSC to the role of empty bodies without any power in defining foreign policy goals. The struggle between civilian and military leaders showed itself in the inability to set a clear, coherent and shared vision of Pakistan's foreign policy.[12]

A thorough analysis of international relations would have shown to the Yahya government that US interests in Pakistan and South Asia were secondary and any reliance on US support, hazardous at best.

The signing of the 'Treaty of Friendship and Cooperation' between India and the Soviet Union, on 9 August 1971, was a crucial development at this point. After Kissinger's visit to China in July 1971, India could see a US–China–Pakistan nexus emerging that would threaten its national and geopolitical interests. 'We shall not allow any other country, or a combination of countries to dominate us, or to interfere in our internal affairs,' said India's Foreign Minister, Swaran Singh, in the Lok Sabha, after signing the treaty with the Soviet Union. The draft of the treaty had been drawn up in 1969, but had remained shelved ever since then. Now, it was updated and presented for signature. Comprising of twelve articles, it put a stamp of legality on the rapidly expanding multi-faceted friendship and cooperation between the two countries and elevated their ties to a strategic level. Under Article 9, if either of the parties is attacked, or threatened with attack, then India and Soviet Union will 'immediately start mutual consultations with a view to eliminating this threat.' This was nothing less than a mutual defence pact, a fact conveniently glossed over by the non-aligned countries and the rest of the world.

The promise of Soviet help, as a counterbalance to US and Chinese support for Pakistan, gave India the confidence it needed to proceed with its war preparations. On the other hand, Yahya and the GHQ in Rawalpindi did not feel any apprehensions regarding this development. Oblivious to the power struggle between Nixon, Kissinger, and Congress, on US policy in East Pakistan, they blindly trusted American and Chinese promises of support.

The Soviet Union had, until summer 1971, remained neutral in the conflict and even after signing the treaty, insisted in an official statement, that 'Both sides "considered it necessary that urgent steps be taken in East Pakistan for the achievement of a political solution… which would answer the interests of the entire people of Pakistan.'[13]

There has been a tendency to evaluate relations between Pakistan and the Soviet Union in a negative light. Such an approach has been unable, however, to accurately define relations between the two countries and it might be useful to recount some details. One major reason for the negativity has been the anti-communist sentiment prevalent in Pakistani politics ever since the country was founded. The Rawalpindi Conspiracy of 1953 and the following ban on the Communist Party, was one major instance, as is the perceived incompatibility of Islam and communism.

Another reason is Pakistan's political ties to the West as a former British colony, its membership in the Commonwealth and the growing overtures of the US, who saw in Pakistan a useful Cold War ally in the 1950s. Liaquat Ali Khan's visit to the US as Prime Minister, instead of Moscow, proved fruitful and Pakistan later joined the western security pacts, SEATO and CENTO. In July 1957, Prime Minister Huseyn Shaheed Suhrawardy approved the leasing of a secret installation, Badaber Air Station near Peshawar, to the CIA. In 1959, Ayub permitted covert surveillance flights of U-2s from that airbase, until the Soviet air defence shot down one of the flights in 1960 and captured the American pilot, Gary Powers. This incident worsened relations between the Soviet Union and Pakistan.

A third major obstacle in relations was Pakistan's close ties with China after the Sino–Pakistan Boundary Agreement of 1963. Incidentally, given the antipathy towards communism and its effects on relations with the Soviet Union, one can never fully explain the deep friendship that developed between Pakistan and communist China.

The Soviet Union desired that Pakistan should not fully side with China, despite its close relations with the US. From there onwards, it aimed at a more balanced relationship with India and Pakistan, trying to remain neutral in their conflicts. As a result, Bhutto, as Foreign Minister, paid a visit to the Soviet Union in January 1965, which was followed by Ayub's visit to Moscow, in April 1965. Pakistan was exploring the possibility of Soviet arms deliveries and expressed its concern about Soviet military aid to India that might be used against Pakistan. Later that year, during the war, although the Soviet Union insisted that Pakistan had started the war, it tried to bring about a reconciliation between India and Pakistan by offering to mediate in

Tashkent. After the 1966 Tashkent Agreement, relations between Pakistan and the Soviet Union improved further, with aid flowing, trade increasing, and a number of other agreements being signed. In April 1968, during a visit to Pakistan, Russian Premier Alexei Kosygin pledged cooperation and promised to finance the Kalabagh Steel Mills and Rooppur Atomic Project in East Pakistan. In June 1968, General Yahya Khan visited Moscow and signed an agreement for the supply of military hardware to Pakistan.[14] After Yahya's takeover, Kosygin visited Pakistan and offered a plan to negotiate transit trade agreements between India, Pakistan, and Afghanistan, as a step towards easing tensions and a provision whereby trade would be extended towards west-Asian states, including Iran and Turkey.

The split came when President Leonid Brezhnev, in June 1969, introduced the idea of the creation of a collective security system in Asia, based on the principle of peaceful co-existence. The intended renouncing of the use of force in the relations between the members and the acknowledgement of territorial integrity of states went against Pakistan's stand in the Kashmir conflict and was tantamount to a rejection of the ceasefire line as an international border. In addition, China cautioned Pakistan that the plan was directed against China and would hurt its security interests. Pakistan's rejection of the Soviet proposal led to the suspension of Soviet arms supplies in 1970. The opening of the Karakoram highway, later that year, naturally reinforced Pakistan's alliance with China and precluded closer relations with the Soviet Union for the time being.

The signing of the Indo–Soviet Treaty in 1971 did not necessarily imply an anti-Pakistan stance on the part of Moscow; the Soviet Union understood that Pakistan was faced with secession on grounds of ethnic tensions. Until late September 1971, it preferred, despite the treaty with India, to look at the East Pakistani conflict as an internal matter of Pakistan and only sympathised with India in the refugee question. It was the stubborn and insensitive refusal of Yahya and his government to allow for a political solution that finally alienated Moscow. It is due to this that one of Bhutto's first visits abroad as

President, was to Moscow, in March 1972, to mend ties that had been fractured because of the events of 1971.

Encouraged by its new alliance with Moscow, India proceeded with its plan to break Pakistan up. A low-intensity war was initiated in August by India—long before war was officially declared. Indian Army and Border Security Forces started raids into East Pakistan. On 3 August, Clare Hollingworth of *The Telegraph*, reported ninety-five Indian casualties in a battle, when two Indian companies were repulsed after attacking Jamalpur, in East Pakistan. On 9 August, according to an official statement, between 29 July and 6 August, twenty people had been killed and others wounded in unprovoked Indian shelling in the border areas of East Pakistan. In mid-August, the GHQ in Rawalpindi announced that the Indian Army had started regular attacks on border outposts in East Pakistan. On 18 August, official reports claimed that the Pakistan Army had beaten back the Indian Border Security Forces in the border area of Rajshahi. The Indian incursions and low-intensity fighting along the East Pakistani border, continued throughout August, despite the monsoon that submerged large parts of East Pakistan and made troop movement for the Pakistan Army extremely difficult.

On 5 August, the Pakistan government published a White Paper on East Pakistan, describing India's role in the crisis. The government had started to feel the international heat because of the continuous flow of refugees into India. President Yahya tried to calm the situation down and told a correspondent of *The Times of London*, that he would welcome British and Commonwealth mediation if it was handled in a strictly neutral manner. That was, of course, not likely to happen. On 8 August, in an official statement from Islamabad, Dr Hermann Schmitt-Vockenhausen, vice-president of the West-German Parliament, who was visiting Pakistan, announced that Yahya was ready to negotiate and reach an agreement with all concerned in the East Pakistan crisis and that he rejected war as a solution to the India–Pakistan conflict. While Vockenhausen seems to have been told this, it was not followed up with appropriate action.

With the backing of the newly signed Soviet treaty, India refused to allow UN forces to check on the border violations and Indian incursions into East Pakistan. In a note to the UN, the Pakistan government asked for a constructive dialogue with India, to facilitate repatriation of East Pakistani refugees to Pakistan, because all appeals by Yahya since 28 June, had failed to bring about any results. The secretary general of the UN pledged to station UN representatives along the India–Pakistan border, despite India's negative response, and facilitate refugee returns. This, however, proved impossible given the international opinion at the time, in which Pakistan was blamed unilaterally for the situation. Indian Foreign Minister, Swaran Singh, is on record saying that nobody could stop India from taking unilateral action in East Pakistan. On 23 August, India rejected Pakistan's proposal to establish a 'good offices committee' consisting of members of UNSC, to defuse the crisis.

While China was supporting Pakistan in the UN against India, the rift in the US with regard to a joint American policy towards the East Pakistani crisis, became even more pronounced. In early August, the US Congress passed an aid bill containing clauses effectively suspending military and economic aid to Pakistan. Nixon's claim on 4 August, that he was against the suspension of aid to Pakistan, did not really change the facts. While he supported Pakistan verbally, the US State Department and Congress refused material support. Nixon sent Yahya a message on 13 August, saying that the American people shared Pakistan's hopes for peace and progress, but on the next day, the US State Department announced that it would not renew the licence for weapons export to Pakistan.

After his visit to East Pakistan in August, Senator Edward Kennedy alleged that the Bengalis were facing genocide. US State Department spokesperson, Robert McCloskey, disagreed and denied the charge. On 21 August, British MP, John Osborn, after a visit to East Pakistan declared in a TV interview to the BBC, that he 'Frankly saw no evidence of genocide' in East Pakistan as alleged by Senator Kennedy. Both the US and Great Britain supported the struggle of the East Bengalis for independence by allowing the opening of a High Commission of Bangladesh in London, in the summer of 1971, thus accepting and promoting the disintegration of Pakistan.

The possibility of a political solution had by then become remote. Yahya's government had underestimated the importance of the international balance of power and opinion that at the time, stood against Pakistan. Yahya carried on with his domestic policy, in which he tried to undo the election results and find a way to install a pro-West Pakistan government in the eastern part of the country. On 7 August, a list was published containing the names of eighty-eight members of parliament belonging to the Awami League, who would be allowed to keep their seats in the National Assembly, implying that all other elected members stood revoked. On 19 August, the government issued another list of only ninety-four members of the Awami League that would retain their seats in the provincial assembly, with all others dismissed.

Yahya also insisted on trying Mujib for high treason and for waging war on Pakistan, despite the fact that Nixon and the US State Department had expressed grave reservations regarding this decision. An effort made by some of the exiled Awami League members in Calcutta led by Bangladesh Foreign Minister Khondikar Mushtaq Ahmed, to explore the possibility of a political settlement with Pakistan through the mediation of the US consulate general in Calcutta and Mujib's lawyer, A.K. Brohi. They offered to withdraw their demand for independence in return for a negotiation summit with the Pakistan government, but this was rejected by Yahya in a meeting with American Ambassador McFarland, on 19 August.[15]

Some who were witness to the conflict claim that chances of a political settlement had diminished as early as May. According to Lt. Gen. Kamal Matinuddin, in May 1971, India and its Prime Minister, Indira Gandhi, were fully focused on the goal of breaking Pakistan up.[16] What seems more credible, however, is that after the successful completion of Operation Searchlight and despite the pains and revulsion that it inflicted, there was a real possibility of salvaging a united Pakistan, if a determined policy of reconciliation had been followed. This would have meant recognising and accepting the election results and rehabilitating Mujib.

Efforts to find a constitutional solution to balance power between the two wings of the country had to take precedence and a confederational setup was one of the options. That possibility was precluded by the political immaturity of Yahya and his supporters in the GHQ, as well as civilian politicians such as Bhutto. They failed, or refused to understand the gravity of the situation and the fact that the conflict needed a political settlement, because a military victory was insufficient.

The East Pakistan crisis became internationalised mainly because of the refugee problem, the effects of the Cold War power blocs and no credible efforts towards a political solution. With China, the Soviet Union, and the US indirectly involved in the conflict, there was more at stake than solely the fate of Pakistan. India found the long-awaited opportunity of breaking its neighbour, but could have been stopped if international power equations had not aided their efforts. Indira Gandhi had already decided to go to war long before August and was only waiting for the monsoon to recede.

A belated peace plan that included the option of a referendum on East Pakistani independence was handed over by Yahya to the new Indian Ambassador, Jai Kumar Atal, in Islamabad. Indira Gandhi rejected it in early September.[17]

Pakistan lost the media war that ran parallel to the civil war. Shrewd handling of the media has never been Pakistan Army's forte; it blundered in throwing out media persons from Dhaka and East Pakistan. This was used by India to manipulate news despite the fact that there was no Internet or social media at the time to challenge official reporting. The military failed to understand that the weapon of misinformation could be used against it. The initial military victory in the civil war, in March, was wasted as the army and civilian political leadership of Pakistan failed to cash-in on it.

Acknowledgement

This chapter has been written while using information from Chronology June–August 1971, *Pakistan Horizon*, Vol. 24, No. 3 (Third Quarter, 1971), pp. 70–110, http://www.jstor.org/stable/41393088.

Notes

1. Matinuddin, *Tragedy of Errors*, p. 237.
2. Safiullah, *Bangladesh at War*, p. 192.
3. Bass, *The Blood Telegram*, p. 189.
4. Sisson & Rose, *War and Secession*, p. 163.
5. Ibid., p. 164.
6. Ibid.
7. Ibid., pp. 164–5.
8. Matinuddin, *Tragedy of Errors*, pp. 267–8.
9. Sisson & Rose, p. 173.
10. Choudhury, *The Last Days of United Pakistan*, p. 197.
11. Sisson & Rose, p. 257.
12. Filippo Boni, 'The impact of civil-military relations on Pakistan's foreign policy,' published by NottsPolitics on 24 October 2013, http://nottspolitics.org/2013/10/24/the-impact-of-civil-military-relations-on-pakistans-foreign-policy/.
13. Hasan Zaheer, *The Separation of East Pakistan: The Rise and Realization of Bengali Muslim Nationalism* (Karachi: Oxford University Press, 1994), p. 307.
14. Ibid., p. 304.
15. Sisson & Rose, pp. 173–4.
16. Matinuddin, p. 268.
17. Choudhury, pp. 198–9.

17

India's Role in the East Pakistan Crisis

India–Pakistan relations have been less than friendly since the very inception of Pakistan. The roots of this lay in the manner in which Independence came about. Congress accepted Partition in May 1947, but believed the concept of Pakistan to be unfeasible and temporary. Thus, instead of agreeing to a power-sharing formula with the Muslim League, it opted for partition to be able to retain full power in its part of the subcontinent. Congress firmly believed that once the Pakistan experiment would collapse, it would establish its writ in an undivided India. India's first goal, therefore, was to gently push Pakistan towards a collapse, first by delaying money transfers to the newly founded Muslim state and then by manipulating the Maharaja of Kashmir 's accession to India. As the years passed and there was no sign of Pakistan collapsing, India thought of means and ways in which to bring this about. The East Pakistan crisis provided India with the opportunity to cautiously influence Pakistan's dismemberment.

However, things are rarely that straightforward. India was a leading force of the Non-Aligned Movement and had to secure its position in that regard. It had to balance its relations with the Soviet Union, the US, and China. Moreover, the East Pakistan crisis touched upon core Indian domestic interests as well. While a Pakistani government dominated by West Pakistan would not give much attention to East Pakistani interests—such as the Ganges water dispute with India—an independent nationalist Bangladeshi government would be more proactive in standing up for its interests. Additionally, while Mujibur Rahman was considered a moderate politician, other leading members of the Awami League were viewed by India as being far more radical.

A government dominated by them could become a liability for India, which was already having trouble with radical leftists on its border with West Bengal.

Since 1967, an uprising of Naxalites shook the Delhi-friendly provincial government in West Bengal and finally succeeded in deposing it. For the elections of 1969, Delhi had to ensure that it would not lose its domination in this important province. With the help of heavy Indian Army contingents that were transferred into West Bengal, a United Front government was heaved into place, even though the Naxalite Communist Party of India (Marxist) won the majority of the seats. The newly instated government, however, did not last long. In March 1970, the chief minister resigned and president's rule was imposed in West Bengal that lasted with short interruption until March 1972. Thus, India watched the outcome of the Pakistani election in December 1970, carefully, while keeping a low profile. The overwhelming victory of Mujib's party was received with mixed feelings at best.

It is difficult to evaluate the events that followed in India–Pakistan relations, especially with regard to the so-called 'Ganga incident' of 30 January 1971, which resulted in the banning of Pakistani flights over Indian territory. This proved a major impediment for the mobilisation of Pakistan Army in the eastern wing, during the crisis. According to Sisson and Rose,[1] on 15 April, a Pakistani commission of inquiry into the incident, presented its report to President Yahya Khan, claiming that the two Kashmiri hijackers were in fact Indian intelligence agents and the action had been launched in order to create for a pretext for banning overflights. This later turned out to be true. Traditionally and because of the lopsided defence concept, there was a small number of soldiers stationed in East Pakistan who, in case of civil unrest or a foreign invasion, would have been unable to defend the country. The belief that the defence of East Pakistan lay in the western wing, had come under criticism as early as 1965, but was never reviewed. Now, it contributed to the dismemberment of the country.

There must, undoubtedly, have been different schools of thought in India regarding what was going on in Pakistan. And while the hawks might well have worked for a dismemberment, there were sober politicians who would have seen a political solution and a power-sharing formula between Bhutto and Mujib as the way forward. The arrest and trial of Mujib and the ban of the Awami League, was not an outcome anticipated by India. Therefore, the breakdown of talks on 25 March and the launching of an army operation on the same night was met with surprise by some in India and with high hopes by others.

The first reaction was to offer refuge to Awami League leaders and party workers, as well as to the Bengali deserters of the Pakistan Army, who soon sought refuge from persecution. The crudeness of the crackdown by the army on the Bengali population resulted in large numbers of Bengalis running for their lives into India. There, they were received well in the beginning and temporarily housed in refugee camps, while official Indian statements on the situation remained guarded.

By early April, however, India changed its stance when it allowed the establishment of the Awami League headquarters in Calcutta helped create a 'Mujibnagar' on Indian soil. As a result of the support provided by India, on 17 April, Awami League leaders issued from Mujibnagar, a declaration of independence and announced the foundation of the People's Republic of Bangladesh. Although, India refrained from officially recognising the new state and its government-in-exile, its tacit cooperation was apparent behind the scenes. A radio station called Free Bangla was set up outside Calcutta with Indian equipment. However, India was very careful with regard to its stature as a leading member of the Non-Aligned Movement and it did not want to be seen as an official sponsor of the breakaway state.

The government-in-exile of the Awami League was allowed to immediately announce the foundation of the Bangladesh Armed Forces and a Military Council headed by General M.A.G. Osmany. The forces were drawn from members of the Pakistan Army, East Bengal Regiments, and East Pakistan Rifles, that had deserted in the wake of Operation Searchlight and attempts of West Pakistani officers to disarm Bengali troops. Later, the Mukti Bahini, or freedom fighters, were gathered and trained from among civilian Bengalis that had taken refuge in India.

During these early days of the crisis, India was keeping its army out of direct involvement. Its borders were guarded by the Border Security Force (BSF), with a central police force charged with the upkeep of border security and with taking stock of the Bengali refugees, directing them to the different camps that had been erected close to the border. In addition, the BSF was made responsible for running the military training camps that India established along its border with East Pakistan, though later this responsibility was transferred to the Indian Army. The BSF was also aiding Bengali fighters who were trained and equipped in the Indian camps, to launch attacks across the border, on Pakistani soil and establish their hold in the border region. It also made some incursions across the border into East Pakistan, as was admitted much later by the Indian General, J.F.R. Jacob in his book.[2] These developments were, of course, not communicated openly at that time and the world was unaware of them for quite some time. The existence of a POW camp in Panagarh, West Bengal, from April onwards, was also kept secret. There can be no doubt that India was actively aiding the break-up of Pakistan from the very beginning of the crisis, even if this was not announced as a matter of policy.

The Indian Army had been involved from the outset, along with trainers and providers of equipment. Large contingents of its troops had been moved into West Bengal since 1969, in connection with the political crisis and Naxalite activity there. From March onwards, the army was increasingly involved in the situation along the East Pakistani border, in West Bengal, Assam, and Tripura. In May 1971, it took over the task of aiding the Mukti Bahini, setting up a coordinated enterprise under the Eastern Command for meeting the logistical and training needs and, to some extent, lending operational support and planning advice.[3] The operation was codenamed Jackpot. The border areas around Bangladesh were divided into six logistical sectors, each to be commanded by a brigadier from the Indian Army. But all this was somewhat of a limited involvement. Sisson and Rose report that when the service chiefs of the Indian military were consulted in late March 1971, about India's capacity for military intervention in East Pakistan, they informed the government that it would take several months before such intervention would be feasible, despite the desertion of most of the East Pakistani military, paramilitary and police units.[4]

Another important aspect of the situation facing India at this point was the rising tide of refugees. Operation Searchlight, which was directed against the civilian population of East Pakistan, had produced thousands of victims and spread terror among the people. Thus, the population increasingly sought refuge in neighbouring India. From about 25,000 departures registered as of 15 April 1971, more than 1.2 million people had taken the road of exile by the end of the month. By May, the movement had assumed a very large scale, with an average daily outflow of 83,000 persons. In June, according to Indian sources, the figure had reached 4.7 million and in July, 6.9 million people were distributed among 1,000 camps and reception centres. These figures continued to increase in the fall, to reach the official figure of 9,899,305 people in December. Of these, 6.8 million lived in camps, the rest being scattered throughout the neighbouring states of India and sheltered by friends and relatives.[5]

Even though India had practically opened its border to East Pakistan, it was nevertheless overwhelmed by the influx of the number of people over a relatively short period of time—all of whom had to somehow be accommodated, fed and clothed. From the very beginning, the Indian government made it clear that it was not going to provide a permanent home for the refugees. In a meeting with economic editors, Indira Gandhi reportedly described the solution to the refugee influx as follows, 'I am just going to send them back. I am determined to send them back.'[6] This policy of 'sending them back' served as a constant reminder that the refugees 'belonged to

Bangladesh...and were going back as soon as the situation returned to normal.'

> The Indian victory and the Bangladeshi Independence paved the way [for] a massive and speedy repatriation of the refugees. As of 7 March 1972, more than 9.5 million refugees had left the Indian territory, leaving 172,908 to [repatriate]. These figures may put into question the voluntary nature of the repatriation. The refugees, at their arrival, had signed a form stating their willingness to return. But filling in this form, necessary for the issuance of identity cards, was also a precondition for the delivery of food.[7]

While the influx of refugees was a considerable burden for India, putting pressure on its economy, labour market, and internal security, it is unclear why India was so adamant on getting rid of them, including the many Bengali Hindus, to the extent that it demanded a clause to this effect be included in any political settlement between the Pakistani government and the Awami League. Describing the situation, Sisson and Rose write, 'There is no question, however, that Indian policy toward the refugees *once they were in India*, was a major obstacle to any political settlement in East Pakistan.'[8] The reason for this categorical refusal to accept East Pakistani Bengalis was that India had trouble with its own population Bengalis, who had repeatedly fought with the central government and who might have felt a sense of solidarity with the Bengali nationalism of the Awami League. The idea of a united Bengal that had been considered in 1947 might have been revived, but that was the last thing the Indian government would have wanted.

Ethnic strife was imminent in a small border state like Tripura, where the indigenous population amounted to 1.5 million, comprising Tripuris, Assamese, and other minority tribal groups, and where almost a million refugees had arrived. India's repeated insistence on a clause concerning the refugees showed that it had limited interest in a political settlement. As East Pakistan's neighbour and a self-styled host of the rebel government-in-exile, India had considerable leverage on the turn of events that she refused to use for a political solution.

The refugee crisis took its toll and the crisis in East Pakistan dragged on for longer than India might have expected. By the summer of 1971, there were signs that the Awami League and the leftists of West Bengal were growing closer to each other. New Delhi grew increasingly suspicious of the government-in-exile it had helped create and in September, it started exerting pressure on it to listen to Indian advice. India increasingly viewed the presence of the refugees and the Awami League government on its soil as a liability and felt that more had to be done to end the East Pakistan crisis.

Public opinion on India's role in the East Pakistan crisis has been moulded by the attitude of second-tier officials, on whom the pressure to uphold a certain image and pretence was less severe. One such person was K. Subrahmanyam, who was then Director, Institute of Defence Studies and Analyses, New Delhi. Writing in the Indian newspaper, *National Herald*, he argued, 'The East Pakistani crisis presented India with an opportunity the like of which will never come again.'[9] Despite denials by the Indian government that Subrahmanyam's opinion had nothing to do with official Indian policy, there are solid reasons to believe that the possibility of Pakistan's dismemberment did appeal to Indian government circles. In any case, it struck a chord in Pakistan that added to the feeling that it was surrounded by enemies and this may have contributed to the determination and rigour of the military to save the unity and integrity of Pakistan.

Subrahmanyam's views can easily be interpreted as a sign of Indian intentions to intervene in East Pakistan more directly than it had already done. After all, the material help for the creation of an exile government and the creation, training, and equipment of a rebel army by the name of Mukti Bahini, supported by Indian commandos, points to a potential plan to push the crisis towards the dismemberment of Pakistan.

The Indian military had been approached as early as April, after the start of Operation Searchlight. It had asked for a grace period of several months, keeping in mind its need for equipment and the forthcoming monsoon that would make large parts of the low-lying areas of East Pakistan inaccessible. According to Sisson and Rose, Chief of Staff General Manekshaw said the Indian Army was not ready for military intervention in East Pakistan and that it would need six to seven months to prepare for conflict.[10] It seems the idea would have been to let the Pakistan Army cope with the situation and the monsoon while the Mukti Bahinis took on the task of fighting. If by the end of monsoon in October, East Pakistan had not collapsed, India could still give the situation the last push by short-term military intervention. They add, 'New Delhi considered it essential to assist in the creation of a resistance movement in East Pakistan, as the political and military basis for direct Indian intervention.'[11]

One major consideration of India—other than Pakistan—was the opinion of the international community. Indira Gandhi set out to visit many countries in Europe and beyond, to garner sympathy for India and its involvement in the crisis. She tried to exhibit Pakistan as the inhuman aggressor against the freedom struggle of the suppressed Bengalis and asked them to end the military action by exerting pressure on Pakistan. The refugee burden won India widespread sympathy, though not much help was offered to cope with it. Most governments were not inclined to take an initiative in the East Pakistani crisis and saw it as a domestic matter for Pakistan.

Even the Soviet Union, at this point, was not a great help to India. In the month of June, Indian Defence Minister, Jagjivan Ram, mentioned for the first time, that 'war may be thrust on us', thus changing the official stance of the Indian government. At the same time, Foreign Minister Swaran Singh told the parliament that if the crisis dragged on, India might have to take action.[12] These words were backed up with action—the Indian Army started moving its units close to the border in May and June and Indian artillery began the intermittent shelling of East Pakistani units across the border. Thus,

India had moved from a denial of military involvement, to a covert engagement in the border areas.

However, India was wary of the reaction of the international community—particularly the US and China, who were on Pakistan's side—to its direct involvement in Pakistan's internal affairs. The US government had not yet suspended its military hardware deliveries to Pakistan, contrary to its official statements. China was no friend to India and the two had fought a war in 1962. China was known to support Pakistan in the UN and other international forums and would have supplied the needed weapons as and when the US had stopped providing them.

In the first round of initiatives, India pleaded with UNESCO in May, to stop economic and military aid to Pakistan. But this did little to change international sentiments. India had to find a way to blame Pakistan, to justify its military intervention as self-defence. It chose to call the East Pakistan crisis an 'indirect aggression' by Pakistan, which had caused millions of refugees to flee to the neighbouring country. Diplomatic missions were sent out by India to popularise this version of the story, first to Europe, the US, and Asian countries and later to Africa and Latin America. However, it met with limited success.

There was another problem as well. India's relationship with the UN had a chequered history—possibly an outcome of the dismal performance of the UN Security Council (UNSC) in the Kashmir conflict. India had approached the UNSC in January 1948, for its approval of the Maharaja of Kashmir's right of accession to India and a condemnation of Pakistan as an aggressor in the war. The UNSC did not condemn Pakistan, nor did it come up with a solution that was acceptable to India.

The strained relationship became quite apparent when, in June, a delegation of the United Nations High Commissioner for Refugees (UNHCR) headed by Sadruddin Aga Khan, arrived in India to assess the refugee situation. India alleged that the delegation was not neutral, but biased in favour of Pakistan. According to Myard:

[The Aga Khan's] June 1971 visit to East Bengal turned out to be particularly counter-productive; the Indian press presented him as a Pakistani agent; it radicalized India's attitude and made him lose any influence on this side of the conflict. The military option was at the time seriously envisaged by New Delhi, and Sadruddin's *faux pas* [of having allegedly said that Pakistan had established facilities to receive returned refugees[13]] was exploited to undermine the credibility of an alternative solution: repatriation without drastic regime change [i.e. the establishment of the Awami League government] in East Pakistan.[14]

Interventions of UN Secretary General, U Thant, were rejected by India and on 3 August, Foreign Minister Swaran Singh categorically rejected the possibility of UN observers on Indian territory. The reason for this might also have been that those observers could have observed the massing of Indian troops at the border, their involvement in arming and training of the Mukti Bahinis and the covert military action of the Indian Army across the border. When, in October, both India and Pakistan started the full-fledged mobilisation of their armies along the border, U Thant again offered mediation between the two for a mutual withdrawal of forces from the border area. While Pakistan agreed to the proposal, Indira Gandhi 'replied with a thousand-word letter that, in effect, accused the international community and, by implication, the secretary general, of trying to save the military regime in Pakistan.'[15]

India was thus denying the obvious fact that the India–Pakistani relations—including the grievances over Partition and the unresolved Kashmir conflict—did play a substantial role in the way it was dealing with the East Pakistan crisis. India would not admit that it was trying to rectify what she perceived as unfinished matter of Partition, by promoting the break-up of Pakistan.

India, as a leading member of the Non-Aligned Movement, had traditionally maintained a distance from the leading power blocs that dominated international politics at the time. As a result, it was not on close terms with the US and the Soviet Union. Additionally, the East Pakistan crisis risked heightening tensions with the UN and the US. The way India saw it, the time for a political solution to the crisis had run out. Thus, in August, the efforts by the US Consulate in Calcutta to try to mediate between Pakistan and the Awami League government were rejected by India. In early September, Indian authorities instructed the government-in-exile to terminate all contact with the US Consulate in Calcutta.[16]

In another development, Indian Prime Minister, Indira Gandhi, visited Washington in November 1971, in an attempt to garner sympathy for India's involvement in the crisis. The US government tried to meet India's expectations by offering full financial support for the refugees and attempted to mediate between Yahya Khan and Indira Gandhi. The latter accepted financial support, but did not respond to any other overtures. According to American sources, senior American officials were convinced that the Indian government had already decided to dismember Pakistan by force, before Indira Gandhi came to Washington and that the discussions were futile.[17]

The relationship between India and the Soviet Union, meanwhile, had suffered since the Tashkent peace negotiations, when Russia acted as a moderator between India and Pakistan, to settle the outcome of 1965 war. Moscow's attempt to accommodate both countries was not taken well by India. As a result of this, Moscow's plan for an Asian Security System, issued in 1969 by Russian President Leonid Brezhnev, was met with little enthusiasm by India. Yet only two years later India had to reconsider its position. In order to ensure that it would not be labelled an aggressor in the East Pakistan crisis, it needed international support. During their world tour to garner this support, Indian diplomats realised that there was little sympathy for the Indian position. Only the USSR had something to offer—the suspension of Russian arms sales to Pakistan in exchange for Indian support in the Asian Security System.

In mid-1970, a draft for a treaty had been prepared that met the expectations of both Moscow and Delhi, but the signing of the document was postponed. Indira Gandhi was heading a minority government at the time and an agreement with Moscow risked undermining India's neutrality in the Non-Aligned Movement. By the summer of 1971, however, the situation had changed. Gandhi's government was secure and she was in need of Soviet support for her plans in East Pakistan. Therefore, on 7 August 1971, the Treaty of Peace, Friendship and Cooperation was signed between India and the Soviet Union. During the negotiations leading up to the signing of the treaty, India made it clear that if a political settlement was not reached in Pakistan within a few months, it would use military force to solve the problem. By then, a political solution was highly unlikely. Despite Russian reservations, Indira Gandhi announced on a visit to Moscow in early September, that the start of hostilities was expected by the end of monsoon.[18] She remained unmoved by the Russian Foreign Minister, Alexei Kosygin's insistence on a peaceful solution. Moscow finally gave up its resistance and in late October, Air Marshal P.S. Koutakhov arrived in Delhi to chalk out India's defence needs. Confident of Soviet support, India went ahead with its plan.

Notes

1. Sisson & Rose, p. 136.
2. Lt. Gen. J.F.R. Jacob, *Surrender at Dacca: Birth of a Nation* (Dhaka: The University Press Limited, 1997).
3. Ibid., p. 90.
4. Sisson & Rose, p. 145.
5. David Myard, *Sadruddin Aga Khan and the 1971 East Pakistani Crisis: Refugees and Mediation in Light of the Records of the Office of the High Commissioner for Refugees*, Global Migration Research Paper 1, Programme for the Study of Global Migration (Geneva: Graduate Institute of International and Development Studies, 2010), pp. 8–9.
6. *Statesman*, 18 June 1971.
7. Myard, *Sadruddin Aga Khan and the 1971 East Pakistani Crisis*, pp. 43–4.
8. Sisson & Rose, p. 148.
9. Ibid., p. 149.
10. Ibid., p. 209.
11. Ibid., p. 151.
12. Ibid., p. 187.

13. Ibid., p. 189.
14. Myard, p. 47.
15. Sisson & Rose, p. 190.
16. Ibid., p. 194.
17. Ibid., p. 196.
18. Ibid., p. 202.

18

Dhaka Daze

In August, my journey home to Dhaka, from the POW camp in Panagarh, via Calcutta, Nepal, and Thailand, came to an end. We had encountered a severe thunderstorm during the journey, but as we approached Dhaka, I could see that its skyline was clear and the lights of the city were visible. Home was now less than a heartbeat away. But was it really home, or another transit stop—to West Pakistan?

Shortly before we landed in Dhaka, I felt a moment of trepidation while recalling Brigadier Ghulam Hassan's remarks that I would be a cynosure here. My views, in any case, were not in consonance with those prevailing in the Pakistan Army at that time. Hence, it would be incorrect to state that I was not apprehensive—I was. However, I was very clear in my mind about the situation in East Pakistan. I did not wish to go and witness what was happening to this part of my beautiful country, I was only going there because I had been ordered to do so.

To me, East Pakistan was home and yet I was well aware that as a Pakistani, I was no longer welcome in my mother's homeland. The time had come to take a final decision. Such being my views, it made my situation even more precarious—I was going to land myself in more trouble. Yet somehow, I was determined to do the right thing; I had been through too much not to blindly put my trust and faith in God. If I was right, I would be vindicated and if I was wrong, then I fully deserved any punishment meted out to me. Yet one obvious question continued to linger: why was I coming to a place where I would be judged 'guilty' of harbouring 'soft' views on Bengalis? My dilemma was great—my father was a Punjabi and my mother a Bengali; unfortunately, Punjabis and Bengalis were involved in annihilating each other and no end seemed to be in sight. What I had witnessed in Dhaka on 25 and 27 March, shocked me. What I saw later with 4 EB and with 2 EB, was no less shocking. I was in a no-win situation. Undoubtedly, many excesses were perpetrated on innocent people belonging to West Pakistan and those of non-Bengali origin.

What does a man feel while returning home after having undergone such a tremendous experience? He is excited and expectant. As opposed to his reticence up till now, he wants to relate his experience to everyone. He thinks he has lived through a miracle—and indeed, he has. The careful hand of God has seen him come safely home. He wants to embrace everyone with joy. He wants to lie down and kiss the soil that he thought that he would never see again or be ever destined to walk over. The emotions well up in him because he thinks everyone knows the experience that he has been through. As time passes and his excitement is not reciprocated, he is unable to understand why everyone is so subdued and remote. He can sense their hostility and suspicion. It is then that he realises that he has allowed his emotions to get the better of the cold professional in him. He calms himself, because he knows he will soon have to submit to the cold, inhuman eyes of those that will debrief him and in their own way, try to cast holes in his narration.

Was East Pakistan 'home' in August 1971? Yes, it was, but anybody who was living there in mid-1971 knew that it was only a matter of time before the country would be torn asunder. I experienced this divisiveness first hand at the 2 EB. In two months, the Pakistani unit had gone from being completely loyal, to outright rebellion. I was in a temporary home. I disembarked onto the wet tarmac of Dhaka airport. The clock had turned full circle. I was back where I had begun. The journey was over and the inquisition was about to begin.

Driving into the city, I was struck by the number of bunkers and check posts on the way. Dhaka was under siege, in the grip of a civil war and it was depressing. We stopped in front of one of the government buildings surrounded by barbed wire. An officer, who was waiting for us, informed me that this was the headquarters of the Inter-Services Screening Committee (ISSC) and that Brigadier Qadir, its chief, was awaiting my arrival. Still carrying our weapons and our bags, we went up a flight of stairs to Brigadier Qadir's office. He was waiting outside and we shook hands. He then said to me, 'So you are the Superstar.'[1]

The ISSC was established to screen those East Pakistanis who were suspected of either helping the rebellion, or for being active Awami League sympathisers—in other words, anyone found working against the concept of a united Pakistan. The ISSC relied on Field Interrogation Centres (FICs), Field Intelligence Units (FIUs), Military Intelligence (MI), and Inter-Services Intelligence (ISI) detachments, for information. I believe it worked under the control of the MI directorate in East Pakistan and a mini-headquarter of this directorate functioned within HQ Eastern Command. The suspects were allocated various shades of colours, used to categorise to their guilt, or lack thereof. These included labels such as 'jet black', 'black', or 'grey,' while those who were cleared, were 'white'.

These rebels, who were captured in battle, were kept in a prisoner camp called the 'Cage'. Lt. Shamsher Mobin Chowdhury of 8 EB, who was wounded at Kalurghat in early March 1971 and captured, was also kept in the Cage. Shamsher later rose to become the Foreign Minister of Bangladesh. His elder brother, Nurul Hasan Khan, (known as N.H. Khan), rose to the rank of a Secretary to the government. He also served as a highly successful Bangladesh Trade Commissioner in Karachi. His daughter is married to Brigadier Majumdar's son. An outstanding human being in all sense of the word, he is like an older brother to me.

The 434 Field Interrogation Centre (434 FIC) was located in the same building in the 'second capital' as the HQ ISSC. The hostel layout for members of the National Assembly (MNAs), adjacent to the parliament building had very nice bedrooms, with attached bathrooms. While others were interrogated, my room remained unlocked and I was free to move around within the compound, but was requested not to disturb the working of the offices. I was free to receive visitors, but they were required to take permission from Major Farooqi (Commanding Officer, 434 FIC). This was almost never refused, or so I had reason to believe. It was a crucial period in East Pakistan, and Dhaka as the capital, was at the centre of the action. From my visitors I was able to get a first-hand overview of what was happening in East Pakistan, especially in Dhaka.

Other than those interrogating me, I had a stream of officers coming to see me from various headquarters and units in Dhaka and elsewhere. Some had genuine queries, while others came out of sheer curiosity, inventing reasons to see me. The visitors included family and relatives—my sister Shahnaz and her husband, Omar Hayat Khan (a distant relative of Mujib), my cousin, Kazi Bashir of Rose Garden (former Mayor of Dhaka)—and politicians who had joined the PPP, or were planning to do so. These included some friends from the university and some politicians and bureaucrats—mostly Bengalis—sent by Maj. Gen. Farman Ali Khan, who was Head of Martial Law in East Pakistan.

Among those who were incarcerated in other 'cells' (and whom I was allowed to meet), were former deputy high commissioner to Sri Lanka, Saidul Hasan; Alamgir H. Rahman, former General Manager, ESSO East Pakistan (my mother's cousin); and Lt. Col. Reza ul Jalil, former CO 1 EB. I knew all three very well; Saidul Hasan's daughter Sharmeen, would later marry my good friend, Adil Hussain, son of Zahir Hussain, the former Governor of East Pakistan. I always met my visitors individually and never in a group. Both Saidul Hasan and Alamgir Rahman were being interrogated on the grounds that they were Awami League sympathisers, and Colonel Jalil for not being able to control 1 EB, when it was disarmed in Jessore Cantonment.

The picture that gradually built up in my mind over the weeks was that the insurrection was gaining momentum. The officers who came from outside Dhaka, spoke of continuous small-unit action, mostly on the border and not confined to one area alone. Invariably, they spoke of supporting artillery and small arms fire from Indian forces, whether the army or the BSF.

Interestingly, those who came from outside Dhaka gave their rendition of facts in a rather matter-of-fact way, without any bravado or bluster, while those who visited me from the headquarters in Dhaka, were far more gung-ho. This did not come as a surprise. Those who engage in battle seldom boast about it, whereas those who do not, tend to be all talk. As the days passed, one could perceive the sense of anxiety among those in the field. One never detected any fear among them; on the contrary, the 'Dhaka boys' remained blissfully on top of the world.

Among the senior officers who came to see me were Brigadier Baqir Siddiqui, Chief of Staff Eastern Command and Brigadier Aslam Niazi, who commanded a brigade. Siddiqui had commanded 6 EB and I knew him well. He was clearly playing second fiddle to Aslam Niazi, who was the first cousin of Lt. Gen. A.A.K. Niazi, the Commander Eastern Command. Brigadier Aslam Niazi did most of the talking, asking some searching questions but both were clearly not satisfied when I told them that the Indian intention was probably to keep us thinking and spread out thinly along the border, so that they could easily break through at any point. Niazi opined that perhaps that was why I had been 'sent'—to change the prevailing strategy, which was to defend every inch of the border instead of concentrating on some well-fortified strong points (or Boxes), like the Dhaka Box, Chittagong Box, Khulna Box, etc. This, however, went against the thought that prevailed among the Guardians of Eastern Command. Niazi's parting shot was, 'That's why you rebelled, [so] that you could become general without having to work for it.'

The feelings of my friends and relatives were divided. Some thought that we could survive as one country, but an overwhelming number in East Pakistan felt otherwise. The rumour mills were working overtime during the war and lurid stories were making the rounds. Some cited instances of rape and pillage, while others categorically refuted these. One could, nevertheless make out that things had heated up considerably outside Dhaka. At night, gunfire could occasionally be heard in the city. It was impossible to sift fact from fiction. As the months passed, the gunfire in Dhaka kept increasing.

The metropolis of Dhaka may have boasted modern residential areas like Dhanmondi and Bonani, but its lanes were narrow and tight. Most of the ambushes took place near crossroads like Farm Gate, near Shahbagh Hotel, Radio Pakistan, Motijheel Commercial Area, and EPR Peelkhana.

Married to my maternal grandaunt, Abdus Salam Khan,[2] President of the Pakistan Democratic Party (PDP) and Shahnaz's father-in-law, came to see me twice—once on the request of Maj. Gen. Farman and again on his own volition. Because of his political standing, the government had repeatedly offered that he become the Governor of East Pakistan. In his two long meetings with me in late August, Abdus Salam Khan asked me searching questions about the rebellion of the East Bengal Regiment, India's involvement and the views of the rebels. He mentioned that the governorship was offered to him, but that he could only accept it if the autonomy envisaged in the Six Points Programme was agreed to. He offered to defend me if my case ever came to trial, but correctly predicted that while I was 'technically' in violation of the Manual of Pakistan Military Law (MPML), my escape from a POW Camp and voluntary return thereof to East Pakistan, was a positive indication of my intentions and patriotism. Once I was cleared in November 1971, I saw him again. While bidding me goodbye, he said, 'You have a long life to look forward to and have every reason to live it with your head up.' He died three months later, in February 1972.

It was quite surreal to be incarcerated in 434 FIC along with Alamgir Rahman, my mother's cousin. Since he and his Hindu wife had no son, he saw me as one. He was the Vice President of ESSO East Pakistan for two long tenures and founded ESSO Fertilizer (now Exxon) in 1966. In 1971, he was picked up by the army for his affiliation with Mujib, as he was the main conduit between the latter and the American consulate general in Dhaka. Over discussions ranging from personal to political, he never wavered from his stance for greater autonomy in East Pakistan. However, he said that after the military crackdown, he was doubtful as to whether Pakistan would remain one entity. According to him, the only realistic chance of keeping Pakistan from disintegrating was to hand over power to Mujib. When my sister passed away and I visited Bangladesh in 1977 with my parents, Alamgir uncle was the Chairman of Meghna Petroleum (the Bangladeshi successor of ESSO Petroleum).

Lt. Col. Reza ul Jalil was considered a star in the East Bengal Regiment. A competent officer, not only was he eloquent, but known for his excellent staff work. On promotion, he deservedly got the command of 1 EB at Jessore. When 1 EB revolted on the morning of 29 March, Colonel Reza ul Jalil's role became subject to controversy. As mentioned earlier, Colonel Jalil found himself in the middle of a mutiny and was uncertain of which side he would take, according to Major Lehrasab Khan. During a lull in the fighting that had broken out, those who did not want to join the revolt went across under a white flag and surrendered, Colonel Jalil was among them, but was later isolated from the others. A day or so later, the Bengali element was separated from the non-Bengalis and shot. In his communication with me while in captivity in 434 FIC, Jalil remained confused about his stance. It came as a shock to see such a tremendous soldier in the state of mind that he was in. Maybe he did not trust me and therefore refrained from revealing his true feelings. When Bangladesh came into being, he was retired and joined the civil bureaucracy, where he rose to a fairly high position.

Lt. Col. Fateh Mohammad Khan Yusufzai was commanding the FF Battalion; he had just been flown in from West Pakistan and was in transit to the forward areas in East Pakistan. He was originally 2 EB and had served under my father. When I was the Adjutant 2 EB in Lahore, he was one of the company commanders. Among his officers was Lt. Arjumand Buttar, the grandfather of former Supreme Court Justice, Javed Buttar. He and his two brothers—Pervez Buttar, a senior practitioner of law in Australia and Lt. Col. (retd.) Jamshed Buttar—

very close friends of mine. As a student, Arjumand would constantly visit me in Lahore and used to say he joined the army keeping me in mind, as a role model. Billeted near ISSC headquarters for a few days, both came to see me a number of times. Colonel Yusufzai knew that I liked *pakoras* with my tea and had his field mess deliver them to me daily. The handsome Arjumand was an excellent professional soldier; he embraced martyrdom somewhere between Jessore and Khulna, during the last days of the war. He was eager and enthusiastic to go into battle and his inherent courage was visible to those who had the privilege of knowing him during the 1965 and 1971 wars. Having lost many friends during the wars, I have always felt strongly about Arjumand's *shahadat* (martyrdom). Full of life and vigour and always in good spirits, he was to me, symbolic of the many young officers who have died for their country.

Major (later Colonel) Salman Ahmed, formerly of 1 EB, was operating with an SSG Company in the Chittagong area when he heard the news of my return. Excited, he rushed to Chittagong airport in Patenga and, upon seeing a Fokker-27 readying itself for take-off, drove his jeep onto the runway, to board it. Salman spent the next couple of hours with me in 434 FIC, alternately berating and embracing me. We had virtually grown up together as friendly rivals—his father commanded 1 EB and my father 2 EB. He was a favourite of General Osmany, who wanted him (as a second generation Tiger) back in 1 EB from SSG, sooner rather than later.

From Salman, I got the first heads-up about the military and political situation in East Pakistan. He made sure that the SSG element posted in Dhaka would get me anything that I needed. A few days later, he came along with another close friend, Major Bilal Rana. This time, both went into detail about Panagarh POW Camp, how far the airport was from the camp itself and the guards at the airport and the camp. It was only a few years later, when the Israeli raid at Entebbe took place, that I realised Bilal's fertile mind was planning something along those lines. Easily one of the most flamboyant SSG officers ever, Bilal embraced *shahadat* near Chandpur, when the launch (boat) evacuating the Division HQ staff was strafed by an Indian jet. Always attempting something daring, this accomplished frogman was also a skydiver. He made me fly him up in an OH-13S helicopter, as high as it could go, in Mangla in 1969 and did a freefall over Mangla airfield. Salman was very easily the most combat-experienced soldier in the Pakistan Army. Besides having participated in several dozen operations in East Pakistan before and during 1971, he trained the likes of Ahmed Shah Masood, Gulbuddin Hekmatyar, Sibghatullah Mojaddedi and several future mujahideen leaders in Peshawar, under Maj. Gen. Naseerullah Khan Babar, in 1974 and 1975. In 1994, Salman gifted my daughter an Afghan horse that he had gotten from Mullah Mohammed Omar. He had a Tajik family look after the horse in his Bedian Farm (near Lulliani on the Lahore–Kasur Road) for many years. No Pakistan officer can come close to doing what he did in Afghanistan, where he was known as 'Colonel Faizan'. It was he who escorted the journalist Sandy Gall into Afghanistan in the early 1980s, when the latter was working on his documentary, *Allah Against the Gunships*. His SSG Company was attached with us in 44 Punjab (now 4 Sindh) during operations in Balochistan, in 1973.

Salman and Bilal had a fair idea of the precarious military situation in East Pakistan, but the senior military hierarchy in Dhaka did not care to listen to them or their commanding officer, Lt. Col. (later Brigadier) Z.A. Khan.[3] Salman knew Afghanistan as no Pakistani does and he is not even a Pathan. The entire south (Kandahar, Herat, etc.) was his area of operation and it was during his time that Mullah Omar entered the equation.

Another emotional visit almost immediately after, was that of my close friend Major (later Lt. Gen.) Ali Kuli Khan Khattak[4] and Major (later Lt. Col.) Patrick Tierney. Both of them were very happy to see me safe and stayed with me for quite some time. Ali and Patrick gave me a good rundown of all the various operations going on in East Pakistan, particularly those involving the Army Aviation. Flying MI-8s in East Pakistan, Ali Kuli was involved in dozens of helicopter assaults and evacuations of injured personnel under direct small-arms fire. I have known him since I was 12 and cannot recall him doing anything wrong.

Pakistan's destiny changed when Ali Kuli Khan, the senior-most qualified and combat-oriented General, was stepped over for the appointment of COAS, which was given instead to Musharraf, who had never seen combat but boasted about it. Musharraf had always been a very good officer. He was the only SSG officer who did not see combat in 1977 in either East or West Pakistan (and neither in 1965, or earlier), but this was not his fault—his postings kept him away from the sound and smell of battle. While Patrick migrated to Canada later, Ali Kuli remains one of my best friends to this day and his wife, Neelofer, is like a sister to me. Ali and I had talked a lot about East Pakistan before 1971 and I had prepared a small brief for his father, Lt. Gen. Habibullah Khan. When uncle Habibullah died, Ali discovered in his papers a file containing the clippings of all my newspaper articles. I have been privileged to serve as a Director on two of his family's publicly listed corporate entities, for over a dozen years.

Major (later Brigadier) Liaquat Bukhari, commanding officer of Log Flight of 4 Army Aviation Squadron in East Pakistan, came to see me, to ensure I did not tell my interrogators how I got an AK-47 and a 7.62 rifle out of the *kote*. This had been done with his permission, but through Patrick Tierney. He said it would get Patrick into trouble. Like a fool, I obliged this blatant liar and suffered the consequences.

For me, another emotionally charged visit was that of Lt. Col. (later Lt. Gen.) Imtiaz Ullah Waraich, who had been my platoon commander (Qasim 34th Long Course) in Pakistan Military Academy. Having been posted out before my last term there, he blamed his absence for my not getting the coveted Sword of Honour. Commanding a unit of the Punjab Regiment in the Jessore–Khulna area in 1971, he had hitched a ride on a MI-8 helicopter to come and see me. Having risen to the rank of lieutenant general, he became deputy chief of army staff, before retiring from the army. As chairperson of Fauji Foundation, he would sometimes turn to me regarding commercial matters, saying 'your teacher has now become your student.' He particularly wanted to uncover the intricacies in the contract concerning the FOTCO Oil Terminal at Port Qasim. This was a great idea, but they had problems with their partner in Singapore. He overcame this to Fauji Foundation's benefit and I remained in touch with him almost on a daily basis after his retirement and even spoke to him on the day he passed away. Other than being professionally brilliant and a war hero, he was easily the smartest soldier I have ever met. His 'turnout' was immaculate and he expected no less than the same from others.[5]

To me, the most important visitor other than my father was my sister Shahnaz, who lived in Dhaka and who came to see me the day after I arrived. Part of her visit overlapped with Salman's; the three of us, as well as Salman's sister, had grown up together as army brats. I could feel her emotions as she embraced me for several minutes, her body shaking. One of the most beautiful women that I had ever seen (or maybe I was prejudiced, being her brother), Shahnaz was blunt and outspoken. She would not mince her words and was perennially fighting for the underdog. Given that she loved the army, she was traumatised as to what was happening in East Pakistan. Being the daughter-in-law of a powerful politician, she would hear exaggerated stories on a daily basis. I tried gently to explain to her during her many visits that excesses tend to be committed in times of war. Shahnaz was always a wealth of information derived from a spectrum of relations across East Pakistan, including that of Bihari origins. Her stance was not prejudiced; she was vehement in condemning the atrocities against small pockets of non-Bengalis. During my meetings with Abdus Salam Khan, one could see that he was disturbed and yet very proud of Shahnaz that she was so outspoken about this. I could imagine his embarrassment when visitors to his house would be subjected to criticism about the atrocities against non-Bengalis. My sister could wear a number of *saris* as a Bengali, but her physique and manner of speaking was clearly that of a Punjabi. Salman, on the other hand, received a tongue-lashing because of the army's 'bad' conduct. Having seen it all first hand, he could only gently remonstrate with someone he loved as a sister since her childhood. Knowing she was pregnant and could come in harm's way, I requested my father to take her to Lahore, just to be safe. One example of Shahnaz's 'free spirit' was that she smuggled into my chamber a small puppy named 'Pinky' in her handbag, to keep me company. When she came to West Pakistan in November 1971, she brought Pinky along. When she went back to Dhaka in March 1972, with her daughter, Shahnoor Hayat Khan (aka Joya) who was born on 8 January 1972, in Lahore, she left Pinky behind.

With the exception of the Major Farooqi and a certain Sub Hakeem, the attitude of the rest of the staff at 434 FIC was positive. When Farooqi and Hakeem asked former Deputy High Commissioner Saidul Hasan—a brave and honourable man—for money to 'ease their situation', he flatly refused. Realising that Said had excellent connections, he was 'shot while escaping' when being 'taken' to another location. Nearly sixty at the time, Uncle Said (as I knew him), had a calm and courteous demeanour and in his frail condition was incapable of even running a few steps. The staff of 434 FIC told me that there had been a number of incidents in which soldiers had been 'shot while escaping'. Brigadier Iqbal told me, without mentioning this particular case, that there were a couple of serious enquiries against Farooqi, a thoroughly despicable human being. Some in East Pakistan did exceed their authority, at times brutally, but most were held accountable. Does this sound like an army running amok?

On 12 November, I was called to Brigadier Qadir's office, where I met Brigadier (later General) Mohammad Iqbal Khan, the Director of Military Intelligence (DMI) at the GHQ. He had served with my father in 1957, in Operation Closed Door in Comilla. Embracing me warmly, he congratulated me on my escape from the POW Camp and said that I was 'cleared' and could resume my duties as soon as possible. Since war was imminent, he gave me a choice of serving in either East or in West Pakistan. I had no wish to serve in East Pakistan and requested that I be posted to an infantry unit. Iqbal Khan said he would convey my request to the Military Secretary Branch, but I should report to Army Aviation Base Dhamial—since then renamed Qasim, after my late instructor. He said that 'technically' I had 'overstayed leave', because I did not report to any unit after my 'joining time' was over. Even though this was not true—I was on 'joining time' and I had done both 'hovering' and 'flight' checks on both the Alouette-3s on the instructions of Liaquat Bukhari and Patrick Tierney—I accepted a 'severe reprimand' from the Station Commander Dhaka, without protest.

Coincidentally, Brigadier Mohammad Iqbal Khan was later promoted to major general in March 1972, and took over 33 Division in the desert, where I was serving with 44 Punjab (now 4 Sindh). Two months after taking over and after consultations with my brigade commander and commanding officer, he selected me to set up a makeshift Desert Battle School in an orchard just short of Umerkot and serve as its first chief instructor. It is now known as the Army Desert Warfare School located in Chhor, Mirpurkhas, Sindh. Major (later Brigadier) Farooq of 12 Baloch, was the commander. The 44 Punjab was a favourite of General Iqbal's—he would select us for all the tough tasks. His brother-in-law, General Muhammad Sharif (who was our GOC in the latter part of the war in 1971), was the first Chairman Joint Chiefs of Staff Committee (JCSC), while Iqbal himself was the third Chairman JCSC. They would make it a point to see me whenever they came to Karachi, while in service and even after retirement. To this day, the families of Iqbal and Sharif are like my own.

In October 1977, when my sister died, I visited Dhaka for the first time since 1971, 2 EB was virtually running Bangladesh. Maj. Gen. Ziaur Rahman was the COAS and the Chief Martial Law Administrator (CMLA); Maj. Gen. H.M. Ershad (later Lt. Gen. COAS and President) was the Deputy COAS; Brigadier Nurul Islam (later Maj. Gen.; nickname Shishu) was the Adjutant General and the Principal Staff Officer to the CMLA (de facto PM); Brigadier A.S.M. Nasim (later Maj. Gen. and COAS) was the Military Secretary. Nurul Islam, who had been the Adjutant 2 EB when I first joined the unit, offered that I should go and visit the building which had housed the ISSC headquarter and 434 FIC, in 1971.

Other than the visits by my friends that uplifted my morale during those days, I did not share positive vibes with the inquisitors of that time. Some were plainly prejudiced and then became increasingly frustrated as the fabricated evidence against me collapsed. I refused Nurul Islam's offer, saying that I had no intention of seeing that place again. However, it did bring back memories of that day in August 1971, when I arrived at the 434 FIC from Bangkok, with Mehr Khan and Nabi Bakhsh.

To quote an extract from my book, *Escape from Oblivion*:

I turned around and embraced Nabi Baksh and Mehr Khan, and handed over the bag containing my AK-47, pistol and grenades to them. I told them that their mission was over. Someone, who they recognised as being from their set-up, was also waiting for them. As they embraced me, they had tears in their eyes. Mehr Khan said to me, '*Khuda Hafiz, Sahib, Allah har waqt aap jaise daler bandey kay saath rahai ga*' (Goodbye Sahib, God will always be with a brave person like you). I knew then that my journey back from oblivion was really over. I have never forgotten Mehr Khan's words to me; God has always looked over me!

Notes

1. Ikram Sehgal, *Escape from Oblivion: The Story of a Pakistani Prisoner of War in India* (Karachi: Oxford University Press, 2012), pp. 123–5.
2. Abdus Salam Khan belonged to Gopalganj, Mujib's home district and was even said to be his distant relative. A fervent activist of the Muslim League, he parted ways in 1949 over the language issue and supported Huseyn Shaheed Suhrawardy in making a breakaway faction of the Muslim League in 1949, called the Awami Muslim League. As a Vice President of the Awami Muslim League, he was elected to the United Front (Jukto Front) alliance, which defeated the Muslim League in the provincial elections of 1954. He then joined the Cabinet. When the word 'Muslim' was dropped from the party's name, he left the Awami Muslim League and resigned from his ministerial post. In 1960, he was disqualified from contesting elections, under the Elective Bodies Disqualification Order.

He re-joined Awami League when it was revived in 1964 and was in its Central Executive Committee when the Six Points Programme was adopted in 1966. He was the Chief Defence Counsel for Mujib during the Agartala Conspiracy Case in 1967, but because of differences, he again left the party in 1969, to form the Pakistan Democratic Party, along with Nurul Amin and Nawabzada Nasrullah Khan.

3. Z.A. Khan's two books, *The Way it Was* and *Weapons and Tactics*, were published by Ikram Sehgal in the 1980s, when he was working with Ikram Sehgal's corporate entity as a consultant.

4. *See* Annexure 5: Lt. Gen. (retd.) Ali Kuli Khan Khattak, HI (M).

5. *See* Annexure 6: Lt. Gen. Imtiaz Waraich, HI (M), SJ.

19

The Theatre of the Absurd
September–October 1971

Since 11 April, Lt. Gen. A.A.K. Niazi, Commander Eastern Command, had taken over the position of Martial Law Administrator in East Pakistan, with Maj. Gen. Rahim Khan as his deputy. General Niazi was not the first choice of the Pakistan Army, or even the government. He was even junior by rank for this position. But Yahya and Hamid had not been able to find an active military officer of the right rank ready to take this precarious position. Niazi offered to take up the position probably due to his characteristic bravado, overconfidence, and limited understanding of the importance of the civilian dimension of the crisis. He was, perhaps, unable to foresee the strategic implications of pursuing a solely military solution in East Pakistan. Brigadier (retd.) A.R. Siddiqi, in critically appreciating General Niazi's performance, writes:

> From day one as commander of all theatre forces—the army, navy and the air force—he would brook no interference or entertain advice from his predecessor and senior General Tikka Khan. This would lead to a tense equation between two serving generals posted in the same place and saddled with the same job of bringing peace to East Pakistan. Niazi's eight months, April 11 to December 16, as the General Officer Commander-in-Chief (GOC-in-C) in the Eastern Theatre were marked by ad-hocism and tactical improvizations outside anything like a strategic framework. He lived and fought for the day without much thought or concern for the next, except perhaps as part of some ongoing action at company or battalion level.[1]

The delicate political situation in East Bengal required careful handling. Coupling military action with civilian affairs did not help improve the situation. Militarily, law and order had been restored in the cities by mid-May, yet no political process was initiated. The reason for this was that General Yahya did not appreciate that a political solution would require a compromise from both sides. He insisted on the trial and imprisonment of Mujib and refused to lift the ban on the Awami League. Such a stance made political progress impossible and garnered criticism across the globe. This became clearer in August, when Yahya felt the need to gain clarity on the implications of the Indo–Soviet Treaty and Russia's stance. For this reason, on 3 September, Foreign Secretary Sultan Muhammad Khan was sent to Moscow to hold in-depth talks with Soviet Foreign Minister, Andrei Gromyko and his Deputy, Nikolai Firyubin. Sultan Muhammad Khan expressed Pakistan's fears regarding the escalating role that the Indo–Soviet treaty could play. Gromyko insisted that this was not the Soviet intention and advised Pakistan that only a political solution would end their problems in East Pakistan and for that Mujibur Rahman was a key figure.

> In the USSR and other countries people believe with anxiety and concern that the well-known Mujibur Rahman will be brought to court. Irrespective of your attitude, hardly anyone would deny his importance as a leader or his calibre, irrespective of one's political sympathies or antipathies… In the present tense situation to take any steps against Mujibur Rahman would be denounced by both the Soviet people and in world public opinion.[2]

Gromyko also expressed apprehensions with regard to the refugee situation. After his return from Moscow, Sultan Muhammad Khan informed Yahya that 'we may henceforth take it in the event of our problems being referred to the United Nations, the full weight of the Soviet Union would be thrown behind India.' He summarised the impact of his report on the President, 'it confirmed my view from the time before going to Moscow that Yahya Khan was not particularly interested in what the Soviet Union might or might not do with regard to East Pakistan developments. Unfortunately, he seriously underestimated their capability for inflicting damage, and overestimated the US willingness and ability to restrain India, and help Pakistan.'[3]

The same caution had been expressed by China and the US regarding Mujib's trial and potential conviction. However, Yahya and his advisors, who were insisting on the trial as a kind of personal revenge for the role they thought Mujib had played in bringing about the crisis, never heeded this advice. Yahya and his circle disregarded the importance of international opinion and sympathy in favour of Mujib. Due to this insatiable desire for revenge, any chances of a real political solution were lost.

Yahya thus went ahead with his idea of a 'political settlement'. He appointed an East Bengali, Dr Abdul Motaleb Malik, as Governor of East Pakistan. Motaleb Malik hailed from the Kushtia district, had studied medical science in Vienna, and was married to an Austrian lady who had converted to Islam and fully adopted Bengali dress and culture. His association with the Muslim League since 1936, provided for his political career in independent Pakistan. He served from 1950–5 as Minister for Public Works and Health in the government of Ghulam Mohammad and from 1956–66 as a diplomat to several countries. In 1969, he joined the Pakistan government as Minister for Health, Labour, Works and Social Welfare and was sworn in as Governor of East Pakistan on 3 September 1971.

On 17 September, a council of ministers drawn from different political parties, including the Awami League, was sworn in to serve as Motaleb Malik's cabinet. The appointment of a civilian governor and cabinet, was meant to be a last ditch effort by Yahya to bring East Pakistan under a formal notion of civilian rule that, it was hoped, could win the support of a cross-section of East Pakistani society and bring about an impression of normalcy to civilian life in East Pakistan. However, this newly inducted government was sidelined by the military administration of East Pakistan—headed by General Niazi—who did not believe in running the province through a civilian administration. For this reason, it remained ineffective. The rapidly developing ground realities in East Pakistan forced Motaleb Malik's cabinet to resign on 14 December, before taking refuge under the International Commission of the Red Cross at the Hotel Intercontinental, Dhaka.

General Niazi was in charge in East Pakistan—militarily and politically. During his period in office, he enjoyed the full support of Yahya and the COAS, General Hamid, for implementing the policies devised in Rawalpindi, especially the nullification of the election results of December 1970. By side-lining the Motaleb Malik government, Niazi made his costliest blunder. He 'militarised' the normalisation campaign wholly to the exclusion of the civilian side and the details that required urgent attention. Part of that campaign was the effort to arrive at a political solution that included the 'loyal' members of political parties other than the Awami League that had been elected in December 1970.

For that purpose, on 5 September, a general amnesty was announced for all civilians and members of the armed forces alleged to have committed crimes since 1 March. A number of detainees, mostly politicians aligned with the Awami League, were released. However, the amnesty did not extend to the majority of the Awami League. Only eighty-eight of the elected members of the General Assembly and ninety-four members of the Provincial Assembly were cleared of criminal charges and therefore included in the amnesty. Most of them had left the country and were in India, only few General Assembly members had stayed in Dhaka. A total of seventy-nine General Assembly members and sixty Provincial Assembly members remained on trial, either in person, or in absentia, under criminal charges and high treason. Their seats were declared vacant and fresh by-elections were announced on 19 September, to be held in November–December. Yahya, however, refused to deal with any political conglomerate under the name of Awami League and ordered to go ahead with his original plan for by-elections. On 18 September, he announced that a new draft Constitution was under preparation by a commission and would be allowed to be amended by the National Assembly, subject to his consent and that of all federating units.

By 12 October, Yahya announced that the draft would be published by 20 December, by-elections held by 23 December and the National Assembly convened on 27 December. In preparation for the by-elections, all parties other than the Awami League and the PPP, were encouraged to come forward and renew their political activity and possibly form a coalition to contest the forthcoming elections. While Yahya considered the Awami League seditious, he distrusted the PPP and Bhutto as well; they were considered uncompromising, divisive in their political stance, and incapable of holding the country together.

Nurul Amin, a prominent Bengali politician of the Muslim League and Chief Minister of East Pakistan in 1948 was viewed as a potential candidate for prime minister—one who would be politically weak and, in Yahya's opinion, acceptable to both parts of the country. Amin could, therefore, head a coalition government consisting of the smaller parties of both East and West Pakistan. Even at this late hour, Yahya was unable to realistically assess the situation and act accordingly. Any window of opportunity that may have existed had been closed much earlier.

Yahya and the East Pakistani establishment closed their eyes on another matter as well. They did not see that it would have been unfeasible to hold elections in East Pakistan at that time. Not all constituencies of the vacant seats were under the control of their administration—or under any control for that matter. Even in districts controlled by the Pakistan Army, it would have been difficult if not impossible to set-up and man polling stations and guarantee the security of the voters and the polling process. Despite all this, efforts continued and on 26 October, Nurul Amin announced that he had successfully cobbled an electoral alliance of six parties. It was announced that some of the vacant seats had been 'filled without contest', while other candidates had been 'elected unopposed'.

On 7 December, in the middle of the civil war, the government announced that the remaining elections had been postponed indefinitely. One senior army officer in East Pakistan spoke of 'Total administrative paralysis and absence of governmental control', in the outlying areas from November onwards. According to Sisson and Rose, 'It was like a scene from the theater of the absurd.'[4]

The security concept for a united Pakistan was, from the very beginning, more focused on West Pakistan. That was partly a result of the fact that the army itself was heavily dominated by Punjabis and Pashtuns and the belief that Bengalis were 'cowards' and not a 'martial race'. But the threat perception of the Pakistan Army since the inception of the country, also supported this view. Ever since the country came into being, West Pakistan seemed much more vulnerable; the Kashmir conflict, which erupted in the first months of Pakistan's birth, festered like a sore wound in the flesh of the country. There were critical developments, such as the Pakhtunistan question and the refusal of Afghanistan to accept the Durand Line as Pakistan's western border. These problems directed the attention of the military towards the western part of the country.

East Pakistan, on the other hand, though surrounded almost completely by India, was not viewed as endangered. Most of the Pakistan armed forces thus remained concentrated in West Pakistan. In case of a war with India, the plan was to defeat it in the western wing.[5] In case of an emergency, China would step-in to ensure the security of East Pakistan. This defence concept was exposed during the 1965 war, when Bhutto mentioned it in an interview with western journalists. It was not taken well by the Bengalis, who as a consequence, added the creation of a separate Bengali army to the list of their political demands. This statement was also not welcomed by the Chinese, who had not been informed of these expectations and it took Bhutto a rushed visit to Peking and quite some diplomatic efforts, to smooth tensions and prevent China from officially contradicting him.

By March 1971, the number of West Pakistani troops in East Pakistan was reported to be 12,000.[6] This excluded the number of

Bengali soldiers and regiments that were considered vulnerable to insurrection and who would either be disarmed or would defect to India and regroup as part of the Mukti Bahini. More forces were brought in to cope with the Bengali uprising and for Operation Searchlight. General Niazi, who was in charge at that time, wrote in his book, that 'The total fighting strength available to me was forty-five thousand—34,000 from the army, plus 11,000 from [the] CAF [civil armed forces] and West Pakistan civilian police and armed non-combatants.'[7]

Moreover, the Indian ban on overflights slowed down troop and equipment mobility. Men had to be flown to East Pakistan via Colombo, while material had to be shipped to Chittagong. With the situation in Chittagong becoming vulnerable, the unloading of ships would become difficult. General Niazi and the GHQ in Rawalpindi were well aware of these limitations, yet the security concept applied in East Pakistan was still not revised.

The Pakistani military were aware of Indian troop movements to West Bengal and the border between India and East Pakistan. Even before September, there had been border attacks from the Indian side and infiltration by members of the Mukti Bahini. This phenomenon gathered strength from September onwards, as the monsoon receded and under the influence of the Indo-Soviet treaty signed in August. With the Indo-Soviet treaty serving as a confidence booster, India had decided to wage war by then and its preparations were known to the Pakistani Army.

Iman Ullah revealed in *The Nation* of August 23, 1990, that the Inter-Services Intelligence (ISI) had 'placed a copy of the Operational Instructions (of the Indian Army) on the table of the President of Pakistan General Mohammed Yahya Khan on 16 September'. It had been signed on August 19, 1971, and fixed November 21 as D-day.[8]

On 5 September, David Loshak, correspondent of *The Telegraph* in New Delhi, stated that the Indian Army had begun a major build-up, moving units into key positions, enhancing its general state of readiness and cancelling leave and retirements. The air force and the Border Security Force had also been put on alert. On 8 September, Pakistani troops repulsed an attack by 300-armed persons, including the Indian Border Security Force, in the Khanjanpur area of Rajshahi district, in East Pakistan. On 25 September, six Pakistanis, including women and children, were killed and eight others wounded, as a result of Indian shelling at Atgram, a border village northeast of Sylhet. In a letter to the UN general secretary, the foreign secretary of Pakistan stated that India was openly interfering in the internal affairs of Pakistan. On 28 September, it was reported that the Pakistan Navy had liquidated a team of Indian-trained frogmen, sent into East Pakistan to sink ships carrying food grains and other relief supplies.

In October, the situation grew increasingly tense and there were daily reports about Indian attacks along the East Pakistan border. In a protest note, Pakistan warned India about the consequences of unprovoked shelling in the border areas of East Pakistan. The commander-in-chief of the Pakistan Air Force, in a note to his Indian counterpart, warned against further air space violations by India and threatened an appropriate response. On 21 October, *The New York Times* correspondent, Sydney H. Schanberg, reported that Indian trains carrying arms for Bangladeshi guerrillas were arriving in Calcutta daily. He reported that the guerrillas were trained in camps on the Indian side of the border with East Pakistan and that the Indian arms build-up was for a 'Frontal push into East Pakistan, to secure a chunk of territory.' *The New York Times* reported widespread military build-up that had 'virtually encircled East Pakistan.' A day later, on 22 October, the *Press Trust of India*, quoting reliable sources, reported that about 1,110,000 army reservists had been called up for service in view of the border situation. In its protest note to India, Pakistan cited twenty-one incidents of border violations in the period between 6 and 12 October. According to J.N. Dixit, 'from mid-October onwards, India had stepped up its support to the Bangladeshi freedom fighters. Indian Army and naval units were put on alert to give support to the freedom fighters…."[9]

In a press conference in New Delhi on 19 October, Indira Gandhi summarily rejected a proposal made by the UN secretary general, for the withdrawal of forces from the border while Pakistan accepted the offer in a letter dated 22 October.[10] British Prime Minister Edward Heath urged Indira, on her visit to the UK, to accept a UN presence in India to help facilitate the return of refugees to East Pakistan. Indira declared that India was totally opposed to UN personnel on either side of India's border with East Pakistan. By the end of October, hectic diplomatic efforts were underway to allay the looming war threat in the subcontinent, with little success.

As previously mentioned, in the wake of Operation Searchlight, a large number of East Bengalis fled their homes and crossed the border into India, giving rise to a refugee problem in the affected areas. The Indian government used the refugee problem in August and September to gain international sympathy and as a bargaining point for a solution that included the creation of Bangladesh. According to official reports in Pakistan, the number of East Pakistanis returning home rose after the announcement of an amnesty by Yahya and due to miserable conditions in the Indian refugee camps.

India refused access to representatives of the UNHCR and Prince Sadruddin Aga Khan, who wanted to check on the conditions of the East Bengali refugees in the camps along the border. India did not like it when the number of refugees returning home rose at the end of monsoon. On 13 September, it was reported that Indian troops had been mining the routes that East Pakistani refugees would take in order to discourage them from leaving. It was a clear sign that the refugees would be used as a pretext for a further militarisation of the conflict.

In two incidents of mine explosions, thirteen returnees died and thirty-four were injured. In October, Labour MP from Glasgow, Thomas McMillan, after a visit to East Pakistan, said that he found no evidence to suggest that there was a continued migration of refugees into India, as was being claimed by New Delhi. He pointed out that in fact, many had returned home from the Indian camps. On 4 October, Prince Sadruddin Aga Khan (UN High Commissioner for Refugees) while addressing the Executive Council of the UN Refugee Programme in Geneva, reiterated that the best solution for the refugee problem was to repatriate the refugees and that India and Pakistan should sign an agreement in this regard. But such an agreement was obviously not in India's interest at this point.

One reason for this was the vulnerable political situation in the Indian state of West Bengal that had seen bouts of President's Rule since 1968. But the more important reason was the opportunity India saw for the dismemberment of Pakistan. As early as April 1971, New Delhi had planned military action in East Pakistan—something the Pakistan Army did not expect and was not aware of at the time. It may have been the reason why GHQ Rawalpindi did not revise its military and political strategy in East Pakistan. The Commander of the Eastern Command until March, was Lt. Gen. Sahabzada Yaqub Khan, a brilliant strategist, who realised the deficiency and could have been asked to review the defence options, but was instead allowed to resign and take early retirement. After that, General Tikka and Niazi failed to even notice this deficiency in the defence strategy. The GHQ under General Hamid did not seem to have been any brighter. Sitting in Rawalpindi, they might also have been deceived by their own media policy that was painting a rosy picture of the situation in the eastern wing.

From August onwards, a third phase of Mukti Bahini initiatives began, which involved—at times with the support of Indian artillery—attacks on Pakistani border posts, to 'liberate' patches of territory along the border. By October, the Mukti Bahinis were carrying out extensive guerrilla activities inside East Pakistan, blowing up offices and army installations, destroying bridges, disrupting supply lines, and killing 'collaborators' of the East Pakistani government. At times, Indian soldiers would be disguised as Mukti Bahini.

INTERNATIONAL SITUATION

In September and October, India doubled its efforts to break Pakistan up. Indira Gandhi went on world tours to promote her version of the East Pakistan crisis. She was in Moscow from 27 to 29 September, attempting to secure support. After this visit, Moscow's attitude changed from trying to keep a balance between Pakistani and Indian sides, to full-fledged support for the latter. On 15 October, Soviet President, Nikolai Podgorny, met Yahya in Persepolis, Iran, where he rejected Yahya's offer of withdrawing the Pakistan armed forces from the border if India stopped supporting the Mukti Bahini.[11]

On 24 October, Indira Gandhi started her tour of Europe, with stops in Belgium, Austria, the UK, France, and Germany. There, she prepared the ground for the acceptance by the world of a breakaway independent state of Bangladesh and the military role that India was going to play in its creation. In New Delhi in September, a Bangladesh mission had been officially inaugurated in preparation for this step. She even visited the US, but could not bring around Nixon or Kissinger. Documents declassified by the US State Department, among others, revealed one key conversation transcript of a meeting between Nixon and Kissinger in the White House, on 5 November 1971, shortly after a meeting with Indira Gandhi, in which they expressed their disdain of the Indian premier.[12] But Europe turned out to be much more receptive to India's intention, supporting the idea that the situation in East Pakistan was a 'war of independence and self-determination', rather than an internal secessionist movement. With that, the arena for the last act of the drama was set.

Acknowledgement

Dates and events in this part are based if not indicated otherwise on the Chronology published by Chronology September–November 1971, *Pakistan Horizon*, Vol. 24, No. 4, The Great Powers and Asia (Fourth Quarter, 1971), pp. 90–145 http://www. jstor.org/stable/41393104?seq=7#page_scan_tab_contents.

Notes

1. A.R. Siddiqi, 'Gen A.A.K. (Tiger) Niazi: an appraisal,' *Dawn*, Features, 13 February 2004, https://www.dawn.com/news/1065607. Accessed on 3 April 2016.
2. Sultan Muhammad Khan, *Memories and Reflections of a Pakistani Diplomat* (Karachi: Paramount Books Pvt Ltd., 2006), p. 320.
3. Ibid., p. 334.
4. Sisson & Rose, p. 176.
5. Niazi, p. 128.
6. Bose, p. 174.
7. Niazi, p. 52.
8. A.G. Noorani, '1971: Kremlin Key,' Book review of Jamsheed Marker's *Quiet Diplomacy: Memoirs of an Ambassador of Pakistan* (Karachi: Oxford University Press, 2010), *Frontline*, Vol. 27, Issue 05, 27 February–12 March 2010, https://frontline.thehindu.com/static/html/fl2705/stories/20100312270508500.htm.
9. J.N. Dixit, *India–Pakistan in War and Peace* (London: Routledge, 2002), p. 197.
10. Thomas W. Oliver, *The United Nations in Bangladesh* (Princeton, New Jersey: Princeton University Press, 1978), p. 64.
11. Matinuddin, p. 317.
12. BBC News, 'Nixon's dislike of 'witch' Indira,' Wednesday, 29 June 2005, http://news.bbc.co.uk/2/hi/south_asia/4633263.stm.

20

The Beginning of the End

Indian Prime Minister, Indira Gandhi, was ready to go to war in April, but the Army Chief, General Manekshaw insisted that the Indian Army needed to prepare for the war otherwise it would risk defeat. The monsoon season ends in East Bengal in October and it usually takes a couple of weeks for the flooded rivers to recede and roads to dry up. That was when troop movement became possible again, in the low-lying territory of East Pakistan, criss-crossed by rivers and streams.

The Indian military command had kept this in mind and when asked by Indira Gandhi, in early April 1971, they announced 15 November as the earliest possible date for the beginning of a full-fledged war in East Pakistan. An additional plus-point from India's point of view was that by then the mountain passes along the border with China would be impassable due to a heavy snow cover, so the danger of Chinese support to Pakistani war efforts was eliminated.

Maj. Gen. J.F.R. Jacob, Chief of Staff to the Commander Eastern Command, Lt. Gen. Jagjit Singh Aurora, made a plan for the conquest of East Pakistan and forwarded it to the army headquarters by the end of May. Thus, the decision to go to war and the preparations for it were taken much earlier than claimed by Sisson and Rose in their book.[1] On 25 April 1971, the first group of officers and men of the Pakistan Army—taken prisoner by the rebels and handed over to India from various locations within East Pakistan—were moved from different prisons to a POW camp set up by Eastern Command at Panagarh, in West Bengal (on the border with Bihar).

While the Indians did not declare war in April 1971, there was no doubt about their involvement in East Pakistan prior to March

1971, through the Border Security Force (BSF) and after April 1971, through the HQ Eastern Command of the Indian Army. The opening of a POW camp many months before the war indicated that India had decided as early as spring 1971, to go for a creeping offensive.

Undoubtedly, the growing number of refugees from East Pakistan pouring into West Bengal and Assam was one of India's reasons for going to war. But another, less-stated reason was the Congress government's belief that Pakistan should never have come into existence in the first place and that its demise had to be promoted more or less silently. This belief is a common thread that runs through almost all Indian political parties to this day.

General Jacob remarked, '...we had very little time to build up the infrastructure and get the logistics in place. I ordered the brigadier in charge of administration of the HQ, eastern command, Brig. Chajju Ram, to go ahead and build up the infrastructure and logistics to support our draft outline plan.'[2]

One of India's major concerns was China's likely reaction to any Indian attack on East Pakistan. In 1962, Chinese troops had overwhelmed the numerically superior Indian Army Divisions in the mountains of the North East Frontier Agency (NEFA) and Ladakh, in a matter of days rather than weeks. What's more, the Chinese army stopped advancing further south of its own accord and not because it had faced a military resistance (no Indian troops of any consequence remained between them and East Pakistan). With such a nightmarish experience in the backdrop, India had adequate reason to be wary of China. This was reinforced when China becoming the major arms supplier to Pakistan after the US imposed sanctions on India and Pakistan, after the 1965 India–Pakistan War.

After 1965, China became Pakistan's main ally. That was why India made it a point to secure the military and diplomatic support of the Soviet Union before making any moves. Therefore, the negotiations for a Friendship Treaty, between India and Soviet Union, were brought to a successful completion in July 1971. Now, India could counter Chinese intervention with military and political support from

Russia. Given Indian attempts to keep war efforts under a shroud of secrecy, another auxiliary force was raised. The Mukti Bahini personnel consisting of East Bengal refugees and deserters from East Bengal Regiment, or the paramilitary East Pakistan Rifles, that had commenced in April and bore fruit by the summer, so that occasional attacks on Pakistani Army installations, with Indian help, were already taking place during the monsoon season.

This tactical device was supported by Pakistan's reluctance to see the East Pakistan crisis for what it is was: much more than mere civil unrest and a war with foreign involvement. India never declared war and did not need to do so. This was left to Pakistan and it eventually did, as late as 3 December, when Indian successes in East Pakistan could no longer be ignored. This shows that the Pakistani GHQ never took the East Pakistani defence seriously; for them war only started when it reached West Pakistan. That happened from 3 December onwards. Therefore, the Indian boast that Pakistan was defeated in only two weeks' time, is less than half of the truth. India had been fighting a creeping war with Pakistan—albeit in East Pakistan—since 26 March 1971.

An undeclared war against the Pakistan Army continued throughout the summer and was sustained mainly by the Mukti Bahini, who by that time had been enlarged, equipped, and trained by the Indian Army that had taken over responsibility from the Border Security Force. Hasan Zaheer, a civil servant posted in Dhaka from May to December 1971, recalls:

The Indian army had taken over the border responsibilities in mid-summer from the Border Security Force, and the *mukti bahini* was operating under its command…. Throughout the period March–November, the highly motivated rebel irregulars kept up the pressure on the Pakistan army…and prevented the resumption of transport, communication, trade, or any kind of economic activity in the province.[3]

The Mukti Bahini were operating directly under army command. On the borders, they were supported by the strong Indian regular forces, during their limited attacks at multiple points of the Pakistan–India border—attacks that were meant to be pin-pricks rather than full-fledged attacks, but nevertheless capable of keeping the Pakistani military engaged along the border. According to Hasan Zaheer, 'Although Indian writers have minimized the role of the rebel force and guerrillas in the "liberation" of East Pakistan, their contribution to the defeat of the Pakistan army was, in fact, very significant.'[4]

By 12 October, Lt. Gen. Niazi had lost 7,700 square kilometres of East Pakistani territory through those attacks. This graphically proved that his plan to prevent the loss of any territory had already become irrelevant and was, militarily, ridiculous.[5] The defensive plan was never updated by Niazi, who did not see the need to do so. No change was demanded by the GHQ either, even though it should have been clear to it by now that the forces present in East Pakistan were insufficient to sustain Niazi's plan for defence. This was professional negligence at its worst and the military hierarchy responsible should have been held accountable for dereliction of duty.

Thus, the plan to fight Indian attacks in the front and the rear was in place when the attack of Indian forces on East Pakistan was launched during the Eid holidays, on 21 November, with incursions in Jessore, Comilla, Sylhet, and Chittagong Hill Tracts. Pakistani troops were thinly stretched out along the border, with battalions holding fronts as long as 30 miles. Lt. Gen. Kamal Matinuddin writes:

> Indian forces entered East Pakistani territory with full force, along with the Mukti Bahini, on the night of 20–21 November. The attacks were no longer limited to border raids or provision of artillery support to the rebels. Proper brigade size operations were now launched against the Pakistani border posts. The Mukti Bahini were directed to bypass the defences and erect blocking positions in the rear to cut off all routes of withdrawal.[6]

No air support worth the name was available to Pakistani troops. Indian troops led by the Commander Eastern Command, Lt. Gen. Aurora, had started to launch probing attacks from different points in the North (Bogra) and West (Jessore), from 15 November. His Chief of Staff, Maj. Gen. Jacob, later recalled that on 20 November an Indian infantry division launched a preliminary attack around Bogra, in East Pakistan, close to the Indian border. The Pakistan Air Force (PAF) struck back, losing three sabre jets in the process.[7]

The situation turned into a full-fledged war from 21 November onwards. Instead of declaring war, Yahya kept stalling. According to Hasan Zaheer, from early November onwards, Ghulam Ishaq Khan, the Cabinet Secretary, set in motion certain preliminary measures to organise the civil machinery for any likely emergency, in view of the deteriorating military situation in East Pakistan. On 6 November, Ghulam Ishaq Khan submitted a note to the President about these preparations and it was implied that he should indicate further action. Yahya returned the note without comment[8] and it was not until 23 November that he officially announced an emergency in the country.[9]

Zaheer recalls visiting West Pakistan during the Eid holidays in mid-November:

As I moved [in] the military and civilian circles of Rawalpindi and Islamabad, I became certain that war with India was imminent.... The people—and they included the well-educated classes—had been carried away by the 'one Muslim equal to ten Hindus' syndrome, which had caught the imagination of even the professional soldier, who ought to have known better.[10]

The Indians knew that they had an overwhelming military advantage in East Pakistan. General Matinuddin estimated the strength of Indian troops around East Pakistan at about 400,000.[11] The topography also gave India the upper hand; it had the advantage of a borderline that almost surrounded East Pakistan from all sides. On the waterfront, it had the overwhelming advantage of its vast navy blockading the coast, while Rear Admiral Mohammad Shariff, the Flag Officer Commanding East Pakistan, had no naval ships to guard the ports of Chittagong and Chalna. A few gunboats were his entire navy.[12]

More importantly, the Indians had the sympathies and support of much of the Bengali population as well as the Mukti Bahini, who were irregulars under their command. Pakistani troops were outnumbered and exhausted by having fought a civil war for the last eight months, with no fresh forces arriving from West Pakistan. While the motivation to fight was there, a lack of support from West Pakistan led even the most optimistic to believe that they would lose. When Indian border incursions began, the over-stretched Pakistani forces faced a hopeless situation.

Archer Blood, the US Consul General in Dhaka, had predicted that East Pakistan was a military liability, 'They could never defend it against India because it is surrounded virtually by India and separated by over a thousand miles'.[13] India knew through intelligence reports that the Pakistani strategy was dividing the troops and dispersing them along the border and for the defence of major towns, thus leaving Dhaka—situated in the fold of the rivers Ganges and Brahmaputra—almost defenceless. Those rivers were two kilometres wide at some points, unbridgeable, and supported by many smaller water flows. This made troop movement from either side difficult, even after the monsoon season. As a result, General Niazi was of the view that the Indians could not possibly move fast and that Dhaka was therefore secure. This must have been the reason why hardly any troops were left in Dhaka.

The Indians, however, worked around this. During the 1971 war, Lt. Gen. (retd.) J.F.R. Jacob was Chief of Staff in the Indian Army's Eastern Command. A major general then, Jacob negotiated the terms of the Pakistan Army's surrender. He explains his war plans:

> The terrain in East Pakistan is divided by the Ganges, Brahmaputra, and Meghna river systems into four sectors. We selected subsidiary

objectives for each sector. In the north-western sector north of the Ganges and west of the Brahmaputra we selected the communication centre of Bogra as the principal subsidiary objective. The western sector lies south and west of the Ganges. Critical objectives were Jessore, Magura, and Faridpur (Goalundo Ghat). Faridpur was to be the final subsidiary objective as it lay opposite the city of Dacca. We asked army HQ for two additional infantry divisions. 9 Infantry and 4 Mountain Divisions were already temporarily located here for anti-Naxalite operations. These we proposed to allot for this sector. The south-eastern sector lay east of the river Meghna. The key objectives were to be Daudkhandi and Chandpur on the river Meghna, an important river port in the proximity to Dacca. We had 57 and 8 Mountain Divisions with no artillery operating in a counter-insurgency role in Mizoram and Nagaland. We could use them in this sector. We would require an additional infantry division. 23 Mountain Division was the reserve for 4 Corps in Assam and could allot this division. For command and control of the sector we could use HQ 4 Corps, whose primary role was to defend against the Chinese in Tibet, [who] could move to this area leaving behind a small HQ at Tezpur. I had no doubt that Dacca, the geopolitical and geostrategic heart of East Pakistan, was the primary and final objective. No campaign could be complete without its capture. We needed one infantry division plus to move from the north, as well as a para-dropped force to capture Dacca. I sent an outline plan based on the above to army HQ in May which was delivered to the then director, military operations Maj. Gen. K.K. Singh by Brig. Adi Sethna, the BGS at our HQ Eastern Command.[14]

General Jacob described the Indian plan as one that involved the bypassing of all small towns and military installations and marching straight for Dhaka. The Indians had accurate intelligence about the lack of fighting units defending the capital city of East Pakistan. Indian air cover would support the advance, which would be carried out using the means of transport and directions provided by the local Bengali population. When the Pakistani troops would come to learn of this tactic, they would have to be prevented from falling back and reaching Dhaka. This strategy was developed because the Indian military command was in a hurry to keep the war short and take Dhaka before the UN and international opinion intervened. Thus, the main goal was not the occupation of East Pakistan territory, but the capture of Dhaka and the surrender of the Pakistan Army there.

The GHQ in Rawalpindi, meanwhile, saw the situation quite differently. When India went to war with Pakistan on 21 November, the UN Security Council (UNSC) should have been alerted immediately but Yahya refused to do this, opting instead to wait until there was a chance that a resolution by Pakistan would be accepted by the UNSC, without a veto. In 1971, there was no defence committee in the cabinet and Yahya took all decisions in times of war and peace, in consultation with the service chiefs and the senior generals close to him. Two days after the Indian attacks of 21 November, Yahya put the armed forces on full alert, declared emergency and ordered the formation of an enlarged emergency committee that would deal with the situation on a day-to-day basis. Hasan Zaheer, who was present in Islamabad at the time, recalls:

> In the meeting of 29 November [Additional Foreign Secretary, M.A.] Alvie presented to the committee a highly optimistic picture of the world's view of Pakistan affairs.... Alvie informed the committee that (a) world opinion had turned to Pakistan's favour... (c) the Chinese Prime Minister had sent a positive reply to the message of the President....[15]
>
> The line in the official media was the same that was being repeated for the last seven months: [that] the overwhelming majority of Bengalis were for [a] united Pakistan, [that] stories of atrocities were fabrications of India and the foreign correspondents, and that any attack on East Pakistan would mean an all out Indo-Pakistan war. ...As I moved round the military and civilian circles of Rawalpindi and Islamabad, I became certain that war with India was imminent.[16]

This shows that the military and civilian leadership of West Pakistan was either oblivious to what was really going on, or that it was a determined to keep the people in the dark while it fought a war—regardless of the outcome. The military and bureaucracy were cooperating on this front. The Governor of East Pakistan, Abdul Motaleb Malik, who also happened to be in Islamabad at that time, was not briefed by either. According to Zaheer, 'Yahya knew that East Pakistan was indefensible and [that] soon, military resistance there would collapse.'[17] He adds, 'The decision to go for an all-out war was clearly not taken on purely military considerations.'[18] He quotes Roedad Khan, who recalled Lt. Gen. Gul Hasan, the Chief of General Staff (CGS), as saying that this action had to be taken and that otherwise they would not be able to wear their uniforms. 'We are being exposed to the charge that we are sitting and doing nothing.'[19] If that were true, it would mean that the GHQ knew that the war would be lost, but sacrificed the soldiers and officers in East Pakistan and may be in the West as well, for their misplaced or fake pride and honour.

The declaration of the start of the war was only one of the many mistakes that were made. From the Pakistani viewpoint, the war had been going on since 21 November and this should have been acknowledged. Sisson and Rose were told during interviews in Pakistan, that the Eastern Command informed the GHQ that war had started on 21 November and that operational orders in East and West Pakistan should be activated, but nothing happened until 3 December.[20] Holding the distance between the two parts of Pakistan responsible for this, they write that the GHQ avoided telephone interaction and communication between East and West Pakistan was almost exclusively by telex. However, the telex messages were said to be open to misinterpretation and confusion, which was what caused the delay. Nevertheless, more than poor communication, the real problem was the inability to understand the political importance of naming India an aggressor.

In any case, Pakistan knowingly missed the point again, when it did not report this attack to UNSC immediately. By deciding to go to war with India on 30 November and doing so on 3 December, Pakistan itself took on the role of an aggressor and devalued the battles that had already been fought by then, as 'border skirmishes'. General Aurora, who mobilised his forces along the border with East Pakistan, later acknowledged that he initiated the attack on East Pakistan soon after the monsoon period was over and long before 3 December.

After the official declaration of war by Pakistan, on 4 December, India launched a full-fledged attack in East Pakistan. The Indian Air Force outnumbering the Pakistanis by three-to-one, attacked the Dhaka airfield and rendered it dysfunctional, while destroying most of the Pakistani aircraft. In the Bay of Bengal, the Indian Navy blocked the port of Chittagong with its aircraft carrier, *Vikrant*, after the Pakistani submarine, *Ghazi*, sank mysteriously with all ninety-two hands on board, while laying a mine, on 3 December. The lack of Pakistani aircraft left Indian troops free to advance on Dhaka, while bypassing the larger towns on their way. When General Niazi realised the precarious situation in Dhaka, he asked the GHQ to send eight battalions, but only two arrived.[21] Thus, the fate of East Pakistan and the outcome of the war was predetermined, as has been argued, conceded, and condoned by the GHQ.

Matinuddin and the Pakistan Army personnel, who fought the war and survived, take pride in the battles that were fought bravely and with determination, irrespective of their outcome. The Battle of Hilli was one such example. Hilli was a small town in the north-west Bogra sector of the borderline between India and East Pakistan.[22] It started on 24 November and lasted for nineteen days, until the Indians gave up and withdrew on 11 December. But this heroic effort went to waste, because while the battle was being fought, Indian troops had already broken through the boundary at Phulbari, about 10 kilometres north of Hilli. Any number of heroic battles could not have changed the outcome of the war, since that had been predetermined by geo-strategic layout of the region, the faulty strategy of General Niazi and the GHQ and the fact that a foreign invasion was coinciding with a local uprising. Matinuddin explains:

General Aurora had over 300,000 men under his command. He had at his disposal tremendous fire power and complete mastery of the skies. The 100,000 Mukti Bahini were giving him real-time intelligence and were operating behind enemy lines to his entire satisfaction. The Indian Navy had successfully established a naval blockade of the war zone in East Pakistan.[23]

On 7 December, Abdul Motaleb Malik's political government had met and voiced its fears in a meeting with General Niazi and General Rao Farman, advisor to the governor on civil-political affairs. They agreed that the situation was serious and decided to send a telex to President Yahya on 9 December, informing him about the state of affairs and asking him to push for a political settlement. In his reply, while referring to the distance that prevented him from a judgement on details, Yahya left any further steps to Malik's 'good sense and judgment.'[24]

In a parallel message, General Hamid authorised Niazi to do what was necessary, keeping in mind the superior forces of the enemy.[25] These exchanges, documented by several sources, were understood to be a permission for a ceasefire. On 10 December, a ceasefire proposal was developed by General Rao Farman and forwarded to the UN, through Assistant Secretary General Paul-Marc Henry who was in charge of the United Nations East Pakistan Relief Operation in Dhaka. However, reports from people close to Yahya, indicate that he was furious when informed about this 'initiative' from Dhaka and informed the UN that the proposal be withdrawn.

With this move of Yahya, the last opportunity for a ceasefire supported by the UN, was lost, despite the fact that it stood a good chance of being accepted within the UNSC and even by the Soviet Union. The only explanation for this move, is that Yahya must have believed, even at this late point, that the US and China would come to Pakistan's aid. This was believed or hoped for in East Pakistan as well; General Rao Farman recalls that on 9 December, when the situation had become critical in Dhaka, a request for reinforcements by airborne forces, for the defence of Dhaka, was sent. Hopes for relief were so desperate that 'when Indian airborne troops later landed in the Tangail area, the Pakistan army mistook them for Chinese troops and went out to welcome them, and were taken prisoners.'[26] It became clear that neither the Chinese, nor the American embassies knew anything about forthcoming military support for Pakistan. For all practical purposes, Farman's message to the UN, delivered through Paul-Marc Henry, on 10 December, was the end of the war. To re-phrase an old saying[27] with apologies, 'it was all over bar the fighting' that had begun in West Pakistan, on 3 December, but kept going on in East Pakistan, since 21 November. This means that the war started no later than 21 November. Yahya and the GHQ, it seems, did not want to admit that things were not going well and they underestimated the importance of naming India as an aggressor. By declaring war on 3 December, Pakistan took on the role of the aggressor. The request for a ceasefire, sent on 9 December, was the logical consequence of the unmanageable military situation in East Pakistan, which could not be mended by the war in West Pakistan.

Notes

1. Sisson & Rose, p. 206.
2. 'JFR Jacob's Memoir: How India Won the 1971 War against Pakistan,' Quartz India, 13 January 2016, https://qz.com/593164/jfr-Jacob-memoire-how-india-won-the-1971-war-against-pakistan/.
3. Zaheer, *The Separation of East Pakistan*, p. 353.
4. Ibid., p. 353.
5. Matinuddin, p. 347.
6. Ibid., p. 362.
7. Bass, *The Blood Telegram*, p. 261.
8. Zaheer, p. 354.
9. Ibid., p. 356.
10. Ibid., p. 358.
11. Matinuddin, p. 355.
12. Ibid., p. 350.
13. Bass, p. 268.

14. 'JFR Jacob's Memoir,' Quartz India.

15. Zaheer, pp. 356–7.

16. Ibid., pp. 357–8.

17. Ibid., pp. 359–60.

18. Ibid., p. 360.

19. Ibid.

20. Sisson & Rose, p. 228.

21. Matinuddin, p. 348.

22. Ibid., pp. 363 ff.

23. Ibid., p. 418.

24. Salik, *Witness to Surrender*, p. 196 as cited in Sisson & Rose, p. 232.

25. Sisson & Rose, p. 232.

26. Rao Farman Ali Khan, *How Pakistan Got Divided*, p. 167.

27. Original saying is 'All over bar the shouting' meaning an activity is essentially finished with an almost certain result but has not yet been made official or announced.

21

The Last Days of United Pakistan

In 1971, Pakistan completely misjudged the international mood regarding the East Pakistan crisis. From the outset, the military-dominated Pakistan government refused to recognise the opinions of various countries and only listened to what they wanted to hear. The ruling junta, headed by General Yahya Khan, was responsible for its inability to handle international relations, including the nature of Pakistan's alliances with its 'friends'—a feature that at times persists until today, among our civilian governments and the establishment. In international relations, there are no 'all-weather friends', but allies, who pursue their own national interest, based on their values and foreign policy. In Pakistan, neither the military, nor the politicians, understood this. The country's fixation on India was preventing a sober evaluation of international power play. This was also true for relations with China, the US, and Russia.

Pakistan's friendship with China gained momentum after the deterioration of ties between China and India, who had fought a war against each other in 1962. The Sino–Pakistan Boundary Agreement of 1963, which included an exchange of territory in the Northern Areas, led to the impression that China would now take Pakistan's side on the Kashmir issue. During the 1965 India–Pakistan war, China supported Pakistan militarily, when the US cut-off supplies. Chinese help was expected, once again, in 1971, but to no avail. Pakistan's military government, claiming a defence doctrine that saw East Pakistan's defence lying in West Pakistan, expected Chinese help for an underequipped military in the east wing. But this was unrealistic, as no such assistance had been discussed with China.

Additionally, China's reluctance was also due to the US–China rapprochement, as Washington fully propped Beijing's permanent UNSC membership. Furthermore, Beijing attempted to sustain its status as a peace-promoting country in the global community, by not engaging in any war directly. The East Pakistan crisis put China in a difficult situation, one that even Pakistan's facilitation of Henry Kissinger's visit to China that year, could not change. By April 1971, China unofficially informed the Pakistan Embassy and the Foreign Ministry in Islamabad that it would not intervene in the hostilities. A message not taken seriously. When the situation in East Pakistan became dangerous after the monsoon, on 7 November, Pakistan sent a deputation consisting of Zulfikar Ali Bhutto, Air Marshal Rahim Khan, and Lt. Gen. Gul Hasan, to Beijing, to ask for thirty fighter planes and other military supplies in the face of a possible war with India. Zhou En Lai is reported to have denied any such possibility, but asserted that if it did happen, China would not intervene directly in support of Pakistan.[1]

The other ally that the Pakistani government had in mind was the US. Despite multiple let-downs in the past, Pakistan had never revised its foreign policy towards the West. For instance, although Pakistan was member of the military alliances of SEATO and CENTO, the US during the Sino–Indian 1962 war, introduced a massive arms aid programme for India that was only 'resented' by Pakistan. During the India–Pakistan 1965 War, the US refused to provide any military support to Pakistan particularly after having brokered the visit of Henry Kissinger, the US foreign secretary to China, in 1971. Pakistan considered itself entitled to US support and ignored the fact that the US was, at the time, actively engaged in Vietnam—a conflict that absorbed most of its military presence in the region. As a result, the US was reluctant to actively interfere in any other theatre of war if no 'vital American' interest was involved. Pakistan did not realise that the US was in fact trying to maintain a balance in its relations between India and Pakistan. This meant not taking sides in a dispute between the two. Thus, on 6 April, the State Department decided a total embargo on new arms licences for Pakistan, while the deliveries under old licences, though not stopped, ran out by late summer 1971. Even economic aid, with the exception of food programmes, was stopped. While President Nixon, who was said to be sympathetic to Pakistan, never criticised Yahya openly, he did not, at the same time, try to offer his 'friend' any advice or persuade him to look at the situation from a more sober perspective. The only American action that could be defined as having a military purpose was the despatch of Task Force 74, consisting of the aircraft carrier USS Enterprise and its escorts, which reached the northern part of the Bay of Bengal on 14 December and then turned south, towards Sri Lanka. This is sometimes seen as a symbolic gesture on the part of the US, in support of Pakistan. It never had any mission related to the ongoing war in East Pakistan, but was most likely a retort to the presence of a Soviet fleet in the Indian Ocean. Thus, Pakistan found itself devoid of any practical help by its 'allies' in the 1971 war.

The Soviet Union was the third power that played a role in the crisis of 1971. As one of the four victorious powers that defeated Hitler's Germany and a leader of the communist countries in the bipolar world that had come into existence thereafter, it had a more pronounced interest in South Asia for two reasons: (1) Russia was a Eurasian power and South Asia was practically in its neighbourhood, separated only by the 15-kilometre Afghan Wakhan corridor; (2) its hostile relationship with China that made Russian politicians think about an Asian mutual security regime to counter it. Therefore, the Soviet Union had a basic interest in a balanced policy towards the countries of South Asia, India and Pakistan in particular. But while India, with its foreign policy based on Panchsheel principles,[2] opted for an independent, third way—involving cooperation with US. Pakistan had, since 1954, decided to join the Western bloc which made good relations difficult. Nevertheless, while hosting the Tashkent peace negotiations in 1966, the Russian Premier, Kosygin, negotiated a settlement between India and Pakistan and from thereon, a more friendly policy towards Pakistan was maintained. One of the reasons for this must have been to counterbalance the growing ties between Pakistan and China. Russia extended economic help to Pakistan and in 1970, even a nuclear cooperation agreement was signed in Karachi. A month later, during President Yahya's visit to Moscow, the steel mill agreement was signed. When Operation Searchlight started in March, the Soviet Union, though no friend and despite being critical of the way Pakistan was handling the crisis, fulfilled its obligations for weapons deliveries though—like the Americans—no new contracts were allowed. It was only after the conclusion of the Indo–Soviet Friendship Treaty in August, that the Soviet Union gave up its balanced policy towards India and Pakistan and started actively supporting Indian military preparations.

The Pakistani government failed to use the UN as a platform to project its policies during the East Pakistan crisis. The main reason for this was that Yahya considered it an internal matter that did not require explanation to the international community. As a possible platform, the UN may also have been unpopular because of its infamous role in handling the Kashmir dispute. For this reason, Pakistan did not trust the UN, or expect it to be an effective international mediator. Nevertheless, 1971 was not 1948 and better representation of the Pakistani stand and the debunking of India's undercover machinations may have delayed, if not prevented, the break-up. For its defeat in the war, the Pakistan Army has only itself to blame. Internationally, India was increasingly viewed as the 'good guy' in the conflict, the defender of human rights, democracy and the self-determination of East Pakistanis.

India skilfully manipulated the platform of the UN from the very start, for its own ends, by forwarding two main arguments. One was to accuse Pakistan of genocide, by putting down militarily an armed uprising within the country; the other was the problem of East Pakistani refugees sweeping the border areas of north-east India. India never talked about the fact that it used the refugees to build up an army of irregulars and sent them back into East Pakistan. When the two delegations of the UNHCR—one led by John Kelly, in July and the other by the Prince Sadruddin Aga Khan, in August—arrived, they were not allowed to go to India and visit refugee camps because the security of the delegates could not be guaranteed. India also rejected UN proposals for the stationing of UN observers, to which Pakistan had agreed. Pakistan, on the other hand, never raised the issue of guerrillas being trained by India in the UN. Agha Shahi, then Pakistan's representative in the UN, was given orders to deny that a growing number of refugees had even crossed the border into India. When, on 21 November, Indian troops carried out the invasion, Pakistan was advised to register a complaint with the UN. Agha Shahi sent a cable to the Foreign Office in Islamabad, asking for advice in the matter. Islamabad answered that he should not act until explicitly ordered to do so. The order never came.

On 7 December, fifteen countries presented a resolution to the General Assembly of the UN demanding an immediate ceasefire and the withdrawal of troops from foreign territory. During the debate, the Soviet representative argued that in case of a withdrawal, the will of the East Pakistani population for secession had to be acknowledged by the UN. Pakistan's representative, Shahi, retorted that the question was not one of self-determination, but autonomy. A resolution demanding a ceasefire and immediate withdrawal was passed, with 104 countries voting in favour, 11 against and a few abstentions. But given the non-binding character of it, it was not implemented and nothing was achieved.

When Yahya did eventually decide to approach the UN, he sent Zulfikar Ali Bhutto instead of relying on Agha Shahi, a seasoned diplomat. On 8 December, Bhutto was appointed Foreign Minister by Yahya and he immediately called Agha Shahi in New York, to inform him that from now onwards he would take over the lead of the Pakistani representation at the UN. The tension that this move created between the two men, would not have been conducive to the Pakistani representation in New York—especially since a seasoned diplomat had to get behind a self-styled and choleric politician. On 9 December, before Bhutto's arrival in New York, Shahi announced that his government accepted the immediate ceasefire demanded in the resolution, but hoped that the UN would ensure the withdrawal of troops from foreign territory and secure it by posting UN observers.

In the midst of the deliberations of the UN General Assembly, Indian Prime Minister, Indira Gandhi was anxious to end the war before any decision blaming India, or imposing an immediate ceasefire could be taken. Therefore, the Indian Army's progress did not come fast enough for her. In a hurry to reach Dhaka, Lt. Gen. Aurora decided to use his parachute brigade to reach Dhaka before the city's defences could be reinforced. Dhaka did not have enough Pakistani troops to put up a fight. All attempts to bring in more troops had failed and further attempts to do so would have depleted other towns of defence (something that was unacceptable to General Niazi because of his ill-conceived defence strategy).

The para-battalion was airdropped in Tangail, close to Dhaka, and securely in the hands of the Mukti Bahini, on 11 December in broad daylight. Avoiding any enemy contact, the Indian troops pushed their way towards Dhaka through outflanking manoeuvres and reached the outskirts of Dhaka on the morning of 16 December. When the troops, under Maj. Gen. Gandharv Nagra, reached the capital, there appeared to be no defence at all. The 26,250 men in uniform that were present there were signallers, service corps, and maintenance personnel. In the annals of modern warfare, this denuding of the vital ground of Dhaka, by the military commander, was not only incomprehensible, it showed a complete lack of military expertise and understanding.

Sensing the disaster, on 15 December, Lt. Gen. Niazi had sent a message to General Manekshaw, asking for a conditional ceasefire. The military hierarchy in Dhaka, however, had already realised the hopelessness of the situation and had requested, on 9 December, a ceasefire in a message to the UN signed by Maj. Gen. Farman, but this was denied by Yahya. Only five days later, it dawned upon Yahya and the GHQ that the battle was lost. On 14 December, Yahya sent a telex message to General Niazi, telling him that further resistance was not humanly possible and would not serve any useful purpose[3] and that they had done all that was possible to find an acceptable solution to the crisis. From there onwards, Generals Niazi and Farman started preparing for a surrender and signalled these intentions to India through the US diplomatic service.

The terms of surrender were prepared by General Manekshaw and presented to Niazi, by Lt. Gen. Jacob, on 16 December. The formal signing of the surrender document was arranged on the afternoon of that day, at the Ramna Race Course, where Mujibur Rahman had delivered his memorable speech of defiance. The document made Niazi surrender not only to the Indian forces, but the Mukti Bahini as well—a fact that was resented by him. The photograph of that memorable event reflects the weight of Indian victory, with the representative of the Mukti Bahini—not General Osmany, who was absent—standing on the side-lines.

After Pakistan's surrender, the Mukti Bahini went berserk. 'Two weeks after the capitulation, the non-Bengalis were in the throes of a slaughter... They had gone so out of control that even the Indian Army had to kill thousands of Muktis after the surrender to put the fear of Allah in them.'[4] While the Bangladeshis today talk about genocide in East Pakistan, they are silent regarding the atrocities committed against the non-Bengali population at the hands of Bengalis.[5]

There is yet another interpretation as to why Pakistan did not make the start of the war known to the world. There is a good chance that the Pakistani military did not differentiate the Indian invasion from the previous Indian policy of 'border pricks' and of sending Mukti Bahinis into East Pakistan for guerrilla activities. Sisson and Rose argue that the Pakistani air attack on India, on 3 December, was considered an 'option of last resort'. The aim at this point, was to even-out, through Western pressure, a losing position in East Pakistan and to induce the US, or China, to come to Pakistan's aid.[6] Yet neither of these was achieved. The war in the western wing was fought primarily as an attack on Indian-held Kashmir and in the Punjab desert. Though characterised by many examples of Pakistani bravery and daring in Punjab, it could not bring any relief in East Pakistan and was ill-managed even in the West. The 18 Division went on an offensive in the desert without any air cover! Why Jacobabad was not activated by the PAF, with or without GHQ consent, has never been fully explained. In fact, India's advantage in the skies reasserted its control over Pakistani skies. In Sindh, troops were moved without air cover and Karachi came under attack through India's Operation Python on the night of 8 and 9 December, in which three merchant navy ships were sunk and twenty-two fuel tanks set ablaze. After 8 December, Karachi's port stopped operating.

The international community remained aloof with both the US and China unwilling to interfere on behalf of Pakistan. The debates in the UN were heavily handicapped by an undecided and uncoordinated Pakistani position. The US was thought to be a staunch supporter of Pakistan on the grounds of the latter's mediation in the reconciliation with China, as well as Nixon's known disdain for Indians. But official US documents of that period show that any such hope in the US was misplaced.

After Indira Gandhi's inconclusive visit to Washington in November, she had launched a full-fledged war.[7] She interpreted Washington's lack of assertiveness as a signal to go ahead. This confirms why, after her visit, Kissinger was sure that war was inevitable. According to Bass, after eight months of slaughter, Nixon told Pakistan's Foreign Minister in the Oval Office that 'he wished he could do more' (meaning that no military support was to be expected from the US) and that 'Pakistan should find a political solution'.[8] But it was too late by then, as the opportunities for a political solution had ceased to exist in September.

Soon after the failure of the Indo–US Summit, the Nixon administration started military sabre-rattling—a customary part of the US foreign relations playbook. Admiral John Sidney McCain, Commander, United States Pacific Command, drew up plans to pull an aircraft carrier task group away from Vietnam and ordered it to sail into the Bay of Bengal. This prompted the cry that 'the Seventh

Fleet is coming', but this rhetoric was the only US support extended to Pakistan during the war.

An important theatre of the East Pakistan conflict was the UN and it was severely mishandled by Yahya, despite the international media's spotlight on Pakistan, during Operation Searchlight. That India had been interfering in East Pakistan, as early as April, was never brought up in the UN. India, on the other hand, used the international theatre much more skilfully; Indira Gandhi's visits to all major powers and the effort of Indian embassies during the nine-month crisis, document this. Agha Shahi, a gifted Pakistani diplomat, was Pakistan's representative at the UN, but could achieve little due to the decisions taken by his government.

India first raised its complaints regarding genocide and the resulting refugee wave, in Geneva, at the meeting of the Economic and Social Council Chamber (ECOSOC), in May 1971. In July, it repeated these, but refused to allow a UN representative to visit refugee camps, as this would have exposed the Indian Army's involvement in training the refugees and involving them in incursions across the border. While India was eager to involve the UN and its organisations in the East Pakistan crisis, it resisted all interference of the UN in India—whether it was the UNHCR, or the posting of UN observers on the Indian side of the border with East Pakistan.

Pakistan did not draw the attention of the international community even when invaded by its neighbour on 21 November. Despite encouragement from some Muslim states, Pakistan did not involve the UN. Instead of putting the blame of aggression on India, Pakistan took the burden upon itself, by declaring war later, on 3 December. The UN's involvement in the crisis started after the war had been officially declared between India and Pakistan and the matter had assumed a dimension that could no longer be ignored in the international arena. Characteristically, India lodged a complaint against Pakistan with the UN Secretary General. An emergency session of the UNSC was summoned on 4 December and for three days the UNSC debated the situation without reaching a breakthrough. The Indian side was represented by the Soviet Union and Poland, while the US and China stood by Pakistan.

India's tactic was to gain time so that Indian troops could reach Dhaka before a ceasefire was thrust upon them. Pakistan tried to stop Indian troops from advancing on Pakistani soil through resolutions that would demand a ceasefire and troop withdrawal. Two such resolutions were put to vote within those three days and both were supported by eleven countries of the UNSC—with the UK abstaining—but both were vetoed by the Soviet Union. During the debates and voting process, Indian troops drew closer to Dhaka. By 6 December, stopping India had become highly unlikely and the UNSC, unable to pass a resolution because of the veto, forwarded the matter to the UN General Assembly, the resolutions of which are not binding.

On 10 December, Agha Shahi was informed by the UN representative in Dhaka, Paul-Marc Henry that Farman, conceding defeat, had asked for a ceasefire. According to Shahi, this announcement was invalid as it did not come directly from Yahya and that Farman, being a military advisor, had no right to demand ceasefire. Only Lt. Gen. Niazi had the power to make this decision. Bhutto, who arrived in New York on that very day, was also shocked by Farman's message. The following day, on 11 December, Yahya denied the validity of the message by the East Pakistani political government and created confusion. But Pakistan faced almost certain defeat, with India reaching Dhaka using a limited force and plans leaking out that it would deploy troops to the western wing as well. Pakistan declared its willingness to accept immediate ceasefire, while India demanded that it recognise East Bengali self-determination above all else.

All the US had done was to send a US Carrier into the Bay of Bengal and demand a new meeting of the UNSC. On 12 December, the second meeting took place. The Indian representative once again blamed Pakistan for the crisis and conceded the withdrawal of Indian troops if Pakistani troops would withdraw from Bangladesh. A fiery

Bhutto spoke for Pakistan and refused to let a country be broken by the force of arms, but he was not heard. Time passed and as the debates continued, Indian troops moved closer to Dhaka. Another resolution was tabled on 13 December, with the same result: eleven votes in favour and a Soviet veto against it. The next day, Poland proposed another draft resolution, demanding a ceasefire and troop withdrawal. This time, Yahya, who was informed about the new draft, seems to have been ready to accept it but was only able to reach Acting Foreign Minister, Bhutto, after several attempts to call him over phone. When they finally spoke, Bhutto is reported to have feigned technical problems, stating that he was unable to understand what Yahya was saying.[9]

When the UNSC met again, on 15 December, news was coming in that the surrender of the Pakistan Army was being arranged. Bhutto, who seemed to have been taken by surprise as far as this development was concerned, was furious. He called the UNSC a farce, stormed out of the Security Council meeting and left for Rome the next day. While the UNSC debate went on without Bhutto, on 16 December, India informed the meeting that a ceasefire had come into effect in East Pakistan, while a unilateral ceasefire had been ordered in West Pakistan. The Soviet Union welcomed the news and demanded that power in East Pakistan should immediately be transferred to the elected representatives of the Awami League, thus accepting the outcome of the Indian war in East Pakistan. A precedent had been set for the break-up of nations by military intervention and the inability (or unwillingness) of the UN to be able to prevent this. The UNSC met again on the same matter, on 21 December—five days after the surrender of the Pakistan Army—and finally adopted a resolution calling for the strict observance of the ceasefire and that the POWs be treated according to the terms of the Geneva Convention. This belated and inconsequential resolution was only possible because the Soviet Union abstained instead of vetoing it.

There is a clear message in the record of the proceedings of the UN and the UNSC. UN resolutions adopted by the General Assembly are inconsequential, as they are not binding. Even UNSC resolutions are of questionable worth if viewed, for instance, in context of its role in the Kashmir conflict and Pakistan's involvement in it. Yet the UN was the sole international forum that had, to an extent, the power to mould international opinion and to negate it was a fatal blunder on Pakistan's part.

After two Russian vetoes, Pakistan should have understood, as Lt. Gen. Matinuddin argues, that the only path towards a timely ceasefire was to agree to the Soviet Resolution put forward on 5 December.[10] It would not have prevented the secession of East Pakistan, but would have prevented a humiliating surrender for the Pakistan Army, saved the lives of many Pakistani soldiers, while preventing tens of thousands of others from becoming prisoners of war. Another opportunity was lost when Farman's offer to surrender on 10 December was rejected. Even in case of a military surrender—by then unavoidable—a conditions-free withdrawal of Pakistani troops could have been reached, without thousands of Pakistani troops becoming POWs. India was ready to withdraw from East Pakistan if Bangladesh was conceded, even as late as 12 December. But Yahya learnt his lesson the hard way, while sacrificing the lives of Pakistani soldiers for a lost cause and leaving the entire nation humiliated.

Notes

1. Sisson & Rose, p. 308.
2. The Panchsheel treaty, also known as the Five Principles of Peaceful Coexistence, is a 1954 declaration of foreign policy that defined the relationship between India and China.
3. Sisson & Rose, pp. 233–4.
4. Matinuddin, p. 238.
5. These have been documented in several well-researched books, including Sarmila Bose, *Dead Reckoning: Memories of the 1971 Bangladesh War* (Karachi: Oxford University Press, 2011; Afrasiab, *1971 Fact and Fiction: Views and Perceptions in Pakistan, India and Bangladesh* (Islamabad: Khursheed Printers Pvt. Limited, 2016); and Junaid Ahmed, *Creation of Bangladesh—Myths Exploded* (Karachi: AJA Publishers, 2016).

6. Sisson & Rose, p. 221.
7. Bass, p. 258.
8. Ibid., p. 260.
9. Ibid., p. 452.
10. Matinuddin, p. 454.

22

The Aftermath of 1971
Lessons to be Learned

The Pakistan Army's surrender in December 1971 was a military defeat. Was any other result possible? In view of a thousand-mile hostile territory separating the two wings; depleted and ill-equipped three-and-a-half infantry divisions against an overwhelming 6:1 superiority (excluding the Mukti Bahini); the eastern wing's ports blockaded; and the local population up in arms against what had essentially become an occupation army. Only the headquarter element of one infantry unit actually laid down its arms prior to the final order to surrender by the Headquarter Eastern Command on 16 December. Even then, despite being cut off and in a hopeless situation, many units and formations surrendered only after repeatedly being ordered to do so.

This military debacle was a consequence of a political defeat suffered earlier, when Yahya Khan and Zulfikar Ali Bhutto, along with the military junta, refused to heed the election result and transfer power to the elected parliament and the prime minister-in-waiting, Sheikh Mujibur Rahman. Undoubtedly, West Pakistan's insistence on keeping power in its hands led to the strengthening of Bengali alienation and the consequent secession of East Pakistan. The political and military defeat of 1971 created two independent Muslim nations in South Asia: Pakistan and Bangladesh.

Bhutto knew after the election that in order to rule Pakistan he had to take East Pakistan and the Pakistan Army out of the equation. This became clear to me in August 1973, when I was called to the Adjutant

General Branch, GHQ, Rawalpindi. The questions I was asked about East Pakistan were meant to assess my feelings about the events of 1971, before allowing me to appear before the Hamoodur Rehman Commission. Having had a harrowing experience while being interrogated by 434 FIC after my escape and return to East Pakistan in August 1971, two years later, in 1973, I was cautious in answering the questions. After three days, I was allowed to leave. The fact that M.I. Qureshi was the Adjutant General at that time and Brigadier Khaleeq was his close aide, would have unfortunate consequences for me later.

I had requested casual leave after my 'temporary duty' at the GHQ and had brought Shahnaz along. My granduncle, J.A. Rahim (Rahim Nana to us in the family) was at that time Minister of Presidential Affairs and Production and had invited us to stay with him in Islamabad. He insisted we have dinner with him every evening. One evening, over dinner, he said that the PPP would never have come to power had the Pakistan Army not lost in East Pakistan in 1971. He repeated this a couple of times. When I brought to his attention the fact that Bhutto had been quite vociferous in his support for military action in East Pakistan, he replied, 'It was necessary. Do you think they would have let us come to power if we didn't?' Rahim Nana was the Secretary General of the PPP and at the centre of party decision-making and thinking, during this momentous period, I could not get over his incongruity. Pakistan's primary political party was willing to let our armed forces be humiliated and lose half the country so that they could come to power!

The odds had been difficult from the beginning. The geographical distance between the two parts of the country and the cultural differences may lead a person who does not have a thorough grasp of ground realities in the subcontinent, to think that running such a country would not be feasible in the long run. It was with fervour and commitment that the project for the creation of Pakistan was started. A large number of people in both wings enthusiastically welcomed independence and their new country in 1947, made efforts for it to succeed, and suffered when it went wrong.

An effort has been made in this book to explain why the break-up of Pakistan happened. Culture, economy, history, geography, internal power politics, international politics and—last but not least—a hostile and conniving neighbour hell bent on separating us played a substantial part. While some of those factors were given not to be changed others were colossal home-made mistakes and self-created problems. As the Hamoodur Rehman Commission later established that army rule had corrupted senior officials involved in the decision-making process, so that they were unable to keep the national interest in mind. The same can also be stated in the case of Bhutto, the leading politician at the time. National interest would have demanded that he concede the prime ministership to Mujib. But the lust for power made him risk the break-up of the country. Even more, we have tried to show the emotional dimension of the crisis, the plight and underlying intentions of the people involved.

Almost fifty years have passed since then and political realities have taught that there had always been space for a second Muslim state in the subcontinent. India seems to be shedding its secular camouflage and openly demonstrating its willingness to be only a Hindu state. Prime Minister Narendra Modi must be recognised for not being a hypocrite and exposing the true feelings of many Hindus in India, thus reinforcing the need for two Muslim states in the subcontinent.

The two successor states, Pakistan and Bangladesh, soon sorted out their relations based on the Simla (now Shimla) Agreement of 1972. In anticipation of the Tripartite Agreement between India, Pakistan, and Bangladesh in 1974, Pakistan diplomatically recognised Bangladesh on 21 February 1974, thus acknowledging the political outcome of the East Pakistani crisis. Since then, the relationship between Pakistan and Bangladesh has been rocky. While most people on both sides were ready to forgive and carry on, the governments of Awami League have, at times, used history to gain political mileage. Thus, the first years of independent Bangladesh were a difficult period of bilateral relations that had to tackle the aftermath of war and secession.

When Bangladesh applied for membership to the UN in 1972, China, on behalf of Pakistan, vetoed its application, because two UN resolutions on the repatriation of Pakistani POWs and civilians remained unimplemented. Pakistan insisted that unless the question of repatriation of the POWs was cleared, Bangladesh should not be allowed into the UN. The POWs included 195 Pakistanis who had been held in India on charges of war crimes and for whom the Bangladesh government intended to set-up a war crimes tribunal. With the matter of their repatriation still unsettled, the National Assembly of Pakistan, in July 1973, granted permission to the government for the formal diplomatic recognition of Bangladesh.

A meaningful change in bilateral ties only came during the preparations for the 1974 Islamic Summit in Lahore. Prime Minister Bhutto invited Mujib to attend the summit by saying that, 'When we have invited Muslims from all corners of the world, how can we keep our doors closed to seven crore Muslims of East Pakistan, who lived with us for twenty-six years'. Mujib refused to come at first, but later accepted the invitation. One day before the beginning of the summit, on 21 February 1974, Pakistan announced the official recognition of Bangladesh. The next day, Mujib landed in Lahore and was warmly welcomed by the officials, as well as the Pakistani population.

The final solution to all problems came on 9 April 1974, when a Tripartite Agreement between Pakistan, Bangladesh, and India was signed. In that agreement, Bangladesh dropped the criminal trials of those 195 Pakistani POWs and Pakistan agreed to repatriate all West Pakistanis left behind in Bangladesh, including all government servants and their families—regardless of their ethnicity—as well as members of divided families. Most importantly, the agreement included a statement by Pakistan's Minister for Defence and Foreign Affairs, Aziz Ahmed, who condemned and regretted any crimes that had been committed by Pakistani soldiers in East Pakistan in 1971. That statement has been made part of the Tripartite Agreement and is part of history. The road towards reconciliation was thus opened by the three signatories of the agreement. After this, all hurdles in the way of Bangladesh's UN membership were removed and the new country was accepted as a member, in June 1974.

I happened to be part of the Pakistani delegation to attend the D-8 conference in Dhaka, in 1998, when the then Prime Minister, Mian Nawaz Sharif, along with Sartaj Aziz, laid a floral wreath on the grave of an 'Unknown Soldier' in Sidhu, near Dhaka. I accompanied the delegation via helicopter to the site of the grave at Savar. When new demands for apologies came up in recent years, President Pervez Musharraf, in July 2002, on a visit to Bangladesh, took a bold step when he implicitly apologised once again for the atrocities that scarred Bangladesh's war of independence. He also visited the war memorial at Savar, and left a handwritten note in the visitors' book. 'Your brothers and sisters in Pakistan share the pain of the events in 1971,' he wrote. 'The excesses committed during the unfortunate period are regretted. Let us bury the past in the spirit of magnanimity. Let not the light of the future be dimmed.'[1]

Therefore, the demands coming from the Bangladeshi side, of more apologies, hold little weight and are politically influenced. How many times can you apologise? The important thing is to mean it and in this regard, there should not be any lingering doubt. What about the thousands of non-Bengalis killed in 1971—particularly in March? The ongoing trials in the Bangladesh War Tribunals are not based on internationally acknowledged procedures and it is unlikely that they will deliver justice or reconciliation. They can also be interpreted as a sign that the history of 1971, its roots and implications, have not yet been sufficiently processed in the minds of the people and their government in Bangladesh.

It took both countries about two years to make their respective peace with the new situation that had come about after the surrender of the Pakistani Army, in December 1971. This was not too long a time. Pakistan had to accept the break-up of its country and the repercussions this would have in regard to its identity and image. It would not be accurate to say that 'the two-nation theory was drowned in the Bay of Bengal'. The dismemberment of Pakistan could have made the Muslims of the subcontinent—especially those in Pakistan and Bangladesh—realise that there is room for more than one Muslim nation in the region, in the same way so many Muslim nations exist in the world. Whatever the size, or form of political organisation, the important thing is that the people of a country should be satisfied and be able to strive for their aims.

The concept of the Ummah—the global Muslim community—remains untouched by these events. While the rulers of both countries may not realise this, the majority of the populations do and continue to cherish their association, despite virulent Indian propaganda. When this lacunae is managed, it will remove many errors and false expectations regarding nationhood and national identity in both countries and as a consequence, help improve national coherence and mutual understanding.

The formal political settlement that was achieved by the spring of 1974 showed that the people of Bangladesh were probably less vengeful and more forgiving than their political leaders. In June 1974, when Prime Minister Bhutto came on his first official visit to Bangladesh, he was welcomed warmly by the public in the streets of Dhaka. Large crowds had gathered at the airport and in the city, shouting 'Pakistan zindabad'. But on the political level problems remained, such as the division of assets. While on the one hand, Bangladesh insisted on the 'repatriation' of those non-Bengalis, who during and after 1947, had migrated to East Pakistan, it irrationally demanded 56 per cent of the common assets, including foreign currency, aircraft etc., based on the population count of non-Bengalis in East Pakistan. At the same time, however, it was not willing to share the burden of liabilities.

Bangladesh's foreign policy during the first years of its independence was largely inclined towards good relations with India. This was understandable, given the vital role that India and its army had played in the break-up of united Pakistan and the fact that without India, there would have been no Bangladesh. India was aware of its decisive role in the birth of Bangladesh and was now trying to use it as an asset against Pakistan.

In March 1972, India signed a Treaty of Peace and Friendship with Bangladesh, on the lines of the Indo–Soviet treaty. It included a paragraph that could be invoked in the event of Bangladesh being attacked by a third country. A trade agreement was signed as well that provided for the creation of a free-trade zone along the Indo–Bangladeshi border, within ten miles and which later turned out to be a problem for Bangladesh, due to smuggling and rising prices.

On 15 August 1975, Mujib's government was overthrown and he and his family were massacred. The political instability was filled by a succession of military coups and military rulers. During 1977–1990, Bangladesh's relations with India cooled down and it got closer to Pakistan. In 1990, the 'restoration of democracy' ran almost parallel to events in Pakistan and entailed the game of musical chairs between the two leading parties, the Bangladesh Nationalist Party (BNP) of Khaleda Zia and the Awami League of Sheikh Hasina Wazed.

The BNP has always been opposed to a renewal of the Treaty of Friendship, Cooperation and Peace with India, which had lasted twenty-five years. Khaleda Zia pledged to 'Free Bangladesh from the shackles of Indian domination and the limitations of Bangladesh's sovereignty, which the treaty imposes due to the lack of foresight of the late Prime Minister Sheikh Mujibur Rahman.'² On the other hand, Hasina Wazed, during her stints in power, upheld friendly ties with India and this naturally distanced her from Pakistan. She last came into power in 2009, after winning the elections that year with a radical programme of pledges to bring prosperity and justice to Bangladesh. Since then, she has sought affinity with India in her foreign policy and naturally promoted the views of her father.

Scratching of old wounds that should rake up tensions with Pakistan is gratuitous from an Indian perspective. For this purpose, the institution of 'Liberation War Affairs Ministry' that is entrusted with the task of keeping alive some of the most vicious and divisive anti-Pakistan themes that were devised during and in the aftermath of the civil war to create internecine hatred and bloodletting, comes handy.[3]

But regardless of the political relations between the two countries, what is far more important is that West Pakistan does not seem to have drawn any valuable lessons from 1971 and its aftermath. The history of the first few decades of Pakistan's existence, leading up to the events of 1971, needs to be thoroughly re-examined and rewritten. Research and publishing initiatives in this regard have thus far remained mostly in the hands of foreigners: Sisson and Rose, Sarmila Bose, and Gary Bass from the US and Yasmin Saikia from India (but who lived in the US at the time of writing). Books by retired army officers, including Lt. Gen. Kamal Matinuddin, although (self)-critical, largely represent the military's perspective on events.

The Hamoodur Rehman Commission Report that contains interviews and classified documents about the events leading up to the loss of East Pakistan and the war with India in 1971. Only twelve copies of the report existed, eleven of which were destroyed while one lies locked-up in the Cabinet division of the government. The Pakistan government had declassified the report in 2002 and made it available in the public domain and on the internet. But it turned out that parts of it had been left out, including, the 1972 interviews of returnees, first published by Vanguard and the 1974 'Supplementary Report' on returnees. While few would want to read the full report, the gist of it should be incorporated into history books.

Questions about 1971 and the reason for the failure of a united Pakistan must be asked anew and answered more accurately. This would be a painstaking process, but the citizens of Pakistan, especially the young generation, should know where they are coming from, to be able to find the best way forward. History plays an important role in identity building and an erroneous historical record creates a false self-perception.

The most important questions are: what must be changed in order to avoid secessions in the future? What consequences do the events of 1971 have in regards to our national ideology? In 2016, the Senate Standing Committee on Law and Justice passed the Constitution (Amendment) Bill 2016 seeking to give major provincial languages the status of national languages—including Punjabi, Sindhi, Pashto, and Balochi.[4] The initiative did not muddy much water in the media, or among academics and until today, the bill has not been made into law by the parliament, despite the fact that recognising those languages as national ones would be a step towards amalgamating those ethnicities into the Pakistani nation.

In Pakistan, history is used as a political tool. It has never been recognised that history has an important role to play in the life of a nation: it explains its past, it supports its present and guides towards the future. It gives identity to a nation, self-esteem and belonging but only if history is written truly and based on the reality of the past. One way in which it has been used to justify the creation of Pakistan, is by drawing parallels with the Indus Valley Civilisation, which remained, throughout history, a distinctly independent and sovereign entity. As such, the creation of Pakistan may not be taken as a partition of India, but a dissolution of Britain's empire in India into its constituent entities.[5] Aitzaz Ahsan, has carried this myth further in his book, *The Indus Saga and the Making of Pakistan*, where he claims that the people along the Indus river have, historically, been different from the rest of the subcontinent and thus, Pakistan's coming into existence was inevitable.

This idea may have been coined by the British archaeologist, Mortimer Wheeler, who published in 1950, *Five Thousand Years of Pakistan*,[6] thus merging the territory that had housed numerous states in the course of history with the political structure that had come into existence in August 1947. It was compiled to present a sketch of the imposing archaeological heritage in the region that comprised united Pakistan. In fact, this territory was based on the Muslim League demand that Muslim-majority areas be made into Pakistan. It was the Radcliffe Commission—named after Sir Cyril Radcliffe—that demarcated the dividing line between India and West Pakistan and India and East Pakistan, thus dividing the British–Indian provinces of Punjab and Bengal against the wishes of Jinnah. When informed of this development Jinnah, who had in mind the undivided provinces of Punjab and Bengal for his idea of Pakistan, is quoted to have described the country that had been carved out as 'moth-eaten'.

Indian politician, Jaswant Singh, after an impressive study of historical documents that were published under the title *Jinnah: India, Partition, Independence* in 2009,[7] convincingly proved that in 1947 there were options other than partition. Despite having adopted the Delhi Resolution in April 1946, that demanded Pakistan, Jinnah, who was solely empowered by his working committee to negotiate with the Cabinet Mission on 19 May 1946, agreed to the plan that proposed a three-tier scheme, with a minimal central union. This would have meant that the central government only managed foreign affairs, defence and communication, while the provinces, 'Should be free to form groups with [the] executive and legislatures,' with each group being empowered to 'determine the provincial subjects to be taken in common.' After ten years, any province could, by a simple majority vote, 'call for a reconsideration of the terms of the constitution'.[8] He withdrew his concurrence on 29 July, when Nehru, in an interview, had questioned his and the Congress' commitment to the Cabinet Mission plan once the British had left. That practically closed the door to the arrangement of a loose federation in independent India.

Archival documents meticulously stored by the British, clearly show that neither the idea of a united Bengal, nor the option of sharing political power with the Muslim League, were acceptable to the leaders of Congress, who decided instead, to opt for Partition. This decision had consequences for both India and Pakistan after independence. India waited for the collapse of the newly founded state and, when this did not happen, did all it could to dismember it.

For Pakistan, this state of affairs meant that it constantly felt as if it was under attack from India from day one. Consequently, its leaders mistakenly believed that the unity of the nation could be made watertight by streamlining its various ethnicities into uniformity. Ethnic differences and identities, it was thought, undermined the nation. Urdu was ordered to be the sole national language to the exclusion of all other mother tongues, despite the fact that only 10 per cent of the population spoke Urdu. Additionally, in mistaking Islam, instead of Muslims, as the founding principle of Pakistan, the founding fathers implemented in the country a rigid interpretation of Islam. When different shades of Shias and Sunnis, Barelvis, Sufis and others were told that they now had to profess the Deobandi version of Islam in order to be 'pakka' Pakistanis, they found it difficult to identify with Pakistan.

Non-Muslims, meanwhile, started feeling insecure in regard to their place in the equation. The matter escalated when Bengalis, who constituted a majority of Pakistan's population, felt economically and culturally neglected. The Punjabi and Muhajir-dominated elite of the country caused hardship not only to Bengalis, but also Sindhis, Balochis, and Pashtuns, creating among them a fervour for concepts such as the Sindhu Desh, Greater Balochistan, and Pakhtunistan. However, none of the three ethnicities were able to muster up the kind of resistance that the Bengalis did. The incongruity of it all is that 'democracy' in Balochistan is supposed to be promoted by Baloch Sardars, who cannot tolerate even a hint of dissent from their tribesmen.

Today, almost fifty years later, many of these problems continue to linger. This time, Balochistan is unhappy with its treatment by the federal government. Secessionist forces, again with the tacit help of India, are trying to apply the model of 1971. This element has been fostered by the Baloch Sardars installed by the British in the nineteenth century. Hybrid warfare has made inroads into Pakistan thanks to technology and feelings of inequality among some. While military action can help to tackle the terrorist aspect of the problem, it cannot solve the underlying discontent and feeling of negligence that has penetrated deep into the population.

The Soviets and their Afghan allies fought a kinetic war in Afghanistan in the 1980s and the US and NATO did the same after 9/11. For the past two decades, using the Afghan platform, India has successfully pursued a non-kinetic war against Pakistan, first through Russian and then through the US. Apart from the economic empowerment that might be achieved through the China–Pakistan Economic Corridor (CPEC), there is a desperate need for a thorough reformulation of Pakistan's national ideology to promote national coherence. The events of 1971 can serve as a strong guideline for that.

This way of looking at Pakistani history clearly explains the looming danger for national coherence if the lessons of 1971 continue to be ignored. We need to rethink the character of our state and national ideology, at a time when globalisation has reached new heights and Pakistan is a vital part of China's One Belt, One Road initiative. Economic, financial, and physical globalisation through expanded communication lines, undermine the structure of nation states, as we have known them so far. In fact, globalisation undermines nationalism and countries based on a national ideology, fixed territory and boundaries, and sovereignty—the idea that a state can take independent and single-handed decisions about how to run the country and that all decision-making power lies in the hands of the national parliaments only.

The inter-dependence of states has strengthening so much that decision-making needs to be adjusted with the neighbours who are affected by those decisions, as well as regional partners. To give up a certain part of independent decision-making is quite a painful process and even the most advanced countries in the European Union cannot easily find a common platform. 'Brexit' is a stark example of this. However, events have shown the contrast between independent political decision-making and the economic advantages of belonging to a larger community. This fact is forcing many in Britain to rethink their plans and if another referendum were to be held, the British might vote against Brexit.

The nationalist slogan 'right or wrong—my country' has to be replaced with the aspiration of being a global citizen. For Pakistan, this means that we will have to tolerate many more cultures and languages, as well as different attitudes towards religion. Given our negative experience with the tough policy of 'unity equals uniformity', the time has come to try another model, one that allows variety and is based on 'unity in diversity'.

South Africa, with a population of 58 million, has eleven official languages. Much smaller countries, like Switzerland and Singapore, have four official languages. India, a much larger country, has two official languages at the national level and as many as sixteen languages are recognised as official because Union States can choose their own official languages. The root cause of the unfortunate insistence on an 'Urdu only' policy is in the idea that a nation needs a national language.

The idea itself is of European origin and has been transplanted by the British onto a subcontinental society that did not meet the parameters of the European idea. Europe had undergone a process of industrialisation, secularisation and individualisation and, as a result, split into multiple nation states based on the modern languages spoken by the population. That was why Indians, while availing of the nationalist idea in order to unite against British colonialism, had to adjust it to Indian ground realities. Thus, we found a mainly secular European template take the form of Hindu and Muslim nationalism and of regional nationalisms, such as Bengali, Tamil and others, all dominated by an overarching all-Indian nationalism. The need was felt to overcome cultural and religious diversity by strongly suppressing it as it was feared to endanger unity, but, tragically, it led to secession.

The idea of 'unity in diversity' is a reality in Pakistan that has yet to be understood fully. It is not understood that identities of humans has developed over hundreds of years and is deeply rooted in their respective cultures, languages, and traditions. A federation in Pakistan must rest on cultural, linguistic, and religious freedom and any negligence of these is bound to have disastrous consequences, as witnessed in 1971 and as can be seen today in the case of Balochistan. The diversity of cultures and languages should be regarded as an asset, rather than an obstacle to unity. This is, of course, a tall order and one that cannot be achieved immediately. The current recourse to evaluate an historical event, which has changed the political map of South Asia, requires serious introspection and self-accountability.

It may be worthwhile to quote Peter Frankopan:

> [A] new world is being born. It is a world of increasing connections, greater cooperation and widening collaboration. None of these are easy or straight forward to get right, and it is important to recognise that rivalry, competition and tensions can be hidden by glossy statements of superficial friendships.[9]

One of the challenges as a historian or as an observer of contemporary affairs is to see the bigger picture. Identifying the ways in which the world is connected and assessing how the dots join up, not only allows for a better understanding of what is going on around us, but provides a platform for a more accurate vantage point too. Assessing how the different pieces of the global geopolitical puzzle are connected to each other also helps to better explain the fragilities and dangers—as well as the opportunities for cooperation and collaboration—that can help frame better decision-making too.

The King of Zhao in north-eastern China, who ruled nearly 2,500 years ago, declared that, 'A talent for following the ways of yesterday is not sufficient to improve the world of today.' Those words of wisdom are as apt today as they were then. Understanding what is driving change is the first step to being able to prepare and adapt to it. Trying to slow down or stop that change is an illusion.[10]

Notes

1. David Blair, 'Musharraf apology to Bangladesh', *The Telegraph*, 31 July 2002, https://www.telegraph.co.uk/news/worldnews/asia/bangladesh/1403185/Musharraf-apology-to-Bangladesh.html.

2. Sanjay Bhardwaj, 'Bangladesh Foreign Policy vis-a-vis India', *Strategic Analysis*, 27:2, pp. 263–78, DOI: 10.1080/097001603084500872003, p. 267,

https://www.tandfonline.com/doi/abs/10.1080/09700160308450087?needAcc
ess=true&journalCode=rsan20.

3. Momin Iftikhar, 'Pakistan-Bangladesh Relations,' *The Nation*, 16 December
2016, https://nation.com.pk/16-Dec-2012/pakistan-bangladesh-relations.

4. Abdul Rasheed Azad, 'Seeks status of national languages: Senate body passes
'The Constitution (Amendment) Bill, 2016',' *Business Recorder*, 9 March 2018,
https://fp.brecorder.com/2018/03/20180309350198/.

5. *Dawn*, 'Five Thousand Years of Pakistan,' 23 October 2011, https://www.dawn.
com/news/668383.

6. R.E.M. Wheeler, *Five Thousand Years of Pakistan: An Archaeological Outline*
(London: Royal India and Pakistan Society, 1950), https://archive.org/details/
in.gov.ignca.17045/page/n7.

7. Jaswant Singh, Jinnah: India, Partition, Independence (New Delhi: Rupa
Publications India Pvt. Ltd., 2009).

8. Source: http://m-a-jinnah.blogspot.com/2010/04/cabinet-mission-1946.html.

9. Peter Frankopan, *The New Silk Roads—The Present and the Future of the World*
(London: Bloomsbury Publishing, 2018), p. 222.

10. Ibid., p. 252.

Annexure 1

Extracts from Ikram Sehgal's Books Published in 2010

Colonel M.A.G. Osmany (later General in the Bangladesh Army), the father of the East Bengal Regiment in all senses, always considered my mother an icon for the Bengal Tigers. Among many initiatives for the battalion and the regiment, my mother gave 2 EB their Bengali marching song, rebel poet Qazi Nazrul Islam's *'Chol, Chol, Chol'*, setting it to music first for 'Bravo Company'. Colonel Osmany soon made sure that it became the regimental song. I believe it is now one of the national songs of Bangladesh. The Bengal Tigers' Family Welfare Center always stood out because my mother made it so. In fact, other regiments of the Pakistan Army followed the model created by my mother, when she got a free hand to do as she wished and got the wives of officers in the battalions, to participate. This was particularly apparent when my father took over command of East Bengal Regiment in Comilla in 1956. When he, at first, lost hope in finding good recruits, she suggested that he screen the jails for volunteers from among those who were not convicted on grounds of moral turpitude—mostly the river pirates from the jails in Comilla, Feni, and Chandpur (some of them belonged to Hatiya and Sandwip). B Company, 2 EB, was mostly from this area and 6 Platoon became the Hatiya/Sandwip Platoon. A least two of the recruits rose to the rank of honorary captain and one of them, Sabed Ali, even became ADC to the President of Bangladesh, as did Honorary Captain, Janab Ali, from Alpha Company 2 EB. My mother would read my articles in *The Nation*, which were translated into Urdu in *Nawa-i-Waqt*. Persian had been one of the languages she spoke as a child at her home in Calcutta. My maternal grandmother was fluent in many languages, including Persian.

The first commanding officer of the battalion, Lt. Col. Zaheeruddin, made me an unpaid Lance Naik (Lance Corporal) at the age of five, for fighting the son of Brigadier Hesky Beg, then commanding 107 Brigade, during the Brigade Boxing Championship at Jessore, where 2 EB had moved to in 1950. I fought him again in Quetta, during the Garrison Boxing Championship in 1952, my father was then at the Command and Staff College and his father was commanding a brigade in Quetta. To me, nothing in the world was as important as my beloved battalion. 2 EB was one of the units in 1953 and 1954, when my father was BM (Brigade Major), 53 Brigade at Comilla. Colonel Zaheer, who committed suicide after leaving the unit, left me his books in his will.

When my father finally took over at the end of 1955 as the seventh Commanding Officer 2 EB, I was nearly ten years old and very much a diehard Junior Tiger, getting into scraps with the brats of the other units in the brigade—2 FF, 2 Punjab (later 1 Punjab) and later, 18 Baloch. Brigadier (retd.) Mujahid Alam, whose father was commanding officer 18 Baloch, was a classmate of my sister, Shahnaz, in Our Lady of Fatima Convent and was one of my best friends. Alam, who is essentially COAS-material, is currently the Principal at Lawrence College, Ghora Gali.

I was well aware that I 'owned' B Company, my father's original sub-unit, particularly 6 Platoon, which mostly consisted of soldiers from the islands of Hatiya and Sandwip. A lot changes when one grows through their teens. Many of those who came to Lawrence College, Ghora Gali, were not from affluent families, but it was hard to live within one's budget when other boys had better clothes and much more to spend (and in some cases, to flaunt). I loved the army and I loved 2 EB, but there was no way I was going to join the army and live the Spartan life that my parents lived, while scraping to send me and my sister to good boarding schools. By the time I was in Notre Dame College, Dhaka, taking part in athletics and playing cricket for the Dhaka University team, I was benefiting from two scholarships—the Burmah Oil Company (BOC) Scholarship, courtesy Maj. Gen. (retd.) Latif Khan (Resident Representative, BOC), and the ESSO Scholarship, thanks to my mother's cousin, Alamgir Rahman (Chief Executive, East Pakistan, ESSO Oil Company). The promise of a brand new car upon graduation as a young oil executive in either of the two companies was a tremendous incentive.

Colonel M.A.G. Osmany, my godfather for all practical purposes, however, had other ideas. He was hell-bent that the 'second generation' be inducted into the Bengal Tiger family. Salman Ahmed, son of Brigadier Mohammad Ahmed (author of Field Marshal Ayub Khan's biography and Commander, 1 EB—Senior Tigers), was already in Pakistan Military

Academy (32nd Long Course) and destined for 1 EB. There was no way Osmany was going to let me off the hook. While my father never forced me, he did encourage me. Osmany convinced Maj. Gen. A.M. Yahya Khan, who was then GOC, 14 Division, in Dhaka, to tackle me with consistency. In short, I had my 'nasal polypus' removed, my 'high IQ' during ISSB Dhaka condoned, and before I knew it, I was entering 34th PMA Long Course, on 14 May 1964.

Once I was in the army, I never looked back and have had no regrets. I topped the first term and nearly made it to the Royal Military Academy (RMA), Sandhurst, but ended up as a 'stand-by' to Salman Ansari, who was deserving. I graduating second on 31 October 1965, as Company Senior Under Officer (SUO) of Khalid Company. The whole of 34th PMA became Khalid Company on 15 September 1965. Earlier, I had been SUO Salahuddin Company for three weeks. I figured in all the three Academy Awards on offer for the shortened PMA Long Course. I was a runner-up for the Sword of Honour and Norman's Gold Medal and winner of the Tactics Plaque.

We had been told in September 1965, that because the course was being shortened, the winner of the Tactics Plaque would get the Sword of Honour. According to both my platoon commanders, Captain (later Lt. Gen.) Imtiazullah Warraich and Captain (later Colonel) Asghar Khan , I would have gotten the coveted Sword of Honour if I had asked for any other unit, particularly a cavalry unit, which everyone knew I would have preferred, had it not been for 2 EB. Major (later Maj. Gen.) Tafazul Rizvi attempted to post me to 20 Lancers and Anwar Jan Babar (later Lt. Col.) was posted to 2 EB. I still joke about it because the Risaldar Major, 20 Lancers, actually came to PMA with the 'Toshdan' for me, as is the custom in good armour units. This was changed when my term commander and platoon commanders realised that I was very keen on 2 EB. After retirement, Anwar Jan was my colleague in the Pathfinder Group for as long as his health permitted. He died recently only a few months after he left us.

While I was destined to join 2 EB, I was also destined to come to grief because of it. Whatever will be will be—*Que Sera Sera*! Colonels Zaheeruddin and Osmany assigned me to 6 Platoon Bravo (B) Company on joining the unit in the field, on 20 November 1965. It was 7 p.m. and raining in Chuadanga, where the battalion HQ was located. An hour or so after reporting to the Adjutant, Captain Nurul Islam, I was sent on patrol by the second-in command, Major Ghulam Sarwar. I almost died on my first night in the unit, on the border near Darsana. Earlier, he had rung my father and asked whether he wanted me to be an officer or a soldier and my father had replied 'preferably both'. When my company commander, Major (later Brigadier) Zair Hussain, who joined the unit a few weeks later, was promoted to unit commanding officer, he made me his Adjutant when the unit reached Lahore. Zair was a wonderful commanding officer, giving me a free hand and trusting me to do the right thing. I learnt a lot from his quiet guidance and the freedom he gave me.

Jamil Hussain (Jimmy) and Maj. Gen. Shakil Hussain (Tony), then 9 and 8 years of age, respectively, are still like family to me. After retiring from the army and serving as Pakistan's High Commissioner in Sri Lanka, Tony is currently COO Wackenhut, in the Pathfinder Group. An Adjutant's job was a difficult task, because the company commanders in Lahore were all heavyweights. They included

- Maj. (later Lt. Col.) Fateh Mohammed Yousufzai;
- the two Maj. Raufs (one later became Brigadier and the other Lt. Col.);
- Maj. (later Gen.) H.M. Ershad;
- Maj. (later Lt. Col.) M.H. Khan (my company commander for ten days in November 1965, before he was wounded);
- Capt. (later Lt. Col.) Rahim Khan;
- Capt. (later Brig.) Wajih Ahmed;
- Capt. (later Brig.) A.K.M. Azizul Islam;
- Capt. (later Maj. Gen.) Moin Chaudhry;
- Maj. (later Maj. Gen.) Ziaur Rahman, who joined the unit in Joydebpur, in 1968, as second-in-command;
- Capt. (later Lt. Gen.) A.S.M. Nasim—my immediate junior, at the time a Quarter Master, later COAS of the Bangladesh Army.

At that time, the army-issued uniforms were too baggy for our Bengali soldiers. I made Nasim have the tailors cut them up (including right-sizing the floppy cap berets). We virtually became a 'Teddy Bears' unit with narrow, well-fitted trousers. With starch and polish, we were the smartest unit in the Lahore Garrison, according to our Corps Commanders, Lt. Gen. Attiqur Rahman and GOC, Maj. Gen. (later Lt. Gen.) K.M. Azhar. Nasim got into trouble with the Condemnation Board, because cutting up uniforms was 'not in conformity' with army regulations. In Lahore (and before I became Adjutant), Maj. Sarwar would make sure that while the rest of the officers were basking in Lahore, in the glow of the 1965 war, I was missing those admirers of the female kind. 'Exiled' in Gandasinghwala, I supervised field training of one sub-unit after the other. After the ceasefire in 1965, the pull-back was covered by an infantry unit located at Kasur (X-Ray Force). The Gandasinghwala Rest House became a training hub. In between training sessions, we were quite content hunting '*Neel Gais*' and fishing in the canals (with mosquito nets). Throughout 11 Division, I was known as the 'Maharajkumar of Gandasinghwala'.

I remained as Adjutant with 2 EB until shortly before I left the unit, in 1968, for Army Aviation. These were my golden years. Virtually being given a free hand by Col. Zia as Adjutant, I could experiment to make the unit better to my heart's content. For me, the route to discipline and comradeship was training and more training. With education endemic among Bengalis, I had all forty-nine Havildars (Sergeants) fit to be promoted to the rank of JCOs. Scrounging additional petrol from the Brigade Major (BM), we managed to build-up 400 per cent reserve of drivers, this along with civilian driving licenses, courtesy a driving school next door. Each specialist sub-unit, including engineer platoon, signal platoon, mortar platoon and intelligence section, had 200–300 per cent reserves. We won the Division Assault Course and all the sporting events, except wrestling and boxing. The reason we lost latter was because in the Light Welterweight category, which determined the championship in the event of a tie, Abdul Jabbar, who had a famous upper-cut, used it on the inviting chin of his 7 Baloch opponents and was disqualified by the referee for 'hitting under the belt'.

I went to Infantry School, Quetta, in January 1967, for my Basic Weapon and Tactics Course. Even though I was one of the junior-most students in a class of 350, my results were among the top five. I was the only lieutenant to get a B-plus at the time in infantry school. Capt. (later Brig.) Saeed Ismat was the youngest captain, and achieved the highest grade in Tactics at that time. We moved to Joydebpur and having the option to choose between the SSG and Army Aviation, I opted for flying and reported to the Army Aviation School in Dhamial, Rawalpindi. I made this decision based on the belief that Colonel Otto Skorzeny, Germany's Commando Extraordinaire, would have chosen a path that prioritised brains over brawn.

To say I liked flying would be an understatement. For me, armour and aviation were the right combination—I loved it. Whether it was flying the L-19 doing STOL (short take off and landing), or the transition from fixed wing to rotary, by way of the OH-13 (S) helicopter, known to us as the Dead man's curse (a military version of the Bell 47G), I graduated second in the course, both in all-round performance, as well as flying. Before doing the Advanced Rotary Wing Conversion (to Alouette-3), I spent one glorious year as Adjutant, 1 Army Aviation Squadron, at Mangla. Not many people know that the station commanders, first Col. (later Brig.) I.R. Sharif and then Col. (later Brig.) Salamat, looked the other way so that we could equip Mangla Airfield with air conditioners and fridges, from what was left in the station yard. Some even equipped the Army Aviation Mess in Rawalpindi. Interestingly, since I could play hockey, I was commissioned by the commanding officer to take over the Mangla Golf Course. I got there just in time to prevent it from being looted by WAPDA personnel, who were hauling away jukeboxes, golf bags, air conditioners and furniture, by the truckloads.

The first annual elections of the Mangla Golf Club were free and fair and attended by three members. Lt. Gen. Hamid, then Commander 1 Corps, was elected president; Col. Kazam Kayani, the vice president; while I became secretary and treasurer (and, I suppose, a member). Luckily for me, soon after Yahya declared martial law, General Hamid moved out as COS, to Pindi. None of the other corps commanders—Lt. Gen. Attiqur Rahman, Tikka Khan, or Irshad—had the same penchant for golf. Rahman, who was into tennis and softball and was my regular tennis partner, requested me as Adjutant, during the corps commander's admin inspection, to ensure my CO wore his belt when he came on parade.

Brig. (later Lt. Gen.) M.I. Qureshi, Commander Corps Signals, took over as the station commander from Brig. Salamat and took an instant dislike of me when I became the club secretary, to which post I was appointed by the corps commander. I invited his ire by not following his dictation and his displeasure was transmitted through his staff officer, Maj. (later Brig.) Khaleeq. Later, this would have very unfortunate consequences for me. As Adjutant, I was given the responsibility for training; it was fun organising Advanced Landing Ground (ALG) and Concealed Area Take-off and Landing (CATO) exercises. The exercises were given exotic names like Crazy Horse, Geronimo, Sitting Bull and so on. I even got away with explaining to my CO with a straight face, that Speedy Gonzales was a famous Mexican General. Flying really started with the Alouette-3, once I was posted to the 4 Army Aviation Squadron at Dhamial. The Alouette 3-B engine is overpowered and in the mountains it gave you that extra power which makes flying exciting and enjoyable, especially with long lost friends, such as Nauman; Agha Humayun; Tahseen; Patrick Tierney; and General Babar (now dead and buried); as well as Hidayatullah Khan Niazi; and Ali Kuli—who are still like brothers to me; Farooq (Ironhead), Saeed Ismat and many others, who taught me to fly.

One can never forget the instinctive flying taught to me by the Chief Flying Instructor, Maj. (later Lt. Col.) Aslam Janjua, a superb pilot and a tremendous human being. He also taught me the 'dead reckoning'—getting from one place to another without a map. When Sarmila Bose was looking for a title for her book, the phrase was suggested by Lt. Gen. Ali Kuli and was befitting, albeit for different reasons. He is a tremendous soul, an outstanding pilot and a great soldier.

We flew far and wide. As the youngest pilot till then to fly L-19s, the OH-13 (S) and the Alouette-3 and as the youngest to be cleared for VIP duty, I had a ball. I got to fly a lot with the Karakarom Highway flight attached to the two Chinese PLA divisions that were constructing the road in the Northern Areas. But the most concentrated flying was in East Pakistan from mid-November 1970 to 12 March 1971. How can I ever forget Maj. (later Brig.) Tirmizi, my flight commander, solid as a rock, calm as a lake. He allowed a degree of freedom that brought out the best in us. I flew hundreds of hours more than I officially logged—who had the time? I flew many more aircraft than I was cleared for; these included the Governor's Amphibian and a PIA Twin Otter. We were literally hauled off the controls of the Fokker on 2 and 3 March 1971, when all PIA pilots and crew had walked out on their jobs. We were needed to be able to cope with the situation and we did.

During the cyclone relief operations from November 1970 to February 1971, as a helicopter pilot, I would fly out in an Alouette-3 before dawn, for the cyclone hit areas in the Bay of Bengal. If I did not telephone Shahnaz by 5 p.m., letting her know that I was back, she would wait on the roof of her house, until I flew over it low, on my way to the base near Dhaka Airport (then at Tejgaon). As I approached Dhaka from the South and neared Baitul Mukaram, I could see her clearly and it remains etched in my memory. Her marriage did not last beyond the sale of all her property, by 1974, mainly for the upkeep and maintenance of her small family. Two years later, she re-married Azimuddin Ahmed, one of twin siblings, who went on to become Petroleum Secretary and then Home Secretary to the Government of Bangladesh. Many of my friends attest as to how Shahnaz fearlessly looked after our Bihari cousins in Dhaka and Bogra, after 1971. Fearlessly standing up for them and ensuring they got onto repatriation flights to Pakistan. None of them now bother to even have a few good words with her children—such is life! Before her death, she turned religious, which was, for her, completely out of character and perhaps a premonition. It is my privilege to be like a father to both of her children, and a grandfather of sorts to their children. Shahnaz died in Dr Feroza's clinic when, during a check-up, she was administered a local anaesthesia injection that contained an air bubble. I lost a sister and a very good friend. She is buried in the Banani Graveyard, in Dhaka.

I loved aviation as much as the cavalry, but would always choose the infantry, because of 2 EB (and later, because of 4 Sindh). In time, I grew to love the infantry. Flying an Alouette-3 was a dream-come-true for any young man; it was like driving a BMW in the air. I must be one of the luckiest men in the world to have been able to fly this aircraft in those days. Flying adds another dimension to one's world—when I look back at my days in army aviation, I realise that they were the sum of the glorious years spent in a world far different from the one we now live in.

I almost gave up my country and my life for 2 EB. I certainly gave up a career, but never regretted it. I had reached Dhaka on 27 March 1971, after being posted to Logistic Flight, Eastern Command and was on 'joining time' and, as such, free to do as I pleased. Dhaka was a killing field, and with a Punjabi father and Bengali mother, it was, for me, an emotional minefield. I was led by my heart and not by my head in choosing to go to 2 EB in Joydebpur, after it had revolted on 28 March 1971, to find out for myself whether all that was being said was true. I could not bring myself to believe that 2 EB had killed its West Pakistani officers, including the family of a JCO, Subedar Ayub, whom I was very close to. His daughters had virtually grown up with me and looked up to me as their older brother. I can never reconcile with this stain. When I finally reached 2 EB in Bhairab Bazar, I realised that my romantic notion that the 'glory and honour of the Regiment must come first' had been turned upside down. Yet even then, how can one ever forget the vociferous adulation that the whole unit gave me on 31 March

1971? Their 'Chand Sahib' was back! I cannot get over the incongruity of it—a Punjabi officer being cheered by Bengali soldiers, in the middle of a civil war based on racial hatred between Punjabis (all West Pakistanis were called Punjabis) and Bengalis. The look of envy on the faces of some of the younger Bengali officers in the unit said it all—I was a dead man, and the only question was when. Destiny had brought me to the unit I loved. And even though I loved Pakistan with every fibre of my being, I was now left with no choice but to die quickly among the troops that I longed to be with.

This narrative is objective and truthful; I know it will not please many and may even cause controversy. The truth is sometimes bitter, yet posterity requires that we look it in the face. I am lucky to have lived to tell the tale. Maj. (later Maj. Gen.) K.M. Shafiulla, then the CO, immediately gave me my last command in 2 EB, Bravo Company, placing Alpha Company under Nasim and an EPR Company under my command. On 5 April 1971, when I refused to cross over into India and my men refused to cross over without me, it led to a revolt within the revolt. Those who truly cared for me—like Shafiulla, Nurul Islam, and Nasim—did not want me to be killed and I was intelligently lured away from my Company and arrested by Maj. (later Maj. Gen.) Khalid Musharraf (along with a squad of 4 EB) and handed over to 91 BSF at Agartala. 2 EB was told I was seriously wounded. Destiny had made the choice for me—I was a Pakistani and a POW in Indian custody. For me, the debt of love for 2 EB was complete, from now our paths would be separate.

After a day in 91 BSF Quarter Guard, I was shifted to Agartala jail. From there, I was taken by air to Panagarh, the first Indian POW camp for hundreds of Pakistanis, including nine officers who had not been declared POWs. Panagarh had been set up by India on 25 April 1971, more than seven months before actual war broke out, on 3 December 1971. The only other Bengali officer incarcerated with me, Capt. (later Maj. Gen.) Amin Ahmed Chaudhry, was later released to join the Mukti Bahini. Amin was a fine human being and a wonderful professional soldier. He became a major general in the Bangladesh Army and the equivalent of the ISI's DG National Security Intelligence (NSI). I escaped from the POW Camp on 16 July 1971 and I reached Pakistan via Nepal, Burma, and Thailand on 16 August 1971.

The narrative of my escape from India was originally penned in 1971, during my interrogation in ISSC HQ. A friendly clerk typed it out on rice paper and I managed to hold on to most of the original manuscript, which would later be published by Oxford University Press, Pakistan under the title, *Escape from Oblivion*. In it, I did not write about my journey from Calcutta, to New Delhi, Agra, Lucknow, Kanpur, Kathmandu, Rangoon, Bangkok, and back to Dhaka. The reason for this was to protect those living in India who helped me—whether knowingly or unknowingly—and also because I did not want to embarrass the US.

I must acknowledge, here, my debt of gratitude to US Marine Sergeant Frank Adair and the US Marine Detachment in the US Consulate General (CG) in Calcutta. I would not be alive if Adair had not allowed me into the US CG Chancery Building on the evening of 17 July 1971. Because of the heavy inflow of refugees, a curfew had been implemented in Calcutta at night and the destitute were being picked up by the police. Since I was already a hunted man, this would have been a death warrant. Frank Adair gave me 'American Aid, 1971-style' because it was (a chapter from my book) in conformity with the US Marine Code. My daughter and I flew to Los Angeles to attend his funeral, in 2017.

I spent 99 days in Indian custody, escaping on the 100th, followed by 84 days under interrogation in the Inter Services Screening Committee (ISSC) HQ in Dhaka. This was located in the 'Second Capital'. On 10 November 1971, I was charge-sheeted for 'overstaying leave' and severely reprimanded. Even this was technically incorrect, as I was on 'joining time'. I was, however, cleared of all other accusations. Two days later, I flew to Lahore, via Colombo, for a few days of furlough with my parents, before reporting to Army Aviation Base, Dhamial.

The animosity in Dhamial was overwhelming, and understandable. The fact that food was refused from the Army Aviation Mess, however, left a bitter memory. My *bhabis* Shazia (wife of Maj. Farooq) and Shama (wife of Maj. Saeed Ismat), made sure I was fed. There was no question of my serving further in Army Aviation. Thinking I would never return, the CO Logistic Flight Eastern Command, Maj. (later Brig.) Liaquat Bokhari, had lied through his teeth, and such were the emotions at the time, that he was supported by others. He made a statement under oath that I had been inciting mutiny and rebellion among the Bengali soldiers in Army Aviation detachment, Dhaka, from 12 March 1971 onwards, and that my actions, from 23 to 25 March, were particularly 'suspect' and that I had attempted to hijack a helicopter.

I had left Dhaka for West Pakistan on 12 March 1971 and only reached
Dhaka on a proper 'movement order' on ten days 'joining time' on 27 March
1971. On 28 March, Maj. Patrick Tierney asked me to do a hovering check
on the Alouette-3, even though I was on leave. After doing so, I realised that
there was some tension in the Crew Room. How can you serve with such
congenital liars and thieves like Bokhari, who, incidentally, took away most
of my music collection and who have no qualms about the consequences
of their blatant falsehood? I had made a request to Maj. Patrick Tierney of
going to Joydebpur and he got permission for the weapons from Bokhari
as the CO. How could I take the weapons from the Quarter Guard on my
own, without the CO's permission? Bokhari told me Patrick would have
gotten into trouble if I said so. And it was foolish of me not to have named
Patrick—out of loyalty to him—when asked how I got an SMG and a pistol
out of the Quarter Guard. Luckily for me, Bokhari's misstatements got me
off the hook.

Because of the impending war, I requested a posting to an infantry unit,
preferably 19 Punjab, which was my father's original unit. I was extremely
lucky in being posted to 44 Punjab. This unit had a core of 19 Punjabis, but
when I heard the name of the CO, Lt. Col. (later Brig.) Mohammad Taj, SJ
(and later Bar) I had grave reservations. There was a general perception that
he did not like Bengalis and I was half-Bengali. At 7 p.m. on 27 November
1971, I got off the train at Rahimyar Khan Railway Station and was received
by Second Lieutenant Hanif Butt, or 'Singhwala', as I immediately called
him, because the lump on his forehead was visible from under his helmet.
He had a wonderful smile that came through despite his large moustache.
The battalion was concentrated in Tarinda and I was asked to see the CO
immediately in his office dug-out. Taj lived up to his reputation. As far as he
was concerned, I was a 'Bengali' and he would shoot me personally if I made
the wrong move. He was going to give me D (Delta) Company, which he
referred as 'Deserter', because it had twenty-five men 'absent without leave'.
His logic dictated I was just the right man to command it.

My Senior JCO, Subedar Mohammad Khan, well briefed by the
Subedar Major, acted defiant and dismissive, as JCOs are apt to do in such
circumstances. I told him that I did not need him and he should report to
the CO. Mohammad Khan hung around till the late evening, and when I
had finished interviewing each and every soldier in my company, he came
to me and admitted he had made a mistake and would never repeat it. And

he never did! In fact, he refused to serve further, after I was dismissed from service, giving up his chance to become the Subedar Major.

I was lucky to be in the company of the wonderful rank and file of 44 Punjab. The three individuals who stood head and shoulders above the rest, were Capt. (later Maj.) Tariq Naseer, Capt. (later Maj. Gen.) Fahim Akhtar Khan and Second Lieutenant (later Maj.) Hanif Butt. When war broke out on 3 December 1971, we, as part of the 60 Brigade and 33 Division, were supposed to strike deep into the Indian desert, aiming for Jaisalmer. As it turned out, this was a pipedream and we ended up being force-marched south by trucks and trains, without any air cover, until we reached Mirpurkhas. The Indians were threatening to take Chhor and Umerkot, and thus enter the 'green belt'. We moved forward by foot under incessant air attacks, to reinforce the 55 Brigade of 18 Division at Umerkot and Chhor, but found the units of 55 Brigade in shambles. While on the move, 44 Punjab brought down two Indian fighter jets short of Umerkot, probably SU-7s, using concentrated machine-gun fire, on 12 December 1971. My company got one!

By the time we reached the gun position of the Battery of 40 Field Regiment, which was commanded by Maj. Gen. Hamid Niaz, near Chhor, they were virtually firing over open sites, without any infantry on the ridges in front of them. Contrary to the training we had received, we had our 'Orders (O) Group' in the gun position and two companies formed at midnight, facing Sanohi Ridge, where the enemy was believed to be. Maj. Hamid Niaz gave us a mug of tea, cheerfully telling us that we might as well drink it as we were going to be martyred shortly. At about 5:30 a.m. of 13 December 1971, while the guns were still booming, Colonel Taj came up to Sanohi Ridge and gave me 'battlefield promotion' to the rank of Major, taking the crowns off his own shoulders and putting them on mine. I can never forget the sun coming up that day. To me, this remains a most coveted moment. He immediately renamed Delta Company as 'Sehgal Company'. I am proud that it still carries my name, forty-seven years later, inscribed in brass lettering on a board in 4 Sindh, even though no one seems to know why this unique honour was bestowed.

Taj was a wonderful companion during war and almost insufferable in times of peace. After 13 December 1971, he looked after me like his own son. I can never repay the debt of gratitude I owe him and Maj. Gen. (later General) Iqbal Khan, who became my GOC (he was Director Military

Intelligence) in late December 1971. Soon after the war, a Desert Battle School was opened up in Umerkot and Maj. (later Brig.) 'Lala' Farooq was made the Commandant, while I was made the Chief Instructor. This School has now a permanent place in Chhor, which has become a full-fledged cantonment. I was being treated for heat exhaustion in the Main Dressing Station (MDS) at Dhoro Naro, in July 1972, when Taj reclaimed me—as usual, without permission from the CO of the MDS, who promptly charged me with desertion—for Internal Security (IS) duties in Hyderabad. We remained on IS duties for months during the language riots, my company looking after Jamshoro and Kotri on direct instructions from President Zulfikar Ali Bhutto.

January 1973 saw us on the move again, this time for IS duties in Quetta. My company was airlifted from Sibi and into the Governor's House, to install Akbar Bugti as Governor in place of Ghaus Bux Bizenjo. After refitting, May 1973 saw us kick-off in counter-insurgency role in the Marri Tribal Area of Maiwand. On the hottest day of the year, dozens of soldiers of the leading battalion 45 Baluch, died of heatstroke and dozens more were hospitalised because the brigade commander insisted on their wearing helmets. This man was later promoted to major general (such people are always rewarded). My company was detached and put directly under brigade and I was given two FC companies, to protect an engineering firm constructing the road from Sibi to Maiwand.

For most of 1973, I alternated between counter-insurgency operations in Balochistan and my relevant army examinations. We suffered casualties and inflicted many more, before a large number of Marri insurgents surrendered. Shahnaz was very worried I would 'get her nose cut off' in the company of the other army wives, by failing in the exam for the promotion from Captain to Major. In the event, I attained the first position in the army, out of the several thousand who appeared, in both the theory and practical sections of the test. When I hitched a ride on a helicopter to show my CO the published results I had borrowed from the Brigade HQ, he was quite angry. 'I kept you under wraps, now they will get you', said Colonel Taj. I decided not to attempt to qualify for the Staff College; my GOC, Maj. Gen. (later General) Iqbal Khan, had other ideas. He ordered me to Divisional HQ in Sibi, to sign my application forms for the entrance examination. General Iqbal asked me that if the Military Intelligence (MI) Directorate cleared me to appear and since he had been Director Military Intelligence (DMI) in

1971, what was my problem? I deliberately left one question unanswered in each paper, and still came first. Clearly, I was bound for Command and Staff College, Camberley.

On 25 January 1974, I was 'dismissed from service with no reasons given'. A mechanism within the Pakistan Army Act allowed for this, in case the army ever wanted to get rid of somebody against whom it was unable to legally press charges. General Tikka Khan, the COAS, was only too happy to take my dismissal papers to the prime minister. Years later, I found out that the officer who did end up going to Camberley as a result of my disqualification, was Maj. (later Maj. Gen.) Saleem Ishaq who had secured second position in the exam and was a cousin of Lt. Col. (later Brig.) Khaleeq.

Many years later, my dismissal was changed to 'compulsory retirement without fault of officer', courtesy of a detailed inquiry carried out by the then Adjutant General, Maj. Gen. (later General and COAS Pakistan Army), Waheed Khan Kakar. He had recommended 'reinstatement with full benefits, rank and service', to compensate for the injustice that had been done. The COAS, General Aslam Beg, however, toned it down. To his credit, he had called me and told me what he was doing. When my own course-mate, Lt. Gen. Amjad Shoaib became the Adjutant General, he somehow 'lost' the file. Lt. Gen. Ziauddin Butt, who was Adjutant General earlier, was annoyed when I told him that he should not have collaborated in bugging the office of the COAS, since he was Private Secretary and thus owed him his loyalty over any other individual.

Annexure 2

Annexure 2 (a) Facsimile of a Letter by General (retd.) M.A.G. Osmany, 30 June 1983

> Tele: Sylhet ~122
> (Alternate, ↗ 6122 ;
> or of order - by writing
> 5754)
>
> NUR MANZIL,
> NAIYORPOOL,
> SYLHET.
> BANGLADESH.
> 30 June 83
>
> My dear Majeed,
>
> The Lord Be Praised! He has Graced you with strength to write and I earnestly pray to Him to Grant you full strength and health, so that next December you and Banu take a trip to Bangladesh and come and stay with me at my partially reconstructed house and visit Hazrat Shah Jalal's shrine and of some of the 360 odd companions who accompanied him in the XIIIth Century, of whom one — Shah Nizamuddin Osmay — was my forebear in this land. Great pity I could neither talk to nor see Chacha!
>
> I am still ill — suffering from very low haemoglobin (I hope I have got the spelling correct!) and during the fasting hours take a nap for two to three hours. One day early this week my servant said a Major Shams had rung up him from Dacca. He (the servant) did not have this phone number nor where he has called from in

353

- 2 -

in Dacca then on the 27ᵗʰ or 28ᵗʰ June came a letter from Dacca by Biman marked I M Sehgal Dhaka 603179. It reached me about 1230 and I immediately dialled the STD (direct dial) to be told he (Chand) had left by the 1100 hours flight to Karachi. What a pity! Please convey my love to him, his wife and children and next time Chand is Dacca-way he must ring up and say Chand of The Tigers from Karachi and insist on walking me up if asleep. And come to Sylhet and stay with me. It must have been a great strain for Bando while you were ill and she must be feeling much relieved now.

I don't know how long more I have but it doesn't matter. Whilst I can't say like Winston Churchill — "I am perfectly prepared to meet my Creator. It is a different matter if He is not so far as to let wait." You and I and Tigers like Sheikh and the second generation Tiger like Chand can at least submit to the Creator — "Our Lord! We have done our honest and dedicated best"

I fear I can't write more. Feeling tired!

With lots of love to you all.

Yours affly Osman

Annexure 2 (b) Facsimile of a Letter by General (retd.) M.A.G. Osmany, 5 September 1983

2

less one thinks about this deterioration the better for one's health. I for one have certainly have not bothered but have not allowed my beliefs, loyalties, principles and attitudes to be impaired, in the least by prevailing attitudes of the fast degenerating human species at home and abroad. I, therefore, sleep undisturbed when I touch the pillow even in my failing health. Bred in The Tiger family, in an atmosphere and amidst traditions so assiduously developed at great personal cost to many of us, you must not get upset but uphold the ideals of a Tiger a Tiger Officer and the motto GRACE STRENGTH SPEED whatever be treading now. Walk or lope you may. All Old Tiger Officers and families here have been deeply grieved on hearing of Majesd's sudden demise and join me in wishing God Bless God's Grace on Danbo and you. God Bless You! You will always be in my thoughts and anything I can do for you anytime, it will my pleasure, indeed duty to do. can't write more. any three – With lots of love to Banu, you and your family Yours affly Uncle Danny

Annexure 3

Operational Details of 'Operation Searchlight'

Basis for Planning

1. AL [Awami League] action and reactions to be treated as rebellion and those who support or defy ML [Martial Law] action be dealt with as hostile elements.
2. As AL has widespread support even amongst the EP [East Pakistani] elements in the Army the operation has to be launched with great cunningness, surprise, deception and speed combined with shock action.

Basic Requirements for Success

3. The operation to be launched all over the Province simultaneously.
4. Maximum number of political and student leaders and extremists amongst teaching staffs, cultural organizations to be arrested. In the initial phase top political leaders and top student leaders must be arrested.
5. Operation must achieve a hundred per cent success in Dacca. For that Dacca University will have to be occupied and searched.
6. Security of cantonments must be ensured. Greater and freer use of fire against those who dare attack the cantonment.
7. All means of internal and international communications to be cut off. Telephone exchanges, Radio, TV, Teleprinter services, transmitters with foreign consulates to be closed down.
8. EP tps [troops] to be neutralized by controlling and guarding kotes and ammunition by WP [West Pakistani] tps. Same for PAF and EPR.

Surprise and Deception

9. **At higher plane:** it is requested that the President may consider the desirability of continuing the dialogue—even of deceiving Mujib that even though Mr Bhutto may not agree, he will make an announcement on 25 March conceding to the demands of AL etc.

10. **At Tactical Level**

   a.   As secrecy is of paramount importance, preliminary operations given below should be carried out by tps already located in the city:

   (1) Breaking into Mujib's house and arresting all present. The house is well-guarded and well-defended.

   (2) Surrounding the important halls of the Universities—Iqbal Hall DU [Dacca University], Jagan Nath Hall, Liaqat Hall Engineering University.

   (3) Switching off telephone exchange.

   (4) Isolating known houses where weapons etc. have been collected.

   b.   No activity by tps in the cantonment area till telephone exchange has been switched off.

   c.   Nobody should be allowed to go out of the cantonment after 2200 hrs on the night of operation.

   d.   On one excuse or the other tps in the city should be reinforced in the area of the President's House, Governor's House, MNA Hostel, Radio, TV and Telephone exchange premises.

   e.   Civilian cars may have to be used for operation against Mujib's house.

Sequence of Actions

11. a.   H Hr—0100 hrs.

   b.   **Timings for Move Out**

   (1) Commando [one Platoon]—Mujib's House—0100 hrs.

   (2) Telephone exchange switched off—2455 hrs.

   (3) Tps earmarked for cordon Universities—0105 hrs.

(4) Tps from the city to Rajarbagh Police HQ and other PS [Police station] nearby—0105 hrs.

(5) Following places surrounded—0105 hrs:

    (a) Mrs Anwara Begum's House, Rd No. 29.

    (b) House No. 148, Rd No. 29.

(6) Curfew imposed—0110 hrs by Siren (arrange) by loud-speakers. Duration 30 hrs initially. No passes for the initial phase. Due consideration to be given only to cases of delivery and serious heart attack etc. Evac by Army on request. Also announce that there will be no newspapers brought out till further orders.

(7) Tps move out to respective sectors with specific missions—0110 hrs. (For tp alert a drill to be evolved). Halls occupied and searched.

(8) Tps move to University area—0500 hrs.

(9) Rd blocks and riverine block estb—0200 hrs.

c. **Operations during the Day Time**

(1) House to house search of Dhanmandi suspected houses, also Hindu houses in old city (int to collect data).

(2) All printing presses to be closed down. All cyclostyling machines in the University, Colleges (T&T) and Physical Training Institute and Technical Institute to be confiscated.

(3) Curfew imposed with severity.

(4) Other leaders arrested.

12. **Allotment of Tps to Tasks.** Details to be worked out by B[riga]de Com[man]d[er] but the following must be done:

a. Kotes of EP units taken over, including Sig[nal]s and other administrative units. Arms to be given only to WP personnel. Explanation: We did not wish to embarrass the EP tps and did not want them to be used in tasks which may not be pleasant to them.

b. Police stations to be disarmed.

    c.   DG [Director General] EPR [East Pakistan Rifles] to ensure security of his kotes.

    d.   All Ansar Rifles to be got hold of.

13. **Info Required**

    a.   Whereabouts of the following:

        (1) Mujib

        (2) Nazarul Islam

        (3) Tajuddin

        (4) Osmani

        (5) Sirajul Alam

        (6) Mannan

        (7) Ataur Rahman

        (8) Professor Muzaffar

        (9) Oli Ahad

       (10) Mrs Motia Chaudhry

       (11) Barrister Maudud

       (12) Faizul Haq

       (13) Tofail

       (14) Nure Alam Siddiqui ⎫

       (15) Rauf   ⎬ and other student leaders.

       (16) Makhan   ⎭

    b.   Location of all police stations and of Rifles.

    c.   Location of strong points and arsenal houses in the city.

    d.   Location of tr[ainin]g camps and areas etc.

    e.   Location of Cultural Centres which are being used for imparting military trg.

    f.   Names of ex-service officers who are actively helping insurrectional movement.

14. **Command and Control.** Two commands be established:

    a.   **Dacca Area**

        Comd — Major General Farman

        Staff   — Eastern Comd Staff/or HQ ML

        Tps   — Loc[ated] in Dacca.

b. **The Rest of the Province**

Comd   —   Major General K.H. Raja
Staff   —   HQ 14 Div
Tps   —   Less those in Dacca

15. **Security of the Cantonment**

a. **Phase I** De-escalate. All arms including PAF deposited.

16. **Communication**

a. Security.
b. Layout.

ALLOTMENT OF TROOPS TO TASKS

DACCA

Command and Control: Maj. Gen. Farman with HQ MLA Zone B.

Troops

HQ 57 Brigade with troops in Dacca, i.e. 18 Punjab, 32 Punjab (CO to be replaced by [Lt. Col.] Taj, GSO I [Int]), 22 Baluch, 13 Frontier Force, 31 Field Regt., 13 Light Ack-Ack Regt., company of 3 Commando (from Comilla).

Tasks

a. Neutralize by disarming 2 and 10 East Bengal, HQ East Pakistan Rifles (2500), Reserve Police at Rajar Bagh (2000).
b. Exchange and transmitters, Radio, TV, State Bank.
c. Arrest Awami League leaders—detailed lists and addresses.
d. University Halls, Iqbal, Jagan Nath, Liaqat (Engineering University).
e. Seal off town including road, rail and river. Patrol river.
f. Protect factories at Ghazipur and Ammo Depot at Rajendrapur.

Remainder: Under Maj. Gen. K.H. Raja and HQ 14 Div.

JESSORE

Troops

HQ 107 Brigade, 25 Baluch, 27 Baluch, Elements of 24 Field Regt., 55 Field Regt.

Tasks

a. Disarm 1 East Bengal and Sector HQ East Pakistan Rifles and Reserve Police incl. Ansar weapons.
b. Secure Jessore town and arrest Awami League and student leaders.
c. Exchange and telephone communications.
d. Zone of security round cantt., Jessore town and Jessore–Khulna road, airfield.
e. Exchange at Kushtia to be made inoperative.
f. Reinforce Khulna if required.

KHULNA

Troops

22 FF

Tasks

a. Security in town.
b. Exchange and Radio Station.
c. Wing HQ East Pakistan Rifles, Reserve Companies and Reserve Police to be disarmed.
d. Arrest Awami League students and communist leaders.

RANGPUR–SAIDPUR

Troops

HQ 23 Brigade, 29 Cavalry, 26 Frontier Force, 23 Field Regt.

Tasks

a. Security of Rangpur–Saidpur.

b. Disarm 3 East Bengal at Saidpur.
c. If possible disarm Sector HQ and Reserve Company at Dinajpur or neutralize by dispersal Reserve Company by reinforcing border outposts.
d. Radio Station and telephone exchange at Rangpur.
e. Awami League and student leaders at Rangpur.
f. Ammo dump at Bogra.

RAJSHAHI

Troops

25 Punjab

Tasks

a. Despatch CO—Shafqat Baluch.
b. Exchange and Radio Station Rajshahi.
c. Disarm Reserve Police and Sector HQ East Pakistan Rifles.
d. Rajshahi University and in particular Medical College.
e. Awami League and student leaders.

COMILLA

Troops

53 Field Regt., 1½ Mortar Batteries, Station troops, 3 Commando Batallion (less Company)

Tasks

a. Disarm 4 EB, Wing HQ East Pakistan Rifles, Reserve District Police.
b. Secure town and arrest Awami League leaders and students.
c. Exchange.

SYLHET

Troops

31 Punjab less company

Tasks

a.   Radio Station, Exchange.

b.   Keane Bridge over Surma

c.   Airfield.

d.   Awami League and student leaders.

e.   Disarm Section HQ East Pakistan Rifles and Reserve Police. Liaison with Sikandar.

CHITTAGONG

Troops

20 Baluch, less advance party; company 31 Punjab present ex Sylhet; Iqbal Shafi to lead a mobile column from Comilla by road and reinforce S.T. 0100 hrs (H hrs) on D-day.

Mobile Column: Brig. Iqbal Shafi with Tac HQ and Communications; 24 Frontier Force; Troop Heavy Mortars; Field Company Engineers; Company in advance to Feni on evening D-day.

Tasks

a.   Disarm EBRC, 8 East Bengal, Section HQ East Pakistan Rifles, Reserve Police.

b.   Seize Central Police Armoury (Twenty thousand Ansar rifles).

c.   Radio Station and Exchange.

d.   Liaise with Pakistan Navy (Commodore Mumtaz).

e.   Liaise with Shigri and Janjua (CO 8 East Bengal) who have been instructed to take orders from you till arrival Iqbal Shafi.

f.   If Shigri and Janjua feel sure about their outfits then do not disarm. In that case merely put in a road block to town from Cantt. by placing a company in defensive position so that later EBRC and 8 East Bengal Rifles are blocked should they change their loyalties.

g.   I am taking Brig. Mozamdar with me. Arrest Chaudhary (CI EBRC) on D-day night.

h.   Arrest of Awami League and student leaders after above accomplished.

Annexure 4

Recommendations Regarding Military Operations, 11 April 1971

1. Mil ops to finish before monsoon i.e. 15 May. Grace period of another 15 days. Monsoon break 1 June 71.

2. **Priorities**
    a. Seal main routes from Indian Border.
    b. Open main routes of comm—own.
    c. Take main towns.
    d. Visit other towns.

3. **Assessment of Tasks**

    Rajshahi Division (16 Div)
    a. Bn – North of Teasta incl L. Hat)
    b. Bn – Rangpur)
    c. Bn – Saidpur) One Bde
    d. Bn – Thakargaon) Rangpur
    (One Arty Reg., One R & S Bn and one Armd Regt)
    e. Bn – Rajshahi)
    f. Bn – Ishurdi)
    g. Bn – Pabna) One Bde Natore
    h. Bde HQ Natore)
    j. Arty – Fd Reg)
    k. Bn – Bogra)
    I. Bn – Noagaon) Div HQ, One Bde & Armd Regt
    m. Bde HQ Bogra)
    n. Div HQ Bogra)

Total Tps

Div HQ, three Bde HQ, 9 Inf Bns, Armd Regt, Two Fd Regts, one R&S Bn
(could economize one inf bn)

Dacca and Khulna Division (14 Div Area)

a. Khulna—Dacca Civ Divisions.
b. Problem of open border in Jessore.

Jessore

a.	Bn	–	Khulna incl Satkhira
b.	Bn	–	Jessore
c.	R&S Bn	–	Jessore
d.	Bde HQ	–	Jessore
e.	Bn	–	Khushtia and Mor Bty
f.	Bn	–	Barisal–Patuakhali
			(Later to be visited through River route)
g.	Bn	–	Faridpur
h.	Bde HQ	–	Faridpur

Total Tps

Two Bde HQ, five bns, R&S, one fd regt and one mor bty.

Dacca

a.	One Bde of three Bns—Dacca City and Cantt.		
b.	Bde HQ	–	Joydebpur
c.	Bn	–	Joydebpur
d.	Bn	–	Mymensingh
e.	Fd Regt	–	Dacca

Total Tps

Div HQ, Two Bde HQ, five bns and one fd regt.

Chittagong Divison (9 Div Area)

a. Sylhet — One Bde HQ, three Bns, Mor Bty.
b. Comilla — Div HQ, Bde HQ, three Bns, One Fd Regt.
c. Chittagong — Bde HQ, four Bns, Mor Bty.

Grand Total

	Div HQ	Bde HQ	Cav Regt	Inf Bn	R&S	Fd Regt	Mor Bty
	1 (Bogra)	3	1	9	1	2	1
	1 (Dacca)	4	–	10	1	2	1
	1 (Comilla)	3	–	10	–	1	2
Present	3	10	1	29	2	5	4
Shortages	3	9	1	23	2	4	2
	–	1	–	6	–	1	2

a. Could possibly economize on one bn.
b. Engr units (RSU, Navy, Rly Bn, Port Bn).
c. Army Avn (Helicopters, a few fixed wing).
d. PAF (Tpt ac)

4. Development of Ops

Rajshahi Division

a. 23 Bde—Capture Dinajpur and develop ops to the North–Thakargaon–Pachagarh.
b. 57 Bde—Complete present op and develop op to Bogra along road.
c. New Bde—To be built up in Rangpur–Isherdi and op to Bogra and seal Hilly.

Jessore

a. Give them one more Bn.
b. Capture area Chaudange–Meherpur–Kushtia and link up with 57 Bde at Paksey.
c. Later one bn to visit Barisal–Patua by river route.
d. Later one bn to visit Faridpur by rd.
e. Addl coy to Khulna. Take Sitkhira and seal border as pri.

Comilla Sec

a.   One more bn to Sylhet and drive South on B Baria.
b.   Comilla grn North to B Baria.
c.   Comilla grn South to Feni and Beyond.
d.   Chittagong grn at present seal Karnafuli and drive North to Feni to link up with c above.

Dacca

a.   Bhairab
b.   Memonsingh–Jamalpur–Netra Kona–Kishore Ganj.

Annexure 5

Lt. Gen. Ali Kuli Khan Khattak HI (M)

On 14 November 2009, I checked into Aga Khan Hospital for an angioplasty. A stent was to be inserted into one of the arteries of my heart. At 7 a.m., three people standing outside my hospital room before the procedure, were Agha Jahangir, his beautiful wife, Rah-i-Naz, and Lt. Gen. (retd.) Ali Kuli Khan Khattak. Ali has been my closest friend since the Lahore days of 1966, when he was in 12 Baluch in 52 Brigade and I was in 2 EB in 106 Brigade. For me, he has always been a 'Pakistani idol'—someone who deserved to be the Head of State, even though he was robbed of the post of COAS due to no fault of his, except perhaps being head and shoulders above the rest when it came to merit. An extraordinary human being, he was an outstanding soldier and he has turned into a highly capable industrialist and businessman. Easily one of the finest officers produced by the Pakistan Army, Ali Kuli had an excellent career, based on an impeccable background. His late father, Mohammad Habibullah Khan (Bibo, to all his friends and relatives) was the second son of K.B. Mohammad Kuli Khan, who was a provincial civil service officer (PCS) and belonged to the Khattak Tribe. His late mother, Mumtaz, was home-educated; she was the daughter of K.B. Sikander Khan, who was also a distinguished PCS officer from Bajaur, Peshawar. She spoke and wrote fluent Hindko, Urdu, Pashto, Persian, and English. Unfortunately, she died rather early, in 1965, in a tragic car accident.

Schooled for the first few years at the Presentation Convents of Peshawar and Rawalpindi, Ali spent nine years at Aitchison College, Lahore, graduating in December 1959, after completing the Cambridge Higher School Certificate (or A-Levels, as they are called today). His late father's passionate love for the Pakistan Army motivated and propelled him through thirty-five of the thirty-seven years he spent in the army. General Habibullah took a great deal of pride and satisfaction in Ali's progress in the chosen profession of arms—an unusual support from someone who was denied the top slot! Ali Kuli was always glad that his father did not live to witness his supersession, because he feared it might have broken even his stout heart.

Throughout his career, General Habibullah had thoroughly outshone and dominated General Musa, his course mate—they were never even in the same league. General Habibullah was considered far superior an officer to General Musa. However, in 1958, when the time came to appoint a successor to General Ayub Khan, General Musa was appointed as the Commander-in-Chief (C-in-C) and General Habibullah as the Chief of Staff (COS). With these appointments, these two officers of infinitely unequal abilities were seen to be working in close proximity of each other and the incongruity of their appointments not only became accentuated, but was also the talk of the town. To remedy the situation, it was considered expedient to retire Habibullah at the age of 46.

Towards the end of his second term at Kakul, in September 1962, Ali Kuli was adjudged as the 'Best Cadet of the Course' and selected to go to the Royal Military Academy (RMA), Sandhurst. The top five who featured in this selection, included Maj. Shabbir Sharif, NH (Shaheed); Captain Zahur Afridi, SJ (Shaheed); Lt. Gen. (retd.) Khalid Nawaz Malik.

From RMA Sandhurst, Ali graduated as a Senior Under Officer (SUO), the only Pakistani to do so at the time and among a handful of non-British cadets ever to achieve this distinction. He was also the first Senior Under Officer (SUO) of his course to command a Sunday Academy Parade. On this occasion, the entire Academy was on Parade and in deference to Ali, the March of the Baluch Regiment was played during the march-past. He was also awarded the Commandant's Cane and declared as the 'Best Overseas Cadet'. Ali captained the Academy's hockey team and was a member of the tennis team.

He joined his father's parent battalion, 12 Baluch, in August 1964, becoming a part of the newly raised 11 Division. 12 Baluch fought the 1965 War at Hussainiwala Headworks. While Ali came out unscathed, the baptism of fire and seeing bullets fired in anger from close quarters was, for him, an unforgettable experience. In 1968, Ali qualified as a Fixed Wing Pilot and was awarded 'The Best Flyer Trophy' of the P-9 Course and posted to 2 Army Aviation Squadron which, in 1969, moved to Lahore. After a short stint as a fixed wing pilot, he converted to the Rotary Wing in early 1969 and in September, was selected to go to the Soviet Union for conversion to MI-8 helicopters. He went to East Pakistan in early April 1971.

On the evening of 15 December, Eastern Command ordered the destruction of all aircraft in preparation for the surrender on 16 December. A plan was made to escape to Burma, taking all the aircraft and whatever else they could carry. Eastern Command agreed to this plan, but kept the responsibility of choosing passengers to themselves. When, at 2 a.m., the crews reached their aircraft, parked all over the cantonment, they encountered total pandemonium and were barely able to take off. The passengers were all women and children and in the chaos and confusion an ambulance-load of nurses got left behind. Apparently, they had kept on sitting timidly in their ambulance, hoping to be asked while others clambered into the helicopters. Ali's helicopter was the second to take off, but for whatever reasons, the first to arrive at Akyab in Burma. 4 Army Aviation Squadron thus because the only unit of Pakistan's Eastern Command which did not surrender.

After graduating from Command and Staff College in 1973, Ali joined his battalion at Maiwand in the Marri Area of Balochistan and in January 1975, was posted as the Brigade Major (BM) of 102 Brigade in Peshawar. In February 1977, he was posted as officiating Commanding Officer of 12 Baluch, which was then located at Kel in the Neelam Valley. In August 1978, he was posted as an instructor at Staff College, Quetta and after approximately a year-and-a-half, was appointed as the Defence Attaché in Egypt. Ali was promoted to brigadier's rank and took over the command of the Rahimyar Khan Brigade. In 1985, he was selected for the Armed Forces War Course and was subsequently posted, in June 1986, as the Chief of Staff (COs) 10 Corps. After three years as a COS, in 1989, he was posted to command another brigade and in 1990 was promoted to the rank of major general and appointed as GOC 8 Division. He commanded 8 Division for a year-and-a-half, during which we went through a fairly tense period of confrontation with the Indians. In early 1992, he was picked to be the Commandant of Staff College, Quetta, where he had earlier been both a student and an instructor.

Ali came to the post of Director General Military Intelligence (DGMI), untrained and inexperienced; some people saw this this as an advantage! During his tenure as DGMI under General Waheed, the MI was used strictly for professional intelligence pursuits. Ali was appointed as Commander 10 Corps in October 1995 and in April 1997, he was posted as the Chief of General Staff (CGS). And so, he sat in the same chair in which his late father had, more than forty years earlier. He had no inkling that fate had reserved for him the same disappointment that had befallen his father.

In Pakistan, merit is often a disqualifier. Very rarely do you find the combination of merit, background and the advantage of seniority; add to that, the qualities of being an outstanding human being. Ali was robbed off his appointment on flimsy grounds. Pervez Musharraf, who took his place, ultimately brought Pakistan to its knees. He gave us the gift of the National Reconciliation Order (NRO), which was declared a black law ab initio by a Supreme Court verdict. Fate does not take it kindly if you interfere with due process. I believe that Pakistan has suffered a decade of misfortunes because of that one solitary appointment of COAS.

Annexure 6

Lt. Gen. Imtiaz Waraich HI (M), SJ

Lt. Gen. Imtiaz Waraich was our Platoon Commander when I joined the Pakistan Military Academy (PMA), Kakul, in early 1964. He brought the best out of us cadets. The PMA Kakul usually has the most brilliant, upwardly mobile officers of the Pakistan Army, as instructors. Waraich was a distinguished officer in this picked lot; a tough and highly professional soldier, who set high standards, both for himself and his command.

Waraich was the prime intermediary in my early army career. Being the youngest in a class of 134 (34th PMA Long Course), it was his encouragement that helped me get selected for the Royal Military Academy (RMA), Sandhurst, even though I did not end up going there. Later, I was a runner-up for both the Sword of Honour and Norman's Gold Medal, winning only the Tactics Plaque and graduating second in the class. This was a major disappointment for my beloved instructor, who believed that I should have got the Sword of Honour. He never forgot it.

Son of a tehsildar, he was born in 1936, in Faisalabad and studied at Government College Lahore in FSC, until 1952, when he was selected for the army. Rising to the rank of Deputy Chief of the Army Staff, General Imtiaz retired with honour, in 1991. According to his old colleagues, as Commandant Infantry School, Quetta, he revolutionised the institution and brought it at par with the Staff College, Quetta, in standard and prestige. The people of Gilgit remember him as Commander, Northern Areas, where he initiated numerous development schemes to make life more bearable for the underprivileged locals.

But for the timing (he had retired a couple of months earlier), he was certainly everyone's first choice for the post of COAS – and a wonderful one he would have made. Wherever he went, he left an indelible mark of organisation, method and discipline, whether it was as Commandant Infantry School or in the raising of the Pakistan Army's new 30 Corps at

Gujranwala. I was privileged to stay in constant touch with him, throughout this period and was with him on his last day in his office, in GHQ, as Deputy COAS.

After his retirement, he was appointed Chairman, Fauji Foundation and Fauji Fertilizer. By the time he had left, the institution was better organised and richer. Fauji Foundation was the strongest, biggest and most successful corporate entity in the public sector. Such was Waraich's charisma, that he could animate a room full of people. Besides the strength and courage he inculcated, he was an admirable conversationalist. Honour, humility, humour, empathy, and heartwarming conversation were his heart-winning qualities. The following is an extract from General Imtiaz's letter, on his retirement,

'My dear friend, believe me that I claim no brilliance, and despite all my limitations I do claim having given my best to the service with ruthless devotion and total resolve. My greatest asset has been the able guidance of seniors, sincere cooperation of the colleagues, and the mutual trust and respect of subordinates. Today I can listen in the far distance bugles sounding the last post. It is my time to fade away. With lot of emotions and veneration I will peel off my Uniform which has become part of my skin. God bless Pakistan Army and the Country'.

Annexure 7

Brief Narrative by Col. (retd.) Salman Ahmed

In 1962, my father Brig Mohammad Ahmed was Director General East Pakistan Rifles, a para-military force with HQ in Dhaka in former East Pakistan. It was here that I met Ikram Sehgal for the first time. Sometime later, we again came across each other in Dhaka Stadium during the inter-college athletic competition. Ikram was participating in discus throw. To his bad luck, he failed to qualify, as in all three attempts, the discus landed outside the sector. Had it not been so, he would certainly have set a new record. In 1963, I was selected for 32nd PMA Long course. Ikram followed a year later in 34th. On commissioning, I joined 1 EB (which my father had commanded) on 13 September at Badian, the unit's war location in 1965 war. I became the first second generation in the regiment.

In 1968, I volunteered for SSG and was selected to undergo 10th Advance Commando Course, which I topped. My first posting from January 1968 to end 1970 was in East Pakistan with 3 Commando Battalion (SSG). In March 1971, on the outbreak of hostilities, I returned to East Pakistan with the 2 Commando Battalion (SSG). With its base in Rangamati the unit operated in the Chittagong Hill Tracts along with a strong force of 1,700 Mizos, who for many years had been waging a guerrilla war against the Indians.

Two months before the start of 1971 war, I rejoined my unit in West Pakistan. My company was attached to the corps responsible for the Narowal–Zafarwal sector. A week before the war started, I was briefed at the Corps HQ and told to obtain information on enemy deployment facing the corps. As such, details could only be provided through interrogation of prisoners we planned accordingly. In the first 72 hours of war, the company captured prisoners from three different locations who were able to provide the required information. The Ebrahim Company, which I commanded during the war, carried out maximum operations and became the most decorated company of SSG in the 1971 war.

In response to hostile actions by the Marri Tribe, the army launched a major operation in 1973 in Balochistan. The plan involved dropping of a heli-borne force comprising an SSG Company and elements of 44 Punjab commanded by Maj. (later Maj. Gen.) Faheem in Maiwand to be linked up by two infantry battalions. Ikram Sehgal was commanding an independent force at Talli Tangi (near Sibi), this was under constant attacks by Marris. I was ordered by HQ SSG to report to the GHQ for briefing by DDMO. Two C-130 aircrafts transported SSG troops to Quetta and from there by train to Sibi from where the operation was launched. The strength of the Marri Tribe was not reliably known and in fact exaggerated as it later turned out. The force landed at first light in Maiwand achieving complete surprise and through swift and speedy action, the operation was over in less than fifteen minutes much to the surprise of the Corps Commander who was flying overhead.

In 1974, I was given responsibility to train Afghan dissidents who had risen up against Sardar Daud in Afghanistan. Two training camps were set up in Attock where weapon, explosives, and tactical training was imparted. Among the students were Ahmed Shah Masood, Haji Din Mohammad (presently President Ghani's Advisor and Client Negotiation of ongoing Peace Talks) and a large number of Afghan dissidents belonging to Gulbuddin Hekmatyar, Burhanuddin Rabbani, Abdul Rasul Sayyaf, Maulvi Younas Khalis, and Maulvi Nabi factions.

In 1976, I joined 23 FF, my new parent battalion since 1 EB no longer remained part of the Pakistan Army. The unit was stationed in Sibi (Balochistan). In the absence of the CO who had not yet been posted I was able to have a free hand in organising the training and acclimatisation of the unit which proved very useful in subsequent operations. After a short stay of a little over one year, I received my posting order to PMA Kakul. I was appointed Term Commander 59 Long Course and Company Commander Khalid Company which in due course was declared Champion Company. While in PMA, I was promoted and posted back to SSG.

On 28 May 1978, I assumed command of 2 Commando Battalion (SSG) at Cherat. A little later it moved to Quetta for an extended stay of over three years. When the time came for replacement, a difficulty arose with regard to its location, as SSG had remained short of a permanent location after East

Pakistan. HQ SSG was of the opinion that the unit should switch over its station to Attock Fort. However, I was insistent that we should be allowed to move to Tarbela which I had earlier visited and found it to be an excellent location. My reasoning was that presently there is not much accommodation available but when the political situation improves, SSG will not get priority. The decision since then has proved to be highly beneficial, as Tarbela now has become a major base of Special Service Group, the best in the world.

On 22 August 1983, my services were transferred to the Inter-Services Intelligence (ISI) in the Afghan Cell. My responsibility was training and operations of Afghan dissidents for the whole of Afghanistan. About this time I took Sandy Gall, a journalist, author, and former ITN news presenter deep into Soviet occupied Afghanistan where he made the BBC documentary *Allah Against the Gunships* depicting the Mujahideen fighting Soviet helicopter gunships with ineffective and outdated SAM-7 missiles. The documentary was instrumental in the subsequent induction of 'Stingers' which turned the tables against the Soviet forces operating in Afghanistan. In 1985, I took over charge of ISI office in Quetta responsible for operations in nine provinces of Southern Afghanistan which being very large had a total area of 50 per cent of Afghanistan. Soviet combatant forces began withdrawing from Afghanistan on 15 May 1988. Soon, major operations against border garrisons and later against district and provincial HQs began. The withdrawal was still underway when all border garrisons and a number of districts were liberated. A little later, the complete Uruzgan province, the first in entire Afghanistan, had also fallen to the Mujahideen. Kandahar province was now cut off from the rest of Afghanistan. Before the final assault, I had planned to flood the city including the airfield by breaching Zahir Shahi Canal carrying high volume of water from Bande Dehla situated at a higher elevation north of the city which would have made the Afghan force, who were guarding the garrison, totally in effective. The plan could not materialise as in 1990 I was transferred to Islamabad.

A delegation of Afghan leadership of Southern Afghanistan, which included Taliban Chief Negotiator, Sher Mohammad Stanekzai, met DG ISI Lt. Gen. Asad Durrani in Islamabad and pleaded against my transfer clearly stating that it would jeopardise their ongoing operations in Kandahar, the capital of Southern Afghanistan and would adversely affect the overall jihadi effort. But they failed to convince him and returned dejected and demoralised. Later, some of them handed over charge and left the area.

This way the trust which took many years to build between ISI and Afghan Mujahideen was shattered. Its after-effects are still there as almost the entire leadership of the Taliban hail from Southern Afghanistan. Sher Mohammad Abbas Stanekzai, presently Taliban Chief Negotiator was head of my military committee in Southern Afghanistan. Two years later while still serving in ISI, I forwarded my case for premature retirement which became effective on 4 May 1992.

Annexure 8

16 December 1971: Lessons not Learned by Brigadier (retd.) Mujahid Alam

'Unexamined life is not worth living'
— Famous dictum of Socrates uttered at his trial

Every year for the last forty-seven years, 16 December comes and passes away as another normal and ordinary day in our national life. It is almost forty-eight years since that dark and ignominious day of 16 December 1971, when our military forces surrendered to the Indian Army in Dhaka, East Pakistan. It was a day of national humiliation and shame. Today, how many of us are even aware or remember what transpired on that fateful day in our national history. Being in self-denial or trying to justify, by self-serving means, our disastrous policies shall not wash away the stain from our national conscience. Such guilt-free apathy and total lack of realisation ought to be a matter of great concern.

Every year, 16 December should be observed as a day of critical introspection, self-examination, reflection and contemplation, not to be used for blame game, settling scores or destructive criticism, but for frank and honest analyses and assessment of all our mistakes—political, military, economic, social, and administrative, in order to ensure we don't repeat them in future. The day should be observed as a solemn and serious occasion, not to rub salt on old wounds, but to educate and enlighten the younger generation through lectures, discussions, seminars, articles etc.

Without facing the stark reality and asking hard questions, we shall never learn the right lessons for our future collective security, well-being, and prosperity as a self-respecting member in the comity of nations. No matter how uncomfortable, unpleasant, and difficult the past may be, we must display collective moral courage to confront it head on. This day must be observed as a day of re-dedication and renewed pledge—never to allow such humiliating calamity befall our nation in future. This collective will, determination, and realisation has to be shown by all institutions of the state—civil and military. The military being much better organised at the institutional level, ought to take the lead in this matter. We must also ask the wider and more profound question as to why we blundered our way into the 1965 war with India within only seventeen years of our existence. How many other nations in history have gotten involved in such self-destructive policies? Nations blessed with visionary leaders ensure the first 75–100 years after independence for peaceful nation building to develop their political, social, economic, military, cultural power, and cohesion. We have been singularly unfortunate to have pygmies masquerading as leaders (both political and military) with a propensity to indulge in disastrous misadventures for their vested and selfish personal interests and misplaced egos. The Kargil misadventure and blunder is another stark example.

The pursuit of wisdom can only be achieved through questioning and logical argument, by examining and by thinking. Nations and cultures that have known great catastrophes develop a sense of national collective introspection and reflection to safeguard their people from any future catastrophe. Reflection and contemplation are vital for leaders to move forward. In the best leaders—those resonant leaders who truly inspire and empower others through their own example—we find in their actions what true wisdom consists of: authentic reflection plus deliberate contemplation over time. Authentic reflection digs deeper and asks questions of ourselves that we might not wish to ask. Just as we should not shirk from facing up to where we can improve, we should also have the courage to recognise and appreciate our strengths so that we might build upon them. Deliberate contemplation focuses on what is significant or important in the immediate future—it is where we derive insights as to the most beneficial next steps to take.

The nineteenth century Danish philosopher, Soren Kierkegaard, once said that, 'Life can only be understood backwards; but it must be lived forward.' In leadership, reflection, and contemplation are vital tools that allow us to chart the best course moving forward by understanding what has gone wrong before. Reflection does not come easily to us. We are, in general, adept at presenting a crafted image to the outside world precisely because we are inclined to construct convincing self-narratives that justify rather than investigate, conform rather than question, and sit in comfort rather than seek to be curious.

Index

388 INDEX

mysticism, 60; voted for the partition of Bengal, 44
Hinduism, 6, 7, 11
Hindu–Muslim riots, 48, 65
Hollingworth, Clare, 253
Hossain, Kamal, 86, 121, 122, 124, 126, 135, 137, 140, 164, 165, 170, 177, 180, 188, 237
Hossain, Kazi Motahar, 23
Hossain, Sara, 236
Human Rights Commission, 232
Humayun, Captain, 187
Hume, Allan Octavian, 4
Huq, A.K. Fazlul, 31, 37, 40, 41, 60, 64–70
Huq, Shamsul, 25, 28, 29, 67
Husain, Syed Shahid, 110, 115
Hussain, Colonel Akbar, 226
Hussain, LCdr. Moazzam, 87, 88, 89, 90
Hussain, Mian Arshad, 77

I

Idrees, Mr, 78
Ikramullah, Begum Shaista Suhrawardy, 41, 42, 66
Iman Ullah, 292
India Doctrine, The, 40
India: ban of overflights of Pakistani aircrafts over Indian Territory, 126, 158, 292; covert engagement in the border areas, 266; division of into 'martial' and 'non-martial' races, 9; Intelligence Bureau, 87; media propaganda, 111, 200, 202; national anthem by Rabindranath Tagore, 8; points out to the Bengalis of East Pakistan that their culture was being 'robbed', 12; refused access to UNHCR, 294; refuses UN forces to check border violations, 254 ; refuses

UN forces to check incursions into East Pakistan, 254; two official languages, 336; Union States can choose their own official languages, 336
Indian Air Force, 307
Indian Army, 75, 76, 199, 209, 213, 216, 218, 226, 234, 242, 253, 259, 261, 262, 265, 267, 292, 294, 298, 299, 300, 303, 316, 317, 319
Indian Civil Service, 10
Indian Independence Act of 1947, 58
Indian National Congress, 4, 6, 34, 36–9, 41, 43, 44, 45, 102, 258, 299, 333; Bose group, 65; Working Committee, 43
Indian Navy, 307, 308
Indian: infiltrators, 234; Mutiny of 1857, 9; nationalism, 4; special forces as 'frogmen', 217; victory, 263
Indian-held Kashmir (IHK), 74, 77, 317
India–Pakistan: border, 75, 254; conflict, 253; Ganges water dispute, 258; relations, 247, 258, 259, 267; threat of war on Bangladesh, 248
Indo–Soviet 1971 Treaty of Peace, Friendship and Cooperation, 252, 268, 287, 292, 314, 330
Indo–US Summit, 318
Indus Replacement Works, 55
Indus Saga and the Making of Pakistan, The, 332
Institute of Defence Studies and Analyses, New Delhi, 264
Intercontinental Hotel, 152, 189, 201, 289
Internal Security Force, 243
International Commission of the Red Cross, 289
International Criminal Tribunal, 237
International Mother Language Day, 30

Z